Oxford in Asia Historical Reprints from Pakistan
Adviser: Percival Spear

THE KAFIRS OF THE HINDU-KUSH

THE KAFIRS
OF
THE HINDU-KUSH

by
SIR GEORGE SCOTT ROBERTSON K.C.S.I.

with an introduction by
LOUIS DUPREE

illustrated by
A. D. McCORMICK

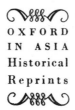

OXFORD
IN ASIA
Historical
Reprints

KARACHI
OXFORD UNIVERSITY PRESS
LONDON NEW YORK
1974

Oxford University Press, Ely House, London W1X 4AH

GLASGOW NEW YORK TORONTO MELBOURNE WELLINGTON
CAPE TOWN IBADAN NAIROBI DAR ES SALAAM LUSAKA ADDIS ABABA
DELHI BOMBAY CALCUTTA MADRAS KARACHI LAHORE DACCA
KUALA LUMPUR SINGAPORE HONG KONG TOKYO

P.O. Box 5093, I.I. Chundrigar Road, Karachi-2

ISBN 0 19 577127 3

First Published in England 1896
Reprinted in this edition in Pakistan 1974

Introduction © Louis Dupree 1974
Index © Oxford University Press 1974

The publisher wishes to thank Fakir Syed Aijazuddin
for allowing his copy of the original edition
to be used for reproduction purposes

Reprinted by permission of the Government of Sind
under the terms of the
Publication of Books (Regulation and Control) Ordinance 1969

New matter set by
Unique Printers, I.I. Chundrigar Road, Karachi
and the whole work printed by
Civil & Military Press Ltd., Karachi

THE KÁFIRS

OF

THE HINDU-KUSH

BY

SIR GEORGE SCOTT ROBERTSON, K.C.S.I.

BRITISH AGENT, GILGIT

ILLUSTRATED BY

A. D. M^cCORMICK

LONDON
LAWRENCE & BULLEN, Lᴛᴅ.
16 HENRIETTA STREET, COVENT GARDEN
1896

DEDICATED

TO

MY WIFE

INTRODUCTION

Scattered throughout the world are various ethnic groups which titilate the tourist, tantalize the dilettante, frustrate the administrator, and alternately inspire and confuse the scholar. We are seldom fortunate enough to find an early visitor who combines the eye of the tourist with the enthusiasm of the dilettante, the attention to detail of the dedicated civil servant with the perceptiveness of a scholar. Such a happy polygamous marriage (in the literate, not literal sense) took place when George Scott Robertson (1852-1916) visited the Kafir region of Afghanistan in October 1889, and later returned, remaining there from September 1890 to October 1891.

The first documented European visit to the Kafir area was the British expedition in 1885, led by Colonel William Lockhart. The 1896 work of Robertson, however, remains the major source on pre-Muslim Kafiristan.[1] For subsequent periods, the autobiography of Abdur Rahman Khan contains a wealth of information on the 1895-6 war to forcibly convert the Kafirs to Islam,[2] and all important studies and documents concerning Kafiristan have been annotated and analyzed by Schyler Jones.[3]

Sir George Scott Robertson, second son of a pawnbroker in Southwark, was born in London, educated at Westminster Hospital Medical School, joined the Indian Medical Service in 1878, and went out to India the same year. He served with the Kabul Field Force in the Second Anglo-Afghan War (1878-80), when 'the people of Kafiristan had first excited my curiosity.... ' (p.2).

In 1889, the Government of India created a political agency in Gilgit to counter the Russians, who, according to reports and rumours, were about to establish a cantonment in Hunza, only sixty miles north of Gilgit. Reactions to real and imagined Russian threats dominated British policy in north-west India during the nineteenth century Colonel (than a Captain) Algernon Durand became the British agent in Gilgit, with Robertson as his surgeon.

After his legendary trip to Kafiristan (with his major base of operations in Kamdesh), Robertson succeeded Durand in 1894, and served during a period of fratricidal strife, the tribal struggles of succession so common in this part of the world. The Mehtar of Chitral, Aman-ul-Mulk, had died in 1892, and in 1895 his successor, Nizam-ul-Mulk, was assassinated. Umra Khan, the Pukhtun ruler of Jandul (and who actively opposed Robertson's peregrinations in Kafiristan), backed Sher Afzal, brother of Aman-ul-Mulk, whereas ultimately the Government of India (i.e., Robertson) recognized the youngest, legitimate male heir, Shuja-ul-Mulk. The confrontation led to the famous Siege of Chitral (4 March to 20 April 1895), which was relieved by two British columns.

A grateful government knighted Robertson (K.C.S.I.), and then to the surprise of his superiors, friends and subordinates, he gave up his distinguished career and returned to England in 1899 to stand (and lose) for Parliament as a Liberal (Sterlingshire), but he gained the Central Bradford seat in 1906.

In addition to *The Kafirs of the Hindu-Kush,* Sir George wrote *Chitral: The Story of a Minor Siege* (1898). He died on 1 January 1916.

The immortality of Sir George will rest on his contributions to Kafir studies, and rightly so, in spite of certain glaring omissions in his data. It has become fashionable to criticize many of the nineteenth century British (and other) traveller-diplomats or scholar-administrators for what they did not do. I suggest we praise them for what they did, and simply list the types of information we need to gather today. What is lost is lost, and no amount of nit-picking can remedy or erase this fact. We would like to have more data on Kafir kinship, inheritance, land tenure, etc. Sir George, however, did not pretend to be a trained anthropologist, although he did try to collect maximum data in several fields. He was one of the many sensitive Victorian observers who with varying ulterior motives served in the shadowy nooks and crannies of the Empire. Some collected raw intelligence data, others information on commercial potentials, and many wanted to understand the exotic cultures of Afro-Asia in order to convert the 'benighted heathen' to Christianity, or to subvert or control for the government. Anthropological research in the service of imperialism is nothing new—and is continuing: the Americans among their Indians, and lately in Vietnam; the French in Algeria and French Black

Africa; the British in East and West Africa.

But whatever their motives, most of these peri-
patetic servants of the Crown left behind valuable
scholarly contributions, still valid and still used. The
many current MA theses and research papers attest
to this. Sir George, often in fear for his life, studies
the macro- rather than the micro- (or mini-) aspects of
culture. What he did observe is generally observable
today; the major change has been the forcible conversion of all Kafirs in Afghanistan to Islam, and even
the Islam practiced in modern Nuristan has under-
currents of the old religion.

Much of Sir George's book reads like a novel.
Understatement wrestles with overstatement, yet never
goes over the precipice. His many lush descriptions of
the geographical and ecological seasonal moods begin
with his first glimpse of Kafiristan (in the Preface),
and few pictures could do justice to his thousand
words.

The history of Kafiristan remains obscure. Classical
sources such as Quintus Rufus (c. A.D. 50) and Arrian
(c. A.D. 100) discuss the Kafir. Even Herodotus
(and those historians who pirated his work) loosely
describes people similar to the Kafirs, but living in
Ethiopia![4] We have definite evidence of bloody
confrontations between the Kafirs and Tamerlane
(May A.D. 1398), and the Moghul Emperor, Babur
(A.D. 1507).

Although much remains to be studied, it is possible
the Kafirs represent the easternmost extension of the
first major explosion (3rd-2nd millennium B.C.) of
Indo-European speakers from south Russia and

Central Asia; possibly the unique Basques of the Spanish and French Pyrenees represent the western extension. Naturally, before anything definite can be said, many intensive studies must be made along lines of potential migration, in particular among the relative isolates of the Caucasus.

Linguistically, Kafiristan presents a bewildering plethora of dialectic variation. The great Norwegian linguist and pioneer in Kafir research, Georg Morgensterne, divides the linguistic picture into Dardic (Indian) and Kafiri dialects, which are often given separate status.

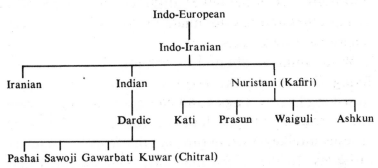

Cultural stubborness (or continuity of identification) partly accounts for the persistence of dialectic differences. Robertson constantly refers to these differences, and his problems of communication, although fortunately he generally had sympathetic interpreters. For example, when different terms for such basic kinship relationships as father, mother, brother, sister, occur in Wama and Supregul, only a few hours walk apart, more appears to be involved than simple linguistic fragmentation. In-group identity and pride are the keys.

	Fa.	Mo.	Bro.	Sis.
Wama	Dai	Arlu	Bra	Saus
Supregul	Bow	Oyyum	Blum	Sawum

Nearly 60,000 Kafirs live in eastern Afghanistan (modern Nuristan), and slough over into Pakistani Chitral. Geographically, the area consists of five major north-south, rugged narrow mountain valleys: Bashgul-Landai Sin-Kunar complex; Waigul; Pech-Parun-Kantiwa; Alingar-Kulam; Darra-yi-Nur. The forests of the region, the most extensive in Afghanistan, include walnut, mulberry, apricot, apple, wild olive, and holly oak in the lower altitudes up to 7,500 feet; Asian pines and firs dominate up to about 9,500 feet, where bare rock takes over.

Wild animals abound: markhor, bear, leopard, flying fox, snowcock, various partridges, and four-foot-long lizards. Eagles and hawks swoop down upon the terraced villages looking for prey. Macaque (rhesus monkeys) swing through the trees in the lower altitudes. In the rivers, men cast their weighted nets for *shir mahi* (milk fish). Winters are severe with heavy snowfalls. Run-offs from spring rains and melted snow swell the many east-west tributaries.

In villages I have visited, I have found between 10 and 40 per cent of the males (few females were examined or questioned) to have blond or red hair, blue or mixed eye colour combinations. The Russian anthropologist, George Debets, measured several groups of Pashai and others on the fringe of modern Nuristan and concluded that these peripheral groups are related more closely 'to the peoples of northwestern

India and Pakistan, than they are to Western Europe.'[5]
He conceded a lighter pigmentation than that of
surrounding groups and partly attributed this to
'isolation'. Whatever the reason, an increase in blon-
dism becomes obvious, even to the most superficial
observer. Obviously, more research, particularly in
genetics (blood groupings, etc.) needs to be undertaken.

Sir George's descriptions of the physical attributes
of the Kafirs are less than scientific, and reveal the
superiority complexes held by many Westerners,
both nineteenth and twentieth century, when discussing the 'races of Asia'. He places most of the
Kafirs in a sort of colour limbo: 'They do not at all
approach the black races, but are equally removed
from those with white skins' (p. 169). He complains
of the difficulties of estimating skin colour because
some Kafirs are covered by 'a particularly grimy
smoke...seldom or never neutralized by washing.'
Modern physical anthropologists realize the best place
to judge skin colour is under the armpit, which has
minimum exposure to sunlight and the elements. On
at least one occasion, the Kafirs had the opportunity
to examine Sir George's armpit when he 'adopted' a
Kafir son, Shermalik, who became one of his chief
informants. Part of the ceremony required the 'father'
and 'son' to 'go through the motion of kissing with
our lips a foot or so apart. But the surprise was in
reserve. My coat and shirt were opened and some
butter placed on my left breast, to which Shermalik
applied his lips with the greatest energy and earnestness. I jumped up as if shot, but the thing was over'

(p.31). Did Sir George become symbolic mother as well as father ?

The comments by Robertson on the sanitation habits and the character of the Kafirs again reflect the general attitudes of Victorian and post-Victorian Westerners towards non-Western peoples. The Kalash were 'a most servile and degraded race' (p.4). He is offered to share the home of a Kafir friend, 'but not being case-hardened to Kafir dirtiness I politely declined' (p.4). 'Civilisation abruptly fell asleep centuries ago in Kafiristan, and is still dormant' (p.162). 'The Kafirs are by no means simple in character; they can intrigue, concoct plots, and then carry them out with the secrecy and tenacity of the average Oriental' (p. 177).

But Sir George also softens many of his observations with sympathetic qualifications:

In his own country, on the other hand, the Kam Kafir is polite, dignified and carries himself with a free, independent, and self-satisfied air (p. 105).

Their present ideas, and all the associations of their history and their religion, are simply bloodshed, assassination, and blackmailing; yet they are not savages. Some of them have the heads of philosophers and statesmen (p. 165).

A Kafir woman and her dirty little baby, when looked at aright, are just as charming to watch as similar human pictures anywhere else (p. 538).

Economically, today as when Sir George was among them, the Nuristani are basically mountain herdsmen, primarily of goats, but cattle are still extremely important for prestige. In most localities, several hundred distinct terms refer to goats, mainly relating to characteristics of the horns; in general only about twenty terms refer to sheep colouring. I have also collected twenty distinct designations for cattle from a single village; about three-fourths relating to cow colour combinations; the remaining quarter refer to horn patterns on bulls.

Women do most of the agricultural labour, though men do perform some heavier tasks, such as removing large stones, and building and repairing the terraced fields. Also, after the women complete the reaping, the men, using wooden flails, thresh the grain before the women winnow. The women use a unique plough well-described by Robertson on pp. 549-50, illustrated on p. 548. The plough, however, can be used only in the lower reaches of the valleys, and in higher areas women usually use a long forked stick attached to a rope to break the ground. While one woman jabs the fork into the soil, the other, standing opposite, pulls the rope.

Crops include: highland wheat and barley, maize, various beans, and millet. The diet consists primarily of dairy products, milk (fresh and sour), cheeses and butter. The Kafirs eat a cheese fondue made in the Continental style without the brandy, although a few old men insist wine was added in pre-Muslim days. From first-hand knowledge (and tasting), I can certify that at least three types of wine are still made in parts of modern Nuristan; one, a mead-like drink laced with honey. As usual, bread is important and baked from wheat, barley, maize and millet.

Kafir table manners (like many other cultural items, including clothing which Robertson discusses in great detail) differ somewhat from those of other Afghan groups. Like other Afghans, they eat with the fingers of their right hands, but, instead of sitting on the floor or ground, use low wooden stools or chairs, seats braided with leather strips. They eat off either wooden tables with twisted, wrought-iron legs, or wicker tables.

Probably the most significant difference in Nuristani material culture when compared to the rest of Afghanistan is the dominant role wood plays in the lives of the people. As one travels up the valleys, house types change slowly from dried mud brick in the Kunar Valley to stone foundations and mud walls at mid valley. Higher up the mud gives way to timber with clay and pebble cement in the cracks between the logs. With only the adze and the knife, the *bari* (former slaves of the Kafirs—pp. 99-103 and elsewhere) craftsmen dress the logs and often carve elaborate designs into the wood, particularly doors, lintels, and the *usultun,* the four pillars centered inside the house around the fireplace. The meaning of most of these symbols has been lost,[6] and even Robertson seemed unable to discover much of value as the Kafirs (as the Nuristani do today) retreated behind the phrase, 'It is our custom,' a quote peppered throughout Robertson's book (pp. 134, 178, 438).

As in many societies, Kafirs considered the fireplace sacred, and today many Nuristani will flick a few drops of butter, cheese, blood from meat, or hunks of bread into the fire before they begin to eat. When asked why, they will again reply, 'It is custom.'

The *bari* function as the artisans in modern

Nuristani society. Generally, a few live in each village, working as masons, potters, silver and goldsmiths, ironmongers and blacksmiths, shoemakers, but most of all, carpenters and woodcarvers. In addition to dressing timber and making the popular walking sticks and *usultun*, the *bari* woodcarvers produce ladders, drains, tables, chairs, stools, beds *(charpayi)*, storage boxes, spoons, bowls (also carved of soft steatite), clothes racks, and, in Kafir times, the grave effigies and coffins.

Although King Amanullah (1919-29) abolished slavery, the *bari*, like many Black sharecroppers in the American South, lived as virtual slaves in some relatively isolated villages. Intermarriage between Kafir and *bari* was—and is—unthinkable. Even today, few *bari* would move to another village without permission.

No bazaars exist in modern Nuristan, and items desired from the outside world are brought in by itinerant traders, or the Nuristanis will trek to the nearest bazaar on the edge of their territory, such as Chitral, Peshawar, Jalalabad, Munjan or Faizabad. Major items brought in from the outside are salt blocks, sugar, tea, *gur* (solidified molasses), guns, ammunition, kerosene and kerosene lamps, cowrie shells for decorating women's clothing, cloth, and cheap jewelry. These items are traded for cattle, goats, hides and skins, butter, lumber and handicrafts.

The Nuristani people retain many elements of their pre-Muslim political structure, but in the past decade have become increasingly involved with central government officials because of the improved road

system around outlying areas. Administratively,
Nuristan is mainly divided between two Provinces
(Kunar and Laghman), but some groups also live in
Kapisa, Badakhshan and Ningrahar.

In pre-Muslim days a man achieved power in three
interrelated ways, *i.e.* wealth in livestock, bravery in
war, generosity to his neighbours in peace. In order to
join the formalized *jast* (an informal grouping of
men who achieve the distinction through 'property-
fighting'—p. 87), a man had to give a specified number
of feasts for the *jast* and for the community as a whole
(p. 449). One obvious function of these confrontations
was to keep the distribution of wealth (at least among
the more wealthy) fairly equal, for all sacrificed
animals were divided equally among the entire
village. Even the *bari* received shares.

In order to maintain his wealth or continue to
participate in 'property-fighting' (which, incidentally,
could be called a 'positive' potlatch, because the
property was not wantonly destroyed but distributed
for the common good), a man participated in livestock raids on other valleys.

Polygamy was common and a man could have as
many wives as his money and sexual prowess would
permit. Marriage usually occurred outside the village,
but within the valley; *i.e.,* village exogamy and valley
endogamy. Robertson, however, does report several
cases of inter-valley exogamy (between Waigul and
Kamdesh, for example). Kinship ties usually extended
the length of the valley, and most inhabitants had
kinsmen in each village. Indeed, in Kafir days, fights
seldom took place between villages in the same valley.

The same is generally true today.

Robertson seems to have been kept in the dark about the *urei* (pronounced ooray), the large silver wine cups, so essential to the Kafirs in the 'bride price', and even today one of the more important objects which changes hands in divorce cases, i.e. the wronged husband demands several of these valuable cups from the family of the wife-stealer.

Robertson failed to appreciate Kafir music, and his Western cultural biases show through. (However, after taping hours of music in Nuristan, I must confess a slight sympathy for his views!)

'In the enclosed space, their music had a surprising clangour' (p. 460).

'The music is most feeble and discordant. My ear could never distinguish between the different tunes which were being played' (p. 616).

He does, however, take time to describe briefly the major musical instruments observed. In addition to small drums, tambourines, and a two-holed flute (p. 616—Robertson calls it a 'pipe'), he mentions (p. 628-9) an unique five- or six-stringed, plucked harp (*wunz* or *waj*, name varies by valley), usually about 50 cm. long by 40 cm. tall, with a skin-covered, wooden resonance box. The harp's origin remains a mystery, but obviously harks far back into the pre-Muslim past of the Kafir.

Afghan Nuristan, so recently converted to Islam, offers a trinity of religious faces: (1) the fanaticism of the new convert; (2) old Kafir customs, now considered Islamic; (3) pride in the Kafir warrior past, dimly remembered by the elderly and passed on in an impure form to the youth.

Some Kafirs (though not many) accepted Islam before Amir Abdur Rahman forcibly converted all Afghan Kafirs, destroyed most of their wooden effigies (the Muslims thought they were idols), overturned the wooden coffins of the dead, forbade the the making of wine, and took many sons of the power elite to Kabul as hostages.[7] Incidentally, many Nuristanis became soldiers, several reaching high command positions.

To speed up conversions, the religious strong arm of Abdur Rahman's army encouraged the Kafirs to believe they were really a wandering tribe of the Quraish (Arab tribe of the Prophet Mohammad—PBUH) lured away from Islam. I have collected Quraish origin myths at many places in Nuristan: Supregul, Wama, Mirdesh, Kamdesh, and Bragamatal. Many Kafir priests slipped easily into new roles as mullahs.

Few in Nuristan profess to remember the old religion. In Bragamatal, for example, only two old men (both over 80) and the wife of one admitted any extensive knowledge. Robertson claimed more fairies and demons existed than could be counted (p. 412), and published a long list of gods, but the three informants in Bragamatal could remember only those indicated in the chart below:

THE KAFIR PANTHEON

Listed in Robertson, p. 381 (1896)		Remembered at Bragamatal (1963)	
God or Goddess	Function	God or Goddess	Function
Imra (two terms : Dezel, Mrar)	Supreme Being Creator, Lord	Imra	Supreme Being; Creator

Listed in Robertson (1896)		*Remembered at Bragamatal (1963)*	
God or Goddess	*Function*	*God or Goddess*	*Function*
Moni	The Prophet; destroyed trouble-making demons		
Gish	War God; most popular	Gish	War God; taught rituals and ceremonies; to return as Messiah
Bagisht	God of Wealth; only deity with normal birth; intermediary between man and gods	Bagisht	God of Wealth: played jokes on men; lacks thumb
Arom	God of Peace; sacrificed to at end of war		
Sataram (Sudaram)	God of Weather; especially rain	Suteran	Rain God
Inthr	God of the Vine; grapes; wine		
Duzhi Nong Parade Shomde	Names only; function unknown (gods)		
Saranji (Sauranju)	Tutelary Goddess		
Dizane (Disni)	Fertility Goddess of Wheat; protects men in battle; mother of Bagisht, his father a demon		
Nirmali	Fertility Goddess; protects pregnant women; protects *pshur* (shaman)		
Krumai (Shumai)	Fertility Goddess of Goats; appears on earth as wild goat		

Several major gods and goddesses (Imra, Moni, Gish, Dizane, Krumai, Nirmali) appear to have been universal in Kafiristan, but every village had its own quota of nature spirits, living in natural objects such as trees, rivers, stones and mountains. Each section of a village and each warrior had a protective private spirit acquired during a trance or dream.

In the old Kafir days, a shaman (*pshur*) went into self-induced (and Robertson suspects, wine-induced) trances and the spirits of various gods possessed his soul in order to answer questions, particularly concerning predicted results of planned raids. Robertson confesses to falling into a trance while watching a dance: 'Then from out of the stamping throng the face of some one long dead and gone would gaze upon me. It gave me no surprise, but seemed quite reasonable' (p. 216).

An interesting story now told in Nuristan concerns a manlike beast which kills cattle, goats, and sheep and even attacks humans at night. Several Nuristanis showed me the marks where they had been bitten by the creature, which, when described, appears to resemble the *yeti* or 'abominable snowman' of the Himalayas. I strongly suspect the abominable snowman stories may relate to the werewolf legends which extend throughout mountainous Eurasia from the Carpathians to the Himalayas.

Death created a major life crisis in the community. The more livestock sacrificed and divided among the mourners, the more honour to the dead man and his living relatives. After the ceremonies (up to three days or more for great warriors), the body was placed in an above-ground four-legged wooden coffin, also used 'for the storage of grain and other property' before being used as a coffin (p. 503): from the staff of life to the end of life.

To the best of my knowledge no Kafir coffin in Afghanistan had been examined by an outsider in the twentieth century until 1965 in Kruen, over the mountain and south-west of Kamdesh. The coffin dates from before 1896 when the soldiers of Abdur Rahman Khan stormed Kruen, one of the last Kafir strongholds to be overrun. The soldiers destroyed all the hillside coffins, and fragments of planks dot the steep non-path leading to the old burial place. However, the coffin I examined had survived because it was the most difficult to reach.

The oak coffin measured seven by two and one-half feet and had an east-west orientation. The skeleton was badly disarticulated. No skull could be found inside the coffin, but a pot buried in the soil, 20 feet south-east and 20 feet higher than the coffin, contained a skull. Whether it belonged to the same individual remains a question. Informants said that in Kafir times when a man was killed in warfare and his body could not be returned to the village, friends cut off his head and brought it back to be buried with the same pomp and circumstance as though the whole body were present. Relatives constructed a straw body replacement, which was later ceremoniously burned (pp. 11, 151, 632-3, 635-41).

In several subtle ways, the Nuristani strike back at Islam either consciously or subconsciously. In and around Kruen, for example, sit several burial shrines dedicated to men who fought and killed 'Musulman'. These heroes died *after* the Afghan conquest of the area, and after they had been converted to Islam. However, each of these heroes is primarily remembered for the number of 'Musulman' he killed, and the local people often use their Kafir (not their adopted Muslim) names in folktales.

Bari artisans carved intricate symbolic motifs into these wooden shrines. All the motifs are pre-Muslim, and today most people claim ignorance of their meanings. Lost and locked in the carved designs on almost all modern objects or still lurking in the minds of some of the older Nuristanis are the true meanings of the symbols, some common with other pre-Muslim and even prehistoric religions of the Middle East and Central Asia. The repeated circles possibly relate to a sun disk and ultimately to Imra, the Supreme Being. The snake may represent the power of Imra, for he killed great serpents in his days as a human (p. 388). In several areas the snake-dragon can be shown in basaltic or granitic geological dikes along precipitous mountain walls. Hazrat Ali, son-in-law of the Prophet Mohammad (PBUH), is the St. George of the Muslims, and in Afghanistan villagers point out similar geological phenomena as serpents killed by him.

Robertson reports the Kafirs believed that Gish (the War God), killed Hazrat Ali, cut off his head, and settled in London, after which the servants of Gish settled in Kafiristan (p. 308). 'He killed Hazrat Ali; he killed Hasan and Husain; in short, he killed nearly every famous Musalman the Kafirs ever heard of' (p. 401).

Another obvious non-Islamic hangover, the goat cult, occurs throughout the Middle East and Central Asia, both in time and space from the Middle Palaeolithic through the Neolithic to the Bronze Age and the present.[8] The devout often cover modern Muslim shrines *(ziarat)* with wild goat horns because, as the people say, it is *adat* (custom). The goat cult possibly relates to an ancient totemic identification by mountaineers with the virility and ruggedness of the mountain goat. Nuristanis (like their ancestor Kafirs) hunt the markhor and Marco Polo sheep (in the north-east only), and ram horns, realistically and stylistically portrayed, occur on many items of folk art; including wooden and stone bowls, *usultun* and doors.

In April 1963, I witnessed a 'Musulman' ceremony at Wama just prior to the spring planting. A mullah decapitated a cow (instead of slitting its throat to make it *halal* or clean, as Muslims would do) at the community meeting area, and sprinkled a little blood in the direction of the fields. He symbolically buried several chunks of meat in a nearby field. The mullah, according to his own interpretation, had performed a Muslim ritual, but I fail to detect an Islamic flavour in this type of sacrifice. The people of Wama, however, all received equal shares of the meat of the sacrificed animal, a traditional Kafir—as well as Muslim—custom. Robertson describes a relatively similar ceremony on p. 468.

The Nuristani have seen the light of Islam, but only fuzzily practise the true religion, and have incorporated Kafir motifs and mysteries into their brand of Islam. They go to the outside world readily, but prefer to keep the outside world away from their relatively inaccessible valleys. They do not have the formalized hospitality of the plainsmen and the nomads, and unless one visits the area with a local inhabitant, hospitality may quickly become strained hostility.

Unlike the rest of Afghanistan, silence characterizes Nuristan. No jet planes whine overhead, no lorries rumble and grind along the narrow trails. At night, the people visit one another, lighting their way with flaming pine torches which they thrust into the wall on entering a hut, and take away when they depart, leaving a flickering trail behind. Time almost stands still in Nuristan. The ticking of the clock gives way to the ecological calendar, and man, working with nature as a partner, survives and prevails. And thanks to the pioneer work of Sir George Scott Robertson, we have excellent research guidelines, eight decades old.[9]

LOUIS DUPREE

King's College
Cambridge
1 June 1973

NOTES

1 Kafir (plural, *Kuffar*) generally means 'infidel' in Arabic; Kafiristan refers to the area of modern Afghan Nuristan before the invasion of conversion by the armies of Amir Abdur Rahman Khan in 1895-6. Nuristan means 'Land of Light'; referring to those who have seen the light and have been converted to Islam. In Pakistani Chitral, between 3-4000 (estimate by Peter Parkes, St. John's College, Cambridge) Kafirs still practise the old religion. In this introductory chapter, I have tried to use the term Kafir in referring to those people met by Robertson, and refer to Nuristan and Nuristanis when making modern comparisons. The people are basically the same; only the religion—and this imperfectly—has been changed.

2 Abdur Rahman Khan, *The Life of Abdur Rahman, Amir of Afghanistan*, 2 vols, London, 1900.

3 S. Jones, *An Annotated Bibliography of Nuristan (Kafiristan) and the Kalash Kafirs of Chitral, Part I*, Copenhagen, 1966; *Part II, Selected Documents from the Secret and Political Records, 1885-1900*, Copenhagen, 1969. For shorter bibliography, see L. Dupree, 'Nuristan: "The Land of Light" Seen Darkly,' American Universities Field Staff Reports, South Asia Series, vol. 15, no. 6, 1971.

4 Arrian (Flavius Arrianus), *Arrian's Life of Alexander*, translated by A. de Selincourt, Harmondsworth, Middlesex, 1958; Herodotus, *The Histories*, Baltimore, 1963; *Ancient India: Its Invasions by Alexander the Great*, translated by J.W. McCrindle, Westminster, 1894 (for Quintus Curtivs Rufus).

5 G. Debets, *Physical Anthropology of Afghanistan, I-II*, Illustrations and Notes by L. Dupree, translated by E.V. Prostov, edited by H. Field, Peabody Museum, Cambridge (USA), 1970.

6 A. R. Palwal, series of five articles in *Afghanistan*, vols. 21-24,

1969-71, published by the Historical Society of Afghanistan, Kabul, does pioneer work on the symbols, and an Indiana University graduate student, Mohammad Alam Nuristani, is working on the same (and other) subjects, the first of his people to do so.

7 Hasan Kakar, *Afghanistan: A Study in Internal Political Development, 1880-1896,* Punjab Educational Press, Lahore, 1971.

8 L. Dupree, *Deh Morasi Ghundai,* Anthropological Papers of the American Museum of Natural History, vol. 50, no. 2, N.Y., 1951; L. Dupree (with others), *Prehistoric Archaeology in Afghanistan: 1959-1966,* Transactions of the American Philosophical Society, vol. 64, no. 4, Philadelphia, 1972; K. Jettmar, Ethnological Research in Dardistan, 1958, *Proceedings of the American Philosophical Society,* vol. 105, no. 1., Philadelphia, 1961; J. Staley, Economy and Society in the High Mountains of Northern Pakistan, *Modern Asian Studies,* vol. 3, no. 3, 1969.

9 Richard F. Strand recently published an important article (with a map) on the distribution of the Nuristani (Kafiri) and Dardic dialects: Notes on the Nuristani and Dardic Languages, *Journal of the American Oriental Society,* Vol. 93, No. 3, 1973. Another paper by Strand includes a critique of Robertson's misinterpretation of the *jast* institution: Notes on Kom Nuristani, Political and Governmental Organisation, *Selected Papers from the Hindu Kush Conference,* Heidelberg 1973.

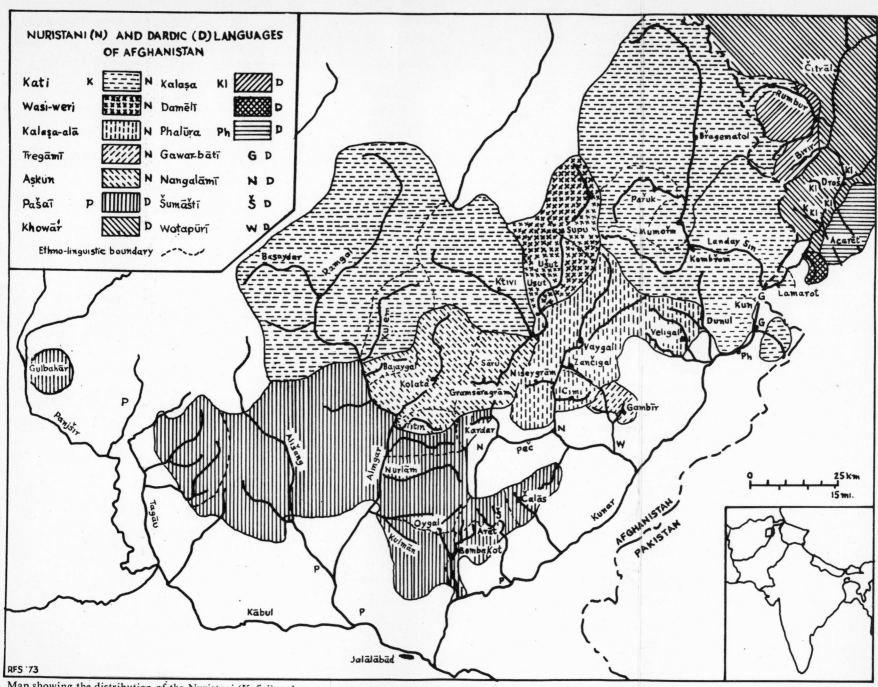

Map showing the distribution of the Nuristani (Kafiri) and
Dardic dialects by RICHARD F. STRAND (1973).

PREFACE

In the year 1888, in company with Colonel Durand, C.B., then a young cavalry captain, I was travelling through the Astor Valley of Kashmir to Gilgit. On one memorable occasion we had made a double march. The track was extremely arduous, and the waning light found us tired and jaded, and still some distance from camp. Silent and slow-footed, we rounded the Doian spur in the gathering darkness, and had begun the descent to the village, when a strange sight to the north-west startled us into open-eyed wonder. And indeed a wonderful picture lay spread out before and beneath us. It was bounded and restricted below by the large spurs which guard the mouth of the Astor Valley. Above, the pure sky domed over all, while in front a filmy veil of cloud was suspended, which seemed to magnify and accentuate, instead of dimming, the noble outlines which lay behind. Through this mysterious curtain could be seen a bold curve of the Indus flanked by mighty mountains, and the light yellowish-grey shades of the Sai Valley, which increased the general appearance of dream-like unreality. Beyond this, again, were the dark mountain ranges of the gloomy Gilgit region, divided by equally sombre ravines, while the eternal snows of the lovely Rakhipushi, calm and brooding, with a single cloud pennon streaming from its solitary peak, completed a background of surpassing beauty. The whole scene was illuminated by a dying afterglow. Swiftly, almost instantaneously, the light failed, and the translucent veil deepened and darkened so rapidly, that the vision-like picture was shut out almost as magically as it had flashed forth upon our senses.

As we turned away silently, the fantastic thought arose in my mind that behind that transparency, that translucent cloud-film, a veritable faery country had been revealed to me, stretching far into the nothing-ness beyond; and an anxious doubt disturbed me lest I should never be permitted to enter that strange and enticing dreamland. I never revisit Doian, and look towards the Rakhipushi mountain, but the memory of that picture recurs to my mind; but now if I gave way to fantasy my reflections would fall upon the countries and people I had visited through the mys-terious cloud-curtain.

This book is the record of a journey to one of these countries, and of nearly a year spent amongst a wild and interesting people.

CONTENTS

ix

CHAPTER XIII

CHAPTER XIV

CHAPTER XV

CHAPTER XVI

CHAPTER XIX

CHAPTER XX

CHAPTER XXI

CHAPTER XXII

CHAPTER XXIII

CHAPTER XXIV

CHAPTER XXV

CHAPTER XXVI

CHAPTER XXVII

LIST OF ILLUSTRATIONS

THE

KÁFIRS OF THE HINDU-KUSH

CHAPTER I

IN October 1889 I found myself, for the second time,
the official guest of the Mehtar of Chitrál at the fort
which constitutes the capital of that country. The previous year had seen me at the same place in a similar
capacity. In those days Chitrál was very little known,
and the Europeans who had visited it could be counted
on the fingers. The people and the country were alike
interesting—the former for their picturesque light-heartedness, the latter for its magnificent scenery, and both
for their freshness and novelty. But it was not only
the Chitrális themselves that had excited my curiosity
and interest, for at the Mehtar's capital, on my first
visit, I had seen several Káfirs of the Hindu-Kush,
and had heard many tales of their strange manners and

A

customs. The people of Káfiristán had first excited my
curiosity during the Afghán war of 1879–80, and seeing
them now in the flesh, my interest in them became so
intensified, that the desire to see them in their own
homes was irresistible. I had accordingly asked the
Government of India to be allowed to make an attempt to
enter the Káfir country, and the permission was accorded
me while actually on my way to Chitrál for the second
time.

It should be mentioned that the only previous European who had attempted to enter Káfiristán was General
(then Colonel) Lockhart, when in command of a Mission
to examine the Hindu-Kush passes in 1885–86. He had
penetrated into the upper part of the Bashgul Valley,
and remained there for a few days ; but jealousies having
broken out amongst the Káfir headmen, he had been
compelled to leave the country and return to Chitrál.

As soon as permission had been granted me to make
an attempt to get into Káfiristán and study its people, my
line of action had at once been decided upon, and by the
time Chitrál was reached, the details of the plan had
arranged themselves in my mind. Lockhart's experiences,
and his partial failure, had convinced me that the great
danger to my enterprise lay in exciting the jealousy of
the Káfir tribesmen one for the other. It also seemed
well for me not to follow in Lockhart's footsteps, and
try to visit the tribe which inhabits the upper part of
the Bashgul Valley, but to make a fresh departure, and
see if the famous Kám tribe would not accept me as a
visitor. There were peculiar inducements to lead me to
try to get into the Kám country. The Chitrális declared
that those people and the Wai tribe were the fiercest

and most intractable of all the Káfir tribes, while of those two the Kám were the most to be dreaded for their military prowess. It also happened that at that time the Kám were on the best of terms with the Mehtar of Chitrál, and acknowledged his suzerainty, which, if only a nominal submission on their part, was nevertheless very convenient for my plans. The Mehtar of Chitrál, on his part, was desirous of showing the extent of his power over the Káfirs, and on my applying to him for help, assured me that there would be no difficulty about my going to Kámdesh, under his auspices, for a few days.

My plan was to get to Kámdesh for a short visit, conciliate the people, and persuade one or more of the headmen to accompany me to India, where, while we were learning to understand one another in the Urdu or the Bashgul language, there would be leisure to gain special information wherewith to equip myself for a prolonged visit to Káfiristán. It so happened that there were at the time in Chitrál several of the Kám headmen, and they readily consented to take me to their chief village, and bring me back again to Chitrál. One of them, indeed, a very rich and influential man, tried to make conditions, while his looks and manner left much to be desired ; but all further objections were anticipated by my riding off at once to the Káfir frontier, leaving my Káfir friends to follow and join me there, which they did two days later; for they are not horsemen, and always journey on foot. My baggage was light, but it was soon seen that it must be still further diminished. Finally, it consisted of a sleeping-bag, a small box of medicines, and a few cooking things.

The third day after leaving Chitrál found me and my Káfir friends at the village of Utzún, a community of Kalash Káfirs, who, as will be explained subsequently, are not the true independent Káfirs of the Hindu-Kush, but an idolatrous tribe of slaves subject to the Mehtar of Chitrál, and living within his borders. The village of Utzún numbers thirty or forty domiciles, which are perched on the top of a conical rock 700 feet high, in the middle of fields which lie in an amphitheatre of hills. The villagers were friendly, and carried themselves with an air of independence which surprised me, for my experience of Kalash Káfirs was that they were a most servile and degraded race. They, however, informed me that the Utzún differed from all the other Kalash in having a strong infusion of Bashgul Valley blood in their veins, and were consequently closely allied to the true Káfirs. These people are known to be turbulent, and to obey the Mehtar's orders with discrimination, reserving to themselves the right of private judgment on such subjects: they generally refused to carry loads.

The headman, Azá, received me with great *empressement*. We climbed the steep, difficult rock together and inspected the village, visited the place where the village effigies were kept under a shed, and finally descended again to my camping-place under a horse-chestnut tree. My friend hospitably invited me to share his home and be his guest; but not being case-hardened to Káfir dirtiness, I politely declined the kind offer, and spread my sleeping-bag under the tree. Azá sat down to entertain me in the kindest way, and told me about his village, and how his mother came from " great " Káfiristán and married the Utzún headman. He spoke with conscious pride of birth, and related with exultation that the village possessed a shrine to Gísh, the great war-god of the Káfirs, which had been erected by his father, no doubt at the instigation of the Bashgul Valley woman and her relations. Finally, he went on to more than hint that his influence was paramount throughout Káfiristán, and that with his help there would be no difficulty in my going anywhere and doing just as I pleased. As every Káfir who had spoken to me had confided to me the same information and the same assurances, and un-doubtedly with the identical object, to get the first milking of the stranger cow secretly and confidentially, Azá's remarks were received by me with considerable mental reservation, although it seemed a matter of con-gratulation that so many people were anxious to help me for pay. But several Chitráli and other friends, who knew the Káfirs well, had earnestly warned me against the positive danger which would be incurred unless my gifts were given discreetly, equitably, and openly. The advice was not only good, it was invalu-able ; and then, and afterwards, it was never disre-garded without my having to pay a penalty.

After Azá had brought me supplies and made all possible arrangements for my comfort, he retired to his home, carrying all my Káfir friends with him, but not before one of them, Torag Merak, had tried an experi-ment upon me. This man was of great wealth and importance in the Kám tribe, and was probably the richest man in the whole of Káfiristán. In his youth he had been a famous warrior, and as a peculiar mark of distinction he carried a walking-stick to which was attached a small brass bell ; so one always knew when he was near at hand. I shall never forget his appearance on the very evening referred to. He had been troublesome at Chitrál, and had tried insolence and fawning by turns with Captain Durand, in the hope of inducing the latter to give him some of the presents brought to Chitrál for political purposes, and had eventually been conciliated (for my sake) with a flaming red broad-cloth robe down to his heels, and one of those bright brass atrocities known as a Benares shield. These he now gravely assumed, and stalked up and down, the last of the sun now and then lighting up his striking coat, or setting the shield on fire for the instant. He had strong Semitic features, and his long locks, matted into rat's-tails, fell upon his gaudy shoulders, while occasionally he turned a proud glance to see if the stranger appreciated his grandeur. He was a delightful object, and made a great impression upon me, especially as this picturesque, fantastic individual was generally credited with having slain, with his own hand, more than a hundred victims, many of them, alas! helpless women and poor children. The exact number of the killed may have been exaggerated, but not very greatly, while about the slaughter of women and children there is no doubt at all. At length, having tired of parading his splendour, he sent me an abrupt message, through my Pathan servant, that unless he was at once supplied with thirty rifles and a large sum in rupees, it would be well for me to return to Chitrál forthwith.

In reply, it was pointed out to Torag Merak, that rifles could not be created on the spur of the moment, and he could himself perceive that the only one with me was an express rifle; and that neither were there

TORAG MERAK.

To face page 6.

more rupees in my possession than the small sum absolutely necessary for road expenses. He blustered and fumed a little, but received no help from his fellow-Káfirs, who, under the influence of the oldest of the party, Dán Malik, a kind and gentle old man—for a Káfir—supported me sufficiently; so the gloomy-eyed Torag Merak went off to the village in all the dignity of sulkiness. I passed the night very uncomfortably, for rain fell heavily, and my sleeping-bag was very unpleasant.

The next morning, the 23rd of October, we were up early, but found it was anything but easy to make a start. The difficulty was to get my light luggage carried. Two of the Mehtar's officials were with me, but they evidently had but little authority in the Mehtar's village of Utzún. Valuable time was passing, and the day's march was a long one. The case seemed hopeless, when old Dán Malik and another old Káfir told me significantly to go on ahead, and that they would see my things were brought after me. The suggestion did not commend itself to me at first, for there was a doubt about my ever seeing my belongings again if once they were left behind; but the two Káfirs explained by signs that they wanted me on ahead, in order that they might put a little pressure on the Utzún people, who were seated all around us, smiling and evidently amused. However, the illustration given of what was intended was quite sufficient, for when the gesture of slapping a man's cheek was made, three or four wild-looking Utzún men at once seized my baggage between them, hoisted it on to their shoulders, and began dancing with it to show how little they thought of its weight.

The next instant they all deposited their loads on the ground, and declared they were too heavy to carry; but on another wink from Dán Malik, I started on ahead. His arguments were conclusive, and we had no more trouble about the baggage that day, the men carrying the small loads easily and cheerily.

For four miles we tramped up the rough bed of a mountain torrent with very little water in it, which was fortunate, as we had to cross and recross the stream continually. It had been necessary to leave my pony behind at Utzún, and the weather was extremely hot. We then started, all together, up the steep track which runs through the pine woods to the top of the Patkun Pass, but very soon we were in two parties; one, headed by Torag Merak, consisting of about a dozen Káfirs, well ahead; the other, consisting of Dán Malik and myself, getting along as fast as we could. It was mortifying to find that this old man, after the first burst, could hold me easily, as the phrase goes, and that I was actually the worst of the party in getting up the hill. As soon as we reached the top, Torag Merak indulged himself in loud yells, and observed that he was still the best man of his tribe on a hill. This was not true, but no one cared to dispute the great man's boastful utterances. We next had a long descent through a delightful pine forest, the path exceedingly rocky and difficult in some places, and eventually came into the open, where a small dwelling stood in the midst of fields. As the people of the place were away, we all sat down to wait at some little distance, as it might perhaps have led to misunderstanding if the owners had come back and found people in their house.

Presently a Káfir woman with extremely rough and dirty hair, but rather pretty for an oldish woman, and clothed in a dark brown tunic edged with red, with a small cotton cap on the back of her head, came up and greeted all the Káfirs warmly, but without taking the least notice of me, although she could have never seen a "Frank" before in her life. Shortly afterwards a young man, her son, also appeared; he was attired simply in a goatskin, the hairy side outward, and restrained at the waist by a leather strap girdle, which also supported a dagger. He also, from shyness, I suppose, looked as if "Franks" were as common in his country as the leaves on the trees, and were equally uninteresting. I was now very tired, and was by no means pleased to find we had not reached our destination for the night. However, all the Káfirs trooped off together, so I followed behind with my Pathan servant. Suddenly one of the Káfir boys, Dán Malik's grandson, came running back to smile encouragingly on me, and repeat the Káfir equivalent for "good" several times, to let me know I was welcome. The ghastly severed head of this nice friendly youth it was my destiny to see brought into Kámdesh, with sorrow and lamentation, not many months afterwards.

If the woman had taken little notice of me at first, she made up for her neglect when reinforced and supported by the women of the small village where we halted for the night. After a sheep had been killed in my honour, and a kind of still-room had been provided for my accommodation, the women, boys, and children of the place besieged my door for hours, and even flattened their noses against the wood, hunting for cracks to see through, after the door was closed upon them. We indulged our common curiosity for a long time, the great feature of the scene being when the man who acts as a temporarily inspired priest at all sacrifices, and about whom there will be a good deal to tell farther on, stepped

DÁN MALIK.

up to me, and gingerly turned back my coat cuff, to expose to wonder, and let us hope to admiration also, my not very white wrist.

Next morning, that terrible old man, Torag Merak, came and told me he had made all arrangements for

having my baggage carried from that village (Gourdesh)
to Kámdesh. He remarked that it was the custom in
that country for the money to be paid in advance. He
then calculated up all the stages and rates for porterage,
which were paid at once. It never occurred to me that
there was no money in Káfiristán, nor any organisation
for the regular carriage of luggage, such as the Káfir
had described. However, Torag Merak had got the
money and my baggage had started, so all seemed well;
but we had not got more than a mile or so, when it was
discovered that the old rascal had left us altogether.
Then the baggage-carriers threw down their loads, and
with the utmost good temper proceeded to make their
own bargain for the journey. As they knew nothing
about money nor about distances, and merely had the
fixed idea that for their own credit's sake they must
make as much profit out of the stranger as Torag
Merak had made, the preposterous nature of their
demands may be imagined. All the money there was
with me would not have satisfied half of their absurd
demands. I do not know how we eventually got on;
sometimes we were on the point of carrying the loads
ourselves; while at others, the only way seemed to be
to abandon them altogether. Every half-hour or so
the discussions were resumed, and the previous bargain
shamelessly ignored by the Gourdesh carriers. It was
worse than useless to get angry, for on the first exhibition of the kind on my part, the people put down their
burdens, quietly but firmly, and announced their intention
of going away. The march was one of extreme difficulty,
the track being over an apparently endless series of low
cliffs, the sides of which were in many places worn so

smooth that there was no foothold, and it was necessary for people who indulged in such luxuries as boots to move along in a sitting position. Then, after each cliff crossed in this way, a halt had to be made to pull out the unanticipated spear-grass which insinuated itself through the clothing. The heat of the sun was excessive. This, combined with the long delays in connection with the luggage and the difficulties of the road, made it impossible for us to get farther than Sárat bridge. So there we camped.

We now numbered a considerable party, for several Káfirs had joined us on the road, and Torag Merak had deputed his Musalmán son, who lives near Gourdesh, to accompany me. Except in religion, the son was very like his father, and it was subsequently found that much of the trouble experienced owing to the absurd demands of the baggage-coolies was at his instigation. It is worth noting here that Torag Merak caused two of his sons to be brought up as Musalmáns, and gave them his property near Gourdesh to live upon. It seems that by this means he intended to be on the right side, whatever might happen. If Umrá Khan, or any other Musalmán power, managed to conquer Káfiristán, then Torag Merak would be safe through the influence of his sons; while as for the latter, they were naturally friends with their co-religionists, while the neighbouring Káfirs, although they disliked having the Musalmán colony in their midst, dare not interfere with it, for the whole of Torag Merak's clan would avenge the death of any one of its members, whether he were Káfir or had embraced Islám. This is only one of many instances which go to prove that the enmity of the Káfirs for Afghan races is one of blood and antagonism, far more than a religious feud.

The night spent at Sárat bridge was sufficiently un-comfortable. Excessive fatigue had destroyed hunger, which was perhaps as well, for the only food procurable was of the roughest and coarsest description. Sleep was impossible, partly perhaps from the excitement of novel

SACRIFICING GOATS: FIRING OFF THE BLOOD-STAINED ARROW.

experiences and from extreme tiredness, but chiefly from the cheerfulness and vivacity of my Káfir friends. I had bought them a huge goat from a grazing-ground close at hand, and this was sacrificed with full ritual, Dán Malik officiating as priest; and the priest, who becomes temporarily inspired on such occasions, going through wonderful antics, perhaps for my benefit. Then they all fell to resolutely, and feasted royally. At the beginning the banquet promised to be a failure. Torag Merak's Musalmán son, already referred to, was named Gul Muhammad Khan, although the Káfirs obstinately refused to know him by any other name than that he received at his birth, namely, Torag, while, in a char-acteristic Káfir way, they always prefixed to this name the word "stout"; not because he was a heavy man, but in the sense of "strong." This young man now came to me and observed that the Káfirs could not eat the big goat unless they were supplied with salt, as it was against their custom to do so. Feeling disappointed and sorry, I expressed my regret at not having the re-quired condiment, on which "Stout" Torag smilingly strolled away, and the cooking and feasting went on merrily. It seems that the people were curious to find out what kind of wealth was in the medicine-box. As they now considered they had proved it was not salt or something valuable to eat, they decided it must be rupees. My sleeping-bag had been placed some dis-tance from the fire where the feast was progressing, but the friendly Káfirs came and slept all round me, not because there was any danger, but to show their sociability. One of the Gourdesh men struck up a droning chant, which apparently had the effect of send-ing them all to sleep except the singer; but this was not so, for the instant he flagged, another man or group of men would take up the refrain, to be succeeded by others, waking up, as it would seem, for no other pur-pose than to make sleep impossible to those who could not sleep at will and in spite of whatever noise was going on.

In the morning every one was bright and refreshed by

MEMORIAL GATEWAY.

a good sleep except myself. The first incident of the day was the general refusal of the baggage-porters to

carry anything farther. They were superior to all remonstrances and reproaches, and perfectly good-tempered.
They had made up their minds not to go any farther,
and to keep all the money they had received for the
whole journey and back again; so they smilingly made
their farewells and departed. No doubt Gul Muhammad
Khan was cognisant and approved of their proceedings.
It is impossible to say what his next manœuvre would
have been, but if he had any little scheme in his mind,
it was spoiled by the Káfir headmen, probably out of
patience with the unceasing delays, making some arrangement amongst themselves, and some of them actually
shouldering my impedimenta, a great condescension for
a Káfir of any rank. So we started for Kámdesh, where
we arrived late in the afternoon, I with my feet cut to
pieces, sleeplessly tired, and almost too hungry to eat;
for, owing to pride of stomach and other causes, hardly
any food had passed my lips for three days. Subsequent
experience taught me to be less fastidious about my
diet.

On the road we had passed a curious memorial gateway with fantastic wooden images on the top, at the
mouth of the Kamu Valley, and farther on had been
kindly received by people of the riverside village of
Mergrom—a kind of Káfir city of refuge.

CHAPTER II

KÁMDESH is the chief village and the tribal headquarters of the Kám Káfirs. It is high up on a great spur, which runs down in an undulating manner from the Arákon ridge four miles to the south of the village, and is bounded on one side by the Nichingul stream, and on the other by another huge spur on which the hamlets of Bináram and Jinjám are built. Between the two is a torrent which turns the village water-mills. Kámdesh is from 6000 to 7000 feet in altitude, according as it is measured from the lowest houses or from those at the top. Including its fields, it covers a large extent of ground. It is divided into three main portions, the upper, the lower, and the east, of which the upper is as large as the other two parts put together. The whole village is built on sloping ground, which is at places extremely steep, except a portion of the upper division, which is constructed along a moderately level ridge. The only other really level spots are the contiguous house-roofs. Kámdesh is about 2000 feet above the right bank of the Bashgul river, down to which

there is a very steep road. It numbers about 600
houses, which are sufficient for the inhabitants. There

KÁMDESH.

are no defences or fortifications of any kind, with the
exception of a picturesque tower, which stands close

to the highest houses in the village. It is difficult to get a good view of Kámdesh, or Kámbrom, as the Káfirs prefer to call it, until the long steep path from the river-bank has been traversed, and the village is nearly approached. Then the view is highly impressive. The houses are well built, and most of them are two or three storeys in height; while the shrines, memorial gateways, and the effigies at the end of notched poles, dotted all about, greatly add to the interest of the scene. A nearer approach does not destroy an illusion, for Kámdesh is remarkably clean for a Káfir village, and is especially free from that smoke grime which gives such a mean and squalid appearance to so many Káfir domiciles. The wood-work of the open, veran-dah-like top storey of most of the houses is generally carefully carved; while the famous shrines of the two gods, Gísh and Moní, which stand in an open space near the east division of the village, are not only elabo-rately carved, but the former is otherwise curiously ornamented, as will be described subsequently.

A few of the tribal elders came to meet me, but there was no pressing curiosity on my account until after I had accepted the hospitality of Dán Malik and adjourned to his house. There my host provided me with a swept room, which opened on to an open verandah. The furniture of the apartment consisted of the common Eastern bed, a square framework, laced together in this instance with leather thongs, and one or two ordinary Káfir stools. The verandah room in front was crowded with the women, youths, and children of the family and of the adjacent houses, for Dán Malik's abode was in a kind of irregular street, with habitations on both sides and in front. This grouping of the houses was, no doubt, accidental, as it was the only instance of the kind I noticed in Káfiristán. After Dán Malik had retired to some other house for the night, the curiosity of the wild-looking figures in the verandah became inconvenient, when, for quietness and rest, I retired into my room and closed the stout wooden door. Recent comers, hearing of the strange individual there was on show, became outraged at the thought that others could boast of having seen what they were not permitted to view, and they would bang open my door to thrust in torches at arm's length, and stare with all the intentness of their keen, strange faces. At first I submitted with as good a grace as possible, but at last, getting really annoyed, I drove away my tormentors, and finding a bolt in the door, secured it properly. It turned out that these troublesome visitors were only people of the lowest rank—slaves and such persons—who were delighted at an opportunity to show off before a stranger, and whom no one ever imagined it necessary to protect me against. All women in Káfiristán rank more or less with the same class.

My stay in Kámdesh lasted three whole days, and until the morning of the 29th October. During those three days I left no stone unturned to conciliate the people, especially the headmen. The former were easily pleased, and came to see me in large numbers; but of the headmen, only a few put in an appearance, while two of them, Utah, the priest of the Kám, and another man, of hardly less importance, named Chandlu Astán, viewed me at first with grave suspicion. Utah luckily had a little son, of whom he was inordinately fond,

TROUBLESOME VISITORS.

To face page 22.

suffering from bad eyes, which were quickly cured by my medicine-box; while Chandlu Astán was very vain of his dancing, and proved easily assailable by compliments on his skill in that exercise. After the second day both these men became friendly, and matters then

UTAH'S CHILDREN.

went on smoothly. These two, with Dán Malik, who was the statesman of the party, with one or two others, —notably a man named Mir Ján—once or twice came mysteriously into my room, closed and locked the door, and discussed high politics, suggesting, amongst other things, that I should bring them many rifles, and they would then open a road for me to Peshawar through Dír and Swát. They were evidently disappointed at my reply, that I was a man of peace, and had only come amongst them purely and solely from the love of travelling, and to study a people that no one of my fellow-countrymen knew anything about.

My offer to take two young men of good family back with me to India was at first openly scouted and derided. It was then taken up enthusiastically. Several suitable youths volunteered to go with me. They were accepted, were carried off proudly by admiring friends and relations to prepare for the journey, and then were seen no more. At length, two young men agreed faithfully to go with me ; one of them belonged to a powerful family or clan, while the other was a man of low rank in life, named Shermalik, who was palmed off on me by the priest and Dán Malik as a relation of both. As a matter of fact, this man, Shermalik, was the only Káfir who eventually accompanied me to India at this time, for at the last moment the courage of the other failed him, and he never put in an appearance after I started on my return journey from Kámdesh. It was afterwards related to me that the reason the low-born man was permitted to go with me to India was because it was considered that if he were killed or enslaved in that distant country, it would not be a matter of much consequence to the tribe.

The march back to the Chitrál frontier was characterised by troubles similar to, or even worse, than those we had before experienced, and also by a somewhat unpleasant episode which occurred just short of

A QUARRELSOME KÁFIR.

To face page 29.

the Chitrál border, where we fell in with a travelling band of Káfirs of the Mádugál or Mumán tribe, under a famous chief, known by the name of Bahdur. Bahdur had been somewhat truculent in his behaviour the same morning near Gourdesh, where I occupied a small hut, and he had refused to leave the room in which I was putting on my clothes until he was practically ejected by me. He had then gone away sulkily. While almost alone in the pine forest leading up to the Parpit Pass, several of Bahdur's men caught me up, and scowling at my Pathan servant, moved alongside of us for a few yards, when one of them suddenly strung his double curved bow, and fiercely and threateningly shouted, "Banát gats," that is, "Give me a present." My Pathan, a plucky boy, unarmed as he was, jumped at the Káfir, but I managed to get in front of him again, and pretended not to understand the nature of the demand, and to treat the whole matter as a joke; so, laughing loudly, I caught the Káfir by his right wrist, and putting my weight on the pull, sent him flying off the narrow path and a few yards down the hillside. He and the others stared at my laughing but rather rough procedure in solemn surprise, while we hurried on, and presently caught up Bahdur himself, from whom I demanded food. This he gave me, and then remarked on the terrible things he would have done if we had not eaten together. He then began to boast of the number of people he had killed. The Pathan quietly but insultingly remarked that he supposed the slain were mostly women and children. The fat was nearly in the fire again, but I angrily upbraided my servant, and got rid of the troublesome Káfirs as soon as possible by getting them to go on ahead. Bahdur, some eighteen months afterwards, gave me much trouble in his own village, where he was on the point of making me a prisoner. He was a terrible homicide, almost rivalling the famous Torag Merak in that respect, but both these men belied their character in their looks. In repose, both had sad faces, a world of sorrow in their eyes, and the identical look which is observable in a certain Chitráli magnate who has killed many people. He has a sad, even gentle face, and is precisely the man a poor wretch would seek mercy from, and is the very last man who would grant it.

At Utzún we caught up the Káfir Shermalik, who, as related, had promised, with another, to go to India with me. I was now confronted with a serious difficulty. Finding himself deserted by his companion, Shermalik, my prize, the chief result of my journey, burst into tears and declared that nothing on earth would induce him to go one step farther. I reasoned with him for hours, painting glowing pictures of the delights of India, and even bribed the people about to add their assurances to mine. For a long time all was of no avail. Finally, however, he cheered up a bit, and said he would accompany me provided I agreed to adopt him as my son on the spot. There was nothing for it but to agree, and so the ceremony, as practised in the Bashgul Valley, was there and then enacted. A goat was procured, quickly killed, and its kidneys were removed. These were cooked at a fire and cut into morsels by an officiating Káfir, who then placed Shermalik and me side by side, and alternately fed us both with the fragments on the

point of a knife. At short intervals we had to turn
our heads to one another and go through the motion
of kissing with our lips a foot or so apart. But the
surprise was in reserve. My coat and shirt were opened
and some butter was placed on my left breast, to which
Shermalik applied his lips with the greatest energy and
earnestness. I jumped as if shot, but the thing was
over. As the objects of my first visit were now fairly
well accomplished, I started for India to equip myself
for a prolonged stay in Káfiristán.

It was at Utzún that a rather curious episode occurred.
It was in connection with my first efforts to persuade
Shermalik to remain with me. We were all seated
round a fire discussing the whole question. A white-
haired Káfir, who had joined me on my return journey
at Kamu, was seated four or five men from me, and
with the garrulity of age was arguing, advising, and
settling matters generally. In a pause, when struggling
to make myself understood in the Chitráli language, of
which I had the merest smattering, the old man began
afresh. Another man, seated by my side, picked up a
small piece of stick and threw it gently at the Kamu
man to attract his attention, and said the equivalent of
"Just you shut up, and let us hear what the Frank
has to say." In an instant the old man was on his
feet, flourishing his axe, while the man alongside of
me whipped round his sword-belt and flashed out his
weapon. I could not understand what had happened to
cause all this commotion. By the time the whole matter
had been explained to me the men were furiously approaching one another. Such a tremendous quarrel for
so slight a cause in some way appealed to my risible

faculties, and instead of being able to intervene, I simply exhausted myself with laughter. The men at once stopped, looked at me in a most sheepish manner, and there was an end of the affair.

At Gilgit, on our way to India, we met. a missionary agent, a converted Muhammadan, whom the Church missionaries at Peshawar had most kindly placed at my disposal. Sayed Sháh was the name of this "native Christian." He had visited Káfiristán on more than one occasion, and was fairly well acquainted with the Bashgul Valley dialect. I engaged him to take care of my Káfir "son," and to return with me the following year as an interpreter. He was a genial, kindly man, and a pleasant companion. Unhappily, he was somewhat timid in disposition and lacking in firmness of character. In the end he proved a bad bargain, but at first he was useful to me in many ways.

CHAPTER III

WE reached India without incident. Having settled several business matters with the Foreign Office at Calcutta, and having made proper arrangements for Shermalik to stay in India for the cold weather, and to be taken to Kashmir as soon as the sun began to get uncomfortably hot, I took short leave to England. The Káfir refused to accompany me, alleging the great distance as his excuse. He never ceased to regret this decision afterwards, and explained that he had been by turns persuaded, and frightened, and bribed to refuse by the people employed by me to look after him, who feared to lose their occupation if he accompanied me to England.

On the voyage home and out I had the good fortune to travel with my friend Captain Parfitt, of the P. and O. Company's service, who most kindly gave me much valuable advice, and many useful hints about observation-taking. This gentleman is not only possessed of high scientific attainments, but has a peculiar gift of lucid explanation, while his patience is as inexhaustible as his kindness. In London, I availed myself of the generous help that the Royal Geographical Society places at the disposal of all would-be travellers and explorers. Unfortunately I made the common mistake of attempting too much in the short time at my disposal. It did not then seem impossible for me to attack, with fair hopes of success, various sciences of which I was practically in complete ignorance. Able and experienced instructors put the subjects they taught in so clear and so pleasant a light that everything seemed easy and simple. But when, after the lapse of a few months, the time came for me to apply all this varied information, I quickly discovered that a short scamper into the fair fields of science, no matter how easy and pleasant the journey may seem, and no matter how vivid all impressions may appear at the time, leaves on the mind little more than vague and confused pictures of a vast and beautiful country.

Having provided myself with toys, photographic apparatus, compressed medicines, and miniature surgical instruments, together with various small articles with which to please and amuse the Káfirs, I returned to India in May to complete my equipment at Srinagar. After receiving the scientific instruments and books which were provided for me by the Government of India, there was nothing more to do except to choose followers and servants who were willing to accompany me on my journey to Káfiristán.

My choice was limited. Volunteers at first were numerous, but no sooner had the nature of the difficulties to be encountered been honestly explained to them, than their enthusiasm rapidly cooled down and they cried off. Finally, I was compelled to content myself with Sayed Sháh, already referred to, and the young Pathan who had been with me before, who, though young, plucky, and hard-

working, was unluckily of a morose and quarrelsome disposition. During the winter this man had been learning
simple cookery and other useful arts. He was most
intelligent, and but for his infirmities of temper would

SHERMALIK.

have been an invaluable servant. Of course, my Káfir
" son " Shermalik, who was awaiting me at Srinagar, in
the charge of Sayed Sháh, also accompanied me. He
had already acquired in India an ungrammatical, but very
useful, knowledge of Hindustáni. At the urgent request

of the other three, but with some reluctance on my part, a powerful, hard-working Kashmiri, named Rusalá, was also engaged. He had a shifty, ill-looking face, with a fawning or bullying manner, according to circumstances. He was, however, undoubtedly intelligent, and quick at learning all menial duties, and there was no one else to be had. In the end, this meek-looking man nearly succeeded in wrecking my plans altogether, and it was only his want of pluck which prevented him from turning my journey into a complete fiasco.

On my arrival in Srinagar, I found, to my extreme annoyance, that Shermalik, the Káfir, had been followed to India by a Kunar Valley Muhammadan, named Mián Gul. This individual I had met in Káfiristán. He was connected by marriage or by ties of friendship with many of the chief men of Kámdesh. He had two homes, one at Mirkani, at the mouth of the Ashrath Valley, the other in the "Gabar" village of Arnú or Arandú. He had travelled down to India by the direct road from Chitrál to Peshawar, through Dír and Swát, a road he knew well, for his occupation was that of a petty trader. He was in the habit of carrying news about the Káfirs to the Peshawar Church missionaries, and with the money he received in return he bought small articles in the Peshawar bazaar to trade with in Káfiristán. His sole object in following the Káfir to India was the performance of a well-laid plan to "exploit" me. In anticipation of my arrival, he took Shermalik to various shops in the Srinagar bazaar, where they together selected a large number of swords, shields, and guns, and all manner of expensive articles of clothing, which they intended me to buy, and in the supposed improbable event of my refusing to comply with their wishes,

Mián Gul hoped to succeed in persuading the Káfir to leave me secretly, and go back with him by the Dír-Swát road to his own country. He promised the man large but impossible rewards if he would agree to do as he wished. Shermalik, however, partly from loyalty to me, and partly from a shrewd suspicion that Mián Gul could never redeem his splendid promises, declined to listen to his treacherous companion, when, hearing my refusal to entertain their wild suggestions for a single instant, the time came for him to make his decision one way or the other. Nevertheless, he was thoroughly demoralised, and in a fury of disappointment when he found his dreams of wealth could not be gratified. If I had bought even half of the property these two men had selected, it would have ruined me, while my baggage train would have extended to an impossible length.

My difficulty was greater than it may appear. Shermalik could be quickly reduced to tears and subjection, and then as quickly restored again to smiles and temporary happiness by small gifts and personal kindnesses; but Mián Gul was a man of different fibre—he knew his power. It was quite possible for him to get back to Káfiristán a full month before us. Once there, he could easily create so strong a prejudice against me that it might be impossible for me to return to Kámdesh at all. It was necessary to be most cautious in my dealings with him. As a preliminary, we had a private interview together, in the course of which he became thoroughly frightened and cowed. He was then paid in a lordly way his own estimate of his travelling expenses, receiving at the same time an extremely liberal allowance for his daily requirements. Finally, as if no unpleasantness had occurred, he was engaged as my servant at a definite monthly wage, and started off at once to Peshawar to buy kerosene oil, and convey it if possible to Chitrál, where, in any case, he was to await my arrival.

I had decided not to ask Government for a guard or an escort of any kind. My reasons were, that a considerable number of armed men could alone be of real use to me in time of danger, while such a number could neither be fed nor supplied with transport. A small guard, on the other hand, would be worse than useless ; for not only would it be unable to withstand any serious attack, but there would always be the fear that the men might begin quarrelling with the Káfirs, and in that way start a disturbance, the result of which might be very serious.

With the four followers already mentioned, I left Srinagar for Gilgit on July 29th. On the road we picked up five Balti coolies, who agreed to remain with me for a year to carry loads and make themselves generally useful. The remembrance of the faithfulness and simple devotion of these five men always excites within me a warm feeling of admiration. No threats nor promises could ever induce them to swerve in their loyalty for an instant. They were childlike in their simplicity, and childlike also in their complete trust in me. For several weeks in Káfiri-stán they were my sole companions. During that period these five men carried my loads, cooked my food, did all my work, and made friends wherever they went, while one of them actually qualified as an interpreter. I have had as good servants in India as any man could desire, but never any so good as these poor Baltis.

On August 17th we reached Gilgit. Two days before a terrible misfortune befell me at Bunji. In crossing the

Indus, one of my boats, containing seventeen Astori coolies, was swamped and sunk. All on board were

ACCIDENT AT BUNJI.

drowned, with the exception of the boatmen, who managed to escape with great difficulty, and reach the bank.

c

Most of the articles so carefully selected in England were lost beyond recovery ; a great part of my photographic apparatus, all my toys and books, my diaries and journals for three years, besides a large quantity of small valuables. All my money went down also. I had to borrow money from the Kashmir Major in charge of the ferry and Bunji fort to enable me to get on to Gilgit. Not the least of my misfortunes was the fact that, with the exception of a light pair of lawn-tennis shoes, which I was wearing at the time, every pair of boots I possessed was lost in the river. Shermalik lost some of his treasures also. They were, of course, ultimately replaced by me, but, at the moment, he was so excited and in such despair at the extent of his misfortunes, that he declared he would throw himself into the river and be drowned also.

At Gilgit, Mr. Manners Smith was officiating for Colonel Durand as British Agent. He did everything in his power to help, and was unremitting in his efforts to start me off for Chitrál, while the clerks in the Agency gave me Kashmiri " chapplies," or sandals, with leather stockings, to replace my lost boots. In a few days we were again in a position to march.

Leaving Gilgit on August 24th, Chitrál was reached on September 15th, without our having experienced any difficulties on the road. The baggage, consisting of twenty-seven loads, was carried by Balti coolies engaged at Gilgit. My idea was to take all these loads to Kámdesh, if it were possible to do so, and then send the porters back at once to their homes in Kashmir. I then intended to try and get a house in Kámdesh in which to store my goods, and for all subsequent journeys to rely upon the five permanent Balti servants, with whatever other help was locally obtainable. This, indeed, was the only possible plan. The experience of relying upon Káfirs to carry my baggage had been instructive, though painful, and was not to be repeated. My entire party, including myself, amounted only to ten persons, which was the utmost number for which food could be ensured. As a matter of fact, the five Baltis always had to carry the baggage without any help, except on one or two rare occasions. This compelled me always to cut down our travelling outfit to its lowest possible dimensions, and often necessitated my leaving the tent behind ; for if ever any of the Baltis fell sick or got over-worked, it was impossible to supply his place and get it carried, and uncomfortable as the arrangement was, it was nevertheless better to abandon the tent than to part with any other portion of my marching equipment.

CHAPTER IV

FROM the 15th to the 21st of September, I remained at
Chitrál as the guest of the Mehtar Amán-ul-Mulk, who
treated me with consistent kindness.

My original intention of marching straight to Kámdesh
with all my baggage by Kila Drósh and the Kalash
village of Utzún, the road I had formerly traversed,
had now to be altered for two reasons. First, there were
secret rumours about that a small band of Dír fanatics
had set out with the intention of intercepting me on the
farther side of Utzún; and second, none of the Kámdesh
headmen had come to Chitrál to meet me.

There were no means of verifying the rumour about
the Dír fanatics. The story was circumstantially told me
by a man who had every reason to wish me well, and he
himself appeared to be convinced of the truth of his
narrative. It was to the effect that the irreconcilable
Mullá of Dír, Sháh Baba, had sworn twelve men on the
Kurán to waylay me on the road between Utzún and
Gourdesh, at some spot in the thick forest on the mountain ridge which is traversed by the Patkun Pass. The
men, it was said, had been given rifles, on the under-

standing that all were eventually to be returned, except in the event of a successful ending to the expedition, in which case the man who actually fired the lucky shot was to be allowed to retain his weapon, while the others were to be given small allotments of land. Umrá Khán of Jandúl was said to be cognisant of the plot. Of the party sent out on this business, a large proportion were understood to be recent converts of Sháh Baba's ; such men are generally held to be extremely fanatical. They had been incited to attack me, so it was said, by the assurances they received that my mission was not only hostile to their religion, but must interfere with their material prosperity also, because my real object was an unavowed attempt to get possession of all the Narsut country on behalf of the Government of India. My informant added that the chief desire of the instigators of the plot was seriously to compromise the Mehtar of Chitrál in the eyes of the English Government, it being thought that he would be held personally responsible for anything untoward which might happen to me.

All this news was given to me secretly, and somewhat dramatically. The narrator had been resident in Jandúl for some months, and was believed to have enjoyed some share of the confidence of Umrá Khán while there. It was impossible to find out the exact degree of credence which should be given to the man's statements. If he merely concocted the story to demonstrate his personal devotion to me, in the hope of immediate or future reward, he had at any rate learnt his lesson carefully and cleverly, and he stuck to the details consistently. However, it was not a matter of supreme importance. I had no particular wish to travel by any special road ;

indeed, it would be pleasant to discover another and easier route to Kámdesh; but the chief reason which made me change my plans was that none of the Kám Káfirs had come to meet me at Chitrál. This looked rather ominous, especially to Sayed Sháh, who confessed that he did not like the situation at all. He was obviously nervous and unwilling to leave Chitrál, so it was decided that he should be put in charge of the bulk of the baggage, and be left behind in Chitrál, while I pushed on through Aiún and Bomboret into the Káfir valley of Pittigul, and discovered for myself the true position of affairs.

I told the Mehtar of my intention, which he objected to very strongly, but finding me fixed in my determination he suggested sending one of his own sons, and a suitable escort to guard me as far as Kámdesh, and at once bring us back to Chitrál.

The chief of the Lutdeh Káfirs, Kán Mára, with five or six followers, was with the Mehtar at the time, and the latter, who had now grown very old, tried hard to persuade the Káfir to go with me, and, taking advantage of my supposed ignorance of the country, to lead me to Lutdeh instead of Kámdesh, and finally to send me back again within ten days to Chitrál. Kán Mára saw the impossibility of carrying out such a childish scheme, and laughingly declined to have anything to do with it. The poor old Mehtar then got more and more depressed; he refused his food, and shed bitter tears at my pertinacity. He pathetically remarked to his courtiers that 25,000 rupees a year depended on my safety.

Finally, being at his wits' end, he implored me to

sign a paper exonerating him from anything which might befall me, and stating clearly that my contemplated journey was to be undertaken in direct opposition to his wishes and advice. Although it was an obvious risk to put my name to a document which might seem to give the Mehtar a free hand to intrigue against me to his heart's content, it nevertheless seemed best to comply with his wishes, for it was certain he must be well acquainted with the firmness of character possessed by Colonel Durand, who was on his way back to Gilgit, and must consequently recognise that, document or no document, it would be dangerous to his interests could it ever be proved that he had a hand in any such intrigue against me as was so lamentably successful against poor Hayward in Yásin, in which the Mehtar was suspected of being concerned. So I signed the paper.

As a last move in the game, the Mehtar sent me over letters said to have been written by Umrá Khán, which stated that the latter intended to attack the Bashgul Káfirs at once. The Mírza who brought the letters explained that they had been intercepted on the road. They appeared to be forgeries, but I sent back word to the Mehtar that, in my opinion, if any letters of Umrá Khán were ever captured, they had been written with the intention of being seized, and that we were both of us so well acquainted with the peculiar character of the chief of Jandúl, that we might fairly infer that if he had written declaring his intention of attacking the Káfirs, then his real object must certainly be to attack some one else in a precisely opposite direction, and that consequently Swát was probably at that moment in imminent danger of an early invasion from Jandúl.

The Mehtar having exhausted all his arguments against my leaving Chitrál, made a final stipulation that his son Ghulám Dastgír, with a strong following, should accompany me over the pass and into the Pittigul Valley. His selection of this particular son indicated that he still hoped that something might yet be arranged to prevent my remaining in Káfiristán, but as it was impolitic to begin wearying discussions all over again, I contented myself with warmly thanking him for his anxiety on my behalf. We parted from one another most amicably.

The old Mehtar, Amán-ul-Mulk, was torn by conflicting counsels. He disliked my journey and thoroughly distrusted its objects. He always, to the end of his days, regarded the Government of India with grave suspicion, and sincerely believed that its real desire was to extend its sovereignty over Chitrál, over Káfiristán, and over all the neighbouring districts south of the Hindu-Kush. His great fear of the power of the Amir of Kabul originally impelled him to seek an alliance with Kashmir, his dread of the Afghans being even greater than his suspicion of the English, and their feudatory the Maharaja of Kashmir. The Mehtar's overtures had resulted, after a time, in his receiving a yearly subsidy of money and other presents, first from the Kashmir Durbar, and subsequently from the Government of India as well. Avarice rarely diminishes with age, and the British-Kashmir subsidy had gradually become such an important item in the Chitrál state revenue, that if anything had occurred to jeopardise or stop it, the Mehtar would have been heart-broken.

His final resolve was sufficiently astute for so old a man. He decided first of all to try everything in his power to prevent me from going to Káfiristán at all, but failing in that attempt, he still trusted in his ability to induce the Káfirs to rob, ill-use, and cast me naked out of their country, and in that way afford him an opportunity of playing a characteristic manœuvre. He would receive me with indignation and compassion, while at the same time he would make urgent application to the Government of India for more rifles and further subsidies, with which he hoped, while nominally avenging my wrongs, to conquer for himself the whole of the Bashgul Valley, and thus effectually prevent the Káfirs from coquetting ever again with British officers. But age had unsteadied his once firm will, and there is more than a suspicion that on several occasions his impatience to carry out the alternative part of his scheme led him to disregard my personal safety altogether, and made him merely desirous of finding a pretext for sending an armed force, paid and equipped by the Government of India, into Káfiristán, to avenge my actual death, which was to be brought about by means of intrigues from Chitrál. The Mehtar had, however, got beyond carrying out a continuous and persistent line of policy. He kept shifting and re-sorting his cards, which his trembling hands could not prevent even the simplest and most unobservant from seeing.

In our personal intercourse, I believe the Mehtar always had kindly feelings towards me, but that, of course, would not prevent him for a moment from sacrificing me, if he thought it the best policy for Chitrál. He is dead now, but he will always remain in my memory as the wreck of a truly remarkable man.

CHAPTER V

LEAVING most of the baggage behind in the care of Sayed Sháh, we started from Chitrál on September 22, with a few coolies only. A message had been previously sent to warn the Kámdesh people of my arrival in Chitrál, but no reply had been received, nor had my messenger returned. The Lutdeh chief Kán·Márá, and several of his fellow-tribesmen, travelled with me on their homeward journey, while the Mehtar's son Ghulám Dastgír, with an armed retinue, composed my escort.

This young Chitráli prince, or Mehtar Jao, was an interesting personage. Owing to his mother being a woman of inferior birth, he occupied a lower position in the Chitrál social scale than some of the Mehtar's other sons. He was, and is, a man of great astuteness and cunning, and this is probably the reason he still survives so many of his brothers, who have murdered one another, or have been otherwise slain within the last four years. This young man, Ghulám Dastgír, was a fine polo-player, a keen hunter, and untiring on the hillside. He was a gallant-looking youth, but an utter barbarian 'at heart, horribly cruel, as all the Chitrál princes seem to be, and incurably vicious. Nevertheless, his Oriental tact and polite genial manners made him a pleasant companion on a journey. He was wonderfully inquisitive, and his naïve questions about England and the British Constitution were very amusing. The British Parliament was a stumbling-block to his understanding, and the reason there was never any fighting and murdering amongst brothers for the succession to the throne or to property was to him evidently as absurd as it was unnatural.

We travelled by Aiún and the Kalash village of Bomboret, and thence over a comparatively low but steep pass to the Káfir valley of Pittigul. We reached Kámdesh on October 1, having been somewhat delayed on our journey by certain occurrences.

On the road to Aiún, Shermalik and the man Mián Gul, who had joined me at Chitrál with the kerosene oil, which he had brought up from Peshawar, relieved the monotony of the journey along the bank by occasionally lagging behind, and then swimming down the river in mid-stream, passing us with great velocity. They put their clothes inside the inflated goat-skins which supported them, or else carried them piled up on their heads, which were high up out of the water. Káfirs and others are very expert in this kind of swimming, and on these inflated skins can easily swim goats and sheep over a river. Mián Gul was said to have reduced the practice to a science, and wonderful tales were told of his prowess in that respect. Shermalik gravely informed me that Mián Gul could take two

unwilling cows across a river at one time by means of
an inflated goat-skin; but the truth of the statement
is open to doubt.

Immediately after leaving Aiún, a ludicrous thing
happened. I was practising measuring distances by
counting my pony's strides, and by shifting pebbles
from one hand to the other, to mark scores and hun-
dreds. With my mind intently fixed on my occupation,
I did not perceive that the man who was running in
front to show the way along a broad deep irrigation
channel was leading me under a huge rock where there
was no room for my pony. The first intimation I had
of it was my coming into violent contact with the
rock, which striking me heavily in the thigh, hurled
both pony and rider into the watercourse ignominiously.
No harm was done, except that it was not pleasant to
begin a march with a ducking. A large number of
Káfirs were accompanying me from Chitrál on their
road to Lutdeh. They were most sympathetic; indeed
far too much so, as all one wished for just then was
solitude. We followed the Bomboret river track the
whole way, the coolies going by an upper road. We
must have crossed and recrossed the river at least twenty
times, always by means of a single-pole bridge. It was
difficult to preserve the balance on the narrow slippery
pole, which was continually shifting about. The water
was running down at a great pace, washing over the frail
bridge. It was impossible for me to maintain my foothold on it at all, and there had always to be a man in
front and another behind to get me across. The Káfirs
and Chitrális were as much at home on the single pine
branch as if they were on solid rock, and we passed

over every time without mishap. The Bomboret torrent
at that season of the year is fordable, though with difficulty, and some unfortunate cows going the same way as
myself were continually being swept down-stream, and
battered against the rocks at the fording-places.

When we got to Bomboret, we found Shermalik's
brother and three companions there. They had gone
to meet us at Utzún, but hearing of our change of
march, they had changed their direction also, and
hurried to join us. They reported that everything
was satisfactory when they left Kámdesh some days
previously.

In the evening the Mehtar Jao provided a Kalash
dance for our entertainment. The music consisted of
feeble pipes supplemented by cat-calls. The appearance
of the witch-like old women dancing heavily their peculiar polka dance-step, singly or in pairs, was strange,
almost weird. They wore their national costume, a
tunic, not unlike that worn by the Siáh Posh women,
but much longer, and a peculiar and very effective
cloth cap, reaching to the shoulders and sewn all over
with cowrie shells. Sometimes they danced in pairs,
side by side, with arms round one another's waists,
at others they formed in a line, each woman's right
hand on her neighbour's left shoulder, and her left arm
round the waist of the woman on the other side of
her. Then led by a woman carrying a spear, the whole
line edged round a group of men which surrounded
the musicians, and helped them by a monotonous chant
in time with the drums, and by a rhythmic slapping
of hands. One or two men were with the women in
line. What pleased the Mehtar Jao best was a dance

of little boys, who bobbed about like corks with the
ordinary Kalash step enlivened so as to be almost
unrecognisable.

The next morning one of the headmen of the Kám,
named Tong Chandlu, put in an appearance. He made
no excuses for the absence of the representatives of his
tribe on my arrival at Chitrál, but brought me greetings
from Dán Malik and the High Priest. He then began
informing everybody, in most energetic tones, that I
ought not to be allowed to go to Kámdesh at all, without first giving the Káfirs rifles and money. This did
not sound encouraging. It turned out afterwards that,
having missed me, he had gone to Chitrál, where the
Mehtar had promised him a glorious robe and a gold
turban if he succeeded in stopping my journey to
Kámdesh. Kán Márá, and his large following of
Lutdeh (Katir) men, left me at Bomboret, to proceed
by the Sháwal Pass to their own country. They had
been very friendly, and, in bidding me good-bye, they
warmly invited me to visit them whenever I was able
to do so.

The next march was delightful, and lay through a
forest of beautiful cedars, which was only in places thick
enough to block out the view of the many-coloured
hill slopes, with the bright sun glorifying their autumn
tints. We could only make a short march on account
of the trouble in getting supplies. Ghulám Dastgír
whiled away the afternoon and evening seated on a
goat-herd's house-top, making my Balti coolies, and
everybody else he could catch, dance incessantly, in
the intervals when he was not praying. One could
not help thinking how well Ghulám's religion suited

him, since its ceremonies could fill up so much of the spare time of an unoccupied, illiterate man. On the 26th October we crossed the Párpit Pass into the Káfir valley of Pittigul. This pass is not very high, being under 14,000 feet, but it is said by the Káfirs to be notorious for giving people headaches. This was certainly true in my case, the reason probably being that it is very steep. Foolishly allowing myself to be overpersuaded by Shermalik and a friend of his, we started from the top to find a short cut for ourselves, with the result that we reached camp long after dark. Everything had arrived safely; but, in my absence, Tong Chandlu had been with difficulty prevented from attacking my servant, Mír Alam, with a spear. There had been some dispute about the best site to pitch my tent. The Pathan and the Káfir had come to loggerheads, abuse had been freely interchanged, and my man had been very near to being murdered. Mír Alam had to be sternly reproved for so stupidly engaging in a quarrel, and I resolved to keep him always with me, for the next few days at any rate. Our troubles began the moment we entered the Pittigul Valley. Extortionate demands were made for food, which had to be acceded to, yet on the following morning the money was returned with a brief remark that it was altogether insufficient. When we attempted to reason with the Káfir seller, he and his companions burst forth into loud complaints. They wanted to know why they were not given large sums for their sheep and goats, and presented with rifles, robes, and money, as they alleged Colonel Lockhart had paid for supplies, and had given presents at Lutdeh. They finally became sullen and very angry. It soon became clear that Ghulám Dastgír and his Chitrális were trying to embarrass me by playing on the cupidity of the Káfirs; so I sent for the Chitrál prince, and then and there politely but firmly insisted on his saying good-bye and returning to his own country. In vain he protested that he must remain with me, that the orders of his father were explicit on the point, and must be obeyed. He urged that, at any rate, the Chitráli guard might remain to protect me, even if his own society were distasteful and displeasing. As I remained politely impervious to all his arguments, he had at length to give way with as good a grace as he could assume, but he left me very reluctantly to start on his homeward journey to Chitrál. I then informed the importunate Káfir headman that the prices he had rejected so scornfully were in themselves extortionate, in my opinion, and that the animals purchased should be paid for after the whole matter had been discussed and settled in Kámdesh. With this assurance he seemed to be fairly content, but there were more serious troubles ahead.

The village of Pittigul is the headquarters of Torag Merak, the wildest and the most impracticable of all the headmen, and the same individual who gave me so much trouble on my first visit to Káfiristán, when he left me altogether as soon as he had obtained money to arrange for my transport. On the present occasion he was violent and most outrageous in his demands. He continually threatened my coolies and servants, and, in conjunction with Tong Chandlu, made things most uncomfortable. He wound up by declaring that we must remain where we were for the present, as he required time to decide whether he should let us go on, or should insist on our returning to Chitrál by the road we came. Torag Merak afterwards confessed that he had been promised a thousand 'rupees by Ghulám Dastgír, on behalf of the Mehtar, if he succeeded in preventing me from going farther into the country. At this juncture another headman arrived from Kámdesh, while a large number of Káfirs were hanging about my camp. Shermalik was one march behind, ministering to an unfortunate hill pony I had foolishly attempted to bring into the valley. I kept cool and very quiet, but refused to give way to any single demand advanced by Torag Merak. On the following day Shermalik caught me up. I made him display

TORAG MERAK.

all his presents to the assembled tribesmen, fire his rifle at a distant mark on the hillside, exhibit his derringer, and then relate truthfully to his fellows how he had been invariably treated by the Franks in India. His account of the kindness and honour he had received made a pro-

D

found impression on his audience. They appeared to feel
a glow of reflected pride on learning that Shermalik used
to ride about on horseback like a Chitráli prince, while
their eyes glistened wistfully as he spread out his
gorgeous robes and other finery for their inspection.
The rifle was greatly admired, its mechanism being
gazed at in a kind of respectful awe. Finally, the latest
arrival from Kámdesh, a well-known headman, sprang
to his feet, and, after making many panegyrics on my
generosity, exclaimed excitedly that every one of the
beautiful garments exposed to view was worth at least
eight or ten cows. On this Torag Merak came to me
hurriedly and breathlessly to say that I ought to start
at once for Kámdesh, and stay there all the winter,
or for as long as the place pleased me, and that when
I went back to India he would send his own nephew
to accompany me. Everything being now satisfactorily
arranged to all appearance, it was decided that early
the following morning my little party should resume
its journey. The Káfirs became friendly and helpful,
chatty and inquisitive, without being troublesome. We
all sat round the camp-fire, talking cheerily till late into
the night.

In the early morning we found most of the Káfirs had
already started on ahead, being probably impatient to
get to their homes to relate the important and interesting news they had to tell about the Frank and his
followers. Among the few that remained behind were
Torag Merak and Tong Chandlu. For some reason or
other, these two men had undergone another change
in opinion during the night. The reason for their discontent was not obvious, but I have a suspicion that

they stole two sheep of mine, which were said to have broken away during the night, and that this successful theft had whetted their appetite for plunder. They kept interfering with the loads, saying that they were too heavy or were badly fastened. As no Káfirs were to carry any of my baggage, these comments were altogether gratuitous. They probably thought my boxes were filled with rupees, and wished to try their weight. Finally, my servant, Mír Alam, irritated by their remarks, returned a petulant answer. This seems to have been what they were waiting for. In an instant they threw themselves into a furious rage, drew their daggers, and began shouting out abuse. I believe now that the whole scene was arranged as a final attempt at blackmailing, for when they perceived me unmoved at the sight of their violence, and prepared to defend my servant if necessary with my double-barrelled pistol, which the occasion had compelled me to handle somewhat ostentatiously, they gradually let their wrath subside, sheathed their daggers, and even made some sort of sullen excuse that my servant was chiefly to blame for what had occurred, because he had begun by abusing them. This was quite untrue. The young Pathan had indeed for a moment hurled back defiance when Torag Merak had infuriated him by vile abuse in far too fluent Pashtu, but the boy had at once pulled himself together, and refrained from adding a single word when the actual crisis occurred.

However, this was the last of our troubles. Torag Merak remained behind at Pittigul, and was still scowling and growling as we moved off. The other man, Tong Chandlu, went with me, and except that he was unusually silent on the road, gave no sign that he was not perfectly contented.

The Pittigul Valley, into which we had crossed from the Bomboret Valley of Chitrál, runs down from a ridge traversed by a road called by the Káfirs the Manjám Pass, which leads to the country of the Lutdeh people, of whom the chief is Kán Márá, already referred to. At its lower end the Pittigul Valley debouches into the Bashgul Valley, its waters flowing into the Bashgul river on its left bank, about four miles from Kamu as the crow flies. At the upper part the valley is rough and stony. Lower down the road is merely a track bordering the stream of a narrow, greatly winding valley, which runs down between steep, in places almost vertical, rocky slopes. The bordering hills come down to the water's edge, and are covered with pines, occasional deodars (cedars), ilex, willow, walnut, and horse-chestnut trees. Boulders and tree trunks encumber the water-way. The path is in places very difficult, running along ledges of rock, widened here and there by timber supports placed together in the roughest way, or traversing smooth rock surfaces which give little or no foot-hold. In the intervals between such places it winds through coarse grass, and over stony tracks or between boulders.

High up in the Pittigul Valley the bridges are unimportant. They consist merely of one or two poles stretched across the stream and placed on convenient supporting stones. Lower down, where the stream increases in breadth, they are more carefully constructed. The superior variety are all built on a rough cantilever principle, which reaches its highest development at a bridge over the Pittigul river close to its mouth, and

is identical in form with the best bridges in the Bashgul
Valley.   The piers of these structures are neatly and
strongly built, the cantilevers being kept in position by
heavy stones.   The roadway is, however, too narrow for

A KÁFIR BRIDGE.

people unaccustomed to cross swift-flowing mountain
rivers by means of a wooden trough high above the
water, and usually under two feet in breadth, while its
sides are not more than nine inches high.   Indeed, these
bridges look more like aqueducts for irrigation purposes

than what they really are ; but they are strong and well
designed, their only fault being the extreme narrowness
of the roadway and the lowness of its parapets.

Near the village of Kamu, where we made our next
halt, the people flocked out to meet us; indeed, the
reception given me at this place might almost be called
enthusiastic. Two of the chief men of Kamu came for
a long talk. They declared that my staying in their
valley would give the greatest pleasure to all, as now
Umrá Khan would certainly abstain from his threatened
attack on the Káfirs. It was easy to perceive that all
the Kám had a wholesome fear of the Khan of Jandúl.
Supplies were brought readily, and the people, with unexpected politeness, refrained from being too pressing
in their burning curiosity about me.   Then and afterwards the Káfirs always withdrew to a distance when,
at a certain time in the afternoon, as at the end of a
march, my bath was being got ready.   They appeared
to attach an exaggerated importance to the proceeding,
and possibly considered it as a half-religious function.
In the restraint the Kamu men placed on their insatiable Káfir curiosity I was glad to perceive a distinct
feeling of friendliness towards me.   On September 30th
we made a short march to the little hamlet of Bináram,
a collection of houses about a mile and a half from
Kámdesh.   This place was Shermalik's home, and his
relatives claimed the right of entertaining me on the
first day of my arrival at the headquarters of the tribe.
We were received with respectful kindness by troops of
Káfirs, men, women, and children, who escorted us up
the steep hill on the top of which Bináram is perched.
Everybody was anxious to carry something for us; not

the loads, of course, as that would imply some measure of degradation, but small articles, such as guns, sticks, and superfluous clothing, were eagerly seized and proudly carried on before. We were most hospitably entertained, all offers of payment for provisions being politely but firmly declined. Shermalik's treasures were once more exhibited and admired, a tall man putting on the vestments, one by one, to show them off with proper effect. The people were outspoken in their expressions of astonishment and delight at the gaudy Peshámar " chappans " (long loose robes).

On the following day we moved into Kámdesh, and pitched near the east division of the village. Crowds of people came to smile upon us in a friendly manner. A kind of deputation of the headmen, led by Dán Malik and the priest, warmly welcomed me, and expressed the hope that my stay amongst them would extend over three or four years at least. They declared that, if I would only take the daughter of some headman as my wife, their satisfaction would be complete, for then they would surely know that my real desire was to remain with them. I was not at all prepared for such a friendly reception, the offer of a wife being as unexpected as it was probably unprecedented. My reply was couched in appropriate terms, and the wife difficulty was got over without offence by my referring to the difference in our respective national marriage customs. They then suggested that I should send for a woman of my own race from India as soon as possible. They obviously placed a curious importance on my getting married. We were shown great hospitality, and every one was most kind and obliging.

CHAPTER VI

HAVING brought the narrative of my visit to Káfiristán
up to the time of my second arrival in Kámdesh, it
seems advisable to pause in the story, and first give
some description of Káfiristán and its people, so that
the remainder of the book may be clearly intelligible to
the reader. Many of the facts now recorded were not
known to me until after a residence of some months
in the country, but, for the reason mentioned, it seems
advisable to insert them in this place.

Káfiristán, then, is a geographical expression used to
describe a small but little known tract of country which
is enclosed between the dominions of H.H. the Amir
of Kabul and those of the Mehtar of Chitrál. The word
"Káfiristán" literally means the land of the infidel,
an appellation given to the country by its Musalmán
neighbours because the inhabitants are idol-worshippers.
Its position is included between latitude 34° 30′ and
latitude 36°, and from about longitude 70° to longitude
71° 30′. The western frontier being very imperfectly
known and somewhat ill-defined, it is difficult to estimate accurately the size of the country. Its greatest
extent is from east to west at latitude 35° 10′; its
greatest breadth is probably at longitude 71°. Its map

area may be put down as somewhere about 5000 square miles.

Its boundaries are Badakhshán on the north ; the Lutkho valley of Chitrál on the north-east ; Chitrál proper and Lower Chitrál on the east ; the Kunar valley on the south-east. The boundary on the south is Afghanistan proper ; and on the west, the ranges above the Nijrao and Panjsher valleys of Afghanistan. The political boundaries of Káfiristán are Chitrál and the Kunar valley on the east, and the territories of H.H. the Amir of Kabul on all other sides.

On the north, the Minján valley of Badakhshán, which has of late years come under the rule of the Afghan Governor of Badakhshán, appears to dip down, so to speak, into the heart of Káfiristán. This valley has never been traversed by any explorer, and my own visit to it was extremely short. My opinion as to its direction is based on the statements made to me by Káfirs, and by other natives of the neighbouring districts, and on conversations with several Minjánís.

All the Káfiristán rivers find their way into the Kabul river, either directly to the south, as in the case of the Alingár, or after mingling their waters with those of the Kunar river at Arandú and at Chighar Sarai. At Arandú the Bashgul river empties itself into the Kunar. The Bashgul draws its highest waters from three main sources, at the head of the valley of the same name. Of these three sources, the stream coming directly from the Mandál is only the second in volume. As it descends, it passes, near its source, through a lake of considerable size and a tarn, and then receives on either hand babbling rills, streams, and mountain torrents. Of these the first of any importance is the Skorigul water, which falls into the main stream just above the village of Pshui. The next is the Manangul, which empties itself into the Bashgul at Lutdeh or Bragamatál. The pleasant river then pursues its quiet course undisturbed by the riotous streams from the side valleys, and winds past Bádámuk, Oulagul, and Purstám, gradually changing its character in its narrowing rocky bed, until at Sunra, on the confines of the Katir and Mádugál countries, it assumes many of the features of a cataract. It becomes a raging torrent in a dark narrow valley, where it dashes against the huge boulders which obstruct its course, and flings high its spray with deafening uproar. There, as in several other places where the tortured water foams and lashes itself against the rocks on its margin and in its bed, the river is beautiful beyond description. Tree trunks encumber the waterway, jam against the rocks, pile up in picturesque confusion, or hurry round and round in the swirl of many a backwater. It races past Bagalgrom and the great spur on which Kámdesh is built, receiving at the village of Urmir the torrent from the Kungani Pass and the drainage of the Nichingul Valley. Below Kamu it is joined on its left bank by the Pittigul river, which has its origin near the Manjám Pass, by the Gourdesh Valley stream, and by many others of all degrees of importance below those particularly named, and ends, as before stated, in the Kunar river at Arandú.

The Presun river is formed by the Wezgul drainage, which includes that of the pass leading to the Skorigul, that of the Mámi Pass, which leads to the Baprok Valley, and that of the Uzhamezhalgul, up which is the road to the Kungani Pass. Just below the Uzhamezhalgul it is joined on the right bank by a considerable stream from the Shidgul, up which valley there is no road, the stream rising in a *cul-de-sac* of lofty, unscalable hills. At the village of Shtevgrom the Presun river is joined by the mountain stream from the Kamah Pass, and flows placidly down the valley through meadow-land set aside for the service of Imrá, and past all the other Presun villages. After passing the last, Pushkigrom, it makes an abrupt turn, which was the limit of my journey, and enters (I was told) the Tsárugul or Tsáru country. Some little distance lower down, now named the Tsárugul river, it receives on its right the Kti river, which drains the small valley of the same name. The point of junction is a very sacred place in the Káfir imagination. On the narrow tongue of land, which separates the rivers just before they mingle, there is a rocky ridge, where the gods were wont to assemble, and a peculiarly sacred stone, placed there by Imrá.

The village of Tsáru, most difficult to approach, is on the right bank about half a mile lower down, and nearly opposite, the Amzhi Valley, belonging to the Wai tribe, empties its drainage into the main stream. The Tsáru river is also said to be joined by the two Ashkun rivers, the upper falling into the Kti river, the lower, which drains the Ashkun valley, inhabited by Shaikhs, (Káfirs " 'verted " to Muhammadanism), joining the Tsáru river direct. A short distance below the village of Tsáru, is a Wai village, the inhabitants of which have recently turned Musalmáns ; and somewhere near that village the Wai river joins the Tsáru, which emerges from Káfiristán and falls into the Kunar at Chighar Sarai. This river, which I have designated the Presungul or Tsárugul river, which flows into the Kunar at Chighar Sarai, is often called the Péch, and is referred to by Bellew and Lumsden as the Kamah, a very good name, inasmuch as it flows along the main road from the Kamah Pass to Chighar Sarai. It might seem advisable to give this river a single appellation. We might call it the Péch, a fairly well-known name, or Kamah, a very good and convenient one; but to prevent confusion, it will be inscribed on my map as the Péch or Kamah river.

Concerning the Alingár or Kao, the stream which empties itself to the south into the Kabul river, I know nothing except by hearsay. My informant told me that the main western valley of Káfiristán was inhabited by the Rámgul branch of the Katirs, and that it was large, and maintained a numerous population. Its river, after receiving many side streams, was joined by the Kulam Valley streams from the left, and ended in the Kabul river at Laghmán. The Kulam river is probably much shorter than the Rámgul river, for the valley of the former only contains four villages, as against the twenty or thirty which are said to exist in the Rámgul country.

To speak generally, Káfiristán consists of an irregular series of main valleys, for the most part deep, narrow, and tortuous, into which a varying number of still deeper, narrower, and more difficult valleys, ravines, and glens pour their torrent waters. The mountain ranges which separate the main drainage valleys from one another are all of them of considerable altitude, rugged and toilsome.

During the winter, Káfiristán is practically converted into a number of isolated communities with no means of inter-communication. Take for example the Bashgul

Valley. During the times the hills are under snow, the only way to reach the Katir people who inhabit the upper part of the district is to travel from the Kunar Valley through the territory first of the Kám and then of the Mádugál tribe. If either of these two tribes is at war with the Katirs, the latter are completely isolated from the rest of the world until the passes open in the spring. The inhabitants of Viron or Presun are similarly cut off from the surrounding tribes, for the only entrance to their country when the passes are closed is up the Péch or Kamah river, which flows into the Kunar at Chighar Sarai. All the passes which lead from Badakh-shán into Káfiristán appear to be over 15,000 feet in altitude. I have only explored the Mandál and the Kamah. These two were both above the height mentioned, but were said to be the lowest of the series. On the Chitrál side the roads over the enclosing ranges are somewhat less elevated, but are still very high, and are completely closed by snow in the winter. There is one low ridge, only 8400 feet high, the Patkun Pass, between the Kalash village of Utzún and Gourdesh, but even that is impassable for two or three months every winter.

Some of the ravines up which regular roads run are of the most romantic and picturesque description; others are bare, rocky defiles. Indeed, almost every kind of mountain scenery is to be met with in Káfiristán, from silent peaks and naked ridges, snowfields and glaciers, to thickly wooded slopes echoing to the bleat of flocks, and wild vine and pomegranate thickets, bordering tumultuous little streams.

At the lower elevations the hillsides are well covered with wild olives and evergreen oaks; very many kinds of fruit-trees, walnuts, mulberries, apricots, grapes and apples, are met with near the villages or growing by the roadside, while splendid horse-chestnuts and other shade trees afford pleasant resting-places from the sun in the hot months. At somewhat higher elevations, say from 5000 to 8000 or 9000 feet, there are dense pine and cedar forests. They contain large numbers of magnificent trees, which even a tired-out hungry traveller cannot pass without admiration. Higher still, the pines cease, the hills become bare, rocky, shaly; the juniper cedar and the wild rhubarb are succeeded by willows, birches, and similar trees, while still higher, say over 13,000 feet, there is no vegetation of any kind except rough grasses and mosses. Numerous wild flowers are met with at different altitudes. The rivers teem with fish which no Káfir could be persuaded to eat. The people declare that fish live on dirt, and shudder at the idea of using them for food, as we would shudder at the idea of eating rats. Immense numbers of "chikor," the red-legged partridges, as well as pigeons and doves, are to be seen, and large numbers of gaudy, "manál" pheasants. The chief wild animals are the "markhor," which are extremely numerous, the "uriál" (wild sheep), leopards and bears. I do not think there are any ibex; none has ever come under my observation, nor has one ever been described to me.

The climate of Káfiristán naturally varies with the altitude, but it is very hot in the summer months at all elevations. In high valleys, such as Presungul, and at Ahmad Diwána, the winter is certainly rigorous. When I was about to leave the former country, a little deputation of the Presuns came to me with a request,

KÁFIR LANDSCAPE.

To face page 68.

which illustrates, not only their simplicity of character, but also the severity of their winters. They begged me to ask Imrá (God) to make their country a little warmer. During the winter of 1890–91 at Kámdesh (elevation 6100 feet), there was an excessive amount of snow, but the thermometer never showed a lower temperature than 17° F. below the freezing-point.

In some of the Káfir valleys the absence of wind is remarkable. On this account low temperatures can be borne without discomfort. In the Kunar Valley, which is wet and windy in the winter, but where snow, if it falls, quickly melts, the sensation of cold is certainly greater than at Kámdesh, for instance, where the thermometer is actually much lower.

The rainfall in Káfiristán is probably greater than in Chitrál, but is insufficient for the requirements of the crops, and has to be supplemented by a somewhat elaborate irrigation system.

The Káfirs do not call the Bashgul Valley by that name—it is a Chitráli word. Indeed, the Chitrális continually refer to all Káfirs as "Bashgulis," as though the two words were synonymous. In the Bashgul Valley there is a village called Bazgul, which may have been the origin of the name now given to the whole of Káfiristán by the Chitrális. The Káfirs themselves have no single designation for their country. They call different parts of it after the name of the different tribes that inhabit it. Thus, the upper part of the Bashgul Valley is called Katirgul (Lutdeh in Chitráli, or Kamtoz in Pushtu), the middle portion Mumán (Madugál in Chitráli), and the lower part Kám (Kámdesh in Chitráli, or Kamoz in Pushtu).

CHAPTER VII

KÁFIRISTÁN, at the present day, is divided among certain tribes who differ from one another in language, dress, and manners and customs. Indeed, the only connection which they have with one another is in the fact that all alike are non-Musalmán. This sole peculiarity, which they have in common, may not be long maintained. Along the fringes of Káfiristán are numerous villages of Káfirs who have changed their ancient religion and have accepted Islám. These converts are known locally as "Shaikhs." But it is not only on the borderland of their own ancestral country that these Shaikhs are to be met with. Close to Kámdesh, the chief village and the tribal headquarters of the Kám, are two small hamlets; one almost exactly opposite, across the Bashgul river, is called Agatsi; the other, on the left bank of the Nichingul torrent, is known as Agaru. Both these little settlements are inhabited by Kám people who have become Musalmáns. Agatsi is a quiet peaceful place, occupied by people who are of the Bilez-hedári clan of the Kám, while Agaru is a most troublesome nest of thieving rascals, who belong by birth to the Utahdári, the priestly clan. The Kámdesh villagers have

assured me that they would gladly be rid of the Agaru
folk ; but on account of their relationships, they can be
no more interfered with than if they were true Káfirs.
Utah, the high priest, confirmed this. He declaimed
against his fellow-clansmen of Agaru, but explained that
if any one killed one of them, it would be just the same
as if he killed an ordinary Káfir. In case of war with
a Musalmán power, I was informed that, even in the
event of an actual invasion of the country, the Shaikhs
would not co-operate with the Káfirs, nor fight on their
side, but would stand aloof, unless the invaders, if
victorious, unduly oppressed the conquered Kám, when
the Shaikhs would probably do all in their power to
protect and avenge their relations. The two small Shaikh
communities, Agaru and Agatsi, are really of no importance in connection with the power for offence or for
defence of the Kám tribe, but the tolerant way in which
the Káfirs look on them, and others of their race who
have changed their religion for that of Islám, is not only
interesting in itself, but has to be borne in mind in all
speculations concerning the future of Káfiristán. What
is true of the Kám people applies with equal force to
the rest of the Bashgul Káfirs, although there are no
other Musalmán communities in the valley. In the
Wai country the religion of Muhammad is making way
strongly. Soon after my arrival in Kámdesh, news was
brought me that another Wai village had destroyed the
shrines of its heathen deities, and to all intents and purposes had become Musalmán. The change was effected
without bloodshed. As soon as the followers of the
Prophet of Arabia formed a sufficiently large majority
of the inhabitants, they threw down the shrines of Imrá,

E

Dizane, and other deities, and cast away the idols. The minority made no great movement in defence of their faith. It is quite possible that before many years have passed, it will no longer be correct to say that the different tribes inhabiting the so-called Káfiristán resemble one another in the one respect, that all are idolaters.

The old division of Káfiristán into the countries held by the Siáh-Posh and those inhabited by the Safed-Posh was more convenient than scientifically correct. The Siáh-Posh, the black-robed Káfirs, are made up of several different tribes, some of which have been at war with one another from time immemorial; but in spite of that, they have a good deal more in common than merely a resemblance in dress. They do not all speak the same language, but the difference in speech appears to be more a difference of dialect than a radical distinction of language. Although it is true that one tribe of the Siáh-Posh uses different words from those employed by another tribe for identical objects, and although even the names of villages are altered by one people, so as to be partly or entirely different from the' names used by another Siáh-Posh community, yet all the tribes who wear the dark-coloured raiment seem at once to understand one another, and to be able to converse together fluently and without hesitation. But if this is true of the Siáh-Posh, it is far different when we come to consider the so-called Safed-Posh or white-robed Káfirs. Among these tribes, of which two stand out as of chief importance, the Wai and the Presun, there is no similarity in dress, appearance, or language; they' cannot converse without the aid of interpreters. The Wai and the Presuns are not more dissimilar from one another than they both are from the Siáh-Posh.

A convenient classification is to divide all Káfirs into (1) Siáh-Posh, (2) Waigulis, (3) Presungulis, or Viron people. There is another important tribe called the Ashkun, of whom, however, it was most difficult to get any information. They are probably allied to the Waigulis. Although the classification given above is convenient, it is necessary to aim at more exactitude by enumerating the tribes in a tabular form by their local names. Every village in Káfiristán has more than one designation, while some have three or four, as, for instance, the village on the road leading from Utzún into the Bashgul Valley, which is called Gourdesh by Pathans, Istorgats by Chitrális, and Istrat by the Kám Káfirs ; every tribe, doubtless, is spoken of in a particular way by different people. The names given here are those I heard in the Bashgul Valley and in Chitrál. Subsequent travellers entering Káfiristán from a different direction, will almost certainly learn various new names for the people I am attempting to describe under the following designations, namely :—

1. Katirs	
2. Mádugál	
3. Kashtán or Kashtoz	Siáh-Posh.
4. Kám	
5. Istrat or Gourdesh	
6. Presun or Viron	
7. Wai	Safed-Posh.
8. Ashkun	

It is probable that, numerically, the Katirs are more important than all the remaining tribes of Káfiristán put together.

The Katirs inhabit various valleys, as Siáh-Posh communities entirely independent of one another; yet they still acknowledge a common origin and a general relationship each to the others.

The Katirs are divided into the following groups :—

(a.) The Katirs of the Bashgul Valley, also called Kamoz and Lutdehchis. This tribe inhabits the Bashgul Valley from Ahmad Diwána (Badáwan) to the hamlet of Sunra on the border of the Mádugál country. It occupies twelve villages, besides several small hamlets like Sunra and Láluk, and others in the Skorigul. The names of the villages are as follows :—

Ptsigrom.	Bádámuk.
Pshui or Pshowar.	Oulagul. .
Apsai.	Chábu.
Shidgul.	Baprok.
Bragamatál (Lutdeh).	Purstám.
Bajindra.	

(b.) The Kti or Katwár Káfirs, a small independent sub-division of the Katirs who live in the Kti Valley. They have but two villages; or, rather, one large village, and a second, Ashpit, hardly larger than a hamlet.

(c.) The Kulam Káfirs, living in the Kulam country, have four villages.

(d.) The Rámgulis or Gabariks. These are the most numerous division among the Katirs. They live in the most western part of Káfiristán, on the Afghan frontier. They probably inhabit several side tracts beside the main valley from which they take the name of Rámgul Káfirs. They are said to have twenty-four villages.

Of the other tribes included under the designation Siáh-Posh, the chief is the Kám or Kamtoz. This people inhabits the Bashgul and its lateral valleys from the confines of the Mádugál country to the Kunar Valley. It has seven villages, and various small settlements or hamlets. The villages are :—

Urmir.	Sárat.
Kámbrom or Kámdesh.	Pittigul.
Mergrom.	Bazgul.
Kamu.	

The next Siáh-Posh tribe in general and numerical importance, is the Mumán or Mádugál Káfirs, who occupy that short tract of country between the Kám and the Katirs of the Bashgul Valley. They are collected into three villages, and possess also a few hamlets. The names of the villages are :—

Bagalgrom, or Mumán.
Susku.
Mungul.

The last Siah-Posh tribe is the Kashtán or Kashtoz, who, with the exception of one or two little settlements, are all located in one village, Kashtán, where they are greatly overcrowded. They formerly had a village in the Dungul Valley, which was taken and burnt by the Asmár people, since which event the whole of the tribe have had to crowd into the village of Kashtán, which is close to, and on the west of Kámdesh.

There is a little colony of Siáh-Posh Káfirs at Gourdesh or Istrat, an extremely overcrowded little village. The Gourdesh folk are said to be very different from all the other Siáh-Posh Káfirs, and to be, in great part, a remnant of an ancient people called the Aroms.[1]

I believe the above list includes all the Siáh-Posh Káfirs.

---

[1] There is a hamlet called Arombrom, up the Arundu or Arnugul, which it is said was formerly a great village, and the headquarters of the Aroms.

We now come to the so-called Safed-Posh. Of these
the Presun tribe, also called Viron by their Musalmán
neighbours, are probably a very ancient people. They
inhabit the Presungul, and are entirely different from the

PRESUN OR VIRON MEN.

Siáh-Posh tribes on the one hand, and from the
Wai and the Ashkun people on the other. They
are remarkable for their more peaceful disposition, and
their inefficiency as fighting men. They have patient,

stolid faces for the most part, and, compared with the Káfirs, are heavy in their movements. The thick clothes they wear add to their clumsy appearance. They are a simple people, very industrious, capable of wonderful feats of endurance, and, with the exception of the inhabitants of one of the villages, Pushkigrom, they are meek and poor-spirited. Why the Pushkigrom villagers should be so different from the rest of the tribe, is a problem that has puzzled me very much. While I was in Káfiristán, the other five Presun villages were at war with their near neighbours the Wai; but Pushkigrom stood aside altogether, and maintained friendly relations with that tribe. In such circumstances it is no wonder that the Presun people were defeated by their enemies; but Káfirs continually behave in this suicidal manner. Sad stories were told me of the straits the people were in. Many had been slain, many carried away captive to be ransomed, or killed in default. Indeed, it seemed probable that the Wai, provided that the Pushkigrom men continued neutral, and the Siáh-Posh tribes did not interfere, could do much as they liked in Presungul; for the only act in the way of reprisal during the three years the war had lasted, of which the Presuns could boast, was the murder of one Wai girl. But just before I left the country, news was brought to Kámdesh that the Pushkigrom men had declared war with the Wai, for some reason or other, and had signified the same in a not unusual Káfir way, by slaying a Wai man captured on the road. Besides this, the Bashgul and the other Káfirs were interested in not permitting the Wai to go too far in their conquest, for fear that there might remain no room for their own exactions. The Kám, for instance, make periodic visits

to Presungul during the time the passes are open, and
return with the presents the Presuns think it expedient
to give them. The Kám, indeed, behave a good deal
like owners of the country. The Presun villagers carry
loads for them, and have to produce food and necessaries;
but all alike have to be circumspect by day, and safely
housed, if possible, by night—the Presuns for fear of the
Wai; the Kám for fear of their inveterate enemies the
Rámgul Káfirs, and the Tsarogul Shaikhs; and the last
two for fear of one another and of the Kám. The high
valley of the Presuns is easy, the grazing excellent, the
flocks and herds good, and the people can be plundered
without much difficulty; but it is a sort of cockpit
for Káfiristán, and no man can wander there in safety,
except when the passes are closed by snow. The
Wai have more than once brought Afghans into the
country to plunder and harry, and have in this way
added to the general state of insecurity which prevails.
At one particular place my escort of Kám Káfirs went
along at a trot, garments girded up, bows strung, matchlocks lighted, and anxious wary looks on every face.
The distance was only a few hundred yards, but all were
greatly relieved when we got past the dangerous spot.
The Presuns have six villages :—

Shtevgrom.	Kstigigrom.
Pontzgrom.	Satsumgrom.
Diogrom.	Puskigrom.

The last tribes on the list on page 75 are the Wai
and the Ashkun. Of the Ashkun my ignorance is
almost complete, for no Káfir was able to give me much
information about them. The small total of my knowledge amounts to this : that the Ashkun people speak

a language somewhat similar to that of the Wai, and
are friendly disposed towards them; that their country
is separated from the Kulam valley by a range of
mountains; that they possess two large villages, one
(Káfir) on a river which flows into the Kti before its
junction with the Péch or Kamah, the other (Musalmán)
on the banks of a torrent which falls directly into the
Péch or Kamah on its right bank. It is also said that
the Ashkun country is surrounded by thick forest, is
practically impenetrable, and is defended by a brave
people particularly well armed with matchlocks, who
are at war with all the other Káfir tribes, with the exception of the Wai.

The Wai people speak a language quite different from
that spoken in Presungul or by the Siáh-Posh, and are
a brave, high-spirited race, remarkable for their hospitality, and for their proneness to quarrel. They are
said to be as generous in entertaining guests as the poor
Presungulis are declared to be niggardly and contemp-
tible. The Bashgul Káfir speaks with admiration of the
two good meals a day which the Wai men offer a visitor,
while he laughs disparagingly at the way in which a
Presun runs into his house and shuts the door when
he perceives a stranger approaching. However, the one
is not so well formed by nature to speak with a possible
enemy within the gate as the other.

The Wai people have ten villages, of which the names
were given as follows :—

Runchi.	Kegili.
Nishi.	Akun or Akum.
Jamma.	Mildesh.
Amzhi.	Bargul.
Chimion.	Prainta.

Of certain of these villages I had frequently heard, particularly of Nishi, near the Péch river, I believe, which is the residence of an energetic Mullah, who possibly himself converted the people to Islám, and now keeps them steadfast in their new faith. The information was volunteered that, in the event of the Mehtar of Chitrál attacking Tsarogul in conjunction with the Kám, who are deadly enemies of that country, the Nishi men and the Musalmán Ashkuns would certainly hasten to the assistance of their Shaikh brethren. The Amzhi Valley drains into the Péch or Kamah just opposite the village of Tsarú. While I was in Káfiristán it was raided by the Bashgul Katirs, who brought away great spoil, but not without severe loss. The Amzhi shortly afterwards retaliated, by surprising and killing every living thing in the little hamlet of Sunra, in the Bashgul Valley. At present it seems that there is no very strong tribal feeling amongst the Wai. They are perpetually fighting amongst themselves. One or two of the lower villages have turned Musalmán, while the Katir raid on the Amzhi was held, by the remainder of the tribe, to call for vengeance from the Amzhi only, the actual sufferers.

Of the slave population of Káfiristán, mention will be made hereafter. A portion of them, at any rate, are probably the remnant of an ancient people subjugated and enslaved by the present dominant tribes. Possibly the Presuns also come under the category of a very ancient people, although they are not only free themselves, but actually possess Siáh-Posh slaves, and none of any other kind. The remains of another ancient race, the Jazhis, are said to exist at Pittigul, in the valley of the same name, and at Gourdesh or Istrat.

From intermarriages with the Kám and others, they cannot now be distinguished from other Bashgul Káfirs; but a tradition remains that they once held possession of all the lower Bashgul Valley, until the Kám invaded it from the west, and drove out or slew nearly the whole of the people they found there. Possibly, Pittigul and Gourdesh, being somewhat out of the direct road for an invader, were not called upon to resist the Kám for some time, or they made a better resistance than the rest of the inhabitants, and finally amalgamated with the conquerors on more or less equal terms. Pittigul is peculiar in certain respects. It is remarkable in having a priest of its own, which no other Kám village has. The Kámdesh Utah, or priest, is not only a village, but a tribal functionary.

I have not been able to get much real insight into the political organisation of any of the tribes, except those in the Bashgul Valley, the Katirs in the north, and the Kám and the Mádugál and others lower down. It is consequently with reference to the Bashgul tribes, and especially to the Kám, that the following description chiefly applies. It is probable, however, that the internal management of the other tribes is formed more or less on the same model.

Although the Rámgul, the Kulam, the Ktis, and the Katirs of the Bashgul Valley have all been considered as belonging to one great tribe—the Katir—yet each of the divisions enumerated is to all intents and purposes a separate tribe. Each is entirely independent of the other, and makes war or peace without in the slightest degree considering its neighbours. For instance, the Western Káfirs have been at war with the Kám for

generations, while the Katirs of the Bashgul Valley are
at the present moment the friends and allies of that
tribe, although Katir and Kám in the Bashgul Valley
still look upon one another with some amount of jealousy
and distrust, and only a short time ago were fighting
furiously. A great source of Káfir weakness is the
readiness with which the different tribes fight with one
another, and the alacrity with which the different clans
of the same tribe, or the different families of the same
clan, engage in sanguinary internecine strife. Among
such people as the Wai and the Presun, it is not uncommon for a single village to stand aloof from the rest of
the tribe, and take no part in a foreign war. The Katirs
of the Bashgul Valley also appear ever ready to start
inter-village quarrels. Indeed, sometimes, if what one
hears is true, portions of Káfiristán must be simply
chaos. The Kám, on the other hand, hold much better
together, and it is probable that it is for this very reason
that, although not a numerous people, they are greatly
respected by the neighbouring tribes, as well as by
Chitrális and Pathans.

A tribe consists of a number of clans, each powerful
according to the number of fighting men it can bring
into the field, and according to its aggregate wealth.
Besides the regular clans, there are a number of men
who belong to groups of families which can hardly be
called clans. Such men are less important than members
of the great clans, because the fighting strength with
which they can support an opinion is inconsiderable;
but such individuals as have amassed wealth are readily
accorded a good deal of respect. Lower still in the scale
is a class of men, the members possibly of once important

groups of families, or small clans, which have died away, or become impoverished from causes difficult to determine at the present day. These men are poor, and without tribal authority of any kind. It is from this class that the patsas, or shepherds, are obtained. The patsas are hired to tend the flocks and herds of wealthy Káfirs during the winter months, on a regular scale of payment in kind.

The lowest class are of course the slaves. The several portions of the Kám people may be shown as under :—

(1) The clansmen belonging to important clans.

(2) Men belonging to very small clans or groups of families.

(3) Men of distinctly inferior family, but free men.

(4) Slaves.

Between classes 1 and 2, there is a point where it is difficult to decide to which category certain individuals belong, nor is there any peculiarity in the appearance of the one class to distinguish it from the other. But with the men of class 3 it is, as a rule, quite otherwise. They appear to approach more closely the slaves than the members of the important clans, and often differ considerably from the latter in features and in general appearance.

The chief clans of the Kám people are as follows :—

1. Utahdári.	6. Waidári.
2. Demidári.	7. Lanandári.
3. Garakdári.	8. Kanardári.
4. Sukdári.	9. Gutkechdári.
5. Bilezhedári.	10. Batardári.

The first six are really important clans. Of these, the Garakdári and the Bilezhedári are probably the largest, the Demidári the wealthiest, while the Utahdári, the clan which produces the tribal priests, though not so numerous as some of the others, and perhaps less rich than the Demidári, is yet as important as any.   Of the remainder, the Lanandári is probably the smallest of all.   It is difficult to determine how many fighting men any of the above clans can muster.   It is also hard to decide which is actually the biggest, for a Kám man belonging to any one of the first six would most certainly declare that his own clan was the most numerous; though probably, whichever clan the man belonged to, he would admit that the Demidári were the wealthiest.

Probably the Garakdári and the Bilezhedári number about 300 fighting men each; while the Utahdári, the Demidári, the Sukdári, and the Waidári have only about 120 men.   The Lanandári contains probably no more than a dozen or fifteen warriors altogether.

Each of these clans has one chief man, or more, to represent it.   These representatives are generally, and in the more important clans almost invariably, tribal headmen or "Jast."   But it must not be supposed that they all have equal authority; some of them are absolutely without weight of any kind in the tribal councils. All the clans are closely connected by marriage ties. Indeed, as all Káfirs are polygamous to a certain extent, and as no man may take a wife from his own clan, or from his mother's, or from his father's mother's clan, it can easily be imagined how closely the people are connected with one another.[1] Nevertheless, a clan is

---

[1] The word *zhame* (brother-in-law) is so constantly heard in Kámdesh, that one of my Baltis fell into the error of supposing it was an ordinary word of greeting, and on one occasion, when helping to raise a house beam, shouted

always ready to act together as a clan, without reference to cousinship or marriage ties.

An individual's importance in a clan is principally gauged by the wealth he possesses; and his influence or popularity depends in no small degree on the way in which he feasts his fellow-tribesmen, and on his willingness to provide sacrifices. If to these important qualifications he adds a reputation for bravery, has a fair record of slain, and is moderately clear-headed, he may reasonably expect to become one of the chief men of the tribe as he gets on in years. But to be of the very first consideration he should belong to one of the biggest of the clans, and also have several grown sons and grandsons.

If he goes several times through the ceremonies connected with the free banquets to the whole tribe, which will be subsequently described, or if he makes his sons go through these ceremonies, and he himself goes into a still higher grade by means of further banquets, then he becomes one of the inner circle of the Jast, of which there are never more than four or five in the whole tribe, and he will be treated with the utmost respect by everybody. The importance of grown-up sons and grandsons lies in their numerical strength in family, clan, and tribal quarrels. It is a most important thing to belong to a big clan for the same reason—where there is strong feeling on any particular subject, abstract justice is apt to be overridden by brute force; by majorities always ready to back up their argument by blows if necessary.

out to the Káfirs, "Now, Zhame, lift!" The priest cheerily exclaimed with a grin, "All you who are Tálib's brothers-in-law—lift," and the Káfirs amused themselves greatly with the joke instead of getting angry, as would have been the case with Hindustanis or Pathans.

The chief clans of the Bashgul Katirs are :—

1. Jannahdári.   5. Charedári.
2. Barmodári.   6. Shtukdári.
3. Shakldári.   7. Sowadári.
4. Mutadawadári.

The divisions of this tribe are, however, of comparatively small interest, as the Jannahdári are so wealthy and powerful that they completely overshadow all the other clans. The chief and high priest of the tribe, Kán Márá, belongs to the Jannahdári, as do also all the other prominent men in the country.

CHAPTER VIII

THE date of my arrival in Kámdesh for the second time, was the 1st of October. The first business of importance was to procure a temporary abode, until the Kám had time to fulfil a promise to build me a house. While negotiations were being carried on with this object, my tent remained pitched close to the east village, and my friends were filled with anxiety about my safety at night. The villagers came in crowds in the day-time, and appeared never to grow tired of watching me, and discussing me with one another. During my former visit to Káfiristán I had taken several photographs, some of which, the portraits of well-known Káfirs, met with the warmest reception. As each face was recognised, the man's name was shouted out amidst shrieks of laughter, as if my audience were gazing upon a ludicrous caricature, instead of upon works of possibly some artistic merit. A small electric battery was as popular as the photographs. At length, my occupation became very much like that of a man with a successful "try your weight" machine at an English fair, and the weariness of death eventually came over me at the sight of fresh candidates

F

for a "shock" or a view of the pictures; but, on the other hand, every one seemed so pleased to see me, and so genially happy, that it was possible to restrain my impatience even after hours of showman's work. My tent was very small, and was surrounded by crowds of Káfirs, whose notions of cleanliness are, fortunately, peculiar and national. The following day was spent much in the same way, but occasionally diversified by house-hunting. My visitors were as numerous as ever, but the difference in their behaviour from that of the year before was very striking. Although anxious to be amused, and to see as much as any one else had seen, they were no longer aggressively inquisitive, and even asked if it troubled me to have so many visitors. This was no doubt the result of Shermalik's account of my greatness and dignity in my own country, which he never tired of proclaiming. The Káfirs were at times very comical, and were usually amusing. The way they delighted to bring up fresh sightseers, ask for the photographs, and then proceed to explain them with the airs of the superior person all the world over, was very interesting. It was curious to notice the influence of age in the power of the people to recognise portraits. No Káfir ever recognised pictures of buildings or landscapes. Boys and youths recognised the originals of the photographs at once, and shouted out their names; men between thirty and forty took time to consider, frequently held the pictures upside down, and required to have them readjusted before they discovered their meaning and recognised the features portrayed; while men a few years older could never make anything out of them at all. The electric battery was their chief delight. They would persuade one of the uninitiated to grasp the handles, and then beg me by winks and nods, or implore me by frantic gestures behind the proposed victim's back, to turn on the strongest current; in this way they showed their keen appreciation of a practical joke at the expense of others.

Concerning a house, there were several placed at my disposal. That which seemed most suitable was the tower at the top of the village. It belonged to a man named Aramalik Chárá, whose old mother, Sumri, had been very kind to me the year before. But it was pointed out that this tower was unfinished in the uppermost story, and must consequently be very cold in winter. It was in its then condition a veritable temple of the winds; but that could have been rectified without great difficulty; while the power of being able to completely isolate oneself at night by merely drawing up the ladder by which the tower was entered, would have been certainly convenient. But it was clear to me in a very short time that the selection of a house was not a matter which was to be left to my private judgment, but was a question which was secretly but decisively being settled for me by others. A transparent little intrigue, in which Shermalik played a prominent part, reduced my choice to one of two houses. The first belonged to Torag Merak, and about it my Káfir son was most enthusiastic; but it was a dreadful building, three stories high, and, from its position on a slope, it was commanded close at hand by many houses swarming with women and children. It was dilapidated, gloomy, and dirty. I decisively declined to go into it. This refusal gave umbrage to Shermalik, who was evidently acting as Torag Merak's secret agent, and who doubtless wanted to conciliate that influential and dangerous headman. The second house was one belonging to Utah the priest. It consisted of one room twenty feet square, built upon the roof of two conjoined apartments, one of which was a cowhouse, and the other, really a woodshed, was at the moment occupied by Utah's brother, and the latter's new wife. There were objections to this house also; but it was no use contending against the influence brought to bear by the priest and Shermalik, so it was accepted and occupied, with many expressions of thankfulness on my part. To make room for me, Utah's youngest, prettiest, but least-loved wife had to remove to her father's abode. The Káfirs themselves promised to carry over my small belongings, for my Balti coolies were busily engaged all day long in collecting firewood in the Deodar forest to the south of the village. The distance the baggage had to be carried was about one hundred and fifty yards over uneven ground; the number of loads was less than a dozen; the number of helpers was perhaps a hundred; the time occupied in carrying the things was about three hours.

After inspecting the tower already mentioned, I went to call on Sumri, the owner's mother, who lived close by. This old lady was the most highly esteemed woman in the Kám tribe. On the death of her husband she had given away enormous wealth in the huge public banquets she provided, not only for her own tribe, but for the Wai people as well. She was proud of telling of the crowds of people she used to entertain daily. Besides the fame she had acquired in this way, she had also

gone through a series of ceremonies, which will be subsequently described, by which she had still further
impoverished her young son by feastings and banquets,
but had in a still greater degree exalted the position of
the family. She was the only woman in the tribe whom
both males and females joined to respect. She did no
work in the fields, and very little about the house, so
high had her rank become, but spent the most of her
time seated on a little Káfir stool on a small platform
outside the upper verandah story of her house, which
was reached by a long notched plank, the local substitute for a ladder. The fact of her sitting on a stool
outside the house proclaimed the high social position
to which she had attained. Anybody may sit on a
stool inside a house or in a verandah; but only those
are entitled to the privilege of using such a seat in
the open who have gone through certain elaborate
ceremonies, and have royally feasted their tribe in so
doing. The number of such individuals in the tribe
was three men—Dán Malik, Torag Merak, and "Lame"
Astán—and the woman Sumri just described. The priest,
by reason of his sacred office, was permitted the same
privilege.

Sumri prided herself upon the good sense she possessed, and was famed for the good advice she gave—
for a woman. She invited me into her abode, seated
me with much honour on a wooden bedstead brought
into the verandah room for the purpose, and composed
herself for conversation. She began by observing, as
sententiously as a weak-looking, pale-eyed little woman
could, that the people would never be satisfied unless I
ate with them. I expressed the great pleasure it would

give me to be entertained by her, and made certain remarks as to the different eating customs of our respective countries, and instanced Shermalik's extreme dislike to cold fowls, of which he had been given far too many on our march down to India. They had usually been pulled out, already cooked, from a saddle-bag, and owing to the extreme cold of the journey, had generally been presented to my adopted son hard frozen, and with their juices turned into ice. It was only necessary to mention this article of diet to Shermalik to set his teeth on edge with agonised memories. She was next told of the surprising behaviour of Shahru, the buffoon priest, when he first put in his mouth some morsels of a hot curry which remained from my plate. These little anecdotes were received with laughter and applause, and the little old woman, with a confident, superior smile, called to her assistance two daughters-in-law, and they all went into one of the two rooms which gave off from the verandah, to prepare me a meal with their own skilled hands. While the cooking was going forward, Aramalik Chárá, that is, Chárá the son of Aramalik, who was Sumri's son and the owner of the house, with several friends who had casually stepped in to see what was passing, proceeded to entertain me after their own fashion; but although it was interesting to watch them for a time, they soon grew very dull. They were on their company manners, and spoke solemnly and in a dignified way about nothing at all for a long time; then a hubble-bubble pipe was handed round by a domestic slave, and every one became more friendly, Shermalik eventually obliging the company with some of his Indian adventures, which certainly lost nothing in the telling.

SUMRI'S FEAST.

To face page 94.

After a time Sumri reappeared with a little feast, which was placed before me on a round, hour-glass-shaped wicker table, about eighteen inches high, and of a diameter of some twelve inches at the top and bottom. There were five or six large, round, thin unleavened cakes, called *chuppaties* in India, made of wheaten flour, and in the centre of the top cake was a small heap of salt, while on one side was a portion of toasted cheese. In a wooden bowl was a quantity of *ghee*—that is to say, butter clarified by the water being driven off by heat. The whole repast was extremely good. The proper method of consuming it was to tear off a piece of the *chupatti*, dip it into the *ghee*, and then deftly convey the morsel to your mouth without dropping any of the oily particles on to your clothes. The cheese was first broken into fragments, which, having been touched with the salt, were then consumed. After the meal was over, the remains were thoughtfully, and with ostentatious fairness, distributed amongst his other guests by Chárá. They had all been somewhat surprised at my clumsy efforts at handling the food, and one or two had tried to instruct me how the thing should be really done. Now they demonstrated the method with conscious pride, and not without some slight exaggeration in giving a touch of added elegance to the performance—a twist of the wrist, an accentuated cock of the little finger, or a graceful toss of the head.

The verandah in which we were seated, which was the only portion of Chárá's house revealed to me on this occasion, was really the front room of the second story. It was closed at both ends by wooden and masonry walls, each pierced by a doorway. In front

were two very large openings, like sashless window-
frames, occupying a space from the roof to within about
three feet of the ground. Behind were two very dark
rooms, side by side. All down the open side of the
verandah room ran a huge, broad, single plank, raised
some six or eight inches from the ground for the
accommodation of guests. On the opposite side, and
between the doors of the two rooms, the ground was
raised three inches, for use as a fireplace. On the wall
on this side of the apartment hung two leather shields,
evidently brought from Peshawar. At one end the
verandah room opened through a doorway, of which the
bottom frame timber was a foot or so above the level
of the floor, on to a square wooden platform, some
eight feet by six, along the edge of which was sitting
accommodation for several people. The platform communicated with the ground below by means of a notched
plank ladder, already mentioned. At the other end of
the verandah room three or four steps led to a window-
like door. On the other side of the door, which was
closed, was evidently a similar short ladder, as was shown
by the way a woman entered, carrying a bright-eyed,
two-year-old child. She placed the little fellow on the
ground, gave him a piece of bread to keep him quiet,
and went out again. To my horror the baby began to
climb up the small ladder after her, opened the door,
and disappeared. I was horrified, expecting to hear the
dull thud of a heavy fall; but none came, and Shermalik,
whose eyes were in the same direction as mine, gave no
sign that anything unusual was happening. No doubt
there is a special Providence which watches over Káfir
babies. They stagger and reel along the edges of house-

tops, a fall from which would mean fracture or death, and crawl along a roof to the smoke-hole, into which they thrust their heads and shoulders, and still live to totter away, to attempt some fresh suicidal-looking exploit.

The sight of the slave who had been handing round the pipe from Chárá to his guests caused me to make inquiries from Shermalik about the bondsmen held by the Káfirs. He gave me much curious information, which was corroborated and confirmed by others, and subsequently by my own observation. While seated in Chárá's house we noticed a low-browed, very dark-complexioned, and wild-looking man of powerful build, carrying on his back an immense load, in size at any rate, of Indian corn from a neighbouring field. I remarked how hard the man worked. The answer was : " Why should he not ? He is a slave ; he sleeps all night, and works all day. If he did not work he would be beaten deservedly." This was said in a tone which implied that the speaker—who probably never did a day's work in his life, except in fighting or in travelling— must seriously reprobate any falling away in devotion to labour, or any remarks which might seem to suggest that anybody could work too hard. The slave community is a curious and interesting class. It is probable that they are partly the descendants of an ancient people subjugated by the Káfirs when they first entered the country, and are partly the descendants of prisoners taken in war. Among the slaves all are not of the same social position, for the house slave is said to be much higher in grade than the artisan slave ; but this is one of the many points in connection with the slaves which have always puzzled me. The skilled mechanics, the wood-carvers, the bootmakers, and the silver-workers, are called "Jast Bari"; "Jast" means senior or elder, and "Bari" means slave. The lowest class of all is the blacksmiths. All the craftsmen of the Káfirs, carpenters, dagger-makers, ironworkers, and weavers, are slaves, as are also those musicians who beat drums. The slave artisans live in a particular part of a village. In Kámdesh the slave quarter is called "Babagrom." The domestic slaves live with their masters. The relations existing between the slaves, their masters, and the ordinary free population, are very curious. It is impossible to insult a Káfir more than by calling him a slave. In a village quarrel that is the epithet used to lash opponents into fury. Slaves are considered so impure that they may not approach the shrines of the gods too closely, nor enter beyond the doorway of the priest's house. They are always liable to be sold, and also, I fear, to be given up to another Káfir tribe to be killed in atonement for a murder. Their children are the property of their master, to do with as he thinks fit. Yet, in spite of all this, their lot is by no means so bad as it must appear. A very curious case I knew, was one in which a master and his slave went through the ceremony of brotherhood together. The master, in talking to me about his slaves, mentioned this fact quietly, and as if there were nothing unusual in it. The slave artisans work for their masters with materials supplied by the latter, and are not paid for their labour. If the slaves work for others, they do not hand the wages over to their masters, but keep the pay themselves; on the other hand, the masters do not supply the artisan slaves with food or clothing; the latter are entirely self-supporting.

The house slaves are fed and worked more in the manner implied by the name. They probably would be beaten, or otherwise punished, if they were not industrious, but I never saw anything like harshness in the way they were treated. A curious circumstance about the slaves is, that they are permitted, after giving certain feasts to the free community, including, of course, their masters, to wear the earrings of the Jast; but this privilege does not appear to exalt the individual, except among the slave community. The bondsmen also adopt, more or less closely, all the manners and customs of the rest of the community, and give feasts at funerals and on other great occasions. But perhaps the most perplexing point about them is, that they are sometimes chosen to be members of the Urir, the annually elected magistrates, provided that they are not blacksmiths, and that they are Jast Bari. In 1891 this actually occurred while I was in Kámdesh. It was explained that it was a useful thing to elect a slave representative, because he knew so much about his own class and their doings. What really happened is what might have been expected. The slave Urir was instrumental in bringing a freeman to punishment by fine. The latter, with his brethren, waited a certain number of days during which the persons of the Urir are peculiarly sacred, and then attacked the slave. The rest of the Urir, all of whom were freemen, rushed to protect their brother magistrate; the different families and clans began to take sides, and what promised to be a bloody quarrel was only averted with great difficulty. There is no distinctive badge either for male or female slaves, but their physiognomy is often quite sufficient to show the class to which they belong. Slaves are just as patriotic as the rest of the community. There was one slave at Kámdesh, a blacksmith, belonging to the most despised class of all, who was pointed out to me as a tall man of his hands, and the slayer of many of his country's foes. Many others fight well when occasion arises.

I was assured that at Kámdesh slaves could only be sold in the village or down the valley, and that if one escaped and ran away to Katirgul, he would have to be given up at once, or there would be war. Slaves are never sold unless the owner becomes very poor indeed. A young female slave is more valuable than a male, because there is the probability that she will bear children. An old woman, or a very old man, is of course worth nothing at all. When a female slave is sold out of the valley she is always sent by herself, for if she were one of a party they would certainly all run away from their purchaser. Musalmáns are always ready to buy female slaves or their young female children, and pay high prices for them, partly, no doubt, because they are thereby enabled to make converts to Islám.

The Presuns, who are a feeble folk, have no slaves of their own, and purchase them from the Katir tribes. It is a strange sight to see Káfirs in the Siah-Posh garb, and therefore presumably manly and independent, owning as their masters the heavy-featured, cowardly Presuns.

There is very little traffic in slaves. Female children of slave parents are sold and sent away to neighbouring Musalmán tribes. The slave population is very limited in number, and as it comprises all the artificers of the village, it would be exceedingly inconvenient to the tribe if such men were always liable to be sold. Nevertheless, I believe that the community lays no claim to a common property in the slaves ; they all belong to their respective masters, to be sold or retained as each thinks best.

On one point I am not clear. It is concerning the position of children of a freeman by a slave mother. I believe that sometimes a slave woman is taken into the house of a freeman, and that her children are not slaves, although they rank much below the children born of a woman of the same rank as the man. One sometimes discovers that the eldest brother, the head of a family, has a half-brother who is looked upon as a man of no importance. He probably inherited nothing at the death of his father, yet he is treated kindly by his half-brethren, and is undoubtedly a freeman. The point I have not determined is this : was the mother of this man of no account a slave woman, or merely a woman of low rank ?

The Utah, the priest of the Kám, who is considered so pure an individual that slaves may not approach his hearth, has two children, a girl and a boy, who are both of much lower grade than his other children. Their mother was a Bashgul Katir, but I never could ascertain whether she had been a slave, or was merely of inferior rank. Utah had given the daughter to a Gújar of the Kunar Valley, who paid an exorbitant price for the girl, believing her to be one of the ordinary children of the Kám priest, and being anxious to proselytise a Káfir damsel of such presumably high birth. Utah told me the story himself, with a grave face, but with his tongue in his cheek, so to speak. I subsequently discovered that he spoke truly.

CHAPTER IX

The narrative continued—Universal opposition to my travelling about the country—Settling down—Appearance of Káfirs—Káfirs in their own country—Anxiety about my safety at night—Necessity for caution— Small swindles and thefts—Torag Merak's threat to expel me from the valley—Difficulty in getting supplies—Adverse and friendly parties— The Mehtar's influence against me—My arguments and assurances— Perpetual sacrifices to Imrá and Gísh—Plans to obtain solitude— Efforts to learn the Bashgul language—Torag Merak's recipe to that end—Visit of Presungulis—Their amazement at my abode—Presungul national dance and music—Visit of Rámgulis—Their attire—Their departure—Their temerity—Rumours of fighting—Raids—Káfir stealthy revenge and cold-blooded murder—Observances upon the return of successful braves.

I BEGAN to settle down in my new house, and the curiosity of the people was still unsatiated. Perhaps the point about the Káfirs which struck me more than any other was the striking difference between the appearance which they present outside their own country, and that which they present in their villages. In Chitrál, for instance, especially if in a conciliatory attitude, Káfirs are singularly mean, shifty, and forbidding in appearance. A scanty and dirty dress, furtive glances, shameless begging, and a prowling step, induce, at first sight, a feeling towards them of dislike and contempt. It needs a close and sympathetic observation to discover that the vile brown robe trailing at the heels, conceals active and athletic forms; that the bland, insinuating faces are keen and well-formed, and can give at times the bold fixed stare, or the swift wild glance of the hawk; that the men playing the part of cringing beggars, with all the subtlety and duplicity of the Oriental, have fierce and impetuous natures, and are capable at any minute of throwing off the mask of humility, and assuming their own characteristics — a fierce independence of spirit, tempered by a clear perception of the exigencies of the moment, and the possible dangers of a situation; and by an hereditary cupidity, which in some instances almost amounts to insanity.

In his own country, on the other hand, the Kám Káfir is polite, dignified, and carries himself with a free, independent, and self-satisfied air. A Jast is rarely seen alone. If only going to a friend's house, he will have one or two men following him. He walks slowly, and with an air of being what he is—a great man. I was quite unprepared for the lofty bearing and the self-possessed manners of some of my wild-looking friends. The younger men are very picturesque. They are much given to posing in graceful attitudes, and show themselves off with a charming simplicity. A warrior who has killed four or five Musalmán enemies is allowed the privilege of wearing a blue shawl, made out of the dead man's turban, in some instances. The young braves took a great delight in wrapping this blue shawl round them, and then placing themselves in some prominent position where I could not fail to notice them. Once or twice, when I made remarks about such individuals, others standing by would hurry off, and a short time afterwards reappear wearing the blue shawl, and then stroll casually near me to show that they also were warriors of repute. All the youths, most of the boys, and not a few older men also, were incessantly shooting with the *galail*, the Eastern variety of the stone-bow, at the season of my arrival in the country. Anything would do for a mark, and the practice they made was very fair. Very small boys brought toy bows and arrows; but every male found something or other with which to show his prowess to the stranger Frank.

My Kámdesh friends were really and sincerely anxious about my safety at night, and continually begged me to be cautious. Dán Malik observed that all Káfirs were thieves and murderers. He did not say this as if he censured his fellow-countrymen for their little failings, but merely to illustrate his argument that my doors should be securely fastened at night, and that my bed should be continually shifted about, so that no man on my roof would know the exact position at which to fire through the smoke-hole when the house was dark. He and others begged me not to light candles in my room for the same reason. There is no doubt that the Kám were for some time in great anxiety lest the Mehtar of Chitrál should bribe some one to murder me secretly. It was known that he was annoyed at my being in Káfiristán, and every one also knew that Torag Merak had been heavily bribed by Mehtar Jao Ghulám, in the Mehtar's name, to stop me in the Pittigul Valley. In acknowledgment of the kindness of my advisers, I took all reasonable precautions for my own safety, and quickly discovered a way to render my room perfectly secure at night without necessitating my having to remain in darkness. I continued to make every effort to conciliate the people and to make myself popular, but great care had to be used that the cupidity of my friends should not be excited. Several little occurrences took place which showed how necessary it was to be cautious. In the Pittigul Valley, Torag Merak had taken twenty-five rupees in prepayment of some sheep, and had never delivered the animals, nor did he subsequently do so. One of Dán Malik's sons, named Kánsta Dán, that is, Dán junior, hurried to me on the day we arrived at Kámdesh, and breathlessly said he was badly in want of money for an urgent and special purpose; that he had two sheep on their way for me to buy — would I pay him in advance, seeing whose son he was? I agreed, and the sheep never arrived. Then Chandlu Astán, the headman who did me such good service when Torag Merak was blocking my way in the Pittigul, being about to start on a visit to Chitrál, was entrusted by me with the care of Sayed Shah and the Balti coolies left behind at Chitrál, and was instructed to bring them to Kámdesh, now that the outlook was so peaceable. He was provided with money to pay for supplies for the party on the road. He took the money, but provided no food for Sayed Shah and the Baltis, and quarrelled with and threatened the men when they reproached him for his bad faith. These little swindles and iniquities would have done no harm if they had not been generally known; but a Káfir cannot refrain from bragging, and each and every one of the above-mentioned peccant individuals boasted loudly of his astuteness, and in this way others were instigated to plunder me, not only from the love of gain, but also because they wanted to be esteemed as smart and able as their fellows. I was consequently expected to buy most miserable, diseased sheep, at the

G

full price of well-grown, healthy animals. Shermalik was drawn into the conspiracy, and brought dying sheep, the property of his friends, for me to purchase, and went off in great anger, knowing the taunts and jeers in store for him when I refused to listen to his blandishments. It seemed at one time that we must go without mutton altogether, because nobody would sell other than diseased animals. Then Barmúk, my next-door neighbour, stole one of my sheep, killed it, and ate it with his friends in broad daylight, during the ceremony of patching up a quarrel with his partner. My wet and dry bulb thermometer was carried off and broken, merely with the idea of seeing what it was made of, and the people round were hungering to devour my substance. I had to put my foot down firmly, lest worse troubles germinated from those existing. Dán junior and Barmúk were kept at a distance and deprived of my friendship, until one had made reparation, and the other had sworn to do so in the spring; the other defaulters also made solemn promises to repay the sums they had received. Then the people, seeing that no one was to be allowed to plunder me, became contented, and we all got on more pleasantly together.

Sayed Shah, with my remaining baggage, reached Kámdesh on the 22nd of October, full of complaints against Chandlu Astán, and rather nervous still about the general position of affairs. But there seemed to me to be no cause for alarm. Several deputations of the headmen had come to me from time to time, to tell me how welcome I was in their country, and to discuss the future. They indeed always wanted me to send off on the instant for rifles; but when I showed

them the futility of making any request on their behalf
to the Government of India on that subject, and explained fully my reasons for having come amongst
them, and my desire to help them and be their friend,
they invariably accepted my remarks and assurances with
the utmost good-humour, and went away from the
conferences with smiles, and in apparent satisfaction.
Sayed Shah had not, however, been in the village four
hours, when he rushed over from Torag Merak, who
had returned to Kámdesh a few days before and whom
he had been to visit, with horror in his face, and breathless with excitement, to say that Torag Merak, speaking
in the name of all the tribe, had declared that I was
to have ten days within which proper arrangements
must be made for a hundred rifles to be given to the
Kám, and that if this was not done, the least of the
consequences would be my immediate expulsion from
the valley. It seemed to me, however, that the old
chief had been working on Sayed Shah's known timidity
as an experiment; so I took no notice of the demand,
but went coolly to one of Torag Merak's public feasts
the next day as if nothing had happened. He received me with grins, and was by no means uncivil.
He exhibited on this occasion a considerable skill in
" chaffing " me, which I accepted as of good omen for
our future relationship with one another. Torag Merak's
jokes cannot be reproduced, unfortunately. He was like
Mr. Vincent Crummles' pony in melodrama—too broad
—too broad.

We soon began to experience considerable difficulty in
getting supplies, especially sheep, as already mentioned.
Fowls and eggs were scarce. They are not used by Káfirs

as articles of food, and the people of the tiny hamlet across the river, Agaru, promised to supply me with fowls, but they only sent me one or two altogether. Even grain and flour were, after a time, only obtainable after a vast deal of worrying. In these circumstances we were compelled to take advantage of the gratuitous distribution of food by men undergoing the necessary ceremonies for becoming headmen or Jast. These compulsory public banquets were continually recurring at short intervals. On every such occasion my coolies and servants were marched off to the feast, where they were entertained in precisely the same way as everybody else. That is the right of every one who happens to be in the village at the time, whether he be a casual visitor or a regular inhabitant. I also sent back all my Balti coolies to Chitrál and Gilgit, except the five who had engaged to remain with me permanently, it being of the greatest importance that we should have no more mouths to feed than were absolutely necessary.

In stating that there was no cause for alarm in the general attitude of the Kám people, it would be more correct to say that there was no such urgency in the matter as Sayed Shah imagined; but there were not wanting signs to show that all the tribe were by no means agreed upon the desirability of having me among them. Two parties were gradually formed. One of these, numerically important, waited with some impatience for an indication that my presence in their village meant a material and immediate advantage to them. A subdivision of this party began to get anxious to try against me the characteristic Káfir tactics of bullying and blackmailing. The second party, my steady supporters, included, amongst others, all the inhabitants of the eastern division of Kámdesh.   These men, although comparatively few in number, comprised many individuals who were the most respected in the tribe for prowess in war, or for the possession of wealth.

Unluckily, all the influence of the Mehtar of Chitrál was steadily directed against me.   He kept sending messengers into the valley to start intrigues amongst the Káfirs; and not content with this plan of embarrassing me, he also summoned various head Káfirs to Chitrál, and there incited them in every possible way to expel me from their country.   He argued, and with a fair measure of success, that my visit to Káfiristán was fraught with danger to its inhabitants, that my design was merely to spy out the land, learn the roads, and study the positions, and then to bring a large army with which to seize the whole valley.   He strongly advised that my avowed friendship for the Káfirs should be put to the test, and suggested, as a crucial experiment, that I should be asked to pay down a large sum of money, and give the Kám one hundred breech-loading rifles.   He more than hinted that I had left behind in Chitrál immense treasure and many stands of arms, which were originally intended by the Government of India as presents for the Káfirs, but which had been wilfully kept back by me, because, in my opinion, the Káfirs were a wretched, savage people, quite unworthy of such splendid gifts.   He wound up by frankly offering bribes to the headmen to induce them to turn me out of Káfiristán then and there.

Of course, the Mehtar overreached himself by showing his impatience and his over-anxiety at my remaining in Kámdesh.   Several men kept me well acquainted with all that was going on; whenever a messenger arrived from Chitrál, private information generally followed that some headman or other was getting unsettled in mind, or had been openly declaring that I should either be made to produce the coveted rifles or leave the valley altogether. My invariable plan on receiving such news was to send for the malcontent headman on the spot and try to reason with him. The arguments employed were somewhat as follows :—I would ask ironically, how long had the Mehtar shown such a warm interest in the Kám Káfirs, and so strong a desire to befriend them, and why was it that he was so anxious to get me out of the country? Did the Káfirs really suppose for an instant that his policy was solely dictated by a desire to benefit them ?—and so on. I invariably ended by assuring my listener that the territory already occupied by the English was quite as much, if not a good deal more than they desired; that the idea that we coveted the poor villages of Káfiristán, where even my small party could hardly get food enough to eat, was an idle and foolish thought; that my sole reason for coming to visit them was a desire to study everything which could be learnt about the people, and when I had thoroughly acquainted myself with all these matters, to try and help them in every way in my power; how it was my hope and intention, subsequently, to write and inform the Government of India of the kindly nature of my reception, and how anxious the Káfirs were to become firm friends of the English ; and other assurances to the same effect.

My words always seemed to have the desired effect at the time they were uttered ; but, of course, all were not equally convinced of my sincerity, nor had every one the power of keeping to one opinion steadily. Again, although every one knew that the Mehtar would never keep his promises, nor pay the bribes which he so freely offered, yet many men remained with a vague sense of injury, because I had not paid them the same amount for abstaining from annoying me that the Mehtar had promised to give them if they made it impossible for me to remain longer at Kámdesh. On the whole, however, matters proceeded as satisfactorily as could be expected. I had the great advantage of being always able to turn a doubtful scale in my favour by the influence which arises from personal contact. There was also a small party of headmen, intelligent and far-sighted beyond their fellows, who attached themselves to me from the first. They acted from the sincere belief that my residence amongst them would ensure a freedom from all attacks by Umrá Khan, the Amir of Kabul, or the Mehtar of Chitrál. These were the men who were so extremely anxious about my personal safety.

During the month of October, which was now drawing to a close, I had been sedulously trying to ingratiate myself with the people, both great and small, and had passéd a good deal of my time in their society, watching their manners and observing their customs. Nothing surprised me more than the incessant sacrificing to Imrá and to Gísh, but especially to the latter deity. His shrine was a short distance below my house, just hidden by the undulating ground; but the smoke of the sacrificial fires arose almost daily, and it was no uncommon circumstance for a dozen or fifteen goats to be offered at one time. When the number and pertinacity of my visitors became unbearable, it was

GÍSH'S (THE WAR GOD) SHRINE.

my habit to suggest that we should go and see the
religious ceremonies enacted ; then, when my com-

panions were actually engaged chorusing with the
throng at the shrine, I would quietly walk home again,
and indulge in the luxury of comparative solitude. I
soon discovered another plan of getting my house
emptied. It was, to study the Bashgul language. At
first my would-be instructors were numerous, and the
greatest delight and amusement was shown at my efforts
to attain the accurate pronunciation of baffling sounds.
But very soon the whole thing was voted a bore, and
it was only necessary for me to beg a repetition of
some strange nasal syllable, for my room to be rapidly
cleared. One by one, without the least ceremony, my
visitors would hitch up their long brown Chitráli robes,
shoulder their walking-sticks, or rather light clubs, jump
for my door, and disappear. For some reason or other,
no Káfir seems able to step sedately over the raised
threshold of a door. He must spring on to it with
one foot, however low the doorway, and however much
he has to bend his head. Consequently, he retires in
a sort of miniature whirlwind, his loose garments float-
ing behind him. All my efforts to get instructors who
would listen to me and reply to my questions for more
than ten minutes, were in vain. I took the dejected
Shermalik, on more than one occasion, to some secluded
spot on the hillside, made him sit down in such a position that he could see nothing but myself, and then
proceeded to ask him the Káfir equivalent for Hindustani
words or phrases; of course insisting on a clear understanding about the—to my ear—unaccustomed sounds
he uttered. He never could endure the proceeding for
more than a few minutes. Before one complete phrase
had been written down in the note-book, he was practi-

cally asleep before my eyes, as though hypnotised. One day Torag Merak came to me and said : " Take a wife, Frank ; women never leave off talking—so you will learn our language—otherwise you will never be able to talk to us." It was quite true ; I never was able to speak more than the simplest and most ordinary sentence, but in a short time my knowledge of the language became sufficient to enable me to prevent any translator playing tricks. This Shermalik speedily discovered, to his annoyance, for it was his custom to try and change any sentence which it might be displeasing for a Jast to hear, into something else which might gratify the great man, quite irrespective of the subject-matter of our conversation.

The Kám people never tired of bringing strangers to see me. Lutkám Chandlu Merak (there was such a run on the name of Merak, that this individual required not only his father's but his grandfather's name to be prefixed to his own, in order to differentiate him from all the other Meraks) brought one day two Presungul or Viron men. They were amazed, altogether bewildered, at the magnificence of my dwelling, and the wonderful things it contained. For a long time they could do nothing but gaze and gaze, shaking their heads from side to side with many soft expressions of wonder. They were very quiet and meek-looking, and daggers seemed absurdly out of place in their belts. After a time they sat down close together with their arms round one another's necks, as though they were alone in a crowd of aliens, which was probably the case. The mystery of the electric battery brought such a look of distrust and horror to their faces, that I

SHERMALIK INSTRUCTING ME IN THE KÁFIR LANGUAGE.

To face page 116.

refused to allow them to be subjected to it, to the great disappointment of the Kám men who were present. A few nights later the same man, L. C. Merak, brought three fresh Presungulis to show me their national dance. By contrast with these people the Kám appeared enlightened — almost civilised. The Presungulis were dark-complexioned, of muscular build and fair stature, and were obviously of an unusually primitive type. Unlike those of their countrymen who came to see me in the daytime, these men were very cheerful, and looked pleased with themselves, and with the performance they gave for my entertainment. A musical instrument was extemporised from a wooden ladle, shaped like the model of a flat-bottomed boat, and with a short straight handle projecting from the stern. The performer simply banged on this with a piece of wood to mark the time, while he sang the alternate lines of a monotonous chant with one of the other men. The same words appeared to be repeated over and over again, without the slightest variation. That, however, had no deterrent effect upon the dramatic expression of the singers, who after a time grew actually excited at their own impassioned utterances. Presently, to the rhythmic beating on the wooden bowl by the one man, the other two began to sway their bodies, and this swaying motion gradually merged into a dance. The movement consisted of the violent shuffling jerk of one foot, about nine inches forward, with a second jerk at the end of the step; then at the next bar the other foot was brought up in line with its fellow, in an identical manner—and that was all. As they warmed to the dance, however, the performers turned and twisted, waved their arms and clapped their hands. To combine all these efforts and still keep within the limits of the step described, is most laborious; but the dancers were in splendid condition, and were so thoroughly happy, that they would have kept on all night if a heavy shower of rain had not fallen and put a stop to the entertainment. The Kám men looking on seemed greatly to enjoy the show; they also helped to indicate the time for the dancers by hand-clapping. It was noticeable that none of the Kám tribe could speak a single word of the Presun language, which they declared it was impossible for any one to learn except in childhood, while all the Presun spoke the Bashgul tongue fluently. A day or two later a very different stamp of visitors came to see me. These were three Rámgulis from the western valley. As the Kám have been at war with this tribe for many generations, it showed great temerity on the part of these Rámgulis to come to Kámdesh. However, they were not wanting in plausibility. When fiercely questioned by the Kám, and asked why they had come, they affected astonishment at their reception, and surprise that their questioners did not know that their particular village had always been at peace with the Kám, and had always admired them also. The result was a triumph for the Rámgulis' audacity. They were strangely attired, but looked fine specimens of strength and activity combined. Their countenances, however, were anything but prepossessing. The dress of the leader of the party was simplicity itself. It consisted of a short pair of loose cotton trousers reaching just below the knee, and a wisp of similar material bound round the head. The body garment was a fragment of a blue turban about four feet long and two broad, in the middle of which was a hole through which the head was thrust. A coarse thick grey Presun blanket completed this individual's outfit, except that he also wore a pair of Chitráli stockings from which the foot part had been severed. Having disposed of the suspicious Kám people, the Rámgulis turned their attention to me, looked with pretended interest but real indifference at everything they were shown, and whenever an opportunity occurred and he could not be overheard, the leader would exclaim with his raucous voice, "Tanga gats" (give us rupees), sometimes so fiercely that it might have been supposed I was in the speaker's power, instead of his life being suspended by a single thread; for several of the Kám were strolling about restlessly, with frowning brows, and at the slightest provocation would have plunged their daggers into the Rámgulis. The latter, finding they could get nothing out of me, went away, and left the valley in broad daylight. It is hardly possible to conceive anything more recklessly daring than the short visit these three men made to Kámdesh. The more I learnt of the Káfirs, the more astonishing this little incident appeared.

There were continued rumours of fighting brought to the village, the best authenticated of which was to the effect that twenty Waigul Káfirs had attacked two thousand Ogani, i.e., Afghans, at a place called Shanur, and had returned safely, having killed thirteen of the enemy, and wounded twenty or thirty or more. This was the Káfir euphuistic way of saying that a few Waigulis had stealthily entered the Shanur country, had killed several

people, and had contrived to get back safely. The Kám
also had their small raiding parties out. On the 3rd of
October two men of the upper village had been brought
to me with stabs on their arms. The wounds were slight.
It seemed that these two men, of whom the more important was named Málding, with two others, had just returned from a place called by the Kám, Tsáru, in the
Péch Valley, where they had murdered a Shaikh (*i.e.*, a
Káfir converted to Islám) and his wife. Everybody
seemed interested about the treatment of the wounds,
but no one seemed to think much of the exploit which
occasioned them. It appeared that Málding, who was
the more severely hurt of the two wounded men, was
avenging his own father, who had been killed by the
Shaikh. The Káfir procedure was characteristic. The
four men crept into the Tsáru country, hiding on the hills
by day, and travelling with the greatest caution by night.
Finally, they reached the habitation of their enemy.
They then patiently waited, concealed near the edge of a
field. After a time the Shaikh and his wife, working in
the fields, gradually approached them. The Káfirs then
sprang upon them, three of them seizing the man's arms
and hands and stabbing him to death, while the fourth
pursued and killed the woman. Nothing then remained
to be done except to strip the dead of as much of their
clothing as possible, cut off their ears as trophies, and get
back to Kámdesh quickly enough to outstrip the avengers
of blood, who would pursue for a certain distance as soon
as the murders were discovered. On their arrival at
Kámdesh, the men were dressed up in all the finery their
relations possessed, and were then ceremoniously escorted
to the dancing-house, which Shermalik, in recollection of

his Indian travels, called the " church." There, with the women of their families, they all danced together to the glory of Gísh, the war god ; and in the intervals of the dance the braves were showered over with wheat grains from the small wicker basket each woman carried. This is a type of what was continually going on in Kámdesh, the marvellous thing being the comparative immunity the warriors experienced in their murderous raids. It was rare for a Kámdesh man to be killed, while it was not at all unusual to hear the peculiar shout or song with which successful braves signified their return to the precincts of their own village. They had to remain there until they were brought in triumphantly by their friends and rela- tions ; while, if they arrived at night, they were obliged to stay outside till the morning, their families carrying them food, and keeping them company during the night on the hillside. There was a magnificent cedar a short distance above the village, and these little encampments commonly sought the shelter of its branches for the night, rousing at intervals to sing their pæan of victory in unison. But the snow was threatening, and it was clear that in a few weeks' time at furthest the raids must all cease, and the Bashgul Valley tribes must confine themselves to their own country, to which there would remain but a single outlet—that into the Kunar Valley at Arundu.

CHAPTER X

IT soon became apparent that in whatever other respects they might differ about me, and about the manner in which they should treat me, all the Kámdesh people, both my friends and my opponents, were united in a resolve to prevent my leaving their chief village to travel about the country. Every suggestion on my part about the desirability of my making a short journey for sporting purposes or for exercise was met by the raising of every possible objection. Direct opposition was not displayed at this time, but unremitting attempts were made to render my desire to move abroad impossible. When I expressed a wish to go shooting up the Kamu Valley, every one assured me that there were no supplies whatever in that direction, that the Kamu villagers were hostile to the idea of my going there, and that consequently the projected journey must be abandoned.

They added that if I had expressed a wish to go down the Dungul Valley in the Bailám direction, instead of going to Kamu, such a journey could easily have been arranged. Upon my eagerly accepting this suggestion, and expressing a keen desire to visit the Dungul Valley, they at once whipped round in the most shameless way, and declared that the first fall of snow, which happened on 21st October, had so completely blocked the pass over the Kámdesh hill that it had become altogether impracticable; that war parties infested the Dungul Valley; and that, in short, the thing could not possibly be done. My reply was that my mind was made up, and that nothing could prevent me from doing as I wished. The Kám headmen appeared to give way and acquiesce in my starting. Utah, Shermalik, and three others of the tribe were told off to accompany me as guide and escort, and a day for the journey was fixed. The night before the appointed day, when everything was packed up, the priest sent word begging me to defer my journey for twenty-four hours, as he had important professional work to do. This seemed a reasonable request, and was of course complied with; but on the following day he sent over a similar message, to which I naturally demurred, and finally declined to wait for him any longer. He then pretended to be offended at my want of consideration for him and his duties, and the following morning, instead of coming over to me, he remained sulking in his house, while Shermalik and the other guides were nowhere to be found. So it was necessary to start without escort or Káfir companions of any kind. On the road to the pass, Shermalik caught me up. He was in a state of

H

great indignation, and kept assuring me, in a loud voice, that it was impossible for me to attempt to follow the dictates of my own judgment in the Kám country as I was accustomed to do in India, and that it was necessary for me to submit to the Jast in all things. He was quickly reduced to tears by my threatening to discard him on the spot. He accompanied me, but was ill at ease all the time, and could not control his temper. The poor fellow was between two fires : he feared my anger and its result in possible loss of wealth to himself; yet he was terrified at the idea of disobeying the orders of the Jast, who certainly have very decided methods of enforcing their mandates.

My party consisted of Rusalá, my Kashmiri factotum, Shermalik, and the five Balti coolies. Sayed Shah elected to stay behind, and, as he was somewhat unwell, his request was granted. My Pathan servant had been giving way to outbursts of bad temper, and had in consequence been sent to Chitrál temporarily, to recover, for a bad-tempered man was an actual danger in Káfiristán. The pass over the curious outcrop of rock which forms a semicircle to the south of Kámdesh, and is called the Arákon range, is reached by a steady climb of about four miles. It is a little over 10,000 feet in altitude, and leads, by a singularly steep descent on the farther side, into the top of the Dungul Valley. About half-way between the village and the pass the deodar (cedar) forest ceases. We were nearing the top, when three Kashtán men passed us on a shooting expedition. All had matchlocks, and each carried a small goatskin bag which contained his food. Their attire was peculiar in respect of its deficiencies. On their heads they wore the ordinary Shín or Chitráli cap, a long bag like an old-fashioned night-cap made of blanket cloth, and rolled up to form a convenient round head-dress. Their legs below the knee, and their feet, were encased in a rough material made from goats' hair, which all Káfirs like to use in the snow. The body garment was merely a goatskin, hairy side out, which reached half-way down the thigh, whence to just below the knee they were entirely naked. I was commiserating their poverty in my mind, and marvelling how they could withstand the cold in such a dress, when the national garb of my own fellow-countrymen, the Highlanders of Scotland, recurred to my mind. This led to reflections on the probable origin of the Highlanders' costume, which were abruptly put an end to by an incident of a startling nature which at this instant occurred.

Aramalick Chárá came round a rocky corner with his flocks and herds, which he was bringing home from their grazing-grounds in the Dungul Valley. He hardly had time to exchange a greeting with me, when he recognised one of the Kashtán men as a private enemy. He at once shouted to his followers and helpers, and fastened on to the Kashtán man with cries of " Vi, vi!" (strike, strike). He, with some difficulty, possessed himself of the man's gun, and threatened him with a sword he waved over his head. Then he struck him several shrewd blows with his walking-club, enough to break any one's skull, one would have thought; but it was not the man's head, it was the stick which broke. I feared for the high-handed Chárá, a somewhat sickly-looking man; but the Kashtán people, thinking we were all of one party, made no real resistance, except that the other two men clung to their guns resolutely and successfully. Chárá's natural attitude as he declaimed and waved his broken stick would have made the fortune of a tragedy actor, except that he did not work himself up to a climax, but ebbed and flowed in his passion, so that at times I thought he would let his prisoner go. The latter tried all manner of blandishments, putting his arms round Chárá's neck and coaxing him like a child, but all without avail. The captor flung off his coat with a fine gesture, seized the Kashtán man by the goatskin coat, and dragged him down a side path. We moved on, but had not gone more than a hundred yards or so when we saw Chárá returning alone, stalking along with the stride of a stage villain. I imagined the prisoner had broken away, but Shermalik acutely pointed out that the Kashtán man's dog accompanied Chárá, and observed that had the man escaped, the dog would certainly have followed him. A short distance farther on my five Baltis were standing transfixed. They had watched the whole tragedy, and had seen Chárá plunge his dagger into the captive, and then hurl the body aside. They also showed where the body was lying exposed to view. There was certainly something dark lying on the ground, and the whole affair made me sorrowful, for Chárá was a friend of mine, and Shermalik told me that to kill a man of a tribe at peace with the Kám meant ruin to Chárá. His house would be burned, and his possessions divided. Shermalik then related the cause of the feud, which was as follows :—Chárá's cousin, a Shaikh, lived at a place in the Dungul Valley, where the Kashtán man also formerly resided. The Shaikh had three Pathan

CHÁRÁ AND THE KASHTÁN.

To face page 128.

servants, whom the Kashtán man murdered. Hence
the feud. Here we get an instance of a Káfir starting
a. feud to avenge three Pathans because they were the
servants of a blood-relation, although the latter also was
a Musalmán. This is another illustration of the racial
rather than the religious origin of the never-ending
fighting between Afghans and Káfirs. The evidence
that Chárá had killed his man was absolute, overwhelm-
ing. It would have convinced any one. Nevertheless,
it was completely false. The Kashtán man had broken
away from Chárá's feeble grasp uninjured, with merely
the loss of his gun and a few bruises. This, of course,
was told me subsequently. We all went on saddened
at having been present, as we supposed, at a tragedy,
and to change the subject Shermalik told me again all
his love affairs.

He never tired of relating the wrong which had been
done him, and which had eventually forced him to
abandon his own wife and child, and seek connubial
happiness in another clan. He began by explaining
that the reason he had been so late in coming to me
that morning was because his night's rest had been
disturbed. It appears that the previous night, to cele-
brate his marriage with a little girl of the Belizhedari
clan, he had taken a goat to his father-in-law's house,
and there feasted with the family. Following the rule
of sleeping where he dined, Shermalik had gone to bed,
but slept very little, because his father-in-law having
caught a Mumán man trying to steal some of his sheep,
had tied him neck and crop and thrown him under
Shermalik's bed. Shermalik remarked that the captive's
groans and writhings were very amusing, but they had

greatly interfered with his sleep.   His love story was
this.   Before going with me to India, he was married
to a woman of humble birth and of Presun descent,
whom Dán Malik called his daughter.   She had been
taken when quite young from her own parents in the
Presungúl, and had been brought up as a field-slave
to all intents and purposes.   It had been agreed between
Dán Malik and Shermalik that the price of the woman
was to be eight cows.   The woman, as in all such cases,
remained at her own home pending the payment of her
ransom.   She had a child by Shermalik, a pretty little
girl, whom her father professed to admire greatly.   When
we returned to Kámdesh, and Shermalik was found to be
possessed of so much wealth, the avarice of Dán Malik
and his family was excited, and they declared that the
former arrangement was no longer in force, and that my
adopted son must pay up his rifle, his derringer, all his
gorgeous robes—in fact, everything he had received from
me—or he should not receive his wife.   In vain Shermalik
offered twelve, and at last twenty cows.   Dán Malik was
obdurate.   He did not demand the bag of rupees my
adopted son had received from me, for that item of
wealth had been kept concealed from him.   Shermalik
was furious, and talked about making a holocaust of
the whole Dán Malik family—at any rate, he would stab
them one and all ; but eventually more prudent counsels
prevailed.   He was a small man, and the great Dán
Malik had always been in his eyes a kind of divinity.
So he quickly dried his tears of rage, washed his garments, and having to pay a high price for a wife, paid it
for a particularly plain and dirty, if high-born, little girl,
and ever after took great pride to himself on account of

his marriage connections.   The first wife and her child
were definitely abandoned.

As we reached our camp for the night on the south
side of the pass, a short distance down the Dungul
Valley, we met two or three little parties of Kashtán
men returning from Asmar with slow steps.   They had
been trying to catch a Pathan or two, but had failed.
When we sat round our camp-fire that night, and Shermalik had exhausted the subject of his loves, his wrongs,
and his marriage connections, he explained that the
Kashtán had been at bitter feud with the Asmar folk
ever since the latter had burnt and completely destroyed
the village of Dungul.   The people of that village
belonged to the Kashtán tribe, and being cut off from
the rest of the tribe by snow during the winter, had
tried to conciliate their Afghan neighbours in every
possible way, even to the extent of adopting their dress.
They succeeded for a time, but eventually the Asmar
men came to Dungul and utterly destroyed the village,
causing its inhabitants to return to and greatly over-
crowd the tribal headquarters near Kámdesh.   Ever
since, there had been severe fighting, and the Afghans
were reduced to such straits that at night no inhabitant
of any of the villages near the Dungul Valley dare leave
his house.   One of the Dungul men, a supposed convert
to Islám, had murdered the Khan of Asmar, seated in
the midst of his own men at the door of his own fort,
and had fled to Kashtán, to be honoured and admired
ever after.   In reply to a question, Shermalik said that
the Kám were at peace with the Asmar Afghans; and
in answer to a further query, admitted that mistakes did
sometimes happen, and Kám people got killed sometimes

instead of Kashtáns, and that a short time before my
arrival in the country Pathans had crept close to Kámdesh over the pass, and had murdered four little Kám
boys, tending goats, and had then decamped. This did
not incite the Kám to open war, but the latter contented
themselves with secretly and privately murdering Pathans
to avenge their own losses. In this way nine Oganis
(Pathans) had already been slaughtered. On my remarking
that the peace of the Kám with the Asmar men seemed
to me to be curious in its nature, Shermalik fell back on
the customary Káfir answer to almost everything, which
also authoritatively closes any discussion, " Insta cháraza "
—" It is our custom." The one point in which their
peaceful killing differs from actual war is, that in the
former there is no dancing at Kámdesh, and the matter
is supposed to be kept a secret.

The next morning we started down the valley, from
our camp under a rock, as soon as the benumbed coolies
could be persuaded to take up their loads. We at once
began to fall in with small parties of ten or a dozen
Kashtán men returning from the Asmar frontier. They
looked upon us with suspicion, although Shermalik was
well known to them. They could not be convinced we
were merely out shooting. "Does a man go out shooting
with five coolie loads of baggage ?" they argued, and they
decided that he did not. They believed we must be
leaving Káfiristán for Jelalabad. Each succeeding group
became more difficult to pass than the preceding. At
one place I was just in time to save my gun, which
Rusalá was quietly handing over to a Káfir who had
demanded it. The only thing to do was to put a bold
face on the matter, swagger up to each little party, give

PACIFYING THE RAIDERS.

To face page 134.

the Káfir salutation, "Nirishtosha"—"Have you come from below?" and then, "Le sher, lickti-le sher, poma mangi adugán ashtá"—"Are you well?—are you very well?—are the people in your house well?" Then I would rest my hand on the shoulder of some one of them, and become curious about their powder-horns and daggers. At a wink from me the poor coolies stole by in almost ludicrous distress. Shermalik and I would hurry after them as soon as possible, to find, almost invariably, that they had been stopped by another band. Shermalik was gradually getting hopeless, while I must confess my anxiety was deepening, when we reached a place called Azharbai, whence a fine valley runs to the north-west in the direction of Kamu. This we entered, and shortly afterwards came upon a "pshál" or grazing farm belonging to a man of Utah's clan. There we felt comparatively safe, and decided to remain.

We had no sooner turned out of the main Dungul Valley than a large force, consisting of some two hundred and fifty Kashtán, Mádugál, and Katir Káfirs, swept down on their way to raid some flocks and herds near the Afghan village of Bailám. On their heels came Utah, who perceiving the danger we might be in from these wild Káfirs, cast aside his sulkiness, and hurried to me with several trustworthy Kám men he had collected together. His arrival was a great relief to us all, for with him as our companion there was no longer any risk, unless the raid failed and the Káfirs returned followed by avenging Afghans; for Utah was known far and wide as the priest, the head of a clan of the Kám tribe, as a wise man, very wealthy, and a

famous warrior. Indeed, if his years were taken into
consideration, he might be considered the show-man
of the Kám. He was a very interesting personage, and
deserves a detailed description. His real name was
Latkam, but he was known, except to his intimates, as
Utah—that is, the priest. He was just over forty, and
his hair was very slightly grizzled. In stature he was
a trifle over five feet eight inches, with shoulders square
and somewhat high, and a splendidly deep chest. The
arms and upper arms were moderately developed, the
flanks of average breadth, the legs very muscular.
His feet were beautifully modelled. He was the most
untiring walker it is possible to conceive; indeed, he
could tramp all round the clock, and cover almost incredible distances over roads of every possible variety,
except that none of them were easy. The fact that he
was the sixth or seventh hereditary priest of the Kám
in regular succession, and the wealthy head of a wealthy
clan, gave him a personal prestige in the tribe inferior
only to that occupied by Torag Merak, Dán Malik, and
lame Astán. His opinion was highly valued by every
one, and if only he had been a little older, and had
finished the Jast ceremonies, on which he was still
engaged, he would have been the most influential, and
also the most respected member of the Kám after the
aged Dán Malik. He had marvellous tact. In a discussion he seemed to perceive almost by instinct the
view which would in the end prevail; he invariably
contrived to identify himself with that view, and to
make himself its exponent and representative. It was
interesting to watch the way he maintained his influential
position and his reputation for sagacity. If hot words

were passing during a tribal conclave, and Utah could
not make up his mind how the popular voice would

UTAH'S HOUSE.

go, he would actually hide himself until the critical
moment, when, his mind made up, he would appear in

the assembly, add a few convincing words in support
of the opinion which was about to triumph, and cover
himself with praises and with glory. He had a somewhat ruddy face fringed with a scanty beard, and eyes
which could narrow into mere slits under the influence
of avariciousness, his chief vice. Ordinarily he was a
shrewd, singularly clear-headed companion, with a considerable reserve fund of geniality and humour. He
had a famous record of homicides, and was emphatically what the Káfirs describe as "le manji"—that is,
a good man. There was no single tribesman who would
not say of Utah, "le manjiz," "He is a good man;" most
would prefix "biluk," which means "very," while enthusiastic supporters would emphasise the word until it became "bil-l-l-l-l-l'-uk," brought out with a flourish of
the right arm, such as that which helps the tenor with
his chest C.

Perhaps I may be pardoned a little story in which
my friend Utah played a chief part, but which occurred
some time before my visit to Káfiristán. Utah and his
cousin and brother-in-law, Chandlu Astán, were down in
the Kunar Valley, hiding near a hostile village on the
left bank of the river. One dark night they crept into
the graveyard, which was to the north, and close under
the dead wall formed by the row of houses in that face of
the square-shaped village, and was an important feature
in the defensive arrangements of the place. Dogs were
barking loudly, and there was actually a party of travellers
camped on the continuous house-tops, cooking their evening meal at a blazing fire. Utah and Astán scaled the
wall noiselessly and peered over the roofs, to find there
was no one at that particular spot. They crawled along

THE STORY OF UTAH.

To face page 143.

the house-tops on their stomachs, till they came to a square aperture leading by means of a notched pole into an apartment below. Such apertures are practically the doors of the houses to which they belong. The two Káfirs listened attentively, then stole down the ladder, and killed with their daggers every living soul the room contained—four people altogether, including a child. Then they quietly withdrew as they came, and started to swim the Kunar river to reach the Dungul Valley. When they reached the farther bank, the alarm had been given, and all the Musalmán males in the village, armed with matchlocks or flintlocks, swords or knives, crossed the river, by a solitary raft the place possesses or by swimming, determined to avenge the murders if possible, and feeling absolutely certain of the road the fugitives had taken. At this juncture, when the two Káfirs were bracing themselves with confidence for a long hard run to the shelter of the pine forests, Utah slipped over a stone and badly sprained his ankle. The agony was so great he could only lie still, and could scarcely help screaming with pain. Astán dragged him into the middle of some bushes, which were hardly any cover at all, except that the dawn was only just breaking, and the pursuers never suspected the Káfirs were still so near at hand. Utah implored Astán to leave him and save himself, as his own condition was hopeless, and on Astán resolutely declining to agree, he threatened him with his dagger. But Astán was equally resolute, and seizing Utah's injured foot, he dragged at it till something or other slipped into its place again. Then Utah, leaning on Astán's shoulder, hobbled on in the rear of their pursuers, contrived in some way to elude them, gained the forest, and eventually, after nearly suffering starvation, reached Kámdesh to dance before their grim war god and tell the story of their exploits.

We camped at the pshal that night and all the next day. The question arose what we should do. Should we, now Utah had joined us, follow the raiding party down the Dungul Valley, or should we go shooting, and try to get a markhor for food. To my intense surprise, Utah, Shermalik, and the others warmly urged me to go down the valley and see whatever was to be seen of the warriors. I assented, made all arrangements about leaving the Baltis behind at the pshal, and was up betimes in the morning preparing for a start. Utah was most genial, greatly admired the long sheepskin coat I wore at night, but could not restrain his laughter at the sight of a waistcoat, and the manner in which it was worn. When everything was ready, Utah and Shermalik pretended they had been misunderstood, and that to go down the Dungul Valley with the possibility, nay, the certainty of coming across Afghans following the returning raiders, was simply suicidal for any man who could not run like a Káfir. Finding that I refused to be cajoled, they finally admitted that the previous night's talk was simply an experiment upon me, and eventually Utah gravely asked me to give up all idea of following out his former suggestion, because he was expecting the raiders to return at any moment. He was evidently sincere, and it was impolitic to refuse his request, so we agreed to go shooting on the hillside pending the return of the braves. We accordingly started off for a hill-tramp, which lasted till four or five o'clock in the afternoon. After ascending eighteen hundred feet steeply through beautiful forest, we skirted a grassy slope, to be finally stopped by a magnificent bluff of rock extending straight down to the Dungul Valley. The hill slopes of rock and forest were so deeply indented, that the huge recesses almost deserved the name of valleys. We passed one or two pshals perfectly concealed from any one who did not laboriously search for them, and I learned that it is an act of good-breeding and politeness to offer any stranger a piece of bread. It is invariably accepted after a formal fear has been expressed that it cannot be spared. We saw no game, for at the place we tried for it, we discovered goats grazing, and a large dog, in giving notice of our arrival, sounded at the same time the knell of our hopes; but we had glorious views, and much curious conversation before we returned to Azharbai. For instance, Utah suddenly stopping and pointing to the south with an animated look would exclaim, "Farang-a (O Frank), do you see that high mountain far away there? That is in Bajour. Just the other side of it, below those two peaks which look like fingers, there is a village. I went there five years ago with two companions. We entered a house at night, and killed six people as they slept."

Then Shermalik: "Tot-a (O father), look over there, where those trees look like a row of towers. There were Oganis (Afghans) camped there. In the night I killed one man, one woman, and one child."

Utah, resuming: "Behind that mountain you see there, twoscore and fifteen Afghans had gone to collect firewood. There I killed a fine man—a very fine man," this in a musing tone, with an abstracted look in his eyes and a slow movement of the head from side to side.

So we returned to camp, at least I did. Utah and Shermalik prepared to go and sit at the cross-roads for an hour or so, in the hope of getting news of the raiders, and perhaps to continue their gruesome reminiscences. After two or three hours they came back, and we sat by the fire talking, and feasting on a sheep we had procured with the greatest difficulty. The wealthy pshal owner asked such an enormous price for a sheep, that Shermalik refused to translate the amount to me, and we were within an ace of going supperless to bed, when a very small proprietor insisted on giving me a goat, for hospitality, as he said. He of course did not suffer any loss by doing so, and his amiable action provided Shermalik with a theme he elaborately discoursed upon, namely, the curious liberality of the poor and the general meanness of the rich. His remarks were couched in the terms with which poor men criticise their rich neighbours all the world over. I wrapped myself in my sheepskin coat and went to sleep, but the Káfirs feasted, talked, and slept by turns all the night through.

Next morning there was still no news of the raiders. This absence of information did not, however, make my friends uneasy. On the contrary, it rather elated them, because it showed that the Káfir force was returning deliberately. We sat round the fire all the morning with a man out at Azharbai to bring us early news.

Amongst the men Utah had brought with him was one named Shtáluk, who came from the Katir village of Purstám to join the raid, but he fell sick and lagged behind, so Utah brought him in to me. We gave him tea, also sympathy, and he rapidly got well from his fever in our camp. This day he, after a long preamble, begged me to adopt

him as my son, and invited me to go to his village, promising to show me on the road some wonderful rock
inscriptions.   This inflamed my curiosity greatly, but
nothing would induce me to agree to his suggestion to
make him my adopted son.   My remembrance of the
ceremony was too vivid to allow me to entertain the idea
for a moment.   He was so greatly disappointed at my
decision, that I cross-examined him to find out the reason
for his insistency.   It then turned out that he had murdered one of the Mehtar of Chitrál's servants a short time
before, and the Mehtar had demanded two males to be
sent to him as an atonement.   This was considered
grasping and unjust, one man being worth one man, and
no more ; but lately the Mehtar had increased his claim,
and demanded four men in recompense for the one slain.
The Purstám men were getting very much afraid of
Amán-ul-Mulk, and Shtáluk's only hope was that I
should make him my son, and that the Mehtar would
then abandon his demand.   Secretly, this information
pleased me greatly, for it was only by such methods as
the Mehtar was then employing that a remedy could be
applied with any hope of success to the incessant murdering of people on the Káfir frontier ; but it also indicated how the prestige and authority of the Mehtar of
Chitrál were increasing in the Bashgul Valley.

About midday we all moved back to Azharbai, and
camped there in the enclosing walls of a ruined house,
for the spot formerly possessed a fort and cultivated
fields belonging to the Chárá family ; but six years
previously, a small force of Pathans had arrived there
and found the fort empty, every one being away tending the flocks.   The Pathans destroyed the building

I

with fire, and knocked down and partially burned the wooden effigies also. The latter had been re-erected, in spite of their being black and charred, but the position itself had been definitely abandoned as untenable, because the snow on the pass prevented its being reinforced during the winter months.

During the afternoon we made a short journey down the Dungul Valley to see if there were any signs of the raiders, but without result. The valley just below Azharbai is a place of extraordinary natural strength for a defensive position. The lateral cliffs, of enormous height, approach so closely, that a stone could be thrown from one to the other; while at one place there is a marvellous lateral rocky ravine, with perpendicular sides which rise at least a thousand feet before the deodars can get a foothold. The entrance to this wonderful ravine is not more than a few yards broad. It looks like a mere crack in the immense mass of rock. The bottom of the valley, down by the stream, is blocked and hidden by immense cedars. The scenery is of a most romantic and most impressive kind.

As our camp was now in an exposed place, many precautions were necessary for the night. We had a big fire built up some short distance in front, and behind this Shermalik and Utah, armed to the teeth, kept guard in a most imposing manner, sitting bolt upright, each with a spear in his hand and a gun across his knees. However, getting up at midnight to see if everything were quiet, I found them both sleeping soundly. Every one had received instructions that if he was roused by an unusual sound during the night, he was at once to awake all the sleepers.

SHERMALIK AND UTAH ON GUARD.

To face page 148.

The danger was not only that victorious, and indeed all, Káfirs are thieves, and most of them ruffianly disposed also, but that there was a fair chance the raiding party might be followed closely by vengeful Pathans.

In the early morning nothing had happened, and I was quietly arranging my clothes by the camp-fire, when a distant shout of " Á-í-Gísh " was brought on the wind from the semi-darkness below. Its effect was electrical. The Káfirs sprang to their feet and rushed out in the direction of the shout, without waiting to give me one word of explanation. It seemed that the cry not only informed them that Pathans had been slain, but also that there had been no Káfir loss, for had there been any such loss, the party would have returned silently, and bringing with them, if possible, their dead and wounded. In the case of utter defeat, they are of course compelled to abandon the dead; but even then they strive to carry away the heads of their slain. The vanguard of the victorious Káfirs shortly reached us. It consisted of nine or ten light-footed, irresponsible young men, all so eager to get home first and tell the news that they could not wait an instant. They shouted their news and passed on rapidly. As far as plunder was concerned, the expedition had been a failure, for the Pathans had removed their herds; but by a stratagem the Káfirs had succeeded in killing several of the enemy. Two Káfirs had gone forward by themselves, surprised a Pathan, killed him, and then retreated. The friends of the slain man had chased the two Káfirs in a body, and had fallen into an ambush prepared for them, in which they had all perished. Of the thirteen thus killed, two were said to be holy men, which greatly enhanced their victory in the eyes of the Káfirs.

When a large band goes on the war-path, as on this occasion, each member of it goes nominally at his own pleasure. There are no acknowledged leaders, and whatever plans are made for the general conduct of the enterprise, each individual may theoretically act upon the dictates of his own private judgment. In this instance, the attack was to have been delivered an hour before dawn, but the Musalmáns having shifted their quarters, that plan had to be abandoned. The spoil consisted almost entirely of arms (matchlocks and flintlocks) and clothes taken from the slain.

We were all starting on our homeward journey when three men in Indian file emerged from the narrowest part of the valley below. We waited for them. At a distance of about 300 yards the leader stopped for his two companions to join him, whereupon the three formed in line and sang a sonorous chant, which made the hills ring again. "Á-í-Gísh" was the beginning of the pæan; it wound up with a loud, sharp, and abrupt "wo," which started the echoes. It was noticeable that in the singing there were none of those high falsetto notes so admired in the East. These men having joined us, we hurried on, Utah, Shermalik and Co. getting very anxious about the main body of the Káfirs, close behind, fearing lest some of my things should be stolen. The Baltis were kept close by us, and were pushed on as fast as they could travel, though they required but little urging. We were soon overtaken by about thirty men from Mumán, headed by Bahdur's son, a friend of mine, and together we began the steep climb leading to the pass over the Arokán

SONG OF TRIUMPH.

To face page 152.

ridge. Half-way up, these Mumán men arranged themselves on a convenient flat stone and sang their song of
triumph. It was similar to that we had already heard.
Two men, side by side, a pace in advance of the others,
chanted a few words, apostrophising Gísh, then all
joined in a refrain, which ended in a loud "wo." As
they finished and moved on, what seemed at first an
echo of the refrain far down the valley continued and
increased in volume, and told us that the main body
was near at hand; shortly afterwards about two hundred wild Káfirs surrounded us. Nothing unpleasant
occurred. They were quite civil, but stared at us with
all their eyes, and crowded round me with the keenest
curiosity. Truth compels me to say that a wilder or
more ill-looking company it never was my lot to behold.
The really fine features of some of the men were lost
in the crowd of evil-looking, bad-shaped faces, with the
hair growing in many cases within an inch of the eyebrows. Indeed, in some instances it seemed as if the
men had no foreheads at all. They were wretchedly
clad, in goat-skins for the most part, while a few had
coarse cotton garments. Firearms of any description
were remarkably few, not more than a third or a fourth
of the number having matchlocks. Bows and arrows
and spears constituted the ordinary equipment. They
were most interested in my sporting rifle. When I
opened the breech to show how the cartridges were
introduced, four ,or five of the younger men dived
down amongst the crowd as if they were gazing upon
a live shell, greatly to the annoyance and disgust of
the seniors at such an exhibition of fear being made
before me; but it was clear that they all had a most

exaggerated idea of the killing power of a rifle. One of
the captured matchlocks was brought for my inspection.
It was a really handsome weapon, ornamented with rings
and brass wire. They informed me it was worth thirty
rupees. Subsequently, to see if Káfirs would sell the
weapons of which they stood in so much need, I offered
to purchase the matchlock at their own price—thirty
rupees. They agreed to sell it, but at once raised the
price to eighty rupees, which I declined to give, when
everybody laughed. They were all extremely happy,
and insisted that I must witness their performance at
the top of the pass. This, by the way, was of a very
poor description. One or two matchlocks were let off
with much deliberation, there was a good deal of
shouting, a little singing, and that was all. After
everything I possessed had been carefully inspected, we
parted about three miles above Kámdesh, the warriors
going to their respective homes, while we went straight
on to that village.

CHAPTER XI

WE returned to Kámdesh on the 5th of November. It
will be convenient to give in the next two chapters some
of the information I had diligently been acquiring about
the Káfirs, their origin and their physical characteristics, and also about the character of the people. This
information was corrected and amplified by subsequent
observation and more extended experience.

It seems probable that eventually the view will be
accepted that, to speak broadly, the present dominant
races of Káfiristán, the Katirs, the Kám, and the Wai, are
mainly descended from the ancient Indian population of
Eastern Afghanistan, who refused to embrace Islám in
the tenth century, and fled for refuge from the victorious
Moslems to the hilly countries of Káfiristán. There they
probably found other races already settled, whom they
vanquished, drove away, or enslaved, or with whom they
amalgamated. It is possible that part of the present
slave population, also the Jazhis and the Aroms, are
remnants of these, while the Presuns are probably a
more or less aboriginal race, who either successfully
resisted the new - comers, or were driven from more

fertile regions and milder altitudes to their present valley. As there is no literature nor any written character of any kind in Káfiristán, it is hardly possible to do more than guess, in an unscientific way, at the meaning of the stories related or the traditions repeated by the people.

The Kám have two versions of themselves to offer. One, proffered by what may be called the Agnostics, is that the tribe originally came from the Salarzai country, and that, beyond that fact, no one knows anything about them. The other version is, that the Kám were originally Arabs, some say of the Koreish tribe, while others affirm that it is the Wai, and not the Kám, who are Koreish. The story goes, that after suffering many vicissitudes in consequence of the fighting connected with the propagation of the Musalmán religion, the Kám found themselves at Kandahar, and, after another interval, at a place called Kamich, in the Rámgul. There they warred furiously with the Wai people, but in the end were victorious, and compelled the Wai to pay them a yearly tribute of four cows and four measures of wine. The collecting of the tribute was, however, always a matter of difficulty, and at length the Kám messengers who were sent to receive it were all murdered. Soon after this, one day when the Kám were engaged at a great dance, they were surprised by a huge army of Wai people. A terrible fight ensued, in which the Kám were successful, but at the cost of a thousand lives. The defeated army suffered still more severely, and lost at least two-thirds of their number. It was immediately subsequent to this great fight that the Kám left Kamich and migrated to the Bashgul Valley. The reason for this move was, that the flesh of the markhor of the Kamich district was found to cause severe and fatal illness, and it was to obtain a better variety of markhor meat that the Kám began to search for a new country. The tradition seems to have been altered in the telling. It looks as if the great fight at Kamich resulted in the defeat of the Kám, who had to take to flight, and find a new home for themselves in their present country. On reaching the Bashgul Valley, continues the story, the Kám found it inhabited by a race called Jazhis, an aboriginal people, of whom there are a few families still remaining in Ishtrat (or Gourdesh), and two households, at least, in the village of Pittigul. The Jazhis were driven out from their lands and homes, which were appropriated by the Kám. The dispersion of the vanquished was complete. None of them were made slaves, nor are the Kalash of Chitrál, nor any of the surrounding natives, in any way akin to the dispossessed Jazhis.

The Kám affirm that the whole of the country, from the Eastern Káfiristán frontier as far as Gilgit, was in former times inhabited by the Kalash, while the true Káfirs extended at least as far as Swát in one direction, while on other sides their extent was practically boundless.

In Káfiristán tradition the Gourdesh (Ishtrat) people are said to be partly descended from the Arom people, and to be partly of Jazhi descent. It is related that a man from Aromgrom, in Arormia, formed a union with an Ishtrat (Jazhi) maiden under somewhat peculiar circumstances, and that their son is the direct ancestor of Shermalik, the chief of Ishtrat.

The Katirs in the Bashgul Valley informed me that they came from the west, and were once part of a numerous tribe which divided into two parties. One division, consisting of all the wealthy and other notable persons, went to London, while the other, comprising menials only, settled in Káfiristán. This depreciation of themselves is in the true spirit of Oriental politeness. They warned me not to trust the Kám, or to believe them for an instant if they declared that they and I were descended from a common ancestor; for it was notorious that it was the Katirs, and not the Kám, who were of my race, the Kám being really more akin to the Russians. This also indicated that the Káfirs of the Bashgul Valley know something of the antagonistic sentiments with which the English and the Russians are supposed to regard one another in the East.

Of the origin of the Presun, the Mádugál, the Kashtán, &c., and of the slaves, there is even less information to be collected locally ; but some of the traditions related to me are of value for two reasons. They show the nature of the evidence placed at the disposal of the traveller by the Káfirs themselves, and they illustrate the crude, bald narrative which suits the present intellectual position of the people. For instance, the Mádugál tribe, according to Kám greybeards, was created in the following peculiar circumstances. One day long ago, the people of Kámdesh were startled by the fall of a thunderbolt from heaven. A great noise and much fire were associated with the phenomenon, and added to the fear and bewilderment of the spectators. After a time, venturing forth from their homes, the Kám perceived seven men, two of whom were playing reed instruments to two others who were dancing. The remaining three were busily employed in performing sacred rites to Imrá. From these seven individuals, who took wives from the Katirs, the whole of the Mádugál tribe is descended.

The slaves also are accorded a semi-divine origin, as the following narrative shows. It appears that one day up in the sky a father blacksmith said to his sons, "Bring me some fire." Just as the lad was obeying the order, there was a lightning flash, and the boy fell through the slit thus caused in the floor of the sky on to the earth. From this youth one portion of the slave population is derived, the remainder being the offspring of Waiguli prisoners, taken in war. Of the Presun the following account was given me. In the beginning of the world God created a race of devils. He soon afterwards regretted having done so, but felt Himself unable to destroy all those He had so recently endowed with breath. But Moni (sometimes called Muhammad by Káfirs, under the impression that prophet and Muhammad are synonymous terms), grieving at the terrible state of affairs, at length obtained a sword from Imrá, and was given permission to destroy all the devils. He killed very many, but seven, the ancestors of the Presuns of to-day, managed to escape him.

As there are no rock inscriptions, no ancient books, nor any literature of any kind to be found in Káfiristán, and as the traditions of the people themselves give such small help in forming any opinion concerning their origin, the only hope which remains that the Káfirs may be eventually assigned their proper place in the general history of the world is from a comparative study of their language, their manners and customs, and their religious ceremonies, as well as from their cranial measurements, and other anthropometric observations. That they are made up of different races appears certain ; that they have

no admixture of Tartar blood seems obvious; that they
came from the west, at least the great majority of them,
is their own fixed idea, and is more than probable. If
there be points of resemblance between present Káfir
and ancient Greek sacrificial observances, and if certain
of their domestic utensils—such, for instance, as the Wai
wooden dish-stand—may seem to be fashioned in Grecian
mould, it may fairly be conjectured that some of the
Káfir tribes, at any rate, are still influenced, as the
ancient Indian populations of Eastern Afghanistan were
also influenced, by the Greek colonists of Alexander;
and that these Káfirs having never been under the rule of
Musalmáns, may possibly represent some of the people of
Eastern Afghanistan as they were before the victorious
Moslem defeated and converted them to Islám. If the
Káfirs resemble these peoples, the resemblance must be
partial, and possibly unflattering. Civilisation abruptly
fell asleep centuries ago in Káfiristán, and is still dormant. A conquering race may progress in the arts and in
civilisation, as it progresses and excels in warlike skill; but
not so an isolated people like the Káfirs. They have degene-
rated until their tribal headquarters are merely robbers'
nests. In the various shifts and expedients to which
they have been forced in order to preserve their freedom
and their lives, lying, running away, and underhand de-
vices have been particularly serviceable. In their mode
of warfare no spark of chivalry is possible. The silent
watcher, his face protruding from a thicket, his wild eyes
glancing swiftly and fearfully around, or the lithe form
wriggling like a snake along the ground to stab his sleeping enemy, man, woman, or child,—these are the pictures
which arise in my mind when I think of Káfir braves;

KÁFIR WARFARE.

To face page 162.

not because this illustrates the sole method of warfare employed, but because continued intercourse with the people, and observation of their silent, stealthy gait and shifty faces, taught me what must be the most popular methods of attack. If it were not for their splendid courage, their domestic affections, and their overpowering love of freedom, Káfirs would be a hateful people. In other respects they are what they have been made by uncontrollable circumstances. For them, the world has not grown softer as it has grown older. Its youth could not be crueller than its present maturity, but if they had been different, they would have been enslaved centuries ago. Their present ideas, and all the associations of their history and their religion, are simply bloodshed, assassination, and blackmailing; yet they are not savages. Some of them have the heads of philosophers and statesmen. Their features are Aryan, and their mental capabilities are considerable. Their love of decoration, their carving, their architecture, all point to a time when they were higher in the human scale than they are at present. They never could be brutal savages, like some of the African races, for example, because they are of a different type, but they are as degraded in many respects as it is possible for this type ever to become.

The physique of the Káfirs is magnificent of its kind. They are lightly-built men, who seem to be almost always in hard training. Fat men are altogether unknown. The average height of a number of Kám Káfirs whom I measured was from 5 feet 5½ inches to 5 feet 6 inches. The shortest was just over 5 feet, the tallest was 6 feet 1½ inches. The biggest man of the tribe was 6 feet 1 inch. He was a splendid object, heavily built, and of prodigious strength.   As a rule, however, the men of medium height are not only the most active, the fastest runners, and the most enduring travellers, but are generally the most physically powerful as well.   I have frequently noticed this when watching Káfirs "larking," and have observed how the taller men could never get away from the others in a short, sharp run over the flat, nor disengage themselves from the grasp of men much shorter than themselves.   Actually the four or five strongest men of the Kám tribe are above the average height, but, with this exception, the rule holds good.

I once came across an old man, a Kashtán, leaning on his long matchlock, who was a striking figure.   He was of splendid, almost colossal proportions, but with all his bigness there was a suggestion of activity about his limbs which was surprising when one noticed his grizzled locks.

Admirers of form would delight in Káfirs in their own country.   They give such an impression of gracefulness and strength when once the eye has become accustomed to the vile robes they wear.   As might be expected of a wild, excitable people, their gestures are highly dramatic. I remember always a group of malcontents leaving a meeting which was discussing me.   The dissentients rose in a body, and moved slowly away, with flashing eyes and white faces, heads thrown back, and walking-clubs pointed upwards at intervals.   As they kept turning back in indignant protest to cast scornful glances at their opponents, they made a fine picture.

Another fine sight is to see two young men in a village quarrel try to get at one another.   All bystanders throw themselves between the belligerents, in the hope of securing them or of keeping them apart. It then becomes more than ever a point of honour for the angry youths to strive to reach one another. In their attempts to evade the peacemakers, they dash up and down the steep village hill, and over the house-tops, at times making remarkable leaps. On such occasions they fly past the spectator like a tornado, really marvellous examples of energy and graceful strength.

Káfirs have well-developed chests. Their arms are muscular, but not remarkably so. There being no special exercise for bringing particular muscles into prominence, and no regular wrestling, their arms would not compare to much advantage with those of a Panjabi athlete. The arms are somewhat long, the wrists and hands rather small. The squeezing power of the fingers is, as a rule, not very great. The flanks, hips, and gluteal muscles are light. The legs are splendidly muscular, but not too big, and the feet are often extremely well shaped, with a high instep.

In repose, a Káfir is usually not seen to advantage. His clothes often obscure his proportions, and he is fond of sitting forward on a stool, his elbows on his knees, and his hands grasping a walking-club erect between his legs. He is generally also conscious of some ceremoniousness in paying or receiving a visit. He looks better when lounging and taking his ease on the ground with his legs stretching out before him. He cannot sit comfortably on his heels like a native of India, but prefers a stool, a plank, or a billet of wood to sit upon, or else to spread out his legs. His well-developed thighs and calves must also make the squatting attitude an uneasy one.

On the march Káfirs travel with a quick, rather short, untiring step. As hillmen they cannot possibly be surpassed, their wind being as excellent as their legs and ankles are strong, while all are comparatively light weights, and not too tall. Their pluck is immense; women and boys, apparently overcome with fatigue, still struggle on till they reach their destination. Káfirs can stand all temperatures. Heat does not unduly disturb them; they can sleep comfortably in severe cold in spite of their scanty clothing. They can go without food when necessary, as well as, or better, than probably any other race.

Their countenances are of a distinct Aryan type, the nose, as a rule, being particularly well shaped. The Kám and the Wai contain the handsomest people I have seen, especially the Wai; the Katirs have fewer good-looking men, and the Presuns are spoilt by their heavy, stupid look. There are distinct gradations in type, from the best-looking of the chief families to the patsas or shepherds, and so down to the slaves. In the highest types, the men have well-shaped heads, good features, and quiet steady eyes. The cast of feature is grave, one might almost say intellectual; rarely of a beautiful Greek type. Of the latter description I know one remarkable instance amongst the Kám young men, and one still more striking example, who, curiously enough, was a young to middle-aged Presun woman. The lowest type of face is of two different kinds. There is the bird of prey type—hooked nose, low forehead, receding chin, and quick-glancing, close-set eyes. In such cases the forehead is particularly bad, being narrow and low, with the hair not unfrequently growing almost down to the eyebrows. In fact, instances may be met with where the only true hairless forehead is a circular space just above the root of the nose, and about the size of a florin. The other variety of the degraded type is often seen among the slaves. It has stupid or crafty, dark, rounded, somewhat heavy features, while the nose is badly shaped and coarse. The hair grows low on a narrow receding forehead, as in the other type. Between the extremes of the highest and the lowest types there is every possible gradation in shape of feature, colour of skin, and size of head. The headmen, as a rule, are the best-looking of the race, but among them are often men with rather bad foreheads and shifty glances, who yet contrive to hold their own among their fellows.

The colour of the Káfirs is, on the whole, less fair than that of the upper classes in Chitrál, and less fair than many Badakhshis I have met. They do not at all approach the black races, but are equally removed from those with white skins. In tint they resemble more the average inhabitant of the Punjab. Of the various Káfir tribes, the Wai seem to be the fairest, and some of the Katirs, some of the Kashtáns, and some of the Presuns the darkest. It is, however, hard to estimate properly the darkness of skin of the villagers of Pshui, for instance, for there the people use a fuel which gives forth a particularly grimy smoke, the effect of which on the Pshui men seems to be seldom or never neutralised by washing. So also with the Presuns. Living in a cold high valley, they are particularly reluctant even to wash their faces, which are often literally sooty. A Presun Káfir taken prisoner and sold to the

K

Khan of Lálpura, made his escape and visited me at Kámdesh. I was astonished at the comparative fairness of his complexion. A few months later, seeing him in his own home, I found him just as dark as the rest of his compatriots. He had probably not washed himself in the interval. The Presun children have often light eyes and fair hair when quite little. The Káfirs, in short, are thoroughly Eastern in colour, as well as in every other respect. Red-haired or more or less albino people are few in number, less than one per cent. of the total population.

With very few exceptions, all Káfirs wear the "karunch" or scalp-lock. This is formed in the following way. The whole of the head is shaved except a round patch some four inches in diameter over the occiput, where it is not cut at all. A tiny lock in front of each ear is often permitted to remain also. Children at the thirty-first or thirty-second day after birth, both male and female alike, have their heads shaved. A Káfir's hair is not very long, seldom more than twelve or fourteen inches, and, with very rare exceptions, is quite straight. It is usually extremely dirty, and matted into rat's-tails. On the heads of some of the boys the crop of hair is prodigiously thick, but that is exceptional. A few of the Bashgul Káfirs do not wear the karunch, but have the hair cut short all over the head. These men can, and occasionally do, pass for Pathans on their various thieving and murdering expeditions. Káfirs who, after turning Musalmán, revert to their old religion, are said to be restrained from wearing the karunch until they have slain a Musalmán in fight. This may or may not be true. The "reverts,"

KÁFIR WOMAN WITH CONICAL BASKET.

To face page 173.

I know, all wear their hair in Pathan fashion, although one of them had assassinated the Khan of Asmár.

The Káfirs admire beards, and love to dye them red as soon as they begin to get grey. The young men are particularly fond of applying antimony to the eyelids, but only a very few have the opportunity of thus ornamenting themselves.

The women are, as a rule, shortish and of light build, with muscular limbs. Pretty faces are rare. Little girls are often decidedly good-looking, but the hard field-work and constant exposure to all kinds of weather quickly darken the complexion and make it coarse. The features are often good, and their type varies precisely as it does in the case of the men. The handsomest woman amongst the Katirs of the Bashgul Valley was a slave, but she was merely one of those exceptions which point an argument. The Wai women are the handsomest of those I have seen, the Mádugál those with the fewest personal attractions.

The Presun women look the most powerful, but all alike are wonderful walkers, and capable of undertaking extremely long journeys carrying loads. Old grandmothers think nothing of marching over the difficult road between Lutdeh and Kámdesh in one day. Girls with their conical baskets lightly laden trot past one on the road, or march steadily and rapidly up the steep hill-paths. At a slower pace they can carry enormous loads, stones for house-building, grapes for the winepress, walnuts for storing, or corn to be threshed.

Their attitudes and gestures are for the most part clumsy. What we call gracefulness is rare, although it is common enough in young men and lads. The little girls from their earliest days run wild, and climb and practise gymnastics just as boys do in other countries. A boy comes to a stranger to be petted, a girl goes into shy contortions at a distance, or climbs trees or the wooden framework of the dance-houses. Women also climb trees with facility. I have passed under a large mulberry tree, and found it tenanted with matronly figures literally grazing on the fruit. It is astounding how big and old-looking many of the Presun girls are before they attain the cap which marks maturity.

All Káfir women roll the hair up and confine it in some sort of cap. Girls confine their locks with a double thread round the brows. Most female heads, like most female faces, are appallingly dirty. The teeth are perhaps the best feature of the women. Their gait seems to depend for gracefulness on the length of their garments, the less encumbered Kám women taking longish, more or less manly strides, while the Presun women take much shorter and quicker steps.

The appearance of both men and women is often spoilt by small-pox and its results, and by a terrible ulceration which frequently attacks the bridge of the nose, the cheeks, or the lower eyelids ; also in the Bashgul Valley by goitre, which seems to be almost exclusively confined to women.

As the result of very many observations of an unscientific kind, I could never discover that the Káfirs displayed any superiority to other races in quickness of eye, certainty of hearing, or skill in aiming with weapons. My eyesight always proved as good as theirs, although they could always see markhor on a hillside long before I could. They are good throwers and good swimmers,

and play skilfully games requiring a good eye and a
good wrist. They never fail when slaughtering cattle
with their narrow axes ; the cut through the neck
vertebræ, which fells and paralyses the beast, is never
bungled. Their most remarkable physical characteristics
are their activity and their powers of endurance. In
these two qualities combined they far surpass any other
people with whom I am acquainted.

They are, moreover, wonderfully good at "locality"—
in remembering places and roads they have only once
visited and travelled over. I have sometimes in winding valleys many miles distant from the village asked
a Káfir in what direction Kámdesh was. He has always
correctly indicated the proper position without a moment's
hesitation. This faculty is almost an instinct, and has
been perfected by heredity. In their raiding expeditions, when small parties set out with the object of
secretly penetrating into an enemy's country and attacking people unawares, the only hope the raiders have of
getting away, after a murder has revealed their presence
in the district, lies in their fleetness of foot and in this
instinct for locality.

The Káfirs, at least the younger men, have the enviable
faculty of being able to sleep at pleasure. Two or three
of them accompanied me on one occasion to Kila Drosh
in Chitrál, where we were the guests of the governor.
As there was nothing for the Káfirs to do, and as it
was not advisable for them to be too much in evidence
outside the fort, they slept nearly continuously for two
whole days and nights. Another time, at the end of
a march, three Káfir youths with me noticed a blanket
which my Pathan servant had cast aside while he was

settling the camp. They pounced upon the blanket in great glee, carried it out of sight behind a rock, spread it on the ground, and in an instant were sound asleep. My servant, hunting for his property, found the little sleeping party, roused up the boys, and took away his blanket. The Káfirs were wide awake in an instant, and merely grumbled a little at the Pathan's selfishness.

On one occasion, as we were crossing a high pass, owing to our late start and the consequent heat of the sun, the journey was most fatiguing for all but the Káfirs. They occasionally raced on ahead, singing, dancing, and twirling their axes. They would then throw themselves down on the snow to wait until we reached them. We invariably, when we caught them up, found them sound asleep.

CHAPTER XII

Káfir character—Intrigue—Intellect of Káfirs—Inquisitiveness—Jealousy and cupidity—Inter-tribal hatreds—Blackmailing—Lying—Love of admiration and credit—Love of freedom—Personal dignity—Politeness—Reception of visitors—Hospitality—Family affection—Kindness to children and animals—Káfirs not cruel—Bravery—Loyalty and self-sacrifice—Quarrelsomeness—Peace-making—Religious tolerance—Sociability and humour—Thievish instincts—Murder—The Káfir ideal of a "good" man.

THE Káfirs are by no means simple in character; they can intrigue, concoct plots, and then carry them out with the secrecy and tenacity of the average Oriental. On one occasion a headman of Kámdesh went on a visit to the Amir of Kabul. On his way home, while journeying up the Kunar Valley, he was waylaid by some followers of a fanatical priest, who formerly lived at Dír, and murdered. The man who actually dealt the fatal blow was a Káfir who had embraced Islám. He escaped to Dír, and lived there under the protection of its powerful priest. The headmen of Kámdesh consulted together how the murder should be avenged. Eventually they decided on a plan which will show the persistency with which a Káfir can carry out a settled resolve. They employed a man to go to Dír to declare himself a convert to Islám, and become a follower and avowed disciple of the fanatic who was the head of the Musalmán religion at that place. Their emissary remained at Dír for more than two years before he could, under the veil of friendship and a common religion, induce the murderer to pay a stealthy visit to Káfiristán, where, of course, he was at once seized and killed by previous arrangement.

The mental powers of Káfirs are often considerable. Many of the headmen have intellectual-looking faces, and are possessed of intelligence, judgment, and considerable mental energy ; but the intense conservatism of the elder men—the result of inherited tendency, the isolated nature of their experience, and their not unjustifiable belief in their own astuteness—make them distrustful of new ideas. They nevertheless thoroughly appreciate the value of rifles, pistols, and other arms, which they do not themselves possess. They have also a considerable respect for the higher civilisation of their Musalmán neighbours, and have as exaggerated an idea of their learning as they have of the destructiveness of Western firearms. All Káfirs have a real admiration for their own customs, nearly all of which they consider perfect. If more efficient expedients are pointed out to them and suggestions made about changes, they reply, " But this is our custom," which is with them a conclusive argument.

Their mental acuteness and strength of memory are considerable. The following are illustrations:—Shermalik was a man of poor family, and of a somewhat degraded type. When we returned together to Káfiristán, among other presents handed over to him by me were some two hundred and eighty Indian rupees. He begged that he might be given the equivalent in Kabul rupees. The Kabul rupee was then worth twelve and a half annas, against the sixteen annas value of the

Indian rupee. I carefully calculated out the number of Kabul coins he was entitled to, and handed them to him. He objected, saying that my calculation was wrong. We had an elaborate argument. I appealed to my figures, and he appealed to his fingers and toes, which he used to represent scores of rupees. In the end he convinced me that he was right and that my calculation was wrong. This man was certainly not above the average of Káfir intellect, and he never could explain to me the means by which he arrived at the correct number of Kabul rupees he was entitled to. On another occasion, having forgotten the arrangement of a certain puzzle-lock, I mentioned my dilemma to a certain friend of mine, a man who was solely remarkable for his splendid courage and his numerous homicides. He took my puzzle-lock in his hand, and sat playing with it, until he actually found out how to open it, nor did he ever afterwards forget the arrangement of letters by which the feat could be accomplished. Yet this man had never in his life seen a printed letter until he saw those upon the puzzle-lock. As a third example of their cleverness in certain respects, I was one day showing the high priest a small conjuring trick, the principle of which, though simple enough, it would have taken me a long time to discover for myself. It consisted of a tin funnel really double, which, when the thumb was placed under the lower narrow end, allowed the fluid poured into it to rise up into the secret middle chamber, where it could be retained or set free at will by the movement of a finger on an air-hole. The trick was to fill the funnel, including the hidden chamber, with wine, which was then apparently all allowed to flow away. Water was run through the funnel, which was then shown to the spectator as empty. Finally, the finger being slipped off the air-hole, the wine was allowed to escape from the middle chamber, and the onlookers were expected to be mightily mystified. When this little toy was shown to the priest, and he was ex- pected to be astounded in the usual way, he sat down thoughtfully for a while, and then looking up, remarked he understood all about it. And so he did. He had thought it all out quietly in a few minutes.

The memory of the Káfirs for places they have visited is remarkable. I have already referred to this in another place. Káfirs are most curious and inquisitive. They long to finger the garment of a stranger and examine him minutely. On my first visit to Káfiristán, before we had come to an understanding on the subject, it was difficult to perform my ablutions except when it was dark. Subsequently the curiosity of the elders could always be kept within bounds, but that of the children could only be combated successfully by driving them away and treating them sternly. They were very curious about the wonders I told them of my own native land, the size of London, the carrying power of a big ship, and particularly about her Majesty the Queen. The headmen on one occasion asked me how it was that such a wonderful nation as mine could submit to be governed by a *jukor* (a woman). I replied that in the first place they must not speak of my sovereign as a *jukor*, and told them the Persian designation of the Queen, which has a fine rolling sound, "Hazur Malika Muazímá Kaisar-i-Hind." This impressed them very greatly, as was intended. I then remarked that rulers of great kingdoms were in the hand of Imrá, and added that it was a small matter for Him to bestow wisdom and justice quite irrespective of sex. To this they agreed.

Among the most striking mental peculiarities of Káfirs are their extreme cupidity, their extraordinary jealousy of one another, and the intensity of their inter-tribal hatred. Their cupidity is indeed a wonderful sight to see. A Káfir will come into your house or tent, sit down on a stool, and talk quietly until he begins to cast his eyes round the place. You may then notice, in many cases, that the man's eyes half close, his face flushes, and his whole demeanour becomes a striking example of extreme covetousness. Káfirs are always ready to starve themselves for the sake of hoarding ; they are remarkably avaricious. Their jealousy of one another is so great that they are often ready to break out into murderous quarrels on the mere suspicion that an English traveller like myself was giving away presents with partiality.

Their inter-tribal hatred is so intense that it often entirely deadens their political foresight. A tribe is always ready to beg the help of its most inveterate Musalmán enemy during a temporary peace, and introduce him into its territory in order to help in the chastisement of some other Káfir tribe.

Káfirs are very fond of blackmailing, and seem to prefer to attain their ends by threats, even when other methods are obviously more promising in their results. The Ashrath and Damir Valleys, and the Kunar district as far down as Sou, at any rate, were favourite hunting-grounds for the Bashgul Valley Káfirs. In those districts almost every villager is a "brother" to some Káfir. This means that he is more or less protected

from the exactions of other Káfirs, and in return supplies
his "brother" with food and lodging whenever called
upon to do so. In times of peace a traveller of any
importance on his way from Asmár to Chitrál generally
finds it expedient to get a Káfir to escort him up the
dangerous part of the Kunar Valley. While I was at
Kámdesh, the Amir of Kabul released a number of
Chitráli slaves, gave them handsome presents, and dismissed them to their native country. The instant news
of this event was brought many Káfirs raced down the
valley, as far as they dared go, to intercept these Chitralis,
go through the ceremony of brotherhood with them, and
then escort them up the valley. The man who made the
most profit by this transaction was greatly envied and
admired by his fellows, and on his return to Kámdesh
related to me with proper pride how he had outrun old
Torag Merak, and subsequently successfully resisted the
latter's insidious attempts to get a share of the spoil.
After bidding good-bye to the victim, from whom he
had received a horse, a valuable coat, and many rupees,
the Káfir a few days later started for Chitrál with a small
cheese as his return present for his " brother," and in the
hope of coaxing something more from him ; but this
attempt was a failure, for a Chitráli on sure ground is
quite a match for most Káfirs. Into such a habit of
threatening do Káfirs fall, that I have heard a man
threaten Imrá. The individual referred to had a little
son grievously ill and likely to die. Talking to me
about the child's condition, he spoke of the feasts he
had given in Imrá's name and the sacrifices he had
made in his honour. "Yet," he complained, "I have
lost twelve sons by sickness." Then he shouted out,

"If this little one dies I shall turn Musalmán." The child did die eventually, but the father did not change his faith, though, like the French king, he ever afterwards felt that God had behaved ungratefully, after all he had done for him.

The Káfirs are very untruthful. A successful lie excites their admiration, and a plausible liar is to them a sensible, sagacious man. Their want of veracity is most striking on first acquaintance, for they, like so many other wild or savage people, evidently hold the belief that telling the truth, merely because it is the truth, must necessarily be harmful to them. Other reasons which make them untruthful are their boastfulness and love of admiration. These three causes taken together made them weave tissues of lies around me, some of which I did not detect until several months had passed, while others have probably remained undetected to the present day. To prevent my starting on some particular journey, on more than one occasion, almost the whole village of Kámdesh must have entered into a conspiracy to give me false accounts of the dangers to be encountered. The knowledge of such facts as these makes it sometimes most difficult for a stranger to decide on his line of action. For instance, on one occasion, believing the people were adopting their usual tactics in dissuading me from a particular journey by exaggerating its difficulties and dangers, I started regardless of their protests, and then discovered that in that particular instance they had spoken truthfully.

Their love of admiration and their desire to stand well in the estimation of their fellows give to public opinion an almost irresistible force. When a Káfir finds himself more or less isolated in his views on some particular question, he seems at once to grow distrustful of himself, and, unless he have some sort of following, will cease to argue the point altogether, and sit shame-faced and silent in council. This characteristic of Káfirs seems to be quite apart from their natural and well-grounded fear of contumaciously opposing the wishes of a majority, which has, indeed, very forcible methods of making its opinions respected. A Káfir, wild and independent as he appears at first sight, has a strange reluctance to act on his own responsibility on any important doubtful question. He loves to go off with his fellows and noisily discuss what should be done. With a single Káfir it is easy to do as you please, provided that you do not transgress his unwritten code of manners or run athwart his national customs. He will probably prove a pleasant and helpful companion. So also with Káfir boys. But if you have a party consisting of several men to deal with, it is necessary to be continually on your guard against little schemes and plots to your detriment. One or other of the men is certain to be always trying to originate some plan by which, at your expense, he may pose as a kind of public benefactor to his friends and excite their admiration for his astuteness. It is not only to get money that these little conspiracies are hatched. It is just as likely as not, that their object is to take you off the road you want to travel in order that the Káfirs may visit some place where they have friends, or to save them crossing a pass, or journeying in a direction which has no interest for them. Káfirs love to talk, to give or receive advice. The giver of advice is always in a more or less dignified position, while the listener is sure of being flattered, unless indeed the conference is to end in a row.

Within the limits which their customs provide, Káfirs love personal freedom. Theoretically, every man acts on the impulse of his own wishes. He changes his mind whenever he thinks fit to do so. He walks into a house and sits down, and gets up and goes away, just as he pleases. If he undertakes to accompany you on a journey, he thinks nothing of breaking his promise. He generally offers some slight, obviously untrue, excuse, which must be taken as it is intended. It is merely a form of politeness. Little boys go off to visit distant friends and relations without a word of warning to their own people. Women also, to a less extent and when not at work, wander over all the districts it is safe for them to travel in.

One of the greatest surprises in store for a traveller who has only seen Káfirs out of their own country is to observe their wonderful sense of personal dignity. When the Jast are attired for the dance, their solemn manner and proud bearing are remarkable. In spite of the frequently grotesque nature of their dress, they are not in the least comical, but distinctly impressive. At all religious ceremonies and sacrifices, even in their games, they strike the onlooker as both merry and self-respecting. Men capering at a funeral while the tears run down their cheeks are only fantastic. Odd they undoubtedly appear to a stranger, and intensely interesting, but they are rarely or never the cause of derisive laughter.

A Káfir in his own way is a model of politeness. He gives precedence to a superior, and unaffectedly takes his own proper position. On a march the most important

individual usually leads the party, all in Indian file.
Everybody gives way to the high priest. In a crowded
assembly indoors, the advent of an important man would
be announced by every one rising and saying, " Here also
is Basti," or whatever the man's name was.

On the road every one met receives a salutation, formal
and kindly. A man travelling up the valley would be
asked, " Have you come from below ? " He would answer,
" Yes," and ask an appropriate question in his turn.
When parting, they would bid each other good-bye. If
they had sat down to talk, the man leaving would use a
particular form of address, and not merely say good-bye,
but give the equivalent of " Good-bye ; please do not
rise." An acquaintance on the road would be greeted
heartily. His hand would be held while he was asked,
" Is it well ?—is it very well ?—are the people of your house
well ? " and after these formal inquiries many kindly questions would follow. At a meal by the roadside, a portion or portions of the food would be offered to any one,
man or woman, coming along the road. It would be at
first politely declined, on the ground that it could not be
spared. It would then be pressed on the wayfarer and
accepted.

There are regular forms to be gone through on arriving at a strange village in the Bashgul Valley. At the
village of Oulagul I arrived one day wet through and
tired. We knew with whom we were to take shelter,
but at a hint from my Kám companions, we all went into
a cow stable and sat humbly on top of our loads. This
gave our host time to clear out a room and make proper
arrangements for our reception. He finally came down
the terraced village and invited us to climb up to his

abode. On another occasion, at Bagalgrom, in somewhat similar circumstances, we sat in a row on a plank on the opposite side of the river, and my companions produced food and began to eat it ostentatiously, as though that were our camping-place. We were then invited to a half-finished house, very leaky. Finally, the redoubtable Bahdur himself appeared, and escorted us to his house with great ceremony.

In visits of this kind it is etiquette to entertain the guest, not only with meat, drink, and firing, but also with conversation. A circle is formed round the fire, every one seated on a stool. The host leads the conversation, which usually is formal and without a spark of interest, for every one has the bearing of a man who feels he is giving and receiving honour by his mere presence. As far as appearances went, the company would, with the help of relays, have sat in this dignified but sociable way all night, while my host was always anxious to sleep in the same apartment with me. In the cold weather, after being entertained for an hour or two, I used to beg that the fire might be put out on account of the pain its smoke caused in my eyes, and that windows and doors might be kept open for the same reason. This always made the company ready to fall in with my suggestion that it should adjourn to some other apartment.

In spite of their avarice, which in some instances almost amounts to a mental disease, Káfirs are most hospitable. No man, however reluctant to expend his supplies in entertaining guests, dare break the unalterable laws on the subject. The only exception to this rule is in the Presungul, where the people are so plundered and bullied by visitors from other tribes, that they try to evade the

L

sacred rites of hospitality in every possible way, and are in consequence generally despised. Among other Káfirs the expenditure on food supplies in entertaining guests must be very great. I was particularly struck with the kindliness and readiness with which visitors were received and fed in the upper part of the Bashgul Valley. At my first visit to any village, a sheep was killed for me as an offering from the whole community. At subsequent visits particular men received me in turn and provided food. It was known that the reward would be liberal, so the chief men decided who were to be my hosts, but for my first visit no payments were taken. I once sat down for a chat at Bádámuk village near Lutdeh. My whole party had been lavishly entertained at another village a short time before, but, in spite of my protests, a goat was immediately killed, and all my followers were regaled, while the question of payment was waived aside, the villagers declaring that they were honoured in being allowed to entertain us. As a rule, the Kám hospitality was of a less generous kind. Their system was once explained to me. I was told that visitors from non-Káfir countries were always entertained well, for it was obvious that the guest on leaving could not, for very shame, refrain from giving a present exceeding in value the food he has received. My experience was that the longer I remained amongst the Kám the more difficult it became to get supplies, even at éxorbitant rates ; but there is no doubt that to feed my following, limited in number as it was, must have been a considerable strain on the resources of a single household, while a village as a whole could seldom or never be treated with. Káfirs among themselves, both by nature and of necessity, are most hospitable.

Family affection in Káfiristán is very strong. Some
tribes are in the habit of selling little girls, and money
will tempt some men even to sell children who are nearly
related to them, but as a rule, it is the offspring of the
slaves that they dispose of most readily. Boys are rarely
sold in this way, but little girls are often looked upon as
goods and chattels. Men of good family in the Bashgul
Valley would not sell female relations other than the children of slaves, except to men of exalted station like the
Mehtar and the princes of Chitrál. In spite of these
sales, Káfirs are very kindly in their family relationships.
I have known a man tend a poor crippled brother, an
epileptic, with the affectionate kindness of a woman, and
have observed innumerable instances of devoted affection
on the part of men for their brothers, their children, and
their relatives generally. A Káfir's delight in a son is
very great. He is fond of his old parents, and of his relatives by marriage, and is obviously of an affectionate
disposition. He is extremely kind to all children.

Káfirs are never rough and cruel to animals. They do
not care much for dogs, though they employ them for
hunting and as watch-dogs. Goats are treated as if they
were domestic animals, and are quite used to being petted
and handled. The animals attach themselves to the
people. A common sight is to see a goat licking a man
or a boy. If a flock of goats is wandering away in a
forest or on the hillside, the herdsman throws stones at
them and abuses them to make them return. He would
rarely think it necessary to run round and head them
back. Goats follow little boys about in an amusingly
affectionate way. Once a boy accompanied by a goat
came to my camp. The boy went to sleep, upon which the

goat went trespassing into a neighbouring field. The boy
was roused up. He threw a fragment of granite at the
animal, which immediately ran to him, bleating loudly.
Then the boy went to sleep again, and the goat remained
by him until he awoke a long time afterwards. Of course
the Káfirs do not show the slightest reluctance to kill their
petted animals. Bulls and cows are so accustomed to
being handled, that no ropes are required to hold them
when they are about to be sacrificed. A man takes hold
of the horns and depresses the head, when a second man
with a blow of a small axe divides the cervical spine.
The kindness with which the Káfirs treat animals saves
much trouble in slaughtering them.

Although a Káfir thinks it a virtue and in accordance
with religion to kill Musalmáns, and gives himself the
benefit of any doubt about their being enemies ; although
in his raids into hostile territory, whether Káfir or Musalmán, he spares neither women nor children ; although he
holds human life as of very little account ; and although,
in hunting, he may appear to employ brutal methods of
getting game, he is not a cruel man by nature. To any
one who considers how wild he is, his comparative freedom from brutality is astonishing.

Káfirs are wonderfully brave. Little parties of two or
three will stealthily penetrate many miles into an enemy's
country, where they would be at once killed if caught.
They will creep into forts and villages during the night,
stab right and left, and then fly to their own hills with a
hue and cry after them. In view of the inferior nature
of their weapons they achieve wonders. The extreme
difficulties which the country presents to an invader have,
no doubt, much to do with their being able to maintain

their independence, but the chief reason, after all, is the gallantry, the reckless bravery, and devotion with which the Káfirs defend themselves, or carry any war into the enemy's country. It is curious to notice the almost superstitious fear the Káfirs have of rifles—a feeling generated by ignorance. At the capture of Nilt Fort, in December 1891, I had six Káfirs with me. The Hunza-Nagar people had a good many rifles, and their fire utterly demoralised the Káfirs. They became so unhappy, then and subsequently, that a few days later I sent them all to Gilgit to await my return when the expedition was over.

Káfirs are splendidly loyal to one another, and are accustomed to acts of self-sacrifice. Two youths were killed on one occasion while I was in Káfiristán. One of them was badly hurt, and could not possibly have got away from the enemy, but the other, a magnificent mountaineer, was killed simply because he refused to run off by himself and abandon his companion.

Káfirs are very quarrelsome among themselves. It is absolutely necessary for a man to take a quarrel up on the instant, to assert his manhood. I have never been at any gathering of Kám or Katir men without seeing one or two rows. Hardly a day passes without a disturbance somewhere, due to this cause.

But if quarrelling is a manly thing, peace-making is a sacred virtue. Men, boys, even dogs, are separated at the first indication of a probable fight. The Káfirs are so extremely quick in their movements that an instantaneous quarrel is followed by a lightning-like onslaught, and so one or other of the combatants often gets more or less hurt, but there is never time for a second blow. The fighters are at once seized, hurled aside, and separated, or thrown down and literally sat upon by the bystanders. Any one who did not lend a hand in stopping a village fight would be looked upon, and would consider himself, as mean and unworthy.

There is nothing like religious intolerance among the Káfirs. There would be something of that nature in Presungul if the people there were braver. They have the desire, but not the power, to be intolerant. Other Káfirs think nothing of a man going away in the sulks for a year or two and becoming a Musalmán. He generally reverts after a time, but many families of Bashgul Káfirs have Musalmán relations settled in the Lutkho Valley or Chitrál, or in the Kunar Valley. They treat these renegades in every way as if they had never changed their religion. The Káfir is always loyal to his blood. It is blood and race that the Káfir clings to; about religion he is comparatively indifferent. If a Káfir slave-boy, sold out of his tribe by its members, were executed, say for murder, in Chitrál, he would be avenged by his tribe.

Káfirs are extremely sociable, as I have already indicated. They have some sense of quiet humour. Their badinage with women is of course obscene, and most of their jokes have the same flavour, but they are greatly amused at ironical remarks, and also at anything, however simple, in the nature of repartee. A man, for instance, came grumblingly and half-angrily to me on one occasion, to complain that the medicine he had received for a sore tongue had done him no good, and that his tongue was very bad. He seemed to infer that I was responsible for his tongue being painful, and spoke rudely to me. My reply was that his tongue must be bad indeed to cause him to speak to me in such a manner. He and the bystanders alike seemed to think this a very good joke, and good feeling was at once restored. Women, of course, are an endless theme of small witticisms. Káfirs never give way to fits or shouts of laughter, but occasionally beam with geniality and cheerfulness. In making little jokes I was careful that they should be of a kindly nature, and by always assuming the expression of facetiousness, left no doubt in the minds of my hearers that a joke was intended. My " son " Shermalik, and one or two others who knew me well, used to laugh in advance when they saw the expression, and before they heard what there was to laugh at. It always showed the Káfirs that I was in a pleasant humour, and also gave them the opportunity of displaying their politeness. There are not a few Káfirs whose conversation, at present principally referring to unworthy subjects, displays an intense curiosity which may perhaps be the germ of scientific speculation.

It is as natural for a Káfir to thieve as it is for him to eat. The children are encouraged to steal. If anything is stolen, traced, and finally returned, the excuse always made is that it was carried off by boys. My maximum and minimum thermometers, dry and wet bulb thermometers, and other meteorological instruments, were all taken away and destroyed by boys the first time they were set up. The villagers thought this only natural. There was one boy, about sixteen years old, who was really attached to me, but he could never resist an opportunity of pilfering. He always had to make restitution, but it did not cure him. Once, in the Kunar Valley, this boy stole a kid from his own particular friend, and carried it for miles inside his shirt without any one knowing of the theft, until the rightful owner, suspicious of his friend, caught us up and recovered his property. In short, Káfirs are born thieves. Little girls are accomplished pilferers. I watched once two innocent-faced little girls persuade a Minján trader to show them a comb. The instant it was in their hands they threw it on a neighbouring housetop, to which the Minjáni could not climb, and could only reach by a roundabout road, while the girls went straight up the difficult walls like monkeys. While the Minjáni seized one child and pulled her down, the other got beyond his reach. He rushed to seize her feet, letting go of his first capture, but he was too late. The girl got the comb, and both disappeared, leaving the poor trader distracted and helpless.

The mere killing of an individual is looked upon as a small affair, provided that he does not belong to the tribe, or to another near tribe with which it is at peace, for in the latter case it might result in war. Killing strangers might or might not be considered inexpedient, but it would hardly be considered a crime.

In the Káfir's opinion, a really fine manly character, what he emphatically calls a " good " man, must possess the following attributes :—He must be a successful homi-cide, a good hill-man, ever ready to quarrel, and of an amorous disposition. If he is also a good dancer, a good shot with bow and arrow or matchlock, and a good "aluts " or stone-quoit player, so much the better. These qualities constitute a fine man ; but to be really influential in the tribe, an individual must be also rich. The pos-session of wealth gives enormous power to any one in

THE TRADER AND THE GIRLS.

To face page 194.

Káfiristán. A man may be brave, devoted to his country, clear-headed, and sagacious, and yet have little or no weight in the tribal councils if he is poor, unless, indeed, he be also an orator, when, to a certain extent, his eloquence may make amends for his lack of riches. It might appear that the knowledge of this fact could be used by a traveller to bend the people to his own ends, but it is not so. Káfirs can be easily bribed, and will do almost anything for money; but their natural boastfulness compels them to publish the fact that they have been clever enough to get money from the stranger, when the cupidity of their friends and relations is at once inflamed, reason is thrown to the winds, and the gravest difficulties arise.

CHAPTER XIII

The narrative continued—Utah takes me to see the rock-markings—Our
journey there—A bad bridge—The Kám frontier village of Urmir—
Difficult pathways—A nerve-trying bridge—Village of Bagalgrom—
Coffins—Effigies—Stone sacred to the god Bagisht—An isolated Káfir—
Markhor hunt—The marks in the rock—The sick, the maimed, and the
blind at Bagalgrom—Embarrassing attentions of the people—Difficult
return journey—Conversation—Lame Astán—Visit to the Kamu Valley
—Unpleasant experiences.

A DAY or two after my return from the Dungul Valley,
my curiosity to see the rock-markings mentioned by
Shtáluk of Purstám became irrepressible, and with some
little difficulty I persuaded Utah to take me to them.
At first he was very reluctant to undertake the little
journey, for although we could go and return in a single
day by starting early enough in the morning, yet the
road lay through the Mumán or Mádugál country, and
the Kám never got over their suspicion of, and their
dislike to, my going among other Káfir tribes. However, finding that, whether he accompanied me or not,
my determination to go was unalterable, Utah, after a
day or two, gave way, and very early on the morning
of the 9th of November we started off in the dark.
Our party consisted also of Utah's brother, Aramalik,
his relative Tong, and Shermalik.   In the darkness I
continually blundered over the rough village paths or
over the smoke-holes, for the road frequently ran over
the continuous roofs of houses; while my companions

moved as nimbly and confidently as only those can move who know a road so well that even in the dark their feet can recognise the locality. Next we passed near the "Shenitán," the place where the tribal dead repose in huge coffin-boxes placed in the hillside— near, but not too close, for such places are impure for the higher ecclesiastics of the Káfir faith—and then by steep zig-zags we trotted down eighteen hundred feet to the Nichingul stream, by which time my shin bones felt as if they were red-hot bars of iron. The old bridge was broken, and a couple of pine poles had been substituted for it. They were, fortunately, not very high above the water, yet still it was necessary to summon all my nerve-resources to enable me to cross the torrent. If Káfirs would only secure such temporary bridges, it would not be so bad; but they seem to think all men are born slack-rope dancers. My companions, not perceiving my difficulty, crowded on my heels, their heads probably turned in every direction except towards me. The biggest jump I ever accomplished saved me from a ducking, and from being carried down-stream as well perhaps. A short distance farther there was a steep rocky mound to be traversed as we turned out of the Nichingul into the Bashgul Valley. At the top of this steep rock, which marks the point of junction of the Nichingul with the Bashgul river, is perched the Kám frontier village of Urmir, which consists of about twenty squalid houses. As soon as we left the precincts of Urmir, we were at once in the Mádugál or Mumán country, which is practically in the absolute possession of the redoubtable Bahdur. It only extends for six and a half miles of the Bashgul Valley, and has but three villages of any size, namely, Mumán or Bagalgrom, Mungul, and Susku. The last two are both hidden up lateral valleys. There are also a few hamlets scattered about. We kept to the right bank of the Bashgul river for about a couple of miles, the pathway being extremely difficult, in one place particularly so, where there was a perpendicular climb which it required considerable muscular strength and activity to surmount, and up which dogs had to be dragged the best way possible. Then we reached a bridge by which we crossed to the left bank. It was quite new and strong, but one of the worst it has been my fortune to attempt, for it was built over the water—some thirty feet—and the roadway consisted of a single plank one foot wide, flanked by two long poles four inches in diameter. In the middle it began to vibrate greatly under my weight, and a glance below at the rushing water caused my brain to swim. I stopped, and bent my knees to try and sit down. Utah, who was ahead, saw my predicament, and ran back to help me, making the bridge vibrate more violently than ever. Suddenly my head cleared a little and my knees unbent. I rejected Utah's help and reached the high built-up pier safely. On my return journey, I swaggered over this bridge as though my heart were not in my mouth and my sight obscured with dizziness all the time. Less than half a mile farther we passed a second bridge which conducts the traveller straight into the village of Bagalgrom, which is built almost down to the water's edge. I stopped to count the number of houses across the river. This is never an easy task in a Káfir village,

for one house runs into another in a most perplexing
way, and buildings which you take to be domiciles
turn out to be cattle-sheds, and *vice versâ*. Bagalgrom
is built at the mouth of a wide, short, snow-bound
valley, between it and the river, and is mostly on the
level. The rocky entrance to the valley behind is
covered with weather-worn coffins for the dead, many
of them broken or falling to pieces from age. The
usual effigies were crowded in large numbers near the
bridge, on some level ground to the north, and at a
distance could not be distinguished from a group of
villagers, until attentive observation proved that they
never moved, and that the whole group never changed
its shape. There were effigies on our side of the river
also, and near them was a blood-stained stone sacred
to the god Bagisht. The people came flocking over
the bridge, and were most cordial in their salutations
and hand-shakings. One man rushed up to me and
carefully placed my right foot on the top of his; he
seemed gratified at the performance, as if he had done
something praiseworthy. Bahdur himself was away at
his pshal, but Utah called upon a friend of his to
accompany us to the rock-markings, as it appears it
would have been wanting in Káfir etiquette for Utah
to have taken me to them by himself and without a
Mumán man; it would have looked as if Utah considered the whole country to be his own.

About a mile or so farther we came upon a hamlet
called Punja, inhabited by a man from Bagalgrom, who,
during times of peace, had slain a member of the Kám
tribe. His house had been burnt, his property destroyed
or confiscated, but he had been permitted to settle in

this place and begin life all over again. A mile and a half farther we had an unsuccessful markhor hunt, and eventually about midday, thoroughly tired, we reached the place where the rock-markings were. It was down by the water's edge, and separated from it by merely a few yards of pebbles and boulders. It was well that I had already become accustomed to disappointments. These markings were about twenty feet from the ground, on the under surface of a cornice-like projection of rock. It was said that they were inaccessible, but they might certainly have been reached without much difficulty by an athletic man helped by others. They consisted of nothing more than some rude rough designs similar to those constantly seen in Káfir carvings. The marginal figure gives an idea of their general form. Some of the rows were horizontal, others vertical, and faded off at the ends into indistinct forms. In places the dentated lines were absent altogether, and only the spots remained,

KÁFIR CARVING.

which looked like the splashes on a target caused by
bullets. The Káfirs looked upon them with reverence,
and said that they were very old, the handiwork of
the Creator himself. It was impossible to get near
enough to see if they were cut into the rock, but it
looked as if the effect had been produced by some paint
of a whitish colour. In any other country it might have
appeared that a practical joke was being played upon
me, but the Kafirs were evidently quite sincere in
their belief that the markings were ancient and holy
writing.

Having seen as much as I cared to, we started back,
and found at Bagalgrom that all the sick, the maimed,
and the blind, had been brought over the river for my
inspection, and that it was necessary for me to say something about each unfortunate. It was with the greatest
difficulty that we could get away at all, the villagers
begging me to stay at least one night in their village. I
had to decline, for having no blankets with me, it was
impossible to accede to their wish. All the time Utah
curbed his impatience with the greatest difficulty. He
was thoroughly disgusted at the friendly overtures made
to me by the people. Their attentions were at times
embarrassing. One fantastically dressed old man related
how he had dreamed a dream in which he had been
adopted by me as a son. When he reached this point
of his narrative he seized my little finger, and, to my
speechless astonishment, put it in his mouth and sucked
it pensively. I was glad to say good-bye to my too
enthusiastic friend.

If we had found the difficult rocky climb hard to
manage on our way up the valley, it was infinitely

more difficult now. The leading man had a most adventurous scramble. Once down, he was able to help us by placing our feet in the niches and crannies we could not see or find for ourselves. At one place in the day's march a very bad bluff had to be passed by wading in the river. When we reached the spot, I was leading, and the sheer precipitous rock in front and on one side, with the swift river on the other, was highly bewildering to me, until the matter was explained. In wading, although the stream at this time of the year was not very rapid, it was terrifying for my poor dogs. In some places they had to be dragged through the water until they were half drowned, or had to be pushed with poles into stiller channels, to prevent them from getting carried into the main current of the river.

On the way our conversation was principally of an instructive kind; the style of talk in which some of the Chitráli princes would have revelled, but which is somewhat difficult to a man who desires to be exact and truthful. It consisted in a great measure of my answering questions and then adding remarks suggested by the subjects under discussion. We, after a time, talked about coal, which Shermalik had seen in India, and had described to the Káfirs. He now evidently desired my corroboration of the statements he had made, and which had not been received with simple faith; so I told of coal-mines, and attempted, in our imperfect medium of conversation, to explain what coal was, and how it was employed in the manufactures of my country. The Káfirs became more and more astonished, until at length Utah merely expressed the sentiment of all when he

DESCENT OF THE ROCK.

To face page 204.

DESCENT OF THE ROCK.

To face page 252.

said, "If we did not know that Franks never lie, who would believe a word of this? It is wonderful."

When we reached Urmir it was getting dark. Just short of the village the Káfirs had suddenly, and in a characteristic fashion, sat down and consumed a meal. The irregularity with which a Káfir takes his food is astonishing. He has no fixed rule about eating when on the march. Sometimes he appears never to leave off eating, at others he seems to do without food altogether. As we passed the sacred stone and the effigies at Urmir, one of the party, at any rate, knew that the most tiring part of the journey had yet to be accomplished—this was the climb up the Kámdesh hill. It was a long, tedious tramp. I got home with my chapplies and leather socks cut into ribbons, and my feet wounded and blistered by the excessively rough road.

Mention has more than once been made of a headman, referred to as Lame Astán. The Káfirs called him Katr Astán, which has the same meaning. He was a man of much consequence amongst the Kám, for he was not only one of the Mirs—*i.e.*, individuals allowed to sit on a stool outside a house—but he was old, reputed to be sagacious, and was a tribal orator. At heart he was a friend of mine, but he was also a time-server. He was very wealthy, and a sagacious, far-seeing man. Five wives owned him as lord, and indeed he possessed every attribute which should have placed him in popular Káfir estimation on a par with Dán Malik and Torag Merak, had he not lacked liberality. He was stingy, and, with all his ambition to be the controller of the destinies of his nation, he could not bring himself to incur the continual expenditure in banquets and in sacrifices by which alone

M

that position could be attained. So he had to fall into the position of sycophant to Torag Merak, and at the latter's feasts he used to run about excitedly helping the servers, going through all the delightful experiences of the liberal entertainer vicariously. This man clearly saw the value to the tribe of my staying amongst them, because he believed that while I remained in the valley neither Chitráli nor Afghan would venture upon an attack. He was, in consequence, a sincere supporter of mine, and would have been of great service to me had he not been obliged to succumb to the wishes of the wild Torag Merak, and change round as often as the latter altered his views, either from caprice, or perhaps merely to show he was powerful enough to change his opinions, and make his followers change theirs, as often as he chose. As it was, I was greatly indebted to Lame Astán for the tact with which he managed, at times, to smooth my path; but after my return from the Dungul Valley on the 5th of November, neither he nor Dán Malik could do much to ease my existence, which was embittered by the persistent endeavours of several of the headmen to obtain a position of authority over me; so I gladly seized the opportunity of going to Kamu, nominally to see some sick people there, and to shoot up the valley at the mouth of which Kamu stands. This little expedition was now urged upon me by the very people who were formerly so opposed to my undertaking it. The Kámdesh folk were very anxious concerning the illness of a certain man named Gutkech, who was not only an individual of considerable importance in the tribe, but was also the officiating priest of the Kamu village. My friends confessed that all that had been told me about the impossibility of my visiting that place was untrue, and that the false statements had simply been made to meet the supposed exigencies of the moment.

We left Kámdesh on November 12th, and after staying two days at Kamu, went a short journey up the Kamu Valley. Shermalik again accompanied me as interpreter, for Sayed Shah, on the ground of old age and indifferent health, still persistently refused to leave our headquarters at Kámdesh. My experiences at Kamu were anything but agreeable. The people who had been deputed to accompany me on my shooting expedition were most troublesome. Their intention was to reduce me to sub-jection, so to speak, and in every small particular to make me obey the directions of the chief of the party. This, of course, was an impossible state of affairs, my position being not very unlike that of a prisoner taken out for an airing. Before I had succeeded in relieving myself of this annoyance, high words had been spoken. Shermalik, terrified at the threats of the Kamu men, became openly rebellious, threw down his rifle and car-tridges, and decamped altogether. I went on my way as if nothing whatever had happened, and tried to demonstrate that my will was at least as inflexible as any Káfir's. After being left alone the best part of the day on the hillside, for the Kamu men also went away in anger, they all came back again, and calmly recommenced their system of directing and ordering my footsteps just as before. However, they gained nothing by this move, and before we reached the village of Kamu on our return journey, I led the march myself, having turned the tables on my companions, who were now

obliged to accede to my wishes. Nevertheless, before
this satisfactory state of things was obtained, there had
been considerable unpleasantness. After this experience
I never allowed any Káfir to go just in front of me on
the march, unless in the capacity of guide. I made an
exception in the case of Utah, partly because he was
extremely helpful to me, but chiefly because it was his
right and privilege to precede everybody of his tribe.

BROTHERHOOD CEREMONY WITH TORAG MERAK.

To face page 213.

CHAPTER XIV

The narrative continued—Return from Kamu—I adopt Torag Merak as my "brother"—The ceremony—Utah takes umbrage, and is also adopted as my brother—Chief reason for this custom amongst the Káfirs—Three days' dancing in connection with erecting effigies to the dead—My attire on such special occasions—The male effigy—Description of the performers, dances, costumes, ceremonies, &c.—The band—The old men dancers—Addresses to the effigies—The choir leader—The female effigy—Declamation by old Astán—Dancing and feasting for the female effigy—*Place aux dames*—November troubles—Growing discontent—Jealousy of Shermalik—Utah's enmity—Squabbling all round by everybody—Bachik's high-handedness—More quarrelling—Kámdesh again—Advantages of not knowing too much of a language—Dinner *en famille* with Torag Merak—Incidents.

THE day after my return from Kamu, the 19th November, I decided to accept Sayed Shah's repeated suggestions to try and disarm Torag Merak's increasing hostility by secretly going through the peculiar Káfir ceremony of making him my brother. The rite was enacted with all due mystery, with closed doors, at the dead of night. A sheep was killed, and the kidneys cooked and served up on a plate. Torag Merak and I were placed side by side, each with an arm round the other's shoulders. Sayed Shah stood in front, and fed us with fragments of the kidneys from the point of a knife, we every now and then turning our faces towards each other, and making the motion of kissing. Torag Merak then uttered a short invocation to Imrá. He was unusually subdued in manner, perhaps the closed doors and the mysterious secrecy of the proceedings impressed his wild mind with some suggestion of solemnity. He quickly recovered from this, for him, unusual state of quietness, and launched forth with perhaps justifiable bragging about the extraordinary expense he had incurred in continually feasting his fellow-tribesmen, a circumstance of which he was inordinately proud. He also discoursed to me for hours on the manners and customs of Káfirs in general, and eventually left me much in the state of mind of a man who has diligently looked at all the pictures in a large collection during one morning, and then tries to remember what he has seen.

I had long become convinced that it was absolutely necessary to conciliate Torag Merak by every means in my power, for, owing to the influence he had obtained through his prodigious banquets, it was a positive danger to have him against me ; but the secret brother-making proved a valuable lesson to me, showing, as it did, how impossible it was to keep anything of the kind from the knowledge of the Káfirs, for the very next day the affair was all over the village ; while the chief result of my action was that Utah, the priest, was greatly incensed, and declared that his prior claims on my friendship had been publicly and openly slighted. There was obviously only one way out of the difficulty, and that was to adopt him also as my brother. He pretended at first that the thing could not be done, hinting that one stranger could not have more than one brother. Subsequently he changed his mind, and entered into the subject warmly. Finally, he became my brother with real enthusiasm.

This custom of the Káfirs of adopting strangers as their brothers is one of their methods of levying con-

tributions in the Kunạr Valley and' in other places, as
has been already explained. Theoretically the Káfir is
supposed to give presents also, but practically he contents himself with handing over some gift of trifling
value, while he himself receives robes, money, and other
gifts, according to the importance of his safeguard. But
it was no part of my plans at this time to excite the
jealousy of all the other headmen by making presents to
one or two of their number. So I declared that Torag
Merak and Utah had become my brothers on precisely
equal terms, and that, as our friendship was from the
heart alone, it was unnecessary to symbolise the sentiment by the exchange of gifts. This was not at all
Torag Merak's idea of the situation, but the priest accepted it readily, so the other was compelled to acquiesce
in this decidedly unconventional arrangement.

For three days towards the end of the month there had
been incessant dancing from morning to night, with
intervals for feasting, at the village dancing-house or
" gromma," in the upper village, in connection with the
erection of two wooden effigies to deceased people—one
to a man, the other to a woman. I went to watch the performances for an hour or two each day, and as usual, on all
special occasions, attired myself in a plain suit of black
at the particular request of the Káfirs, whose admiration
for such a costume had been imparted to me in India by
Shermalik, at whose suggestion I had brought the garments with me. A stranger or more fantastic ceremony
it is difficult to imagine. Perhaps to an onlooker my
own appearance, dressed in the quiet garb of English
civilisation, the black coat of a London tailor, would
have been sufficiently remarkable amidst its uncommon

surroundings. The people behaved like wild men, in a manner, but did not look the part. Some of the old men amongst the spectators had faces of an intellectual type, quite up to the average of Orientals. Many of the dancers were my own friends, and to see them for the first time in their changed attire, posturing in such unusual attitudes, with, of course, a complete absence of shyness or self-consciousness, made me at times, when lulled by the monotonous music, or by the Gregorian-like chant of the singers, start as if from a dream. The continuous stream of people always dancing round in one direction made me dizzy and drowsy. Then from out of the stamping throng the face of some one long dead and gone would gaze upon me. It gave me no surprise, but seemed quite reasonable. The sudden change to some other face caused no astonishment, and when with an effort I roused myself, it was most difficult to discover what trick of feature or expression had created the illusion.

The dancing-place was just outside the gromma, which borders it to the north, and is used in bad weather. The building also formed a stand for spectators. On the opposite side, a dwelling-house with a large porch formed a similar vantage-ground for the show, and was crowded with sightseers. Behind, the steep hillside was covered with densely-packed spectators. In front, projecting over the slope, was a large square wooden platform, supported at its outer extremity on long posts firmly planked in the hillside. This platform was furnished with a rail, and with seats on three sides. It looked dangerous enough, but was much stronger than it appeared. There were collected all the fathers of the tribe, the wise greybeards,

A DANCE WITH EFFIGIES.

To face page 216.

who solemnly discussed current affairs and family matters. Amongst them I was given a place. The actual dancing space was perhaps twenty yards square, the largest flat expanse of ground in the village.

When I arrived the first day, escorted by one or two young braves, friends of mine, the performance was in full swing. In the centre of the dancing-place, close by the rough altar, was the effigy of a man. It was carried on the back of a slave, above whose head and shoulders it towered a couple of feet. The long straight legs were covered at the ends—there were no feet—by tufted dancing-boots. A Badakhshán silk robe was thrown over the shoulders, and the head was bound round with a silk turban, into which eight paint-brush-shaped contrivances of peacocks' feathers were thrust. The odd-shaped face, huge and solemn, the white stone eyes set close together, and the bobbing up and down of the big image as the slave bearing it shifted from one foot to the other in time to the music, and every now and then gave it a sudden bunch up, made a curious picture. The effigy bore a look of such massive grotesqueness that it ought to have been comic, but for me such figures always had something repellent; the sight of one of those sinister faces (of the small variety) peering through the foliage would at once extinguish the charm of the loveliest thicket, and invariably excite me to thoughts of iconoclastic anger. The monotony and the evil expression of these conventional shapes became more and more irritating as time went on. In the, present case it seemed a wonder that one man should be able to sustain so heavy a burden. He always looked tired, and was frequently changed, but, nevertheless, the wood from which the image was cut must have been extremely light for one man to be able to uphold it. During the intervals of the dance the image was propped up against the altar, and left in charge of the women. Of these during the dance, about two dozen, including little girls, the seniors wearing horned headdresses, circled slowly round the figure, keeping time by a slow bending of the knees, and moving the feet only a few inches at a time. They incessantly moved one hand, palm upwards and breast high, slightly backwards and forwards, towards the bobbing effigy. This action of the hands is intended to symbolise the words, "As this dead person is, so also shall I become." All the women and little girls were shockingly dirty and unkempt, their garments being much torn. The women wore the large serpentine earrings, and two or three had on silver blinkers also. Outside the women was a dense throng of men, all dancing round from left to right. The women of the inner circle were of the family of the deceased, while their male relations in the dancing crowd were distinguished from the others by wearing bright-coloured clothes and all the bravery they possessed, and by each carrying a dancing-axe. They wore gorgeous sham *kinkob* chappans or long robes and white cloth turbans.

The attire of some of these men deserves description. In the ears they wore long silver earrings, in shape similar to those seen in old-fashioned portraits, while the neck was frequently circled by a silver, or what looked like a silver ornament, solid and heavy, such as those worn by Hindu women. If an individual were the proud possessor of two chappans, he wore them both, exposing some of the glory of the one underneath by slipping an arm out of a sleeve of the one above. The waist was girded by a narrow shawl, or the usual metal-studded leather belt of the country, supporting a dagger. The feet were covered with curiously worked dancing-boots, with red woollen rosettes on the instep, while from the long, soft, drab-coloured uppers, which reached nearly half-way to the knee, there depended a long fringe of white goat's hair, dyed red at the tips. The boots were secured to the legs and ankles by narrow tapes of list. Above them appeared Chitráli stockings, into the tops of which the loose, baggy trousers of coarse white cotton cloth were carefully tucked. This, with a dancing-axe, completed the full dress of a swell, but there were all gradations in attire, according to the wealth or position of the wearer. Some merely had a silk turban, worn as a sash over one shoulder and under the opposite arm, the ends hanging free. Others had for their only ornament a diadem or fillet, consisting of two rows of silver half-spherical buttons, behind and at the sides, while the portion over the forehead and brows consisted merely of two narrow black strips. This circlet was much affected by the young girls also. I observed that some of my friends wore only Chitráli stockings, or a scrap of turban cloth as an additional ornament; while those dancers not related to the deceased wore their ordinary clothes, which they had not had washed for the occasion, probably fearing to appear conspicuous. Almost everybody wore "watsás," the soft reddish leather boot of the country, but there were exceptions to this, and bare feet stamped and pranced with the liveliest. The music was supplied by professionals, kindly assisted at times by amateurs. It consisted of three tiny drums and two or three of the ordinary wretched-toned reed pipes. The drums did not exceed four inches in the diameter of the heads, and were contracted in the middle like hour-glasses. The performer beats with a small stick, while he keeps up the tension of the drumhead by pulling at certain leather thongs with his left hand, by which the tightness of the stretched hide surfaces could be regulated. I was told that these little drums are costly, being each of them worth a cow, because, out of many, not more than one or two turn out a credit to the maker. The "time" allowed great latitude to the dancers, who indulged their individual fancy, either walking slowly round and round the dancing circle, taking several steps of not more than six inches in length to the bar, or two skips on each foot alternately; or sometimes prancing, stamping, or rushing forward. It was a question of pace.

A favourite movement seemed to be to march round more or less steadily, merely raising the knees slightly, and then suddenly to rush violently at the orchestra with the head bent, as in the act of butting. Nearly all the dancers were in pairs, with arms over one another's shoulders. Characteristically, if a man wanted to scratch his nose, he was just as likely to use his encircling arm as the free one, without the slightest thought of the discomfort he was causing his partner by twisting the latter's face round. The splendidly dressed relations danced singly. Often in the mob, especially when near the musicians, the leading pairs would face round to those behind them, hammering their feet with great force on the ground, and bending over to watch the effect. Round and round they went, round and round, smiling, very happy, fully conscious of the excel-

lence of their own performances, and never tiring. Aged
men, with that touch of nature which makes us all akin,
danced with an added grace, from the consciousness that
they were showing their juniors how the thing should be
properly done. With wooden step they doubled up their
knees, gyrated, performed the back-step, side-kick, all
the figures of the highest style. These men never smiled,
while they were frequently out of time. The axes were
twirled by some, jerked with both hands by others, or
were merely bobbed up and down on the shoulder.
Every time the band stopped the head-drummer sounded
a few last taps to show his finished touch and his reluctance to stop. The intervals in the dancing were
filled up by extemporary addresses to the wooden image
by an individual specially appointed for that duty.
He extolled the liberality of the deceased, his bravery,
and his good deeds, as well as the virtues of his ancestors.
As the orators on these occasions are always members of
the dead man's family, they probably say all that is to be
said on the subject, and never err on the side of false
modesty. His style was curiously like that of certain
uneducated itinerant speakers one sometimes hears in
England. Breathless staccato sentences, with pauses,
all the speech broken up into passages of nearly equal
length, while the pauses show a constant tendency to
grow longer and longer. I could hardly understand a
single word uttered until my companions made it clear
to me ; but it was obvious that the orator thought little
of repeating himself over and over again.

While the orator declaimed, the dancers refreshed
themselves with wine ladled from a tub with wooden
cups. The same not particularly generous fluid was also

circulated among the spectators constantly. Sometimes the musicians would stop altogether, and the dancing would recommence to the chanting of men's voices. The singers crowded round a central figure, a lame friend of mine, who was the highest musical authority in the tribe. In leading the choir he vibrated violently from head to foot with the rapture of his song or hymn, but his notes were inaudible in the accompaniment of his fellows. Poor fellow! I hope he did not know this, for, like all really fine singers, and some others also, he liked to be heard. The men's voices intoned a perfect church chant. Shut your eyes, and you would believe a full-voiced choir was sounding a Gregorian prayer; open them, and it was something quite different.

The greybeards and seniors, all importance, sat round the platform drinking wine and talking politics. Occasionally a notable would emerge from the dance, take off his finery, hang it over the rail, pay my sheepskin coat the tribute of a rub between the fingers, and then join in the general conversation.

After a time I proposed to go home, but was requested to wait to see a woman's effigy which was being brought up to the dancing-place. The figure was very large, much larger than that for the man, and must have been very heavy. It required a crowd of people to carry it. The deceased was a Waiguli woman, married in Kám-desh, and evidently belonged to a wealthy family, as there were to be two days' dancing and feasting in her honour. The massive effigy was brought into the dancing-ring, preceded by two men waving flags, one white and the other red, each being about two feet square, and made of coarse cotton; the white flag had a small worked centre about the size of half-a-crown. As soon as the image was placed in a proper position, lame Astán limped forward and addressed the stolid wooden face. At the end of his speech he went through the form of kissing the effigy, an action which was immediately imitated by every one present. The dancing in honour of the man's effigy was then resumed.

At the next interval old Astán stood forth again, and declaimed against three absent individuals who had stolen a cow belonging to one of Umrá Khan's people. He wound up by saying that unless restitution was at once made, the culprits would be sent to Umrá Khan, for him to settle matters with them. At that time the Kám were most anxious to keep on good terms with Umrá Khan, and nobody seemed to think there was anything unusual in introducing the topic of the theft in the middle of the effigy ceremonies.

On the 21st, the dancing and feasting for the Waigul woman began. The only remarkable feature about the performance was that no one wore dancing-dresses or dancing-boots. The two flags were carried in the middle of the dancers and were waved energetically. They can only be carried in procession in this way when the effigy is of a certain value. I was told that the large price of three cows was paid to the slaves who carved the Waigul woman's image. At one period of the dance women brought forward an immense number of quarters of cheeses. Each fragment was impaled on the end of a stick. One of these sticks was given to every woman present, both dancers and spectators. The dancers carried their portions over the shoulder, and revolved as before. One of the women dancers kept twirling a white metal bowl above her head as she circled round the effigy. This was to signify that the dead woman's relations were giving three feasts in her name. It was a symbol of distinction and honour. The feasting was of a lavish description, and was remarkable for the fact that the women were fed first, the only instance of the kind I ever noticed in Káfiristán. When the ceremonies were completed, the images were taken away and placed in their appointed positions. Although these images are respected, and even honoured, I do not think they are ever renewed or repaired when they once fall into decay.

The last days of November were full of trouble, and more than once we had consumed all the food we possessed and there seemed small likelihood of our getting more. The weather was abominable. The sleet and rain pouring through my roof forced me to retreat to the woodshed below, which still remained dry, but which had the disadvantage of possessing no outlet for the smoke. It was necessary, therefore, whenever a fire was lit, to keep the door wide open, and for all within to save their eyes by crouching as near the floor as possible.

In the discontent on my account, which now began to increase considerably, poor Shermalik suffered greatly. All the headmen, without one exception, seemed to have taken a strong dislike to him, the real cause of which was jealousy at the amount and variety of the wealth he had received from me. While he literally fawned upon them, and adopted most conciliatory and ingratiating manners even to the smallest boy on the road, it was declared that he had grown conceited—that he gave

FLIGHT OF SHERMALIK.

To face page 229.

himself airs, and I know not what else. Finally, Utah, his old friend and patron, not only abandoned his cause, but announced publicly that if Shermalik remained with me, he, Utah, must stop away. Poor Utah was too much married. The wife he liked best, a strong-minded, opinionated, but unprepossessing woman, lived down the village, while I occupied the house of pretty Number 2, who had gone to reside with her father, a one-eyed scoundrel who gave me much trouble. The pretty wife was excessively jealous of the plain wife. Madam Jealousy, seeing Shermalik butchering a sheep for me, asked him for the skin. He answered that he intended to cure it for my use. Shortly afterwards Utah passed by, whipped up the skin, and carried it off to his chief wife. Then there were alarms and excursions. The father of the injured wife, the one-eyed villain aforesaid, whose name was Bachik, retaliated by stealing and eating the last of my sheep. There was no doubt on the subject, although Bachik attempted to prove an alibi both for himself and the sheep. Then his wife and other female relations came down to assail Shermalik with their dreadful tongues. To my great joy, Shermalik incontinently fled, but poor Utah was forced to assume his father-in-law's quarrel as his own, and declare Shermalik his mortal enemy, whose life he spared merely out of friendship for me. In my diary of this date I find a note that it was snowing hard, and no one could see more than a few yards from his door; yet my Káfir friends took good care I should not feel dull.

On the next day the first sentence recorded is, "Squabbling all round by everybody." It was finally decided

that Shermalik must go away to Bináram until matters
went more smoothly. Utah's miserable father-in-law,
Bachik, paid me another visit, demanding all sorts of
things from me. In my most finished Bashguli I bade
him begone. He retorted by ordering me off my own
premises. There are various ways in the Bashgul tongue
of telling you to go away. " Imma," for instance, means
"let us go," and is polite ; so is " prits-i," which also
means "go ; " but "pis-boh" is excessively rude, and
means "get out of this"—"disappear"—"make your-
self scarce," or some similar vulgar phrase ; yet " pis-
boh " was the phrase Bachik employed. I could do
nothing but send for Utah, who promptly hid himself ;
so I bade the wrathful Bachik do his worst. This he did
effectually by sending down all his women-folk to show
their eloquence in abuse ; but they soon tired of a one-
sided skirmish, and retired defeated, having expended
every harsh word in their vocabulary. Then everybody's
attention was diverted by one of those quarrels which
occur daily, almost hourly, one might say, in a big Káfir
village.

My next-door neighbour was also a connection of Utah,
having married the latter's sister. He was a poorish
man, and could not afford "patsas " or shepherds ; so he
managed his dairy farm in partnership with another Káfir.
They joined their flocks and herds, so that when one partner
was at Kámdesh, the other was usually with the flocks.
Together they possessed but nine cows ; Burmuk, Utah's
brother-in-law, owning four, and the other man owning
five. On this particular occasion both partners happened
to be in Kámdesh together, and it occurred to the five-cow
man that he ought to have a larger share of the common

stock of cheese than Burmuk. He said so. The other demurred. Then each called the other "kuri" (dog) and "bari" (slave), reached for sticks, and fell to fighting. Din Malik, a splendid young Káfir, and other stalwart men, swung the fighters apart. Burmuk, a little man, dissembled. He pretended he was quite content, and strolled down to talk to me; then, suddenly snatching up a block of dried firewood, he rushed down a big grass stack behind which his foe was orating. He was rewarded by a blow across the head which would have broken any skull except a Káfir's or a Pathan's. I know a Pathan has a tough head, for a fortnight before I had been obliged to try its resisting power to the stroke of a club. On that occasion it was the club which broke, the Pathan being merely a little dazed and entirely subdued. However, the combatants were quickly separated again; a goat was sent for and eaten, and peace established; while it was decided that as Burmuk had been the aggressor all through, he must pay for the peace-offering. He ingeniously and successfully shifted this responsibility on to my shoulders.

Soon after I reached Kámdesh, an old Káfir came to see me, and examined my belongings with great care. He shook his head sadly on my india-rubber tub being exhibited to him, pitied my innumerable wants, and finally asked me if the English ever fought themselves. He had been present when I was compelled to show the strength of my arm in quelling a little mutiny—the episode already referred to. To stop the perpetual small thefts which were occurring, I asked him and several other of my friends in a very innocent way if they thought it advisable for me to shoot the next thief who stole my property.

My counsellors gasped with amazement—such a punishment for such a small offence ; and then hastened to tell me of the dreadful events which must necessarily follow such a shooting. My own views entirely agreed with theirs about the nature of the punishment, but I pretended to be only partly convinced, and promised to consider the point with care, reserving my opinion until I had looked at it in all its bearings. Then the people said that Franks had very strict notions, and liked to be obeyed.

About this time I also found it advisable to be sometimes very angry, even when feeling most lazy. The total result was good. All my stolen property was sooner or later returned to me, and although the people sometimes said extremely impudent things, they uttered them in a subdued voice, and their general behaviour greatly improved.

There is a certain advantage in not knowing too much of a language. When I wanted to be quiet, it was my custom to send away all my interpreter people. Káfir visitors would sit down and ask me questions as usual. My only answer was a friendly smile. This quickly took effect, and the men would soon go off muttering the hope that Imrá's curse might strike Shermalik and Sayed Shah for being absent. So also when differences of opinion arose. It was a common plan of mine to affect complete ignorance of the details of the controversy. If a man were really angry, he had to keep repeating his observations till he was tired out and had cooled down. He invariably changed the nature of his remarks under the treatment, and at last would have given anything to get away from my bland

and puzzled interrogations. On one occasion, in the middle of a hot dispute, I begged to be excused for a few minutes, went off to take a meridian sun observation, and then returned to resume the conversation. I then had it all my own way, and was able to dress down my friend handsomely.

In spite of the cold and snow at the end of November, the Káfirs seemed to be even more scantily clad than before the weather changed. Most of them discarded their boots, that the poorly-tanned leather might not be spoiled. So nearly all went about bare from the knees downwards. On entering my house, their un-usually clean feet steamed under the influence of the genial warmth. The women carried grain to the water-mills as usual, also going bare-legged. Children were carried about attired merely in a short sheepskin, open all down the front, except at the waist. Babies were kept warm by being tucked inside the man's or woman's garments, so that the naked bodies came into contact. Luckily there was no wind. There never is at Kámdesh.

On the 25th November, to show the close nature of our friendship, I went to dine with Torag Merak. My own servant accompanied me, carrying knives and forks as well as plates, in the hope of thereby ensuring some amount of cleanliness in the proceedings. Torag Merak met me in the road, and on arriving at his house, pre-ceded me up the rough, notched pole which did duty for a staircase, and led to the upper apartments. This enabled him to clear my path by kicking out the numerous dogs which were precariously perched on the different notches, knowing well that some eating enter-tainment was going forward. We were ushered into

a room of the usual description, and about eighteen
feet square. In addition to the stools of the country,
it contained three bedsteads covered with coarse blankets.
I secured a stool, placing it against one of the corner
wooden pillars of the hearth, refusing the bed-seat prepared for me, which, though more honourable, had
dreadful possibilities lurking in the thick blankets.
Torag Merak and his wife dived into the treasure-
room of the house, in the middle storey, and presently
emerged, carrying the food with which we were to be
regaled. The repast began with walnuts and wine.
The latter was strong and good, and was declared to
be three years old. A small earthen vessel of honey
was placed by my side, into which the walnuts were
to be dipped before being eaten. As Torag Merak's
women folk were indifferent cooks, it had been ex-
pressly stipulated that no unleavened bread cakes were
to be provided. Therefore rice, a great luxury according to Káfir ideas, since it has to be imported into
the country, was provided, and cooked in a large earthen
vessel over the fire in front of us. Torag Merak, to
show the lavishness of his hospitality, so recklessly
salted the rice and ladled so much ghi into it, that
when it was ready to eat I had to content myself with
one small mouthful, for fear of consequences. My
surroundings also were not of a kind to favour the consumption of food. The place swarmed with the dirtiest
of dirty children, some belonging to the house, others
the offspring of servants. Among them were two infants in arms, one Torag Merak's, the other a visitor's.
The son of the house began to cry miserably, upon which
the visitor, politely putting her own child away, which

TORAG MERAK ESCORTS ME HOME.

To face page 237.

at once began to howl dismally, proceeded to suckle the other. A three-year-old son of Torag Merak's, a marvellously spoiled child, ran riot all over the place. He was a horrible nuisance. This urchin, wanting he knew not what, began crying for food. His fond father fed him with rice, ghi, wine, honey, cheese, everything there was which was edible ; but nothing satisfied the young cormorant until he was handed an enormous meat bone, the mere application of which to his face nearly suffocated him, and so kept him partially quiet. The way the other children ran about, staggering and tumbling all round the big fire, was a wonderful sight. Old Torag Merak, who was his own head-cook, stirred and fiddled about with the food in a most unpleasant way. He has the appearance of a gipsy king, and though darker than the average of the tribe, is wonderfully picturesque. In his gloomy eyes there is a world of pathos. They belie him utterly. He is at heart a howling savage, while in repose his features are those of a man saddened from gazing on the sufferings of a troubled world. As a matter of fact, a ferocious-looking Káfir is rarely seen. The greatest cut-throats are often the quietest-looking individuals. I was glad to get away to my own house. Torag Merak escorted me almost to the door, lighting my steps with sticks of resinous pine, similar to those he had employed to see how the cooking in the earthen pot was getting on, and to show me where my plate was in the grimy room we had just left.

CHAPTER XV

DECEMBER, January, and February were destined to be a period of great trouble to me, although it opened auspiciously enough by my being invited to join the Jast in a ceremony of a very exclusive kind. It is probable, indeed, that on no former occasion had a stranger been permitted to view such proceedings. Although I had been particularly asked by the priest to go to his house for this special ceremony, both Shermalik and Sayed Shah declared that it would be impossible for me to obtain admittance into the inner room, where none but headmen or those who exercised religious functions were ever permitted to enter. But, as a matter of fact, the priest and his companions warmly welcomed me on my arrival, and conducted me to a seat with great politeness. The respect with which they treated me on this occasion seemed a good omen for the relations in which we should live together. Indeed, on looking back to my residence in Káfiristán, after comparing different dates in my diaries, the con-

clusion is forced upon me, that if the Káfirs had no
warm affection for me, which, from our different mental
training, our different modes of thought, and our different rules of conduct, was in the nature of things
quite natural, yet in their hearts they bore me no ill-
will ; probably they had a kind of liking for me, based
principally on the idea that they could trust my word
as well as my kindly disposition towards them.   It seems
to me that the Káfirs, if left to themselves, were always
inclined to be friendly, provided their friendliness did
not cost them too much trouble, and that many of them
were not so greatly desirous of getting hold of my
property as they were fearful that others of the tribe
were being given presents in which they themselves
had no share.   It was this peculiar but characteristic
jealousy, not only of neighbouring tribes, but of one
another, which was the real origin of more than half my
troubles.

In the beginning of December small-pox broke out
in the village, and a few days later nearly every one
was suffering from severe colds, the forerunner of an
epidemic of influenza.   The whole tribe was in a state
of consternation about the small-pox ; inoculation was
practised, which merely had the effect of spreading the
disease, and constant offerings were made to Imrá to
stay the pestilence.   The children suffered terribly.   If
they escaped with their lives, they frequently got in-
flammation and suppuration of joints, especially the
elbow-joint.   Káfirs are quite careless of infection.   At
the effigy dances, described in the last chapter, a baby
was brought one day whose face was covered with the
small-pox rash just on the point of pustulating, and the

infant was handed round and discussed. Hearing about vaccination, every one was anxious for me to send to India for lymph, but there was no time nor opportunity for me to comply with such desires. The weather was pitiless. Several feet of snow fell, and my wood-shed became nearly as wet as the room above, through which the snow-water melted by my fire poured incessantly, forming pools which drained through into my apartment. I had to camp on my bed under a waterproof sheet used as a rough tent.

On the 2nd of December, when strolling about the village, I was riveted with astonishment to see at a spring a short distance from me a perfectly white-skinned woman with golden hair. On seeing me regard her so attentively she fled to her home. This, however, was from coquetry, for on my passing the house in which she had taken refuge, I observed her peeping at me from behind a door, and also assuring herself that her antics were perceived. Having paid a long-promised visit to the Debilala, my road home ran over her house-top, and my companions shouted to her to let the Frank see her hair. The damsel readily came out to show herself. At such comparatively close quarters her hair proved to be outrageously "carrotty," and the young woman herself to be so fair that she was almost an albino, while her face, arms, and legs were covered with yellow freckles. She was dreadfully ill-favoured, and a most unpleasant object; so it was not difficult for me to decline her and her friends' kind offer to come for a still nearer inspection. The Káfirs, I believe, hoped for a romance, and that at last they had found a wife for me. They were quite cast-down when, in answer to their eager questions, my reply was, "Lilliwik shingera na zánum" — "I do not think the young woman beautiful;" but they afterwards confided to me that in their opinion she was distinctly ugly, and that it was for this reason she still remained unmarried.

Utah Ding, Utah's brother, was very ill, poor fellow, so we looked in at his house to see if he could be helped in any way. As we approached the door we heard a terrible noise as of fierce altercation inside, and Lame Astán's voice, as usual, drowning all others in its strident and penetrating tones. Indoors, a mass of people were so busy gesticulating and shouting, that they could not pause for more than a smile in our direction. It turned out that there was a conference arranging the terms of peace between Aramallik Chárá and his Kashtán enemy.

On the 6th of December a Lutdeh Káfir, named Gazab Shah, with several followers, came to see me in the afternoon. He was the individual who, with a cousin named Kán Jannah, also a headman, actually prevented Lockhart's Mission from coming down the valley. He was by no means reticent on the subject, and in answer to my questions said that Lockhart was a good man, a very good man, and as it seemed certain that his journey to Kámdesh would be attended with difficulty and trouble, he, Gazab Shah, kindly made it impossible. He is a man of the coolest effrontery.

In the evening Shahru the "pshur" came for a long talk over the events of the day. He even endeavoured to explain his own position towards the gods during sacrifices, but our limited means of intercommunication

left the subject still obscure. He told me he had
attended four sacrifices that day, and four times had he
become possessed, speaking with tongues. The obvious
result was that he was very tired. Tobacco had a good
effect for a time. We discussed the looting and destruction of a house which was going on two hundred yards or
so in front of us, in a philosophical spirit, much in the
same quiet way in which we referred to an earthquake
which had startled us during the day, for it now took
a great deal to turn my curiosity into keen inquisitiveness. Under the combined influences of warmth, tobacco,
and friendliness, Shahru revived greatly, and on Utah
coming in, the three of us, with my Pathan servant, Mir
Alam, sat round the fire, and discussed everything in
the world, from the general inferiority of the Presungulis
in comparison with all other Káfir tribes, to the family
connections of her Majesty the Queen-Empress. I invited my guests to take some brandy, or rather I should
say they led up to the subject in so marked a manner
that I could not do otherwise than send for the spirit.
They only drank a very little, greatly diluted with water,
but even in this condition they were astounded at its
fire and potency. We were continuing the conversation
quietly when Shahru suddenly jumped to his feet, powerful
tremors shaking his body. He sprang to the door, where
he turned and faced us. His face was pallid, his lips
uttered indistinct words, while he held his down-stretched
writhing hands tightly clasped together. He kept raising
himself on his toes, and then lowering his heels to the
ground. If other assurances had been necessary, a glance
at Utah's face told me that no farce was being enacted.
Utah, serious and priestly, had risen to his feet. Mir

SHAHRU SEES A SPIRIT.

To face page 242.

Alam had done the same, while I sat and looked on. Shahru presently recovered himself with many strokings of the beard and long-drawn sighs. Utah made him sit down by his side, and gave directions in low but authoritative tones for more wood to be quickly placed upon the fire, which had burned somewhat low. Then the explanation came. Shahru had seen a female spirit, a *vetr*, just over my door. As was customary on such occasions, whatever the spirit wished to say she spoke through him. It appears she had come all the way from London, and, after merely asking, " Is the Frank here ? " at once disappeared. Her face, Shahru said, was like the moon, especially in its shining qualities. Utah requested me to send at once for some very pure article of food to eat. I produced the remains of a box of sweets which were considered to fulfil the stated requirements. We each solemnly took a morsel of toffee, and munched it silently and thoughtfully. I had summoned up my most sympathetic look, and was rewarded for my trouble. Utah begged me on no account to go to sleep before midnight, adding that he himself, after what had happened, would be afraid to sleep at all that night. He said that on one occasion, near Utzún, he saw

SHAHRU.

Shahru seized by a spirit and whirled away some distance before being thrown to the ground with such violence that all his clothes were torn into ribbons. He now doubted the wisdom of leaving me at all during the night, and proposed that he and his brothers, Utah Ding, and Aramallik, should sit with me by turns. If there had been a certainty of further "manifestations" their company would have been most welcome. Shahru was not humbugging. He remained tired and silent until we all made a move, my friends to their homes and I to keep a vigil, if I would be ruled by priestly advice. Utah, in his quiet, steady way, appeared to have been really startled and impressed by the scene. He was a very interesting man, while his experiences and illustrations were of the strangest kind. For instance, during the evening I had been trying to learn the Bashgul word for a fat man, in contradistinction to a stoutly-built, powerful man. Utah for a long time was puzzled. My meaning dawned upon him as he exclaimed, " I remember killing a man near Asmar who was just as you describe—the word is *skior*, not *katr*."

The following day a young brave of the Kám, a strikingly handsome, genial, kind-hearted man, recounted to me his homicides, which he totalled at twenty-five, including three women. He also showed me various scars where hostile bullets had entered into, and emerged from, his body. He described his exploits, most of which consisted in stabbing people while asleep, or in shooting his enemies with matchlock or bow and arrow from an ambush. He was a famous young warrior, but his exploits, in comparison with those of his brother Shyak, were as Saul's to David's. The thought somewhat naturally occurred to me, "How was it that any Musalmáns remained on the frontier if only a portion of what I heard was true?" The reverse of the shield is, that among the Kám the men are disproportionately few in number. Bragamatal (Lutdeh) has many more fighting men than Kámdesh, and fewer houses. The explanation usually given is that the Lutdeh men live farther away from the fighting-grounds, and consequently the mortality amongst the males is much smaller. This is probably correct. This same pleasant, kindly young man subsequently came to me one day with a look as if he had made an interesting discovery. He asked if I remembered the derringer pistol I had bestowed on Shermalik in India. Well, the latter had lent the little weapon to his friend, my interviewer, who declared he had merely put the muzzle to the head of a sleeping Ogani, and just touched the trigger, and lo and behold the man was dead!

But the story which startled me most was that of Chandlu Torag. He subsequently went to India with me. When I first knew him he was very youthful-looking, and, although he may have been sixteen, he looked much less, being boyish and short of stature. His father, Torag Chandlu, had been the richest man in all Káfiristán, and was Torag Merak's brother. Torag Merak, on his brother's decease, achieved great fame by distributing the latter's property in lavish feasts, although, apparently, it was not his to deal with, but belonged of right to Chandlu Torag. However, this young boy had been well brought up from a Káfir point of view, and nothing could exceed my astonishment when I found that, in spite of his tender years, he had actually slain two men, one of them a Kaka-Khel, at Ashreth, from an ambush ; the other, however, had been surrounded and disarmed, and the boy had simply been the executioner.

To atone for dining with Torag Merak, I had to go through a similar ceremony with Utah. He was most thoughtful, knowing my ideas about cleanliness, and he carefully abstained from using other than my own spoon and fork for stirring the food while it was cooking. But the people present behaved as ingenuously as usual. The ordeal was a terrible one. I had to sit it out, for the priest was an extremely sensitive man. His favourite wife was lying on the bed with an open wound in her skull, caused by the fall of a heavy beam. She was also expecting a baby, and groaned in the dignity of her mis-fortunes and to compel my sympathy. Utah's mother-in-law, lying face downwards on another bed, with a girl of eight or nine years of age walking up and down her back to relieve the pangs of rheumatism, was as nothing by comparison.

My relations with the Kám people were at this time becoming more friendly again, and would probably have continued to improve had I not been unlucky enough to contract a somewhat serious illness, which kept me in bed, with only one or two days' interval, from the 8th to the 25th of December. It was during this short illness that the dormant cupidity of the Káfirs was aroused, and their inveterate jealousy and suspicion of one another accentuated in a very curious way by the bad behaviour of my Kashmiri servant Rusalá. The special character-istics of the people were by this time well known to me, and it had been my constant endeavour to keep the men on good terms with one another by never in any cir-cumstances giving any one a present except for services

RUSALÁ TURNS THIEF.

To face page 251.

actually performed, and by uniformly acting on the sup-position that the real danger of the success of my visit lay in the springing up of inter-tribal dissensions. It may be interesting to show how careful and well-laid plans may be completely upset by apparently trivial causes.

There was an epidemic of influenza raging in Kámdesh. Every household had one or more of its members attacked. I caught the disease also, and while under the influence of high fever dosed myself with opium and other drugs in a way which no doubt greatly delayed my recovery. Several of my followers were also ill, but Rusalá and two of the Baltis escaped infection altogether, and waited on us invalids in the usual kindly Oriental way. On the night of December 15th, when the fever was high, and, no doubt, appeared very bad indeed, Rusalá thought the time had come for him to look out for himself. He took the keys from under my pillow and went to a room above where the two faithful Baltis kept watch over my boxes. He proceeded to rummage my property, the timid guardians not daring to interfere, and appropriated money principally, but also sundry articles of warm clothing, and trinkets of little or no real value. In the morning my fever abated, and the Baltis told me what had occurred. A portion of the stolen property was recovered, Rusalá was disgraced and mildly punished, and the affair seemed at an end. But Rusalá, fearing that vengeance was in store for him, and that he would probably be imprisoned in India "for life," made up his mind to run away then and there, and get back to Kashmir as speedily as possible, while, in the apparently improbable event of my ever returning, he intended to bring a false charge against Sayed Shah, and accuse him of being the actual culprit.

o

He thought rightly that it would be difficult for any one
to convict him of the crime after a lapse of time, especially
if witnesses- could only be produced with the greatest
difficulty or not at all.   In pursuance of this plan he
bribed the Káfirs right and left with my property.   He prevailed on the priest's brother, Aramalik, to conduct him
out of the valley, and, as it subsequently became known,
was actually able to induce Utah himself to adopt him as a
son in the usual Káfir way.   Rusalá went away altogether
on the 20th, but returned a few days later with a considerable following of Káfirs.   He had become so certain of
his own position, and also of his power eventually to
outwit his new friends, that he had the assurance to
return for more " loot," and to make absurd demands on
me for back-pay, which he falsely alleged was due to him.
He made his attack through his Káfir accomplices.   It
seems he had promised certain definite sums to each of
his supporters, payment to be contingent on their forcing
the money out of me.   He had succeeded, in short, by
bribing with my money and by lying promises, in buying
over some of my best friends.   Yet it must be confessed
that they were very shamefaced when the matter was
brought to an issue, while some of them purposely kept
away on the Chitrál frontier.   The only people to be
relied upon were those who had become enraged at being
excluded by Rusalá in the general distribution of my
goods.   Matters shortly assumed a dangerous complexion.
Rusalá and his friends attempted to dictate terms to me,
the chief of which were that Rusalá should return to my
service, that all the rest of my servants should be sent
away, and that Rusalá should be placed in sole charge of
all my property.   I was ill in bed when these conditions

were excitedly laid before me and argued by eloquent
Káfirs, Rusalá himself keeping carefully out of sight.
Shermalik, out of an intense enmity he had acquired for
Sayéd Shah, brought a little party of his own to wait upon
me. They declared that in their belief Sayed Shah was
the man who had stolen my goods, and that Rusalá was
an ill-used man, and ought to be reinstated at once.
They also, with their tongues in their cheeks, affirmed
that Rusalá had a right to the absurd rate of back-pay
which he demanded. Although very weak and ill, I was
not idle all this time, and gradually a small number of
trustworthy Káfirs came over and took my side in the
dispute. One of them sent me word that the only way
out of the difficulty was for him to murder Rusalá—a task
which he professed himself both able and willing to
perform. Of course I refused him permission to kill my
rascally servant. My unswerving determination not to
yield to any demand made by the Rusalá party gradually
told on them and wore them down, while public opinion
by degrees began to turn in my favour, and several important men openly or privately declared themselves on
my side. Rusalá was at length abandoned by all his
friends, as soon, indeed, as they were convinced that there
was no more of my property to be divided amongst them.

Promising him full protection from personal injury,
they brought him over to me. He approached with a confident air. But I insisted on his being unconditionally
surrendered. After much argument this was granted,
and the chief headman amongst Rusalá's supporters provided the stick with which justice was done.

My triumph may seem to have been complete; nevertheless, before Rusalá was escorted from Chitrál to Gilgit

there were several minor troubles which had to be met. On one occasion Utah threatened to murder all my servants in revenge for the indignities heaped on the head of his adopted son, and when, after more intrigues and much discussion, Rusalá eventually left the valley, he marched off in a state of cheerful defiance, for, although abandoned by the priest, he had been openly acknowledged as the adopted son of that worthy, and in consequence there was a kind of special sanctity which clung to him, and his person was inviolate. A kind of poetic justice befell him. He had buried a considerable sum of my money in a stolen silk handkerchief at the foot of a tree on the road to the Kunar Valley when he first left me. Snow hid the spot and prevented his finding it when he went away for good. The treasure eventually became the property of a lucky Káfir, whose little son found the money, which had become exposed by field-rats digging up the handkerchief.

The total result of the Rusalá episode was unfortunate in every way. The Káfir appetite for unearned gains had been whetted. Ever afterwards they looked upon me as a person of extraordinary wealth, who could not possibly have brought so many rupees into the country for his own private use. A gradually increasing suspicion arose in the tribe that my own personal adherents gained much profit by my continued residence in Kámdesh, while the bulk of the Kám people derived no benefit from it whatever. The suspicion that a few favoured individuals received presents and money was quite unfounded, but it had the unpleasant effect of persuading my friends that they ought to receive what every one believed they actually were receiving. These growing feelings of suspicion on the part of some, that gifts were being distributed with partiality among a people claiming equal rights, and the impatience of others at finding themselves gradually incurring the dislike of their fellow-tribesmen without any compensating advantage in the way of increasing wealth, eventually led to my expulsion from the Kám Valley.   An entire reversal of my policy, the open giving of money to a limited number, a deliberate but straightforward attempt to create a party enthusiastic for my return, and another larger party hopeful of personal advantage by my being again among them, enabled me to get back again to Kámdesh after having been once expelled, although my return journey was naturally undertaken in circumstances of considerable difficulty and danger.   But this is anticipating.   The chief annoyances at the moment were, first, the envious, covetous eyes with which my visitors gazed always round my room ; and secondly, the impossibility of my entertaining my guests properly with tea, tobacco, sweetmeats, and so on, for Rusalá, taking advantage of my illness, had made unto himself friends of the mammon of unrighteousness, by distributing my little stock of luxuries with a carelessly lavish hand.   At the termination of the Rusalá episode it seemed advisable, on many grounds, for me to leave Kámdesh for a short period.   By removing to a warmer climate I could alone hope to regain my health and strength, while the somewhat unsatisfactory relations which still existed between the Káfirs and myself made it advisable that, for a time at least, we should not see too much of one another.

CHAPTER XVI

THE moment my intention of leaving Kámdesh was announced, the greatest opposition was aroused on the part of the people, and I was so absolutely boycotted, that no Kám man could be induced to accompany me, either as guide or escort. That nothing should prevent my carrying out my fixed resolve, we started down the Kámdesh hill through the deep snow, but were compelled, on account of my bad health, to halt for a few days in great discomfort at the village of Mergrom, which is a kind of city of refuge for those Káfirs and their direct descendants who have killed fellow-tribesmen, and who continue unable or unwilling to pay the necessary ransom for the shedding of blood.

From Mergrom a message was sent to Gul Muhammad Khan, the " 'verted " son of Torag Merak, who lived near Gourdesh. He came at once at my summons, bringing with him several hunting-dogs, and we went shooting together up the Charadgul Valley.

On the 30th of December a Kám friend of mine had caught me up. He was called by the appropriate name of Zanr (red) Malik ; he remarked that he had followed to help me secretly, but no one else was coming. The Kám people, however, when they perceived that they were out-manœuvred, hurried off two of their number to overtake me, and to offer all manner of excuses for leaving me to wander about the country alone, and then to try, on various pretexts, to persuade me to return to Kámdesh at once ; but I refused to listen to these messengers.

We got one or two markhor, and as we had run out of all supplies, we had to live exclusively on the flesh of that animal, while Gul Muhammad's servant, Yara, and one of my Baltis were away getting flour at Gourdesh. On the 2nd of January we moved our camp, the baggage going straight up the Charadgul Valley, while we proposed to shoot on the hills and meet it at the pshal (goat-pens, &c.) where we intended to camp. Gul Muhammad led the way with his dogs. Mir Alam followed behind. He was to have strapped my greatcoat on to his back, but forgot all about it. After a climb of three or four thousand feet the dogs were slipped, but the result was disappointing. We saw several markhor, but Gul Muhammad's dogs were wild and ill-trained, and separately hunted the animals in different directions. After an hour or so the dogs returned one by one, completely exhausted. We wandered about for a few hours aimlessly, when Gul Muhammad, pointing to a distant ridge, asked me to go and wait there for a time, when, if nothing happened, we were all to proceed to our new camp, the precise position of which he indicated in fluent Pashtu to Mir Alam, who declared, with characteristic "cock-sureness," that he fully understood, and could go there without a mistake. Pathans are scarcely less infallible than a last-joined Indian Civil Servant. It was now four o'clock, and we had a steep and difficult descent before us. Mir Alam at once came to grief, wounding his hand severely in the fall. We marched on confidently enough until it grew dark. It seemed we must have lost our way, but Mir Alam in a superior manner pointed to certain tracks in the snow which he identified as those of my dogs. He even particularised which man each dog was following. It seemed wonderfully clever, but at length the tracks ended in a clean sheet of snow, and it was clear we had been following old marks. Upon this, even Mir Alam had to acknowledge himself at fault. We were both very tired, the cold was intense, and, as bad fortune would have it, we had nothing with which we could light a fire to warm ourselves, and at the same time to signal our position to Gul Muhammad Khan, who would certainly be on the hills with a search party. I finally determined to follow the Charadgul stream down to our old camp, near which was a pshal, and to rest there for the night. We blundered in the dark down the bed of the stream, twisting our ankles in the crevices between the water-worn stones, and crossing and re-crossing and wading the stream fifty times, when once would have been sufficient had we only known the way, or had we been able to see

IN THE PSHAL.

To face page 261.

our path. In the end, all out, as the phrase goes, we arrived at the place we had quitted in the morning, and soon found the pshal. The Káfirs were immensely surprised, but received us with hospitality. We had little to say in reply to their many questions, we were so hungry, cold, and fatigued. The pshal was of the regulation size, about twenty feet square, and was strongly built in the usual Káfir method. It contained over a hundred goats, many kids, four men, and two girl-wives, thirteen or fourteen years old. In the corner blazed a huge fire, in front of which a youth sat superintending the cooking of some markhor meat in a big earthen pot with a small mouth. He was attired in a too abbreviated goat-skin. In his hand he had a wooden cup with a handle a foot long. The bowl of the implement was too large to be of any real service in skimming the boiling fluid, but the boy worked away at his task as if he were employed most usefully. He possessed an abominably shrill voice, which lacerated one's exhausted nerves. There was a small door-shaped window near the fire, but this was only opened when drinking-water was required from a vessel placed to keep cool on a shelf outside. Watching the cooking and offering occasional remarks, were the rest of the company. I was given a block of wood to sit upon, and supplied with some delicious goat's milk, while one of the Káfirs produced from a bag something which looked like a stone, but which turned out to be a kind of bread. The bleating and familiarity of the goats, the cries of the kids from their little enclosed platform, the piercing voice of the cook, in addition to the general smell of ordure and the closeness of the atmosphere, counted for nothing against the delightful warmth and the pleasure of stretching out one's wearied limbs to the cheerful blaze. I soon slid off my block of wood and lounged on the ground. Dinner was served soon after we entered. Chappaties were handed round and eaten heartily; then, when the bread was all finished, the meat was found to be sufficiently cooked. It was served out in large fragments, one piece being with much care selected for me. It was extremely tender and seemed delicious, although I ordinarily abhor the flesh of the markhor.

After general conversation, the two little wives, who had been yawning frankly for some time, prepared for bed. Just behind me was a platform, about nine feet long by six feet broad, and three feet from the ground. It was made of light branches, sufficiently elastic to vibrate under a man's weight on mounting it. This was the common couch. I was invited to follow the girls, but in a dubious way, as though my hosts were prepared for my excuses. I expressed my preference for remaining by the fire. All the men then prepared for rest by loosening their not very well secured garments and by shaking themselves, and all climbed on to the platform. I was about to lie down in a brown Chitráli robe, which the owner of the pshal perceiving, he jumped down and put the garment aside with an authoritative, peremptory gesture. He dragged out of some recess a fine black bearskin, and spread it for me with the air of a man who knows how to entertain a guest. I suffered horrible tribulation for a fortnight afterwards on account of that bearskin. My head hardly touched my pillow, the wooden block before mentioned, before I was sound asleep, nor could the goats, many of whom seemed to be asthmatical, with all their nibbling at my back and hair, prevent my sleeping as soundly and peacefully as a baby. But about four o'clock Gul Muhammad and Red Malik arrived, and roused us all up to tell us their adventures in search of me. The boy with the dreadful voice placed himself directly behind me, and proved unhappily to be a humourist, for his remarks were received with general laughter by the company. He told the story of my having been robbed by Rusalá with great gusto, and looked to poor Mir Alam to corroborate the details. The money actually stolen had become greatly magnified, and both hands and feet were required to show its amount in scores of rupees. There was no more sleep possible save an occasional dose. At seven o'clock the ceremony of sweeping the pshal floor was enacted, and the huge, reddish-brown heap of manure outside was perceptibly increased.

Then we started to find our camp, which was accomplished in less than two hours' time. It was so carefully hidden up a ravine, suitable for a stage brigand, that I might have wandered about for a week without discovering its position. I had, in fact, passed the narrow chink between rocks, a mere water cutting, without suspecting that there was room beyond for a pshal. The next day we went on another markhor hunt with dogs, and I was soon convinced that the sport is by no means so easy as it is supposed. Afterwards I found it preferable to stalk them in the usual way. We first climbed up two or three thousand feet, when the dogs were slipped. We raced after them over most terribly difficult ground for probably a couple of miles, when we found a markhor standing at bay on a difficult, smooth, sloping slab of rock, upon which the dogs could find no foothold. The quarry was guarded above and below and on both sides by dogs. We approached very cautiously, for the sight of a man deprives a markhor of all fear of dogs. When near enough for Gul Muhammad to begin his careful preparations for taking aim, and at the same time to run no risk of wasting a cartridge, one of the dogs, a callow brute, ran to greet us, wagging his tail. In an instant the markhor jumped away, darted past us, and made for the place whence we had started. We again followed, but the pace we went over the frightful ground was too much for me, and about half way I was lying prone, wondering if my breath would ever return. Subsequently from a spur I saw the markhor again brought to a standstill by the dogs, and watched a Káfir miss it with his matchlock at less than twenty paces, and so let the animal escape. However, the valley swarmed with game, and with hunters also. On that day we saw four sets of dogs, belonging to four different hunting parties, chasing markhor at the same time. A small party of Kashtán men at one camp had killed twenty-three markhor in ten days. Our average was one or two a day. As the creatures are shot for food, male and female are almost equally esteemed, except that the former, being larger, are on that account more highly prized. A goat markhor is really, to my taste, most unpleasant, so I shot always at females for the pot. The Káfirs were delighted with the execution of my express rifle, and would rush forward in great glee, shouting "tum-bah" in imitation of the sound of the rifle, to carry away a slain animal.

In the spring large numbers of markhor are caught on
the snow behind Kámdesh on their way up the valley;
but the supply seems practically inexhaustible, though
probably in consequence of the harrying the animals get
with dogs, and when they are blundering through deep
snow, there are few large heavy animals. The biggest
horns I saw were but forty inches in length.

At my second camp in the Charadgul my tent was
pitched on the top of the pshal, that being the only level
place anywhere about. All except myself retired into
the pshal at night, and enjoyed themselves greatly. They
sang a monotonous chant which acted as a lullaby upon
me for a time, and then towards dawn kept me wide
awake. It had a curious refrain, which I in vain tried to
catch. They said it was a Wai song, but it seemed to me
very like that the Presungulis sang in Kámdesh.

Our first march from the Charadgul was to the village
of Birkot, just below and on the opposite side of the
river to Arandú. Birkot is one of the so-called "Gabar"
villages of this particular part of the Kunar Valley, which
is called Nursut by the Chitráli, and Satrgrom by the
Káfirs. These Gabars are all Musalmáns of the Sunni
sect. They have a particular language of their own, and
are believed to have anciently been Fire-worshippers.
The Ramgul Káfirs are also spoken of as Gabars or
"Gabariks," but of course they have no relationship with
the Gabars of the Kunar Valley.

Birkot is on the right bank of the Bashgul river, and
two hundred feet above its stream. It is built in the
form of a square, which also answers the purpose of
a fortification, as there are no external windows. At
one or two positions, where houses are absent, a wall

fills up the vacant space, a rimmed parapet between six and eight feet high surmounting the conjoined roofs. The centre of the village is a filthy open spot, a farm-yard, in fact. From it narrow lanes run, just wide enough for a man or a cow to pass along to the houses they seem to share in common. So contracted are these lanes, that they present no difficulty to people walking, as they always do walk, on the house-tops. Birkot has a tower twenty feet high at the south-west corner. The village altogether contains no more than twenty domiciles. We entered by climbing a practicable breach in the parapet and on to the roofs, in preference to using the doorway on the east or river side, which opened into the accumulated filth and mud of ages. Most of the houses have man-holes, through which the people, on the roofs, can dive into the interiors, unless they prefer to drop down into the narrow lanes in front of the door they desire to reach.

The Gabar has no very distinctive appearance, except that one occasionally sees a face like that of a panto-mime Jew. There are one or two fair-visaged, well-looking men belonging to the better class, who would compare on equal terms with the similar class in Chitrál; they, however, are the exception. The re-mainder, both high and low, seem no better than the poor cultivator class in other parts of the Mehtar's dominions, and have a singularly furtive and mean look and manner. The women have a much better appear-ance. They dress in loose blue garments, which fall naturally into graceful folds. The head is covered with a blue skull-cap from which escape long plaits of hair, one over each shoulder, and two hanging down behind.

White metal or bead neck and wrist ornaments contrast well with the dark blue material of their clothes. At a short distance these women are pleasing and picturesque. Here, and at Arandú across the river, there is much cultivable land, which at this time of the year is simply a bog.

Arandú, or Arnú, or Arnui, is a large and important village, nearly opposite where the Bashgul torrent joins the Kunar river. It has some two hundred habitations. There is no attempt at fortification, and it may be considered a semi-defensible place on account of its position. It is remarkable as being the only Gabar village which is not built on the plan of Birkot. After visiting Arandú, I got back to Birkot over the delightfully easy rope-bridge, which even my dogs could trot over, just in time for the inevitable Káfir quarrel. An official of the Mehtar of Chitrál, of good position, came to see me with his son, to offer me every assistance in his power. He promised to take me to Nári the next day, or wherever else I desired to travel; but half-an-hour later his amiable intentions were completely changed. His small son came to loggerheads with the son of a Káfir we met in Birkot named Dach (Slender) Shyok. The two boys were proceeding to settle their differences with sticks, when Dach Shyok must needs rush in and drag the Chitráli boy all about the filthy passages where the quarrel occurred, by the hair of his head. The boy's father naturally went to his assistance, when Dach Shyok drew his dagger, and things looked bad. However, Lutkám Chandlu Merak, one of the Kám men sent to get me to return to Kámdesh, jumped down from a roof and seized Shyok, upbraiding him severely for his ill-behaviour. Matters at length appeared to be amicably settled; but the Chitráli official came and announced that he would not go to Nári or anywhere else with me, and that he intended to start for Chitrál forthwith. He did not trouble himself to behave respectfully in my presence, and there was little doubt that Lutkám Chandlu Merak, taking advantage of the obligation the man was under to him, had been practising his Káfir arts upon him in the hope of preventing my going down to Nári the following day. The following morning we marched to Nári. The Káfirs all the time gave me great trouble, and succeeded in weaving round me such a mesh of falsehood, that to this day it is impossible to say whether it was true that thirty Shál men hurried up the valley in the hope of firing a volley into my tent at night, but only reached Nári the day after we left it on the return journey. Even if the story were true, and the Shál men had arrived at Nári a day or two earlier, they would still have been doomed to disappointment, for although my tent was temptingly exposed on the camping-place formed by the contiguous house-tops of the fortified village, we were all securely and comfortably ensconced within good walls, whence we could observe whatever was going on. Nári was, moreover, so full of Káfirs that the Shál men could only have fired at my tent from a distance, and must have then decamped as quickly as possible.

The people of Nári, on this, my first visit, behaved very badly. The Malik, or headman, on our arrival came with an angry-faced crowd to watch our proceedings. He refused to afford us any help or to sell any supplies, and shouted out insolently, " Who is this Frank? What

does he want here?" He was told that the Frank was
a friend of the Mehtar of Chitrál, his sovereign, and
that he claimed hospitality in the ·name of that prince.
On hearing this, the Malik violently exclaimed that he
was a subject of no prince, and had but one superior,
Heaven. We finally got the food we wanted through
Gul Muhammad Khan, while some men with a Káká
Khel caravan, on learning that a year or two previously
I had been kind to a certain Mián well known in Chitrál,
and a relative of several of those present, crowded round
me with offers of friendship and help. Various Chitráli
officials, who had joined me on the march, were ostentatiously helpless.

All along there had been a suspicion that the Malik was
not only playing a part, but was playing it badly; nevertheless, he and his followers were rapidly becoming an
intolerable nuisance, while there is always a danger in permitting oneself to be openly bullied. So a little plan was
arranged to bring matters to an issue which it seemed
could not be other than favourable to me. On the following morning, therefore, observing the Malik approach
in an exaggerated blustering manner, my Pathan servant,
who was on guard over my tent, received a prearranged
signal, while I turned my back, ostensibly to talk to some
Káfirs. The Malik swaggered up to the tent and expressed his intention of going into it. The delighted
Pathan, in the most insinuating manner, politely assured
him he must not do so, and when the Malik persisted in
opening the hangings of the tent, the Pathan, suddenly
changing from suavity and gentleness to ferocity, hit him
cleverly between the eyes and knocked him over on his
back. The Malik was at once cowed, and hurried off

P

weeping and explaining in a deprecating way, to any one
who would listen to him, that he was merely going to
look into my tent, and nothing more. Most carefully
watching what was going on, but seeing that it was unnecessary for me to interfere, I pretended to know nothing
of what had occurred, until the headmen of the Káká
Khels came and told me of it. The Malik was then at
once summoned and talked to seriously about his behaviour. He was then forgiven all past offences, at
the same time that he was warned to be careful of his
conduct in the future. Two or three Káfirs who were
standing by then asked him threateningly what he
wanted interfering with my tent. The poor Malik was so
terribly nonplussed at hearing this, that there was little
doubt left in my mind that he had been instigated to
annoy me by the Káfirs themselves, in order to prevent
me from prolonging my stay in Narsut, and to compel me
to hurry back to Kámdesh. However that may be, our
late turbulent host became at once extremely civil, not to
say servile, and almost enthusiastic in his helpfulness.
We met several times afterwards, and were always very
good friends.

Nári is a Gabar village on the left bank of the Kunar
river. It contains a hundred houses, and is built on the
same plan as Birkot, except that the lanes between the
houses are broader, and require rough bridges of boughs
across them. As the important Gicha festival was approaching, we left Birkot on our return journey to Kámdesh on the 14th of January, and the next day reached
Mergrom. On the road rain fell in torrents, drenching
us to the skin. The Baltis trudged along bravely. We
were delighted when the abominable wooden bridge

THE PATHAN AND THE MALIK.

To face page 270.

which there spans the Bashgul river at Mergrom came in sight. Our pleasure was effectually lowered, however, when we heard that—thanks to the inoculating which had been carried out there—no single house in the village was without one or more people suffering from small-pox. The rain had now turned into snow, and we were in a sad plight. The tent was put up, but the heavy snow soon knocked it down again. At this juncture I inquired if there were no stable we could take shelter in. A little reflection told the bystanders there was such a place. On going to inspect it, we found the most delight-fully dirty cow-stable it is possible to imagine. Two men and one woman slept with the cows, so in one corner there was a lively fire, in front of which several big calves were standing warming their tails in a comically human way. We all crowded together round the fire, thankful for the heat and shelter. Soon a mighty steam from wet garments arose, which added another poignant odour to the many others in the place; but we were all happy and contented. We made our arrangements for the night. I vacated my place at the fire, and occupied, with my bed, a distant corner of the stable. The com-plaining calves were driven behind a barrier which ran down the centre of the building. The top of this barrier was surmounted by a long hewn plank about a foot broad, upon which the cow-keepers slept. I imagine that no one but a Káfir would have selected such a sleeping-place, where the slightest movement might result in a bad fall. Partly by persuasion, and partly by keeping our backs against the door, we managed to exclude the female human element. She went off indignantly to some other house. Then all was peace. In the morning

our stable was invaded to overflowing by inquisitive villagers, until it was almost impossible to move. One
youth stared at me fixedly and stolidly for at least an
hour. At length I stared at him unblinkingly until
he was compelled to alter the direction of his eyes. In
reply to my question why they continued to stare at
me so intently after they had had sufficient time to learn
and remember my features, a Mergrom man promptly
and politely assured me that it was because they considered me a very good man ; they never permitted themselves to see the faces of those they thought wicked, but
upon the good they could not gaze too long.

The terrible bridge was hidden in deep snow, which
had to be cut away before we could cross. We all got
over safely enough, but two of the Baltis had to be helped,
besides having their loads carried for them. The march
up the Kámdesh hill was extremely arduous for the poor
Baltis. They kept slipping off the narrow hardened track
which ran between snow-walls breast-high, and each
slip meant disappearance in the soft snow, and a great
hauling and pulling to get them on to the path again. They
were, however, very pleased at getting home once more,
and they persevered like heroes. We reached Kámdesh
about three in the afternoon, wet through and steaming,
as it had begun to snow heavily again. The Káfirs had
their oldest inhabitant brought to assure me that never
within his memory had there been such a terrible winter.
The toothless old creature was full of senile cheerfulness,
and mighty proud of being called upon to relate his experiences. We found we had arrived in time for the
Gicha festival. During my absence Torag Merak had
lost a little son. He was really in the greatest distress,

BALTIS IN THE SNOW.

To face page 274.

but nevertheless he sent over word to say, that when such events happened, "brothers" were expected to bring over a goat and pay a visit of condolence. Having no flocks, I compounded for the ceremony by a money payment, which, with my excuses, was very kindly accepted.

After my return to Kámdesh, I noticed that the common people of the village were much less cordial in their manner, while several headmen, notably the priest, made various determined but unsuccessful efforts to over-awe me.

About the same time also the Mehtar of Chitrál recommenced his intrigues, but he worked so clumsily, that although he undoubtedly increased the general distrust of my intentions, yet he contrived at the same time to awaken the suspicions of the Káfirs against himself; so that at length it came to be generally believed that the Mehtar wanted me to be killed or badly injured, so that he might have a pretext for invading the Bashgul Valley, with the help of the Government of India. It is possible that he had some such design in his head at this time, but Colonel Durand at Gilgit seemed to have some pre-science of my position, for about this period he wrote one or two firmly worded letters to the Mehtar, which caused him to pause and reconsider the matter. At any rate, shortly after receiving them the Mehtar changed his plans altogether, and his sole remaining desire was to get me out of the Káfir country as safely and as quickly as possible. This sudden change of front from bribing men to do me injury, to impressing nervously on the same men the absolute importance that no harm should happen to me, bewildered his hearers. They whipped round also, and to many my remaining in Kámdesh now seemed a

matter of vital importance ; not because they believed in
the honesty of my intentions more than they did before,
but because they believed the Mehtar had been warned
from Gilgit not to do anything which might endanger my
personal safety, and on no account to attack the Káfirs
until after my departure from the country.   Consequently
the headmen thought that the date of my leaving Káfiristán might be the signal for a Chitráli invasion of the
lower Bashgul Valley.   My short journeys were in each
instance believed by many to be my actual departure from
the valley, although the majority of the people trusted
my word, and raised only a tacit resistance each time to
my leaving the village.   They all, friends and opponents
alike, always seemed greatly relieved at my return.

On the 14th of January it was seriously debated
whether it would not be advisable for the Kám to
keep me a strict prisoner for at least three years.   It
was argued that by so doing the tribe would not only
secure a valuable hostage, but would also be in a position
to apply the screw, and compel me to send to India for
rifles, or whatever else the Káfirs wanted.   This last consideration had a great hold on the national conservative
instincts of several of the headmen.   News of what was
going on was brought to me.   Although pretending to
laugh it to scorn, it was, at the same time, necessary for
me to take the precaution of sending for the instigators
of the notable scheme, to talk it over seriously with such
as answered my summons.   After reminding them of the
sacred rights of hospitality, after instancing once more the
way in which Shermalik had been treated in India, and
after assuring them yet again that whenever I left Kámdesh it would be openly, in broad daylight, and never

as a thief or a prowling animal, I finally disclaimed all intention of going away in the spring, and challenged any one present to say that he doubted my word. Thereupon every one gave me his assurance that he believed me implicitly. At the termination of all these interviews, my guests invariably parted from me with cordial expressions of friendship.

After a few days the clouds appeared to be slowly drifting away, when a formidable intriguer appeared on the scene in the form of Mián Gul of Mirkani and Arandú, the man who once caused me so much anxiety about Shermalik at Srinagar. This individual, as already mentioned, had met me in Chitrál, with some kerosene oil he had brought, at my request, from Peshawar. He had been most liberally recompensed, and was also given a monthly salary for acting as my nominal agent in the Kunar Valley; but Rusalá had excited him greatly by untrue stories of the enormous wages my servants received, until Mián Gul became firmly convinced that he himself was most badly treated, because he only received a certain number of rupees a month for doing little or nothing. He always maintained that, because he had carried information to the Peshawar missionaries about the Káfir tribes, he held the gates of the Bashgul Valley, as he phrased it. Sincerely believing himself to be a thoroughly ill-used man, he became an active intriguer against me, and attached many of the Kámdesh headmen to him by promising them a large share of the money he intended to force me to pay—for his avowed object to his friends was simply to blackmail me. His tactics were so similar to those employed by Rusalá, that the inference that he inspired the latter is almost irresistible. Mián Gul was an abler man than Rusalá, but resembled him in the fact that he was wanting in real pluck. He began craftily, and there was no indication of what was going on until it was discovered that some letters of mine, given a month previously to Mián Gul to send to Peshawar, had never been taken farther than Mirkani, at the mouth of the Ashrath Valley, where they were detained in his house. Unfortunately, this man always had some personal fear of me ever since an interview we had together in Srinagar, on which occasion it had been necessary for me to speak my mind to him freely, so that when he came to Kámdesh to press his imaginary claims, he opened his attack through certain of his Káfir wife's relations and through his own personal friends, instead of coming straight to me to tell his grievances, and in doing so give me the opportunity of explaining matters to him. Every one in the village knew what was being attempted, and eagerly awaited the result of this flagrant attempt at blackmailing. It was announced that my letters for the time being must remain where they were, and it was plainly hinted that Mián Gul must be propitiated. To this undisguised attempt at bullying my reply was that unless the letters, which by tacit agreement were made a test question, were produced on a particular day, Mián Gul must consider himself as dismissed from my service, and would never be employed by me again in any circumstances. It was added that no excuses of any kind would be accepted ; that my determination to dismiss Mián Gul if the letters were not produced at the time mentioned was fixed and unalterable, no matter what happened—sickness, falls of snow, or anything else. The letters were not produced, and Mián

Gul was formally dismissed. A deputation of headmen at once waited upon me to ask, or rather demand, that Mián Gul should be reinstated in his old position. I declined to comply with this request, giving my reasons in full. Then we had a very bad time indeed. The air was full of threats. Every single headman of any importance in the tribe had attached himself to Mián Gul's cause, and every kind of menace was conveyed to me, often by very circuitous roads. Shermalik became thoroughly frightened, and with tears implored me to leave the valley secretly and at once, before worse befell me. He said he had made his own arrangements to go away also, for he had now become so obnoxious to the tribe from his connection with me, that it was no longer safe for him to remain in the valley; but there was nothing for it but to remain firm and pretend to ignore the possibility of any danger.

For several days no Káfir came near my house. We were regularly boycotted. Then, on January 23, I was summoned to Torag Merak's house to meet, or one might more truly say to appear before, the chief headmen, who were assembled there. This was the first time such a request had ever been made to me, for it had been the invariable rule for a deputation of Jast to wait upon me whenever there was anything for us to discuss together; but as it would not have been safe to refuse to go, and as my chief anxiety was to get at once into close contact with my opponents, I waived all ceremony and started as soon as the summons from the headmen was delivered to me.

On my arrival, the most important of the Jast were already collected together in Torag Merak's house, and

Mián Gul was lying half concealed upon the roof close to the smoke-hole, from which position he could see and hear all that went on below. On entering the room where the Jast were collected, I affected cordiality, and tried to appear unconcerned and genial, and partook of a meal which was in progress. As soon as the eating was finished, the Káfir batteries were opened on me. Cajolery, arguments, threats, all were in turn employed. They told me of the danger involved in disobeying the orders of the Jast, the mildest of which, it was explained, comprised the burning of the delinquent's house and the plundering of his goods and chattels. To this my answer was, that it was most right and proper that the authority of the headmen should be strictly maintained, and this led me to remark on the different customs among Englishmen and Káfirs, and to explain how remarkably law-abiding the men of my race were ; but I refused to accept any suggestions which tended to support the idea that I, a guest, must necessarily submit my strictly private affairs to the authority of the Jast. My contention was that as Mián Gul was my servant, paid with my money, my right to dismiss him if he failed in his duty to me was un-doubted ; that he had so failed, and that consequently he had been dismissed. I added that my decision on that point was irrevocable. Torag Merak then got very ex-cited and abusive, but I particularly noticed that Dán Malik, Lame Astán, and the others, tried persuasive methods only, after the failure of their attempts at coer-cion. After about three hours' incessant talk the Káfirs got exhausted and bored to death. Observing this, and assuming a rage I was far from feeling, I sprang to my feet, declaiming against Mián Gul, his treachery and disloyalty, and concluded by stating positively that nothing on earth would move me from my position, nor would my gaze ever willingly fall on the face of such a rascal again. Torag Merak came in for a share of my invective also, in that he, my brother, had openly sided against me. The headmen present looked at first doubtful, then surprised, and finally they applauded, while my interpreters had their work cut out to follow my rapid speech; but my gestures no doubt helped my hearers to understand my meaning. The victory so obviously remained with me, that Mián Gul sent down word from the roof that he would accept my decision if he were paid a preposterous sum of rupees, which he declared was still due to him. Even the Káfirs shouted with laughter at this impudent demand, while, taking advantage of their humour, I brandished my stick and threatened Mián Gul with all sorts of calamities in English, which, though not understood, was evidently accepted as the outpourings of natural indignation. This was practically the end of what at one time promised to be a troublesome if not dangerous business. The Káfirs became most friendly again, as was shown by their once more urging me to marry and settle down amongst them for good. In the evening Utah came to my house to make a last appeal for Mián Gul, so that he should leave no stone unturned in getting some of the promised presents out of him. Utah's request had also to be refused. It appeared from his remarks that he had purposely abstained from being present at the meeting at Torag Merak's house, because, he said, he was sure the Jast would be defeated, and he could not bear to witness such a dreadful sight. From this observation it seems possible that the Káfirs had only been playing a game of bluff with me all through. If so, it must be confessed that they were extremely good actors. Following up the advantage gained over Mián Gul, I next insisted on my letters being given up forthwith. They were eventually brought to me by that worthy, who then received his arrears of pay up to the time he was dismissed from my service. He returned to the valley only once during my residence there. He continued his intrigues, but the failure of his direct attempt at blackmailing had discredited him to a great extent in the eyes of the Kám, who formerly looked upon him as a man of almost superhuman wisdom. He still remained a thorn in my side, but not a very painful one. On one occasion active steps had to be taken by me to prevent his being murdered by an over-zealous partisan of mine. To the end, he chiefly worried me by his persistent statement to Káfirs that he knew for a fact that the Government of India had entrusted me with many valuable presents for the Káfirs, which I was engaged in "eating" myself instead of handing over to their legitimate recipients; but he at the same time started a second report, that I was a "small" person, of no importance in my own country, the robbery or murder of whom would be allowed to pass unnoticed. In his anger he thus made conflicting statements about me, which made it easy to turn the tables on him, and laughingly ask my hearers if a "small" person, such as Mián Gul described me to be, was likely to be entrusted by the Government of India with the presents he mentioned. It was, indeed, an easy matter to make the Káfirs perceive the glaring discrepancies of Mián Gul's story, provided that my audience was in a sufficiently cool and reasoning humour.

However, it seemed advisable to get away from Kámdesh again for a few days, to allow angry feelings to cool.
So we moved camp, and crossed the river to take up our
abode for ten days at Agatsi, immediately opposite Kámdesh, in a pshal belonging to Málkán, a headman of the
upper village.

CHAPTER XVII

The narrative continued—Difficulty to obtain service of Káfirs—Lutkár—
Road to Agatsi—Bridge—Cool reception at Agatsi—Misery of life in a
"pshal"—Lutkár's love story—Utah's apotheosis as one of the Jast—
Improving relations with the Káfirs—Sayed Shah's defection—His de-
parture for India—Kila Drosh—Shah-i-Mulk's proposed fort at Narsut
—Straits for food—Second visit to the Kunar Valley—Chitralí escort—
Riot at Arandú—The "bloodshed" season — Umrá Khan of Jandúl—
Káfir discontent with the Mehtar of Chitrál—Schemes of Mír Ján—Dis-
putes between the Chitrális and the Káfirs reach an acute stage—The
Mehtar's ultimatum—My journey to Lutdeh—Pleasant welcome.

I HAD not yet become convinced of the utter hopelessness
of attempting to get a Káfir to accept regular service in
his own country. Many disappointments had not deterred
me from making further attempts. My last experiment
was with a youth named Lutkár, an adopted son of Kán
Márá, the chief of the Bashgul Katirs. This young man
was smart and active, and gifted with a quick intelligence. He now accompanied me to Agatsi on a regular
monthly wage as my servant, really as a kind of companion. Agatsi is a tiny settlement of Káfirs of the Bilez-
hedári clan converted to Islám. The road from Kámdesh
is a steep descent of two thousand feet to the river, and,
thence over a bridge universally admitted to be an admirable specimen of Káfir engineering. The centre trough
part is, however, only nineteen inches broad, with parapets
eight inches high. The stanchions which lead up to this
portion, which is actually over the water, stop abruptly
where they are most wanted, so that it is necessary to
cross with the utmost care and exactitude. Snow lay

thick on the roadway of the bridge, while all recent travellers had stepped exactly in each other's footsteps, which looked as if made by one Colossus. The problem was, how to get over this narrow, slippery track without allowing the roar of the river, thirty feet below, to interfere with the even balance of one's mind—and body. Of a group of girls carrying wood on the opposite bank, one found her nerves unequal to the strain; upon which Lutkár handed her over with polite dignity. Her stronger-minded companions were so much amused at this scene that it suggested a doubt whether the young woman's fears were as bad as she made them appear.

Our reception at Agatsi was certainly wanting in cordiality. As we approached Málkán's pshal, the owner of which, Káfir-like, had not troubled to keep his promise to accompany me, an old man emerged from the adjacent hamlet, and in a loud voice wanted to know why the Frank had been brought there, and observed that, under the instructions of his spiritual guide, he must not look on the face of a Frank Káfir—the very worst of all infidels. My companions retorted by asking him if he were a dog that he barked so at the approach of strangers. Then Málkán's own nephew, a man called Gazab Shah, came to make sulky complaints about my arrival. By this time I was neither cheerful nor good-tempered, and I retorted by using some of the less-prized phrases of my own vernacular with considerable effect; for Gazab Shah immediately asked angrily why I was angry? Was he not Málkán's own nephew, and quite ready to bring me milk, firewood, everything which might be required? He was even prepared to sell me an emaciated goat at the price of three healthy animals. In the end, we became good friends by my giving a great feast to everybody, and by my showing how profitable my visit could be made for the people of Agatsi.

The misery of life in the pshal was great. It was hardly any protection against the rain, sleet, and snow which fell incessantly. The floor of the building had to be traversed on stepping-stones, while even under the driest part of the roof it was impossible to keep one's bed from getting wet. All Málkán's goats had died, so there were no animals to crowd on to the roof to harden the earth by their incessant movements. The only compensation for all the discomfort we had to undergo was the enormous number of magnificent pheasants and chikor (red-legged partridges), which swarmed everywhere. There were plenty of markhor also, but owing to the snow on the rocks they were inaccessible. After one attempt to reach them we had the greatest difficulty in climbing back again to our camp, and did not succeed without one or two awkward falls.

One morning at Agatsi I found, on returning from getting some chikor, a fine handsome-featured woman, whose appearance was marred by small-pox, seated on a stool on the exact spot where I wanted to change my sopping clothes. Behind her, in a modest attitude, stood my new servant Lutkár. The latter at once advanced, and having used all his persuasions in vain to induce me to adopt him as my son, sent away the woman and poured out his sorrow. It appeared that Kán Márá, his adopted father, had provided him with a wife; but his heart was not with the damsel, and was faithful to the woman who had just gone away; so he had left Bragamatál, and now lived anyhow in Kámdesh, so as to be near the object of his affections. She, unhappily, was in the power of Chandlu Astán, the famous Jast of the Utahdari clan, because her father had died in his debt, and she was the pledge or security for the payment of the money. Chandlu Astán would not allow Lutkár to take away the woman until he had paid the whole sum due upon her; an impossible condition, for Lutkár was poor. The lovers had made up their minds to run away together to Chitrál, and the idea was that if I adopted Lutkár as my son, they might be safe from Chándlu Astán's vengeance. The sequel of the story may be here related. Lutkár went to Mehtar Jao Ghulám at Aiún, and became a Musalmán. He then returned and ran away with the young woman, and after that deed dare not show his face again in Kámdesh country; but in the Katir country we met again. He was then the strictest of strict Musalmáns in all the ceremonials connected with the killing of animals, but had not learned the customary prayers. He was full of the kindness which had been shown him by the Chitráli prince, and especially delighted in referring to a beautiful pair of trousers which his wife had received from that magnate; for this not only showed how favoured they had been, but explained, without further words, that the woman had turned Musalmán also. At a still later interview I found that Lutkár, in spite of the protection he had received at Aiún, and the high favour in which he stood with Mehtar Jao Ghulám, had been obliged to make peace, and, with the help of his patron, had paid Chandlu Astán everything the latter demanded. This is only one of many instances of the caution displayed by Chitrális of even the highest rank in doing nothing to incur the resentment of headmen in Káfiristán.

Q

Lutkár, having finished his story at Agatsi, remarked that his personal devotion to me was so great, that while I remained in the country he intended never to leave me, for he delighted in being my servant. Two days later, after wasting many of my precious cartridges in missing sitting birds, he got thoroughly bored, and left me without a word. This had been the result of all my former attempts to get Káfirs to remain in my service, and was obviously a national characteristic; so I made no more efforts in that direction.

The 3rd of February was the Viron festival, but the snow was so heavy that we did not attempt to climb the Kámdesh hill for the occasion; but on the 11th, in reply to most urgent messages, we all went up to help at Utah's apotheosis as one of the Jast. On the way to my house we rested for a time at Utah's house, and admired the garments which were being got ready for the great man to wear in the evening. It was then suggested to me that it was the privilege of a brother on such occasions to provide a "kullah," a peaked Afghan cap. This was, particularly insisted upon by Shahru, the soothsayer, but the only article of the kind which could be produced belonged to my servant Mír Alam, from whom I purchased it. It was sent down to Utah, who was delighted until he heard how much Mír Alam had received for it, when he returned the cap, declaring it was not suitable for his purpose. It seems that, handsome as he thought the head-dress, he yet thought it more desirable to get the somewhat heavy price I had given for it than to possess the article itself. He came over to partake of tea at five o'clock, but rushed off in a hurry to dress, although his entertainment did not begin till eight o'clock. About that time his son-in-law, Nílíra, came for me with an urgent request that for this occasion I would wear my best clothes. Accordingly, in the admired black suit, a striped flannel shirt, and a kháki-coloured turban, I went to witness the strange ceremony.

During the months of March and April 1891, my relations with the Káfirs continued steadily to improve. The spring festivals kept them fairly employed, and although the populous upper village left me rather severely alone, there were no more individual attempts to worry me. Of course there were various small unpleasantnesses to be undergone. The Káfirs, for instance, were unremitting in their endeavours to corrupt the loyalty of my followers, and their efforts were not without some measure of success, except in the case of the Baltis, whose unswerving fidelity neither threats nor promises could affect in any way. Sayed Shah did succumb to these sinister influences. He maintained close friendly relations with Mián Gul, and caused me considerable annoyance. He became very ill, and from the date of his recovery, gradually detaching himself from me, fell completely into the hands of Mián Gul and the intriguing Káfirs. He then became frightened out of his wits at his new friends, and secretly left the house of the chief man of Kamu, with whom he was staying for the benefit of his health, the climate of that village being considerably warmer than that of Kámdesh. He was at once followed, and, as if he had been a prisoner instead of a guest, was severely beaten and robbed. My influence, however, was sufficient to enable me to recover all the stolen property. Shortly afterwards Sayed Shah was sent off to India. He had proved in the end a bad bargain. His natural timidity had increased with age, and he fell an easy prey to the intriguers by whom he was surrounded. As he invariably refused to accompany me on any of my short .journeys, declaring that he was too old and too unwell to leave Kámdesh, there was small opportunity of my exerting continuous personal influence over him.

While on a short visit to Shah-i-Mulk at Kila Drosh, I discovered that that prince, with the full consent of his father, the Mehtar, was desirous of erecting a fort at the village of Nári or Narsut. He asked me to select an appropriate site for the building, and to perform what is the Chitráli equivalent to laying the foundation-stone. The Mehtar's object was to create a general impression amongst the surrounding tribes that the proposed fort was being built by order of the Government of India. This compelled me to excuse myself, as politely as possible, from doing as was wished, and necessitated my hurrying back to Kámdesh to be relieved from further importunities on the subject. During the short stay in the Kunar Valley we ran short of supplies on more than one occasion. Once, on the way to Kila Drosh from Arandú, being entirely without food and almost starving, we were compelled to take by force a goat which the owner refused to sell me out of his flock. He was a fanatical-looking Musalmán, who admitted he was a subject of Shah-i-Mulk. The incident was unpleasant, but happily it was also unique. We were at the time in very great straits. The man was eventually told that the whole circumstances of the case should be related to Shah-i-Mulk, and the value of the goat paid over to that prince. On hearing this, he expressed a wish that the money should be paid into his own hand. He was accordingly given the price of the animal with a small addition, as compensation for a buffet he had invited and had received. We left him apparently quite contented. His refusal to supply me with food was dictated by pure churlishness, and because he considered me a Káfir of the worst type. This was the only instance of the kind which occurred during my stay in these regions.

In April I paid another visit to the Kunar Valley, going as far down it as Upper Bailám. A Chitráli guard accompanied me, in addition to my own Káfir escort. The Chitráli soldiers were a company of the regular troops which the Mehtar was at that time forming. It was a custom of this guard to stand round me with fixed bayonets whenever we rested, even for an instant, guarding my person with unnatural alertness until they became wearied of the occupation, when they one and all would march off and leave me. During one of the many intervals in this spasmodic vigilance, a somewhat serious disturbance broke out between the inhabitants of Arandú and my followers. The villagers used as missiles the smooth water-worn stones which they keep ready on the house-tops for such purposes. We all had to turn out and fight, until the lagging Chitráli guard came to our help. There were a good many bruises and contusions, but no one' was seriously hurt. After the tumult was suppressed, the leaders of the disturbance were bound and delivered over to me for punishment, it being carefully explained that they might be dealt with in whatever manner seemed proper in my eyes. An inquiry, however, elicited the unpleasant fact that the quarrel had been undoubtedly caused by the high-handed behaviour of my own Pathan servant. The prisoners were, therefore, at once released, and the Pathan, who had suffered rather severely in the fray, was suitably admonished. A short time afterwards he had to be dismissed from my service altogether. This unhappy incident was followed by no bad result in the village in which it occurred, for the people of that place were, from that time forward, invariably helpful and friendly to me. For any expedition similar to mine it is most desirable that all followers should be good-tempered men. This is, indeed, a far more important qualification in selecting servants than any other with which I am acquainted.

During this second visit to the Kunar Valley the fort at Narsut was rapidly approaching completion. On my return to Kámdesh on April 27th, the village seemed nearly empty owing to so many men being away with their flocks and herds; but those who remained received me with more than usual cordiality. Little crowds came daily to see me, and many sick people were brought for medicine, so that my time was fully occupied.

What may be called the bloodshed season opened in 1891 at the beginning of April, when the pass which leads into the Dungul Valley from Kámdesh was sufficiently clear of snow to allow the hardy Káfirs to cross it.

On April 5, two Kashtán men returned in triumph, after having committed a couple of murders in the Asmár direction. The Kám men also had achieved some similar small successes, which delighted the tribe, and these, in conjunction with the Gísh ceremonies, kept them all in a high state of good-humour. There was daily practice with bows and arrows, and much preparation of weapons on the part of young men hungering for fame.

PRACTICE WITH BOWS AND ARROWS.

To face page 294.

In the prevailing general satisfaction I was especially honoured, and Shahru, the individual who is temporarily inspired during sacrifices and other religious functions, took every opportunity of performing his antics before me. He, no doubt, helped to increase my general popularity, which at that time seemed considerable. Utah, the priest, after many doubtings, had settled down as my firm friend, and even my avowed opponents had begun to abandon their intrigues against me, as hopeless speculations. In short, the general aspect of things was decidedly encouraging, and the only rift in the lute was the dislike and impatience with which the Kám listened to any suggestion of mine about visiting other tribes. So long as I was content to remain with them, and never speak even of other Káfirs, so long would a majority of the Kám be delighted to have me with them; but the moment a word was spoken of my wish to go to Lutdeh, every brow lowered and every face grew sullenly angry. The Kám people had no objection to my going to Chitrál or to the Kunar Valley, both of them Musalmán districts. They reserved all their jealousy for their co-religionists in Káfiristán.

For some time past, also, a cloud no bigger than a man's hand had appeared on the horizon. It had increased a little, but as yet gave no portent of a coming storm. This was Umrá Khan, the ruler of Jandúl. He was engaged in making secret overtures to the Kám, who, on their part, had shown themselves perfectly willing to send and receive emissaries bearing friendly messages.

The Káfirs were extremely discontented with the Mehtar of Chitrál. The cause of quarrel was the grazing grounds about Narsut. The Kám claimed both banks of the Kunar river at the place mentioned, while the Chitrális wished to restrict them to the right bank only. There had been threats and recriminations on both sides, which culminated in a straining of the relations between Chitrál and the Kám, almost to the snapping-point. The Mehtar re-affirmed his intention of introducing Gujars[1] into the Narsut district, while the Káfirs roundly swore that they would murder all such intruders. The Mehtar's action in building a fort at Narsut had also given great offence to the Kám, who were secretly assured by Umrá Khan of his entire sympathy. There had, consequently, come to be a considerable *rapprochement* between the Káfirs and the wily Khan of Jandúl.

I felt certain that the Chitrális were only "trying it on," and would never really come to an open rupture with the Káfirs for the paltry increase of revenue which the settlement of a few Gujars would afford the Mehtar. Besides, although Umrá Khan had expressed a desire to meet me privately, while nominally on a shooting expedition—a meeting, by the way, that never came off—and although he was apparently inclined to be friendly towards me, it was, nevertheless, well known that he was using all his new friendship with the Káfirs to induce them to send me out of the country. I never tired of pointing out to the Káfir people that Umrá Khan's real object in being so anxious about my leaving Káfiristán must simply be that he himself was desirous of being in a position to attack the Bashgul Valley, without at the same time running any risk of compromising himself with the Government of India.

For a long time past the Káfirs had been dreading an

[1] An unwarlike nomadic Indian race.

attack from Umrá Khan, and had been in much doubt as to the willingness, and also the ability, of the Mehtar to help them against the Jandúl people in case of need. Yet, in spite of this dread of Umrá Khan, and although my words had some slight weight with them, they were greatly elated, almost intoxicated, at the uncommon friendship which Umrá Khan was displaying towards them, in expressing his willingness to help them covertly in their present quarrel with the Mehtar. This feeling was sedulously worked upon by one of their own headmen, named Mír Ján, a man of considerable repute amongst his followers for political sagacity and astuteness, who himself really believed in the good faith of Umrá Khan. Mír Ján had several times visited Jandúl, where he had been well treated, and had received many valuable presents. He was one of the Kám orators, and possessed much influence over the people. It was well known, also, that he had much to lose if Umrá Khan proved faithless; for his grazing grounds were in an exposed position, where they were liable to be raided by the Jandúlis at any time. Doubtless the knowledge of this fact had no small influence in convincing Mír Ján that the true policy of his tribe was to ally itself with Umrá Khan. In the end no definite conclusion was arrived at, for the Káfirs wanted me to stop with them, and yet did not want to disoblige Umrá Khan. There the matter rested, but it was obvious that should I ever become unpopular again, Umrá Khan's party would rapidly increase in strength and influence, and might tell heavily against me at a critical moment. This, as a matter of fact, is what actually did happen. When I eventually left the valley for good, my departure was

generally accepted as an assurance that Umrá Khan
would become a firm friend of the tribe. Unhappily,
however, my predictions were confirmed to the letter.
Umrá Khan promptly raided the Káfir grazing grounds
in Narsut, killed several people, and carried off others
for ransom, and thus started a war to the knife, accompanied with lamentable bloodshed, between him and
the Kám.·

During the early part of May the disputes between the
Chitrális and the Káfirs concerning the grazing grounds
at Narsut reached an acute stage. Shah-i-Mulk, the
governor of Kila Drosh, brought in a family of Gujars,
all of whom were immediately murdered by Red Malik
and some other Káfirs. One of the assassins was captured and detained by Shah-i-Mulk, who, however, refrained from punishing him in any other way. Both
sides then assumed a threatening attitude. Finally, the
Mehtar sent an ultimatum to Kámdesh, that unless the
Kám at once and for ever gave up all claim to the grazing grounds on the left bank of the Kunar river at Narsut,
a Chitráli army would forthwith invade the Bashgul
Valley. The tribe naturally got very excited on hearing
this, and a deputation of the headmen waited on me,
bringing the Mehtar's messengers with them. The whole
question at issue was then discussed in my presence, and
I willingly agreed to do everything in my power for
the maintenance of peace. In the fulfilment of this promise I wrote at once to Chitrál. Although it was nearly
certain that the Mehtar was merely trying to extort by
threats what he had failed to obtain by other methods,
yet there was considerable danger that the inflammable
Kám might take these threats literally, and anticipate

any hostile action on the part of the Chitrális by raiding across the frontier. To me it was absolutely certain that the Kám would never give up their immemorial rights to the Narsut grazing grounds—rights which they had established once and again by hard fighting—unless they were thoroughly beaten in war.

I had, after very great trouble, at length succeeded in making arrangements for visiting Lutdeh. The Kám strongly disapproved of my going there, but were just then in a conciliatory mood towards me on account of the help I had been able to give them in their negotiations with Chitrál. My journey, however, had to be postponed for a few days on account of an outbreak of inter-tribal fighting at Lutdeh. It was of the usual fratricidal kind, for which the Katirs have so unenviable a notoriety. It is the intense enmity of family to family, of brother to brother, in that district which has given the Mehtar of Chitrál a predominating influence over that part of the Bashgul Valley. Many of the Kám who were connected by marriage ties with the Katirs rushed off to Lutdeh to try and arrange peace. Happily their efforts were crowned with success, and in a few days we were able to make a start.

Three Kám men were told off to accompany me, one of whom, a headman, had secret instructions from the Jast to bring me back to Kámdesh on a certain definite date, and to watch and see that I did not become too friendly with the Katirs. In short, my Kám followers were to be as much my custodians as my escort. To reach Lutdeh from Kámdesh, that short portion of the Bashgul Valley inhabited by the Mádugál Káfirs has to be traversed. This tribe had always been friendly towards me, but their chief, Bahdur, was a man of insatiable cupidity, and always looked on me as a barred tiger just before feeding-time might gaze on a stalled ox; but the Kám were far too powerful and far too close at hand for Bahdur to give me any trouble while I was under their escort, and we were treated extremely well by his people.

On the border of the Katir country my old friend Kán Márá of Lutdeh was ready to receive us, as well as several Káfirs belonging to the western branches of the Katir tribe, who were then, and still are, at war with the Kám people. My reception was most agreeable. The greatest hospitality was shown me, and my entrance into Lutdeh itself was signalised by drum-beatings and by other attempts to do me honour. The people were very polite. It was by this time well known throughout the Bashgul Valley that curiosity which took the form of personally handling me or my garments was a thing I never permitted, and that certain topics of conversation were most distasteful to me. It was amusing to notice how a man would pull himself up when he found he was approaching dangerous ground, and then, with apologetic looks, would change the conversation. The quiet behaviour of the women left nothing to be desired; they kept themselves entirely in the background. The Káfirs did not know whether to think me a confirmed woman-hater, or such a superior person that their women had no attraction for me.

CHAPTER XVIII

The narrative continued—The village of Bragamatál—The Manangul torrent
—The old village—Its destruction—The Jannahdári Clan—Kán Márá—
Fort-villages peculiar to this part of the Bashgul Valley—The story of
Karlah Jannah—His stronghold in Badáwan—Káfir etiquette—Conver-
sation upon religon — Karlah Jannah's surprise at Franks' ignorance
of Gísh—His own ignorance about Gísh—Attempt to prevent my cross-
ing the Mandál Pass—Karlah Jannah's pertinacity—The customary
change of tactics—Strange behaviour of Shermalik—A difficult climb—
Descent to the Minján Valley—Camp—A day of trouble—The masterful
Mersi—Peip—The Minjánis—The women—The Mandál Pass—The
village of Palul—Return march—Reach Bragamatál—Letter from the
Mehtar of Chitrál—Unsatisfactory news from Kámdesh—Return to
Kámdesh—Friendly relations—Journey to the Presun planned—False
rumours—Umrá Khan's messengers—Calm before storm.

BRAGAMATÁL, or Lutdeh, or Deh-i-Kalán—the last two
names mean the same thing, " the big village," in Chitráli
and in Persian respectively—consists of two portions, a
smaller on the right bank, a larger on the left. They
are connected by a good bridge across the river. The
smaller or western village is built on a rock of inconsiderable altitude close to the water's edge, and on the
level ground to the south-west, where there are many
houses and the dancing-place. On the left bank the
houses are so arranged on a low hill as to form half of
a regular hexagon open towards the south, the semi-
enclosed space being occupied by the dancing-platform,
the dancing-house, and a few other buildings. The
total number of domiciles is about six hundred, much
the same number that Kámdesh possesses, although the
population of the latter village is comparatively small.

Bragamatál is a pleasant village, requiring no laborious climbing to reach any portion of it, while the river close at hand, with its clear, moderate stream, is an added charm. From the east the Manangul torrent from the Sháwal direction joins the Bashgul river a short distance below the bridge, and at the end of May is bright and clear till about two o'clock in the afternoon, when it changes, becoming turbid and laden with soil. Over this torrent there is another good bridge which leads to the road running down the left bank of the river to the village of Bajindra. There are the remains of an old bridge over the Bashgul river, a short distance below the existing structure. On the right bank, immediately above the village, and on the west slope of the valley, are the effigies and coffins, but little above the level of the river, and separated from its bank by a short space of level ground. This proximity of the dead discovers itself to the living in a very unpleasant way when the wind is in a particular quarter.

On a hill to the west are several ruined walls, which mark the site of the former village of Bragamatál, which then consisted of two portions; part being on this hill, and the remainder being on the low rocks on the right bank, now occupied by part of the west village. As is so common amongst the Katirs, a deadly fratricidal feud broke out some fifteen years ago between these two divisions of the same place. The lower village people called in the aid of Amán-ul-Mulk, the Mehtar of Chitrál, who sent not only foot-soldiers, but horsemen also, and the hill-villagers were completely vanquished and dispersed. Some eventually settled in the Lutkho Valley of Chitrál, some fled to the western valleys, while the

Mehtar received sixty as prisoners to be sold as slaves. At the dancing-place in the east village, beside the altar to Imrá, constructed of two rough stones, there is a pole surmounted by an iron trophy which looks like a small iron four-cornered hat. It commemorates a victory of the Bashgul Katirs over the Pomora or Minján people "many years ago."

Bragamatál is a cheery village owing to the fact that traders and travellers from Badakhshán, Minján, and Chitrál make it their destination. The inhabitants boast that traders come to their very door, while the poor Kám folk have to travel all the way to Chitrál or Narsut for any small articles they may require. There are many shrines just above the village on both banks.

In the Katir country, although there are many clans, there is only one of real importance, namely, the Jannah-dári. Kán Márá, Kán Jannah, and four or five other brothers, as well as Márá's former great rival, Ghazab Shah, all belong to this family. So also does Karlah Jannah, of whom more hereafter. Kán Márá is not only the hereditary priest, but appears to be the undisputed chief of the tribe, a place he has obtained mainly through the aid of the Mehtar of Chitrál, Amán-ul-Mulk, who was also his son-in-law.

With the help of this ally, eight or nine years ago, he defeated the Ghazab Shah faction and caused its chief to flee from the country. Peace now prevails, but the two households are not yet on visiting terms. Kán Márá has very few other enemies; he has killed them all.

After resting a day or two at Bragamatál, we marched leisurely up the valley, being warmly welcomed and hospitably entertained at the fort-villages, which are peculiar to this part of the Bashgul Valley.

Just beyond the Skorigul we met Karlah Jännah, who is a kind of outlaw amongst the Katir tribe. He has a house at Bragamatál, but he may not venture there, partly from fear of Kán Márá and of his own brother Ghazab Shah. but chiefly because to do so would be a great lowering of his dignity. His story is somewhat curious. Some years ago he was so rich and influential that he posed as a rival of Kán Márá. To declare his wealth and become famous for ever, he announced his intention of bestowing a cow upon every family in Bragamatál. Kán Márá, startled at this determination, sent round to each intended recipient of Karlah Jannah's favour, and, by threats and promises combined, induced them all to refuse the proffered gifts. This was a dire insult; so Karlah Jannah left his home and tribe, and established himself at Ahmad Diwáná, where he hoped to be able to induce the Afghans to invade the Bashgul Valley from Minján.

Karlah Jannah was most gorgeously attired in Badakhsháni silk, and wore a most striking chappan. His whiskers were newly dyed the fashionable scarlet colour. He met me just above the bridge, mounted on a stout pony, on to which I was immediately transferred, and in this unusual manner—on horseback—I reached Jannah's stronghold at Badáwan.

This was a delightful country, pleasantly cool; indeed the snow bridges remained at many places spanning the river. Badáwan is a considerable tract of country, three miles or so in extent, with a tower at each extremity, and Jannah's house in the middle. He possesses two towers overlooking his cow-sheds and goat-pens, while on the

KARLAH JANNAH'S STRONGHOLD.

lower ground to the west there is sufficient cultivable
ground. In his service were two or three Minjáni

R

refugees from the alleged tyranny of the Amir of Kabul, as were many other people we had met in this part of the Bashgul Valley. Most of these people had asked for permission to return to their former holdings, but had been informed by the Amir's officials that their places were already filled up, and that as they had chosen to go away of their own accord, they must now stop away altogether.

My picturesque host entertained me in a most lavish manner; a goat was killed in honour of my arrival, and also a sheep for my special eating; while food of all kinds was pressed on my servants and followers. A bed covered with a carpet was carefully placed in the shade for my use, and it was easy to tell from the style of my reception that Jannah had spent a good deal of his time at Chitrál. His little sons, unlike other Káfir boys, were dressed up in gaudy Badakhshání silk robes of extraordinary patterns.

We had arrived just before midday, and all the afternoon the Káfirs played at stone quoits (*aluts*). As the evening set in the cows came home to be safely housed for the night, while my host conducted me to the upper room of the smaller of the towers, where he, his friends and retainers, visited me in relays, lest solitude should make me feel dull. This is Káfir etiquette. We talked about religion, and Jannah was astounded at the information that Franks knew nothing of the god Gísh. Nevertheless, he seemed to have very little to relate himself about the famous war-god. He knew that he had fought with and killed "Hazrat Ali," and had cut off the saint's head, and he also knew that eventually the god went to London, while his servants settled in Káfiristán. There his knowledge ended.

Next morning it was evident that Karlah Jannah had been won over by my Kám friends. He did everything he could think of to prevent my going beyond Badáwan. The Kám men the previous morning had gone the length of trying to lead me by false assurances up the Skorigul Valley, which debouches into the main Bashgul Valley a short distance above the village of Pshui or Pshowar, and had become furious when I could not help laughing at this puerile device.

All manner of terrible things were now predicted. Four Afghan officials had been living in Pomaru (Minján) all the winter, and were there still, waiting for us just the other side of the pass ; the snow was so deep no one could cross ; the Minjánis would be enraged at seeing us, and would not only refuse us supplies, but would drive us back. At last, at Imrá's shrine, where there is a bridge over the river, Widing Chandlu, the Kám Jast, had an inspiration of genius. He brought an old Minjáni, who with tears in his eyes begged me not to enter his country, for if the Amir heard of it he would make my visit an excuse for oppressing the people. For the moment I was on the point of retracing my steps, and should have done so had it not been that the night before I had sent forward a man secretly, to waylay and cross-examine any party of Minjánis who might be travelling down the valley. As it was, I determined to merely go as far as the top of the pass, and then to return at once if there were any real danger of the Minján people having to suffer for allowing me to enter their valley. This resolve, however, seemed to give even less satisfaction than my former arrangement, so I determined to press on.

Widing Chandlu, declaring he could not face the snow

on the pass, took leave of me at Imrá's shrine; but his pernicious influence was preserved in the person of Mersi, the man he sent as his substitute. Mersi was an extremely intelligent but wild Káfir, who knew little or nothing about me, and whose ideas of influencing any one were confined to bullying. He was a Kám orator, and so possessed great influence over his companions. He was, moreover, much admired for his astuteness and business capacity, which he had many opportunities of showing; for he was the man usually entrusted by the Kám with any arrangements which had to be made with the Wai; he was also a kind of agent of the latter people for selling their little girls as slaves. Karlah Jannah, with Káfir pertinacity, kept reiterating all his arguments against my crossing the Mandál, but he was kept at bay by my urging on the pony he had lent me, by which means he was reduced to breathlessness, and also left behind.

At a place where we made a short halt he caught me up, and began his expostulations all over again. All the Káfirs present took their cue from him, and solemnly assured me, guides and all, that they had been deceiving me, and that no one present knew the road over the pass. In the end Jannah had to be politely told by me to mind his own business, upon which he at once mounted the pony and rode off in high dudgeon. For the rest, I began ceremoniously to shake hands and say farewell, and expressed a hope that we should all meet again in a few days on my return journey. My real authority only extended to my three Baltis. Ordering them to follow me, and waving my hand in friendly gesture, we started away from the Káfirs; but we had not gone more than a mile or so when they all came trooping after us, and declared their intention of accompanying me. They were not in the least abashed at having to gainsay their former statements, but laughed cheerfully at the false stories they had related. At a spot by a mountain tarn, where the slope begins to grow steep, we halted, and spent the rest of the day in preparations for the morrow. We cooked all the flour we had, collected wood to carry up to our sleeping-camp, and plaited rings of birch twigs to pull over the soft leather *pubbus* (boots), and so prevent the feet from slipping over the frozen snow. Every one was merry and busily occupied, and at sunset we ascended a thousand feet, and just at the edge of the snow, building up rough stone walls to keep off the wind, we prepared for the night.

A very strange thing now occurred. One of my companions was a nice, cheery, but rather stupid Bragamatál Káfir named Lutkám, the son of Kán Márá. Being in high spirits, he and Shermalik, who was also with me, enacted a little scene, and pretended to quarrel; whereupon the other Káfirs, entering into the fun, acted the part of peacemakers with great gusto, and the whole crowd went rolling about shouting with laughter. Shermalik and Lutkám, hoarse with screaming at one another, and apparently exhausted with their vain endeavours to reach each other's throats, played with the greatest spirit and simulated earnestness. The whole performance was rather clever. I looked on, and laughed with the rest. Shermalik, greatly excited with this struggle, and bursting with pride and arrogance at being treated on such equal terms by Kán Márá's son, knew not how to get rid of his superfluous energy. Strange to say, he turned on me, and angrily demanded a certain robe which he said had been improperly given to another. Knowing nothing about the article in question, Shermalik's insolent manner made me really angry ; but it was at once apparent that my anger must be strictly repressed, for my adopted son raved like a maniac, and was entirely beyond self-control. My silence made him, if possible, even more angry than before ; he almost foamed at the mouth. He raved and shouted himself absolutely speechless from sheer fatigue. Mersi and the others applauded him under their breath, partly from love of mischief, but chiefly in the hope that a quarrel would occur and put an end to my journey. I told Shermalik that henceforward he was no longer my son. After this repudiation of our relationship I pretended to sleep, but he kept on murmuring hoarse threats far into the night.

We started for the pass at half-past four next morning, Shermalik being sulky, half defiant and half frightened. He required all the moral support of his friends to maintain his attitude of sulky dignity. Our trackless path lay over frozen snow, but the distance to the top of the pass, 15,300 feet, was greater than we had estimated. The last three hundred feet were as steep as the side of a house, but not steep enough to be quite clear of snow. The sun was very hot, and I came near to the knowledge of what extreme exhaustion means ; for the snow let me through at every step up to the hips, and at least a dozen times caused me to slide back helplessly many yards in a miniature avalanche. The Káfirs fairly romped over the undulating frozen snow-field, but even they had hard work to accomplish the last piece of climbing. They could not understand my being unable to keep up with them, or my getting so breathless over the hard

KÁFIRS ON THE SNOW.

To face page 315.

snow. One of them said to his fellows, not suspecting his speech was understood, " What is the matter with the Frank? he must be very fat." They would sometimes race on ahead, shouting and singing, and either spread out their brown Chitráli robes on the snow to sleep placidly but soundly till the panting Baltis and myself caught them up ; or else they would form a circle, twirl their axes and clubs, and prance, shuffle, and stamp round and round in a wild fantastic dance ; a singular spectacle to witness on a wide snow-field more than fifteen thousand feet above the sea-level. The snow was strewn with myriads of dead butterflies.

The descent on the Minján Valley side was also difficult on account of the treacherous snow continually letting us through ; but the farther we went, the easier became our path. Finally, it seemed advisable to halt in some willow jungle in the middle of a large level plain. The Káfirs demurred to this, declaring it was nonsense to say that the Minjánis might be punished by the Afghans on our account, or that Afghan officials were in Minján. They now urged me to push on to the hamlet of Peip, and swore that all their former statements were false. However, we were now a fairly large party, quite strong enough to overawe the mild Minján villagers, while the Káfirs were turbulent, entirely out of hand, and were robbers and raiders by heredity ; so I kept to my determination, and sent on one man for news and to buy provisions.

Next day was full of trouble. Shermalik had returned to a state of sulky obedience, but Mersi and the others became noisily and openly rebellious. At length they were proceeding to actual intimidation, and got more and more excited every instant. Their object was to force me to give them the money they demanded, and to then rush off and do the best they could with my rupees and their own threats at the nearest Minjáni village, where they hoped to get black robes and Badakhshán silks to trade with on their return. They had received the wherewithal to buy sheep, provisions, and other necessaries, but the sight of the money only inflamed their cupidity. Mersi screamed out threats, and with him all the Káfirs were marching off together. They had persuaded themselves that renewed threats, violent wrangles, and mad behaviour generally would compel me to agree to their demands. Finding milder methods of no avail, I was at length obliged to take the floor and face and browbeat the violent Mersi, dismissing him on the spot; at the same time I sternly ordered Lutkám to sit down in a place indicated, under the penalty of his never being allowed to come near me again. Somewhat to my surprise, Lutkám, after wavering an instant, complied with my demand, and his example was followed by all the men of lesser note. Finding my orders were being obeyed, the turbulent and masterful Mersi rushed off white with passion, but stumbling in crossing a torrent, he fell heavily and broke two fingers. Sick with pain, he had to return humbly to get the bones set and to have his agony relieved.

Two of my three Baltis were snow-blind and in great distress.

About eleven o'clock a Minjáni was brought to me, an interesting, rather intelligent man. He had come to conduct me to the village of Peip, stipulating, however, that we were not to start until it was nearly dark. He

gave me a great deal of information about the Kti and
Rámgul Káfirs, and about their trading with their young
female relatives. As evening drew near, the Minjáni
suggested we should make a start. On the road he
nervously suggested a fresh plan, which was that he
should go on ahead and prepare for my reception at Peip,
while I sat on a particular stone and awaited his return.
To this suggestion it was impossible to agree. He then
remarked that he was not a resident of Peip himself.
All further observations from him were checked by my
declaring that he must remain with me, or rather that
we intended to accompany him wherever he went. We
shortly afterwards reached Peip, when our guide disappeared into the upper story of a tower, and calmly
shut and locked the door. The only other man about
suggested that we should move on to some other village,
as Peip had no supplies of any kind. In reply to a
question about fowls he said that there were none in the
place, though all the time a great clucking was audible
from a neighbouring house. After waiting about for
some time rather hopelessly, I called sternly to my friend
in the tower that he must come out, and that he must
get us food, as we were starving. With one of those
sudden changes of front so common in the people of
these regions, Bík Muhammad, as the man was called,
suddenly produced fowls, flour, and milk, and ushered
me into an apartment where a good fire was blazing. All
this time my Káfirs had been foraging, and they now
appeared with a fine sheep, flour, butter, and all manner
of luxuries. It is too probable that they had not paid
for these supplies. Káfirs always prefer to keep back
he price and to obtain what they want by violence, or

by threats of violence. There was no longer any doubt about the Afghan being near at hand. Some of his baggage coolies had already arrived, and the people implored me to go away lest the Afghan official should make my unauthorised visit an excuse for wreaking vengeance upon them. So there was nothing for it but to return the way we had come, and to leave unsolved an interesting geographical problem connected with the Minján Valley; for it was absolutely necessary that the kindly but wretched Minjánis should run no danger of being plundered and oppressed because of their hospitality to me. Peip is merely a hamlet consisting of two towers and several small circular apartments and en-closures. Some of the latter were roofed in, others were open to the sky. Most of these enclosures appeared to be for cattle. Both towers were inhabited. There seemed also a superfluity of walls and lanes for a place so limited in size, but perhaps these were erected merely for the sake of getting rid of the superabundant stones. Bík Muhammad and his friends first conducted me through a small semicircular anteroom which fitted on to a round room behind, as a watch-glass fits on to a watch. It contained a small plough of similar construction to those used in the Bashgul Valley. The farther room was curiously arranged. Down the centre ran a sunken path, a foot and a half lower than the rest of the floor, which was divided on either hand by a series of mud walls which caused the enclosed spaces to look like the stalls in a stable. In one of these a rough carpet was spread for my use. The sunken path terminated in a fireplace, the top of which was level with the floor. It was built solidly of clay, the centre being scooped out so that the fire blazed and crackled in a neatly shaped cylinder, twenty inches in diameter and one and a half feet high. The cylinder was open at the top, where on either side there was sufficient room for a seat, or to place cooking vessels or other utensils. The cylindrical fireplace was also open in front for one-sixth of its circumference. The towers were low, two-storied buildings, the upper apartment being reached in the usual way by a solid outside ladder. In the construction of all the buildings a great economy in wood was apparent. The upper story of one of the towers was placed at my disposal for the night. In the centre of the apartment was another great mass of clay containing a cylindrical fireplace such as that already described, the whole forming a table and a seat as well as a fireplace. All walls are built of smooth water-worn stones cemented with clay. The central smoke-hole in the roof was in shape and appearance similar to those seen in the Bashgul Valley, but with this difference: that instead of hewn timber shaped into scantlings being used for supporting the earth on the roof and to form the sides of the aperture, branches two or three inches in diameter were alone employed. In my apartment two stout square wooden pillars in the middle of the room strengthened the roof beams.

The Minjánis seem to be a singularly meek people. They have patient, simple looks, and the slow heavy movements of men who carry loads or who spend their lives working in the fields. They are of the Maulai or Ráfizi sect of Shiah Musalmáns, and speak Persian fluently. The clothing of the men consisted of thick grey blanket robes secured at the waist, wide and easy woollen trousers, and soft leather boots. We saw few women. They were swarthy-looking, like the men, and had something of a Tartar appearance. They were unlovely, dirty, and careless in their attire. Long unkempt locks were permitted to obtrude from under a small cap, while a long sack-like garment of woollen material, and sad in colour, reached to a little above the ankles. The loose baggy trousers, of the same thick cloth as the body garment, fitted tightly to the ankles, in the usual fashion adopted by Musalmán women. There was a heedlessness about fastening the clothes about the neck and breast which was surprising. As may also be said of the Káfirs, the men, as a rule, are cleaner and pleasanter to look at than the women.

The Minján Valley itself is practically treeless, but it is noted for its good grazing. It would be most interesting to discover the precise direction in which it runs. The river-banks are, in places, at any rate, formed of immense masses and cliffs of boulder clay and drift, backed by steep rocky slopes of metamorphic origin. The narrow valley leading down from the Mandál Pass to Peip opens out in two places into broad and level expanses; the lower, on which we encamped (at 11,500 feet), was covered with willow jungle and intersected by streams. It was a mile and a half in length by a third of a mile in breadth. It had the appearance of an old lake-bed, and was remarkable for the appearance of the rocks on the western side. They looked as if they had at one time been continued down into the plain as well-defined spurs, but had been broken off regularly and uniformly by glacier action. Between each remaining bluff there is a "talus" of shingle and small rocky fragments. Higher up, towards the pass end, this level

KÁFIR LANDSCAPE.

To face page 320.

expanse is encroached upon by a huge rounded mass of shining, dark-coloured rock. At the lower end the plain is closed in by a long, low rampart of rock, which leaves just sufficient room for the main river, swelled by the smaller streams and water-channels, to wind its tortuous way round the western free extremity. From this point the valley narrows, and by an easy gradient flows slightly to the west in the direction of Peip, whose altitude is 10,000 feet.

To the west of Peip, on the high drift bank on the opposite side of the river, is the village of Palúl. This village has two conspicuous towers, and apparently numerous lower buildings. It must be several hundred feet higher than Peip.

The next day, the 3rd of June, we marched back, keeping a good look-out all round us; but we started so early that we passed our old camp before the sun was well up. There the shallow streamlets were covered with a film of ice.

At 11,800 feet the birches and the willows ended altogether. At 12,300 feet we reached the second level space, where the grass and low scrub invited us to camp; but we went forward till, just short of 13,000 feet, we came to a crevice in the rocks which had been cunningly turned into a small, well-sheltered apartment. This the Káfirs appropriated, and soon filled with smoke from the branches they had carried up from below. I slept outside under a small wall of loose stones.

Next morning we started at two o'clock, and reached the top of the pass just before six. We found it most difficult to keep warm in spite of our exertions. On the pass an icy blast was blowing, which numbed fingers,

nose, feet, and ears. The descent on the Káfir side was
also fatiguing, the slippery snow surface betraying all of
us several times ; and when the sun appeared we began
to fall through the snow in a most unpleasant manner.
A short distance beyond our first camp we rested for two
or three hours by the edge of the tarn, and we finally
spread our blankets for the night by the river-edge, close
to a pshal a mile or so above Ahmad Diwáná. We were
extremely tired, and all night long the cow-flies revelled
on our hapless bodies.

From Bragamatál I wrote a letter to H.H. the Amir of
Kabul, expressing a wish to visit the Minján Valley, and
asking for permission to do so, and also explaining the
circumstances which had led to my finding myself on his
frontier while travelling in Káfiristán. This letter was
never delivered. It was burked ; and so well was the
secret of my journey kept, that three months later, when
I met in the Presungul some Minjánis of the lower villages, they assured me that they had never even heard of
my short visit to their valley.

We reached Bragamatál on the 6th of June. The
Baltis who crossed the Mandál with me, although their
eyes quickly recovered, remained weak and ill for some
days, on account of the severity of the march they had
undergone. A fourth Balti had been left behind at the
village of Pshowar in charge of my baggage. He had
been particularly well treated by the villagers. The
remaining Balti was sick at Kámdesh. He had been instructed to follow me, bringing my tent as soon as he
was fit to travel.

We remained at Bragamatál for ten days, very pleased
with the general friendliness of the people. A letter

reached me there from the Mehtar of Chitrál, in which he assured me he never had the intention of attacking the Kám people while I remained in their country, but had simply been trying to frighten them into compliance with his wishes.   This was satisfactory, but the news from Kámdesh itself was less so.   It appeared that the Káfirs had stripped and beaten two of the Mehtar's messengers on the road, and that a small armed force of Chitrális had been very nearly attacked in Kámdesh itself.

On June 14th the Balti who had been left behind arrived at Bragamatál, but without my tent.   He had been told by Dán Malik to leave it where it was.   My somewhat prolonged absence had created a suspicion in the minds of the Kám men that I was not going back at all, so Dán Malik detained my tent as a kind of hostage for my reappearance.   Another man was therefore sent to fetch it, who met me with it on the road.

We returned to Kámdesh on the 19th of June.   Before leaving Bragamatál, Kán Márá declared he could and would take me to Presungul (Viron), but he strongly deprecated my making any attempt to get into the more western valleys.   However, he said that if I was determined to try and get there, he would do all in his power to help me.   As the Katirs were just then on most friendly terms with the Presungul people, it would obviously be a great advantage to go into that country under Kán Márá's auspices.   The Katirs, moreover, were at peace with the Wai and the Rámgul Káfirs.   The Kám, on the other hand, had been at war with the Rámgulis for generations, and were always liable to be attacked by them when travelling in the Presun country.

Nothing could be pleasanter than my relations with

the Kám from the date of my return up to the end of the month. The Chitrál difficulty was settled, the Mehtar had admonished Shah-i-Mulk, the Káfir prisoner had been set at liberty, and friendly relations were again established. The Kám headmen rightly thought that I had had a principal hand in bringing about this satisfactory state of affairs. They talked about building me a house, there were no longer difficulties about supplies, and an unusual deference was paid to my real or supposed wishes.

We planned a journey into the Presun (Viron) Valley. It was arranged that I was to go with a few Kám Káfirs up the Baprok Nullah, and cross the Mámi Pass into the Presun country with the help of the Katirs; while Utah, with a strong escort of Kám men, was to travel by another road, meet me in Presungul, and escort me back to Kámdesh. Nearly everybody seemed amiable and helpful. There were, indeed, false rumours flying about that I had distributed large sums of money at Lutdeh; but as the authors of those rumours were known to be men persistent in their hostility to me, their statements were received with a good deal of reserve. The inveterate enmity of the men referred to could only have been overcome by bribing, when the remedy would have been worse than the disease, for the thing could not have been kept secret, while to bribe an enemy often means paying a premium for ill-will. Umrá Khan continued to send in his messengers, who explained that the only obstacle to a complete *rapprochement* between their master and the Káfirs was my continued presence in Kámdesh, and to assure them that as soon as ever I left the valley he was prepared to enter into a firm alliance with them, and use all his military power to help them against either the Mehtar of Chitrál or the Amir of Kabul. These matters were openly discussed, but the great majority of the people were still quite satisfied with things as they were. Whether at that time we were living in the calm which precedes the thunderstorm, or were merely in a fool's paradise, I have never been able to decide; but it seems to me that the end of June was really the period when my popularity reached its zenith, in spite of the discontent which my journey to Lutdeh had undoubtedly awakened in the minds of many.

CHAPTER XIX

The narrative continued—Mersi again—Widing Chandlu in disgrace—Mír Ján's efforts for Umrá Khan—The question of building a house for me —Quarrel between the three divisions of the village—The issue—General disturbance in the upper village—From bad to worse—Testing my friendship—Impossible demands—I am dismissed from Kámdesh—Utah escorts me out of the valley—Arrival at Lutdeh—The tribe absent raid-ing—The women dancing to Gísh—General ill-fortune—March up the valley—Pshowar—Unpleasant experiences—Karlah Jannah receives me kindly—We become brothers—He escorts me up the Skorigul—Return to Lutdeh—Ten weary days there—Resolve to go to the Mádugál tribe —Shermalik joins me at Chábu with good news.

EARLY in July there was clearly something wrong with the people of the upper village. One or two of their headmen came to tell me they feared the Kám people had lost favour in my eyes since I had been to the Katir country. They were assured that such was not the case, and they went away apparently satisfied with my assur-ances. Nevertheless, there was obviously some soreness in the minds of many of the villagers concerning my visit to Lutdeh. The ungrateful Mersi, who had left me at that place on our return journey to Minján, brimming over with gratitude for my kindness in treating his broken fingers, and for the wages he had received for accompanying me, no sooner arrived in Kámdesh than he began to grow dis-contented with the money he had been paid. He appears really to have convinced himself, against his own reason, that I had given much more money to the Katirs than to him. He went all over the upper village complaining of the treatment he had received, and gradually infuriating himself with his own eloquence.

Widing Chandlu, the Kám headman who started with me from Kámdesh, was in much disgrace with his fellows, for allowing me to cross the Mandál Pass. Public opinion was indeed so strong against him that he kept to his house and was terribly cast down. It gradually came to be accepted as a fact that not only had I given a splendid largess to the Katirs, but that the headmen, particularly those of the eastern village, were receiving regular payments from me.

Mersi attempted openly to blackmail me. He was so obviously in the wrong, and had behaved so badly throughout, that he could get no single man to openly support him. He uttered vague threats about murdering me, and conducted himself so violently that there was no possibility of our coming to terms. Indeed, he had gone to such lengths before my return to Kámdesh that he had closed every door of possible reconciliation. He had so furiously excited himself, and had indulged in so many wild vapourings, that if an attempt had been made to buy him off, his sudden change of front would certainly have been attributed to its true cause. He would have been admired for his successful tactics, and would at once have found many imitators.

All this time Mír Ján, Umrá Khan's adherent, among the headmen, was untiring in his efforts to impress the people with his own belief in the irresistible power of the Khan of Jandúl, and with the sincerity of his wish for a friendly alliance with the Kám.

My old friends of the east village remained fairly firm, although the rumours of the excessive favours which had been bestowed on the Katirs were not without an unfortunate effect on their minds also. Their jealousy of the Lutdeh people did not make them exactly hostile to me, but somewhat sore and a little indifferent.

On July 14th there was a large gathering of the headmen to decide whether a house should be built for me, and if so, where it was to be erected, and who was to do the work. It seems that the proceedings opened quietly enough, when some remark was made which stirred up those feelings of jealousy so characteristic of the Káfirs. Soon the representatives of the three divisions of Kámdesh—the upper, the lower, and the east villages—were hard at work quarrelling. At first they were all against one another, but before the end, the east division had to contend against the other two united. No news came to me of what was going on, but subsequently it was reported that my friends in the assembly grew more and more excited, and finally quitted the council in great anger. A small deputation from the east village afterwards waited on me to say that in future they alone must be relied upon to make all my arrangements. They would build me a house, arrange for my supplies, and act as guides and escorts, while the rest of the tribe were to have nothing whatever to do with me. It appeared, also, that in the acrimony of discussion the upper villagers had declared that the Frank was of no use to them, as he gave them nothing, but reserved all his favours for the eastern villagers; while the latter indignantly, and with truth, denied the accusation.

The next few days were busily employed by me in pouring oil on the troubled waters. These efforts were attended with a fair measure of success, when an unlucky fight between two women in the upper village led to a general disturbance there. The quarrel itself was soon settled, but the general excitement remained, and soon found an outlet for its energy by re-starting the old contentions about me with the east village.

And now matters went from bad to worse. The malcontents were careful to explain that against me personally they had no complaint, and several of them added, that should existing dissensions go to an extreme length and fighting occur, every one respected me so much that not a hair of my head would be injured. But my friends were rapidly becoming cowed by the majority, and there was no real danger of a fight. They were alternately accused of receiving my money and taunted with not supporting me better. It was at length agreed that a certain test should be applied, to discover if my friendship for the Kám were sincere or not. Acting on this suggestion, headmen representing the whole of the tribe, came to ask me to send for a force of Chitrális, to co-operate with the Káfirs in a raiding expedition. The spokesman declared that it was well known to all the village that the Mehtar would do anything to please me, and that if he were asked for rifles, he would certainly send them. They argued, also, that the Mehtar would be delighted at the chance afforded him of capturing prisoners and selling them as slaves. It was fairly obvious that no raid was contemplated ; nevertheless, the question could not be trifled with. Quietly, but in unmistakable terms, I declined to do as they asked, pointing out that my mission was one of peace above all things, and winding up by saying, that although they were well aware of my readiness to help them to the extent of my power if they

ever were wantonly attacked by an enemy, yet such a pro-
posal as the one they were advancing could not be entertained for an instant. My answer was listened to in
sullen silence, and the people shortly afterwards went
away without offering any comment on what they had
heard. The next day Torag Merak came to me with
another deputation; indeed, the suggestion to test me in
the way described originated with him, and on getting
the same reply, he, in a real or simulated fury, ordered
me to leave the valley forthwith. Then followed two or
three days of interminable talk, until it was at length decided by the great majority of the Kám that I must go
away. My own friends acquiesced in this decision. They
argued that it was not worth while, nor were they strong
enough, to fight. In this they were perfectly right, but
as they felt a little ashamed of abandoning me, they kept
murmuring half-hearted complaints against my having
rewarded the Katirs excessively.

One or two tentative experiments on a small scale,
to see the result of bribing antagonists, did not answer.
It only made the recipients shamefaced and silent in
council, where they had before been vociferous and
leather-lunged.

So, bearing in mind the extreme friendliness of the
Katir people, and their obviously sincere promise to take
me to Presungul (Viron), it seemed to me useless to
struggle any longer against the inevitable, and that my
dismissal must be accepted as gracefully as possible.

At the last moment I determined on a plan which
might not only enable me to return to Kámdesh if it
were absolutely necessary, but would, at the same time,
enable me to reward all those who had served me,

although it was certain to cause great dissensions amongst the people. So every man, woman, or child who had in any way been helpful to me received a present of money after my departure from the village. Every one knew what each individual received, and that it was payment for actual service rendered, while all those who had opposed me, or who had looked on passively, of course got nothing.

Once more the village divided itself into parties, the minority not only devoted to me by the payments they had received, but driven into my arms, so to speak, by the resentment of those who got nothing; while among the majority there must necessarily have been a certain number who, whatever they might say, would be naturally anxious to curry favour with me at some future time, in the hope of being handsomely repaid for their good offices.

In spite of all that passed, we parted on very fair terms. The only discordant note was the determination on the part of the majority of the Kám, that whatever my destination might be, the straight road up the Bashgul was closed, and that the only way for me to get to Lutdeh (Bragamatál) was by first going to Chitrál.

Utah, the priest, who had expressed his intention of escorting me out of the valley, was told that my determination to go to the Katirs was fixed and unchangeable. In reply to a question if, in the event of my wanting to return to the Kunar Valley through Kám territory, any objection would be raised to my doing so, he scouted the idea of my being opposed by force, or indeed in any way, adding, "You have done no one any wrong, either with their wives or female relations; no one would dream of interfering with you." This was satisfactory enough as far as it went, which was perhaps not very far.

My real intention was not announced until we had passed the village of Pittigul, in order that there might be no tribal discussion on the point. The general belief was that as our road was up the Pittigul Valley, we intended to enter Chitrál by the road we had left it, viz., over the Párpit Pass leading to Bamboret. When my Kám companions were informed of my determination, they raised no objection. Utah detailed his brother and several other Kám men to accompany me, as well as two or three of the Pittigul villagers.

Many little kindnesses on the part of poor people were shown me when quitting the Kám valley. Men brought me goats and sheep in acknowledgment of my surgical treatment of their relatives. Of course all were handsomely rewarded in return, but the offerings were certainly not made in the hope of getting presents. Just before we left Kámdesh a number of poor people went to the headmen without my knowledge, and begged them to accept certain cows and other property, and then to ask me to remain in the country. They had to be threatened with a beating before they desisted from their amiable but mistaken efforts on my behalf.

We left Kámdesh on July 24th, and reached Bragamatál (Lutdeh) on the 30th by the circuitous mountain road already mentioned.

A severe disappointment awaited me at Lutdeh, which was as entirely unexpected as the fantastic ceremonies of the women which we were in time to witness.

It appeared that during a sacrifice to Gísh, the Katir Pshur had announced that great Gísh was offended at the paucity of his offerings, and had instructed him to order the people to "attack." After he had delivered himself of this sacred mandate, the inspiration of the Pshur suddenly ceased.

The headmen collected together to consider the question. It was eventually decided that it was undesirable, on every ground, to raid either the territory of the Amir of Kabul or that of the Mehtar of Chitrál, while there were many objections to attacking the fierce Kám people. It was also known that in a certain valley belonging to the Wai tribe there was abundance of flocks and herds, so it was ultimately decided that the raid should be made there. A few days before my arrival the expedition had started, and there was no single male remaining in the Katir district over twelve years of age, except the Pshur, and such as were too old or too ill to undertake the journey. The women meanwhile, abandoning their field-work, collected in the villages to dance day and night in honour of, and to propitiate, the gods.

All this was bad enough, but it was not till two days later that the full measure of my bad luck disclosed itself, for in their progress through the Presungul Valley the Katirs had managed to come to loggerheads with the Presun tribe, and had slain two or three of them. So when the warriors returned with immense spoil, but lamenting many killed and wounded, they found themselves involved in war with the Wai and with the Presun Káfirs as well. All idea of the Lutdeh men being able to take me to Presungul had to be given up. In fact, the only people by whose assistance the Presungul could now be reached were the Kám, who had just turned me out of their territory, not unkindly, but most decisively. The problem to be solved was how to get back to the Kám again. It was a most difficult one, yet it had to be faced.

Kán Márá, the chief of the Katirs of the Bashgul Valley, acting under instructions from the Mehtar of Chitrál, obviously wanted me to leave his village, although he was reluctant to tell me to go in so many words, while two other of the headmen of Lutdeh were beginning to grumble about my remaining any longer amongst them; not that they had any strong feeling on the subject, but because they thought there was an off-chance of their being bribed to silence when their discontent was made known.

I decided at length to march up the Skorigul Valley, and there pay a second visit to Ahmad Diwáná, in order to gain time for Shermalik to try his utmost to carry out my new plan of inducing the Kám to ask me to return to them. He was carefully instructed in all the details of the scheme, and was to keep me informed of the course of events by sending trusty messengers to Lutdeh at frequent intervals. Kán Márá, who maintained a predominating influence over his tribe by reason of the consistent support he received from his son-in-law, the Mehtar of Chitrál, gave a great sigh of relief when he heard of my intention to leave his village and travel about the country; he hurried me off with as much haste as decency permitted.

On reaching the village of Pshui or Pshowar, we found the people in anything but an amicable frame of mind. They conceived that they had been badly treated by the Lutdeh men in the division of the spoils taken in the recent raid. They absolutely refused to allow any of the Lutdeh men to enter their village. The latter laughingly admitted that the Pshowar men had been swindled, but remarked that they were "slaves," and it did not matter. However, the "slaves" made our visit very uncomfortable; not because they had any personal resentment against me, but because, knowing me to be a friend of Kán Márá, they hoped to annoy him by being rude to me. As a matter of fact, old Márá, provided that he was able to retain his unjust share of the plunder, cared little or nothing about the inconvenience any one else might suffer on his account.

One of the headmen of Pshowar, a man who had accompanied me into the Minján valley a month or so before, agreed to conduct me through the Skorigul. Everything was settled, when a second headman swaggered up, and positively declared that unless he were promised that his son should be taken to India as Shermalik had been taken, he would not allow us to travel in the Skorigul. This was merely a prelude to many other demands of a toll-paying character. We passed a most uncomfortable night. In the morning one of my cooking-vessels was stolen from a Balti in a most impudent manner in broad daylight, while the men of the village looked ripe for anything. A formidable Rámguli desperado, who was also present, wavered in his mind whether to join forces with me or incite the Pshowar men to further mischief. He wanted me to buy him over, but in an emergency of this sort it would have been dangerous to have shown any symptoms of wavering; so high-handed proceedings were adopted, and the Rámguli was sternly warned off. The villagers were threatened with the vengeance of my old friend, Murid Dastgir of Drusp, a prince to whose attack they were peculiarly exposed, if they gave me any further trouble. Then, ostentatiously examining my pistol, cocking both barrels of my rifle, and putting myself at the head of my frightened coolies, we marched out of the village with as much dignity as possible.

The Pshowar men evidently did not wish to proceed to extremities, as they knew that but a short distance off, at Badáwan, there was a firm friend of mine in the person of old Karlah Jannah, who, although he was an outlaw from the Katir tribe, was yet sufficiently strong to inspire fear in such people as those who inhabit Pshowar. So we went on our way unmolested. Karlah Jannah received me with great warmth and kindness. We became "brothers" in the usual Káfir way. We were both of us more or less outcasts, and each had a liking for the other. We remained together at his fort for several days, after which he escorted me up the Skorigul in defiance of Pshowar people, but had to confess his inability to take me anywhere else without several months' previous preparation and tribal negotiation.

Impatience for news from Kámdesh now impelled me to return to Lutdeh, in the hope of meeting some Kám messenger from Shermalik; so we said good-bye to Karlah Jannah, who shortly afterwards, finding the valley too hot for him, retreated over the Mandál Pass, and went over to the Afghans in Badakhshán.

The Pshowar people on my return journey gave me no trouble, but were clearly anxious to be friends again. They had found a strayed dog of mine, and made the *amende honorable* by feeding the little animal to such

WATCHING FOR THE MESSENGERS.

To face page 341.

an extent that it was scarcely able to walk. Their overtures were accepted in the spirit in which they were
offered, but an invitation to stay a night in the village
was declined, everything being now satisfactory, and it
being undesirable to run any risk of a rupture to our
newly restored friendship.

Ten weary days passed in Lutdeh, during which period
my time was incessantly employed in watching with field-
glasses for Kám messengers who never came. At length
I resolved to march leisurely to the Mádugál tribe, and
see what effect my presence on their actual border would
have on the Kámdesh people. While halting at the
village of Chábu, Shermalik joined me, bringing the best
of news; indeed it was altogether too good to be true.
He asserted that the Kám hungered for my return, and
that since my absence there had been such unhappiness
in the tribe, that wives would no longer speak to their
husbands. The upper village headmen were prepared
to do anything they were asked, for a consideration,
while the common people would know no happiness
until they saw me again. One piece of information
was decidedly cheering. The Káfirs had allowed my
baggage to be taken away to Chitrál immediately after
my departure, and in their scrupulous honesty had
insisted on sending away also various articles which
had been discarded as useless. This was intended to
show that the tribe was friendly towards me personally,
and that we had no ground of complaint against one
another.

Shermalik's roseate account of the friendly feelings
the Kám had for me was somewhat discounted by a
row, nearly ending in a fight, which he had with two

compatriots we met on the road; the latter abusing him for trying to take me back to Kámdesh.

Nevertheless, we started down the valley in high spirits. We arranged that two of the upper village headmen were to meet me at Bagalgrom (the chief village of the Mádugál Káfirs), and thence conduct me up the Kámdesh hill. Shermalik hurried forward to warn the people of our approach, while my party followed slowly behind.

CHAPTER XX

WHEN we reached Bagalgrom, on the 3rd of September, there were no Kám headmen to meet me, but on the following day one of the lower village Jast made his appearance. He was the orator, L. C. Merak. So far from helping me, he at once set to work, in conjunction with Bahdur, the chief of the Mádugális, to bully me. We could get little or no food, and those two rascals behaved most violently.

Finding at length that nothing was to be got out of me, even in the way of promises, by such tactics, L. C. Merak went away vapouring. Bahdur at length demanded that my "native doctor," Gokal Chand, who some time previously had joined me from Chitrál, should be left in his hands.

A man well instructed in surveying and in road sketching had been sent up to me from Peshawar, and had actually got as far as Lutdeh, when, at the sight of the Káfirs, his courage failed him, and although he

343

was then within a few easy miles of my camp, he turned
round and fairly bolted back to Chitrál. I thereupon
sent for Gokal Chand, who had been with me once
before in Kámdesh, a man whose single-hearted loyalty
could be implicitly relied upon, and whose premature
death in India in May 1892 I shall never cease to
deplore.

Gokal Chand was really a compounder of medicine
in the Chitrál dispensary, but he possessed an extraordinary amount of empirical skill in the treatment of
ordinary diseases, while his earnestness and industry
delighted the Káfirs, who could sincerely admire many
qualities of which they were themselves totally desti-
tute. Gokal Chand was unusually even-tempered and
kind-hearted, and was as popular in Káfiristán as he
was in Chitrál, where for some reason or other he was
universally known by the Hindustani word meaning
" Uncle." His professional enthusiasm was great. To
watch Gokal Chand prepare a poultice, affectionately
pat it, and then apply it with pedantic care and exactitude, was amusing and interesting. He was courageous
to fearlessness in his own peculiar way. On the march
I once offered him a spare revolver to carry, but he
turned his head away with something like annoyance,
and declared he did not know how to shoot. At the
village of Bádámuk, where we were staying for a few
days on one occasion, he hurried indignantly to where
the headmen were seated round me in solemn conclave,
and declaring he had caught a culprit throwing stones
at one of my thermometers, produced a little boy certainly not more than two years old, who smiled upon
us, while he sucked as many fingers of one hand as

he could cram into his mouth. Gokal Chand demanded that the prisoner should be punished, but we could not restrain our laughter or give him any answer, so he hurried off, his shrugging shoulders and outspread hands disclaiming all future responsibility concerning my instruments. He was born devoid of all sense of humour, but possessed that strong feeling of conscientiousness which frequently more than atones for the defect.

It was this man that Bahdur announced his intention of detaining, ostensibly as a doctor, but presumably for ransom. When his demand was refused, Bahdur informed me that we were his prisoners, and he behaved so outrageously, that I made an excuse to pitch my tent by the village bridge, and carefully studied the ground with a view to making a bolt with my baggage to Kámdesh if necessary, as it would be better to go back to the Kám uninvited than to run the risk of an almost certain conflict with the Mádugál folk. Bahdur was so sure of his position and so careless, that it is probable we should have got away in the night, and, with ordinary luck, have had no necessity for using my firearms.

We were, however, saved this experience by the opportune arrival of two Kámdesh headmen, C. Astán and Málkán, who represented the upper and lower villages respectively. They were accompanied by several followers, and announced that they had been sent from Kámdesh to escort me to that village. They further declared that all the tribe were gratified at my coming back to them, and were prepared to receive me warmly; but private information reached me that this was hardly a true description of the sentiments of the tribe, and

T

that these two headmen, with a few others, were playing a bold game to take the Kám by surprise ; all the
conspirators feeling sure that they would be handsomely
rewarded for any help they were able to give me.

The 5th of September was a somewhat exciting day.
The following extract from my diary gives some
details :—

" Bahdur furious, but dares not oppose the Kám Jast.
At suggestion of latter I gave Bahdur handsome present,
which he shortly afterwards thrusts back into my pocket,
demanding five times the amount. I make no sign.
Bahdur rages, but eventually heads procession over
bridge, and sulkily bids me farewell. We reach foot
of Kám hill, and begin ascent. Half-way up meet
scared messenger, who says village has gone mad,
and Shermalik's house has been burnt because he was
suspected of bringing me back. Resolve to go on.
Rioting at north end of village. People rushing about
with mad cries, waving weapons. C. Astán views proceedings from top of small rock, jumps down girding
up his loins, and swears he is prepared to die for me.
Málkán had gone on ahead. Troops of women have
followed us for some time. Thought women disliked
me, but at a word from Astán that I am in danger
they rush to collect my friends. Utah Ding, Shyok,
and other fighting men, few in number but nearly all
famed in war, collect around me. A big fight seems
inevitable. Coolness of little Gokal Chand. Clever
suggestion of my friends. They advance up the hill
in a body, while I, conducted by one man, slip through
the Indian-corn fields and down to the lower dancing-
platform, where my friends are rapidly collecting. They

receive me respectfully, many kissing my hands; meanwhile men of upper village, finding I am not with advancing party, rush to upper dancing-platform, whence there comes terrible uproar. Málkán makes admirable suggestion. Acting on it, I, accompanied by him alone, start for his home in upper village. Malcontents astounded at our quiet and matter-of-fact approach. They sit in silent wonder. I greet all I know in the customary manner, and try to express by my features my entire ignorance of what is going on, and what the row is about. Our triumph complete."

The success of this little *coup* was due to three causes. First, Málkán was the head of one of the clans most hostile to me, and no one suspected that he was my friend, as he had been bought over secretly. Secondly, there was no strong feeling against me personally. I should probably only have been attacked if surrounded by my own friends. Thirdly, most important of all, the rioters were taken by surprise. Káfirs almost invariably require time to sit in conclave and decide on a definite line of action.

. But our troubles were very far from ended. In my diary under date 6th September is the following note :—

"There seems no doubt that had I gone to C. Astán's house last night there would have been a severe fight, and in all probability many men must have been killed. Most violent discussions everywhere. At big conference this morning, the disaffected, white with rage, left the dancing-platform in a body at nine o'clock in a most dramatic manner. Old Sumri, A. Chárá's mother, had come down to cheer me up. The feeble old woman with her big heart is quite capable of fighting on my behalf, or rather, of getting badly hurt by persistently sitting in front of my door. The Káfir idea of comforting one is peculiar. A man just observed to me that there was not much risk for me personally ; that if people were killed they would be villagers, and that did not matter. About ten o'clock C. Astán, the 'Debilála,' and several others, came to say they would have no other 'king' but me ; they intended to build a fine house for me at once, and so on. All the time a furious rabble were rushing up and down outside with deafening outcries, which were sometimes actually drowned for a few seconds by the clamour in my room. I repudiated all wish to be a king, declaring that I only desired friendship, and adding that my heart was so sad at the internal discords of the village, that until peace were restored it would be impossible for me to discuss such questions."

It was shortly after this that C. Astán performed a miracle. The mob outside had been growing more and more furious every moment. My room was full of friends, stripped to the waist, waiting for a general attack. They looked anxious but determined. Once or twice there were false alarms, when the men jumped to their feet. The last of these alarms was peculiar. The mad crowd sweeping backwards and forwards over my house-top (my roof was contiguous to many others, which together formed a thoroughfare of the village) suddenly seemed to gather itself about my smoke-hole. The general shouting and excited speaking all at once collected itself into one swelling roar, when one of the Demidari, named Chárá, was dragged in through the door. It seems he had made some remarks on my behalf to the crowd, which at once fell

WAITING FOR THE ATTACK.

To face page 348.

upon him. Luckily, a few friends were at hand, who dragged him out of the clutches of the maniacs, and then rushed together into, and in front of, my room. Most of my friends in the east village were lying low, fearing to excite still more the already raging crowd by showing themselves ; but Utah had sent me word secretly that they were all ready, and the instant there was a real attack he and the others would hasten to my assistance. I think that, in spite of the numbers against it, my party would have won in the end, although it must have been a touch-and-go business. It was just at the moment when Chárá was pulled in, and the end seemed to have at last come, that C. Astán performed his miracle. He rushed out, and in some extraordinary way managed to make himself heard above the awful din. In an instant there was absolute silence, and almost immediately after-wards the riotous throng quietly dispersed. Waking up from a nightmare could not have produced a more remarkable effect on the senses. I was never more astonished in my life.

The truth was that the wily Astán had shouted out that sixteen thousand rupees would be paid by me to make friends again ; and that the Káfirs believed this daring lie. But knowledge of this did not reach me till afterwards, and at the time Astán's power over the people seemed simply marvellous.

On the morning of the 7th the village was quiet, but on that day, when every scrap of good fortune was re-quired to enable me to weather the storm, a surprising piece of bad luck happened. Two youths, Sunra, the grandson of Dán Malik, and Nílíra, Utah's son-in-law, were killed during a raid on the Tsárogul people. These lads belonged to the party most devoted to me, and were personal friends of mine; indeed Nílíra, in virtue of my adopted relationship to Utah, always addressed me as "father."

The whole village was in an uproar again, and when the heads of the slain were brought in for funeral ceremonies, all the women wailed piteously, while the men were furious for vengeance. The bereaved fathers threw themselves from their house-tops and rent the air with their lamentations. The grief of these unhappy people was most tragic. Nílíra's father in particular, ordinarily a mean-looking man, now became like an inspired seer. Though badly hurt by his fall, he yet with outspread hands kept crying out in a mighty voice, "O Nílíra, Nílíra, my son, my son!" No wonder his sorrow-laden accents touched the hearts of the people. It is difficult to imagine anything more intensely pathetic. On my going to try and comfort him, he, all bandaged as he was, threw himself at my feet and implored my help, although how he was to be helped was not apparent. But on the following day, two of my firmest adherents from the east village came as a deputation to again ask me to write to the Mehtar for a large force to help the Káfirs to destroy Tsárogul. Although in declining to accede to the request all my reasons were given as convincingly as possible, and all my tact was expended in trying to soften the disappointment my reply must necessarily cause, my interviewers left me in sullen anger, scarcely able to conceal the resentment they felt.

During the next few days the funeral rites of the two youths and of a third man, a famous warrior, who had died suddenly, fully occupied the attention of the village,

LAMENT OF NÍLÍRA'S FATHER.

To face page 352.

and my own personal following became a little more
reconciled to me, although the greatest caution was
necessary in dealing with them.

At the time Sunra and Nílíra were killed, two others
of the Kám were made prisoners by some of the Wai
people, although the latter were at peace with the Kám.
On the 14th the prisoners were returned with honour,
and a Káfir equivalent for an apology. This was good
news, but on the same day C. Astán came to ask me to
pay down the sixteen thousand rupees he had promised
the people in my name. Mián Gul, the ancient thorn in
my side, had fully convinced the tribe, who knew nothing
about money, that more than double that sum was in my
possession ; so C. Astán.played a bold game, and declared
he could not go back and face the Jast without the
money. His ambition was to pose as the wisest man and
the greatest benefactor of the tribe. He was impervious
to reason, and kept repeating, "How can I now face the
Jast? what can I say?" My reply was, "Speak the
truth." He went away sorrowful. For the next three
days the village was simmering.

On the 17th an envoy from the Mehtar arrived. He
also brought me a letter from the Chitrál news-writer,
which told me that the Mehtar had determined to help
me in every possible way, and had promised to help the
Kám against the Tsárogulis on certain conditions, among
which was that he must be sent beforehand a certain
number of beautiful girls. On the 20th the Chitrál
diplomatist brought the headmen to me with much com-
placency of heart, but the meeting quickly resolved itself
into something approaching a faction fight ; and on the
following day the Mehtar's ambassador left the country

in consternation at the state of affairs, and at the contempt with which the Mehtar's advice was received. A
strange thing then happened. The headmen had practically all more or less come over to me, when a new
danger arose. The young men, the "braves," believing
that they were shut out from all my favours, openly
revolted against the Jast, and there was a general temporary overthrow of authority in the tribe. The headmen were at once cowed in a way which showed that
their authority was a matter of sentiment only, but a few
of the more astute immediately placed themselves at the
head of the new movement to try and retain some portion
of their *prestige.*

Then began a series of continual changes in popular
opinion, which it was difficult or impossible to prognos-
ticate or understand. On September 22 the people
informed me that they had no objection to my going
to Presungul, nor to my selecting my own escort and
arranging with it myself, while on the 23rd it seemed
almost impossible for me to do other than start at once
for Chitrál. On the 24th, in the morning, affairs were
once more arranged, definite payments were to be made
and divided equally by the Káfirs themselves. In the
evening of the same day they passionately ordered me
out of the valley. During those days my opinion of the
questions under discussion was never asked in a single
instance, nor was I consulted in any way.

On the 25th there was another complete change of
front, and we started in a hurry for Presungul, taking
advantage of the fair wind while it lasted. My adherents
in the east village had by this time lost all patience with
their opponents, and had resolved, in the event of my

forcible expulsion from the upper village, to conduct me to a certain tower, and there settle the matter in dispute by force of arms. My party in the upper village, which was gradually increasing, also met together and secretly agreed to have recourse to force if Málkán's ultimatum was not accepted. Málkán's arrangement was this : he was to give security for my promised payments by placing all his portable property in the hands of the opponents of my journey, while my escort was to be composed exclusively of my enemies, who were to be paid a definite sum for their services.

It was a curious plan to start in this way, with the wildest and most turbulent of my opponents as my companions, yet it was the easiest way out of the difficulty, and the only method of avoiding bloodshed. I trusted also in my ability to make the men behave properly as soon as they had once got away from the village ; for if you can only prevent Káfirs from going off together and holding excited conferences, they are much less difficult to manage than might be supposed.

We crossed the Kungani Pass on September 28th, and began our march down the Presungul Valley.

CHAPTER XXI

MY escort behaved abominably. Utah, the priest, and two other of my friends followed secretly from Kámdesh. When they caught us up there was trouble, but Utah, with much tact, soon secured his usual ascendency by posing as the bitterest of my opponents. The chief danger of a turbulent people is when they are left in disgust by their natural leaders, and are ruled by mere demagogues. From this extreme danger Utah's presence relieved me.

My rough experiences in Káfiristán were now beginning to tell on me. Fever seized me and sore throat, and one of my heel tendons became swollen and inflamed, so that it was impossible for me to put a stop to the excitement, and try to restrain the insane cupidity which had seized on my escort; but all their insolent demands fell on a deaf ear. The Kám declared that supplies must not be paid for by giving money to the villagers who brought them, but that the price must be paid to the Kám to divide amongst themselves. When they were informed that this could not and should not be done, they waxed

358

furious. But it was no part of my plans to leave behind in the minds of the Presun people the impression that the first Englishman they had seen had bullied and swindled them. It required great care on my part to ensure that every man received his just due ; the payments had to be made secretly, for fear the Kám, of whom the villagers stood in the greatest dread, should force the money from its lawful owners. My escort kept holding daily conferences, which it was impossible for me to prevent or be present at. These meetings gradually became noisier, and our general relations more and more strained. At a village called Pushkigrom, the only dangerous village in the Presun Valley, there was a disturbance between my escort and the people, which was only stopped when the former remembered in time the paucity of their numbers.

On the following day, having fully incited the villagers against us, as they supposed, my escort left me in a body. As a matter of fact, to get rid of the troublesome rascals was a source to me of great pleasure. Fraternising at once with the villagers, I took the opportunity, on being deserted, or rather on being left unguarded, to limp down the valley to inspect a certain stretch of country. As soon as they found that they had failed in their attempt to frighten me by leaving me alone in the middle of the excited village, the Kám trooped back again, and my return journey had to be made in their company. Utah and my few friends dared not say a single word, but were compelled for their own safety to side with the majority.

At length, at Shtevgrom matters came to a crisis. We were sitting round a great fire in the gromma. The Kám men for the two preceding days had been growing more

and more excited. The daily march had been short, and
all the rest of the time was spent by them in heated
conferences, where they harangued one another violently.
I had somewhat forgotten my caution, and had just expressed my determination to visit the Kamah Pass, when,
at something one of their number said, there went up a
shout of approval, while Shermalik looked scared and
burst into tears. Most of the men half started to their
feet, and, in spite of Utah's "Matah-matah" (gently,
gently) and his imploring gestures, they glared at me
furiously. I was obviously within an ace of being seized,
and there was no time to be lost. My worries had been
so incessant, and I had been so badly used of late, that
for an instant a thought of the delight it would be to
give two of the ringleaders the contents of my heavy
Lancaster pistol if an actual attack occurred, clouded my
judgment. But in a flash of thought I saw that such a
proceeding must inevitably result in the massacre of my
whole party; and as I got up from my seat and looked
at the wild faces, the first part of my subsequent plan
formed itself in my mind. I moved slowly to the door,
but once through it, jumped hastily on to the house-top
where my tent was pitched and flung the pistol on my
bed. The next instant I was several yards away walking
up and down and whistling unconcernedly, looking over
the parapet. Presently the Kám came slowly towards me
from the three other sides. One or two of them began
to speak soothingly, telling me not to mind what had been
said, that it was all Shermalik's nonsense, and so forth.
All the time they edged up to me continually. By an
assumed natural movement I flung open my rough ulster
and put my hands in my trousers pockets. By this

THE TENT RUSHED.

To face page 363.

action they discovered I was not wearing my pistol. At the same instant a shout from that little rascal Chandlu Torag, who was spying into the tent, told them that the weapon was lying on my bed. They at once rushed the tent and seized all my firearms. I tried one last act of "swagger," and loudly ordered them to put the guns back. They were so surprised at my manner and tone that they seemed on the point of obeying, when some one cried out, "You obey this Frank as if you were his dogs." Then there was no more hope. My Baltis had been all put under arrest and warned that on the least disobedience of orders they would be killed, while I was now bluntly informed I was a prisoner and was to be carried away to Kámdesh tied to two poles. For the first and last time in Káfiristán I was in imminent danger of being subjected to personal ignominy. I replied quietly that I was seriously annoyed with them, and did not wish to speak with them any more. They stood and whispered for a few moments, and then all, except two or three, went back into the gromma.

After walking up and down for half-an-hour, just as if nothing had happened, I shouted as usual for Mir Zaman, one of the Baltis, to bring me hot water for my teeth. He was allowed to do so. The poor fellow was trembling with fear and weeping. Without detection I managed to tell Gokal Chand to get hold of Chandlu Torag, and promise him anything he liked if he would procure me a guide to take me out of Shtevgrom during the night. Gokal Chand in the middle of the conclave in the gromma gave my message to Chandlu Torag, who was the only one amongst them who could speak Chitráli. In the meantime, I had ostentatiously undressed and got into bed and put out my light, to arise immediately afterwards and redress myself. A goat was just then being sacrificed in the gromma, and all the Káfirs went to the feast, believing me safe for the night. While the ceremony was proceeding and the responses were being made, Gokal Chand, Chandlu Torag, and a Presun man crept into my tent. In a few minutes we had packed up a few stale chappaties, and two or three blankets. The parapet was only a few feet distant, so holding our breath, we silently dropped over it on to a slope of stony fragments below, all except Chandlu Torag, who crawled back to the gromma, where he made himself prominent, and took care of his alibi. On the moving stones it was a little difficult to keep our foothold, and poor little Gokal Chand more than once sat down unintentionally and violently, on each of which occasions the shingle slipped with him, making an appalling rattle. We stopped, palpitating, and listened intently; but the stars in their course fought for us, for a war-party of the Presungulis just then issued from the village with anticipatory shouts of victory, and under cover of this, the only kind of pæan they were ever likely to raise, we managed to get clear of Shtevgrom. Our guide would at times bid us lie still, while he crept forward to reconnoitre. It was impossible not to remember the stories which had delighted one's youth. It almost seemed as if we were playing at Indians over again. Finally we crossed the river and hid in a labyrinth of goat-pens, where the only possible fear of discovery lay in our being tracked by my dogs.

Our hiding-place was perfect. Not only were we in the labyrinth of pens already mentioned, but we were

THE ESCAPE BY NIGHT.

To face page 364.

also concealed in an inner small apartment, the presence of which could have hardly been suspected by any one, while in the big outer room a woman came at daylight with her children, who played about noisily and unconsciously, although it is certain that the woman must have known where we were. Chandlu Torag himself could not find us in the evening, until we revealed our presence by whistling, although he knew the particular block in which we were concealed. In the evening the coast being reported clear, we emerged from our hiding-place. We learned that our absence had not been discovered by the Káfirs until the early morning, when Chandlu Torag had at once been suspected of helping us; but he declared, and most of the Káfirs believed, that he had never left the gromma for a single instant during the night, while all remembered that he was one of the foremost in rushing my tent. They knew instinctively that he must be in some way connected with our getting away, but he had managed so cleverly, that they could prove nothing against him. He had confided everything to Utah, who contrived to be left behind, on the remote chance of my having gone down the Presun Valley. From our hiding-place we had watched the Kám people hunt everywhere, scour the country to find us, and eventually start off with my poor Baltis as prisoners, under the impression that I had gone to the Katir part of the Bashgul Valley.

Next day we ascended and examined the Kamah Pass, which leads from Presungul to the Minján Valley, and after a night's rest, hurried after the Kám men, rightly conjecturing that they would be hard put to it to explain in a satisfactory way to my friends, or even to my opponents, in Kámdesh, the cause of my absence. The Baltis were certainly safe, provided I put in my appearance without delay, while it was nearly certain that, after a few days' reflection, my late companions would cool down, and, after separating each to his own home, would rapidly grow shamefaced and depressed when deprived of the support of their fellow-rascals.

I got back to Kámdesh on October 14th, after we had suffered considerable hardships on the road, when, on account of my inflamed heel-tendon, we had been obliged to take up our quarters in a cave for a time, to find my prognostications were true. The men who had behaved so badly to me were now become humble. The whip was in my hand, and it was applied as freely as was consistent with prudence. After haranguing the people many times, I only consented to return to my house in the upper village after receiving profuse apologies, and when we had reached a point beyond which it would have been unsafe to carry the matter farther. When Káfirs are excited, it is necessary to keep absolutely calm and cool ; but when they are ashamed of themselves, it is good policy to assume anger and indignation. In all circumstances a traveller should seek, at all hazards, to maintain his personal dignity in an unbending manner. There was now a considerable revulsion of tribal feeling on my behalf; nevertheless it was clear that the time for my going away had arrived. My sole remaining object was that my departure should be a friendly one on both sides. The Kám had become tired of their internal dissensions, and were more desirous than ever of entering into an alliance with Umrá Khan of Jandúl. They were prevented with difficulty from adopting the suicidal policy of introducing a large Jandúl force into their valley to help them against the Tsáro-gulis. They indeed stopped short of this mad scheme, but they were all agreed in the opinion that they had nothing to lose and everything to gain by accepting the Khan's overtures. He had always made a great point of the necessity of my going back to Gilgit before he and they could become friends. It was a knowledge of this fact which made the Kám willing and anxious for me to leave their country without further ado. I also wished to start for Gilgit, where frontier troubles were threatening, and where it occurred to me that my presence might possibly be useful ; besides which, it was extremely doubtful if my temper could have borne the strain of a longer residence in Káfiristán, without a change of some kind. My best friends thought it expedient for me to go away from Kámdesh for a time. We all parted on good terms. At our final interviews the statesmen of the tribe begged me to remember them with good-will. They were evidently well assured of my kindly inten-tions towards them, and plumed themselves greatly on having secured my friendship, while they at the same time felt certain of securing the alliance with Umrá Khan. My warnings against the designs of that wily and ambi-tious ruler were entirely disregarded. Only a very few people paid the slightest attention to my words, and those were men of little or no influence in the village. The Káfirs were simply fatuous on the subject of Umrá Khan, and paid dearly for their credulity.

Just before starting, the Káfirs were informed of my readiness to take a certain number of the Kám tribe to India with me as guests of the Viceroy. Nearly the

u

whole village clamoured to go. Instead of finding it hard to get men to accept my invitation, as was the case on my first visit to Kámdesh, the difficulty was how to make any selection from the crowds of volunteers. Once more angry discussions broke out all over the village. The different clans became jealous of one another, and fighting was only avoided with difficulty, and not before one or two dagger-wounds had been inflicted. To prevent further disturbances, it was decided by the Jast that no one should be allowed to go. To enforce this decision, a large company of the Kám was deputed to escort me to the frontier, nominally to ensure my suffering no inconvenience on the road, but really to prevent any of the tribe going away with me. It was also decided and proclaimed that, should any one be presumptuous enough to disregard the orders of the Jast and accept my invitation to India, his wives, his houses, his flocks, and his herds, would be seized and sold, and the proceeds divided among the clans. At the time it was my fixed resolution to return to Káfiristán after a winter's rest, to penetrate into and explore the western valley. I had, therefore, been careful to secure young men of good family belonging both to the Kám and the Katir tribes to go with me on a visit to India. It was all very well for the Kám elders to threaten all kinds of penalties to any one who accepted my invitation, but it was perfectly certain that nothing would or could be done to anybody who accompanied me, provided that he belonged to a sufficiently powerful clan.

I left Kámdesh on October 22, and crossed the Chitrál frontier three days later. The large number of Káfirs who escorted me bade me good-bye in a cordial and friendly spirit just short of the border. It certainly did not surprise me when, an hour or two later, the young men invited to accompany me began to catch me up one by one. They fell into their places calmly and naturally, and listened with the greatest fortitude to the messages that were sent after them by the Kám headmen. They knew well that the clans to which they belonged were not only strong enough to protect their property from being pillaged, but were at heart delighted that their representatives were with me.

We halted five days in Chitrál to collect the whole party and make final arrangements for the journey to Gilgit. The Mehtar was extremely kind and helpful, while the Chitrális, especially Shah-i-Mulk, the governor of Kila Drosh, and others who lived near the Káfir border, viewed me with great interest, not unmixed with some feeling of disappointment. They had predicted, with conviction, that I should never be seen again, especially after the disturbances broke out in Kámdesh consequent on my return to that village; and they were, perhaps, just a little hurt at finding their prophecies falsified. Shah-i-Mulk never tired of slightly paraphrasing an old saying, "It is all very wonderful, but the most wonderful thing is that you have returned."

CHAPTER XXII

My party reached Gilgit on November 16th. The
Hunza-Nagar expedition was on the point of starting,
and shortly afterwards, owing to the unhappy accident
of Colonel Durand being wounded at the storming of
Nilt Fort, it fell to my lot to officiate as British Agent
at Gilgit until the end of the war. Since then my time
has been so constantly employed on frontier "political"
duty, that my once cherished design of returning to
Káfiristán will now never be carried out.

My work in that country is consequently most incom-
plete, but one chief object ever present to my mind has,
I believe, been accomplished. It was this : that in everything I did or said, the possibility of some other Englishman following me must always be remembered. I
invariably acted on the supposition that I was the first
of a series of travellers about to visit Káfiristán, and
that the success of those coming after me would largely
depend on the way the people were managed by me,
and on the general impression they were given of my
fellow-countrymen.

Without being didactic, it may be well to put down
my opinion of the methods which should be adopted by
travellers who may have dealings with a people like the

Káfirs. The first thing is to try and impress their minds with the idea of a strong personality. Geniality and grave kindness of manner are as valuable as anything like buffoonery or "chaff" is hurtful. The Káfirs would at times shout with laughter at good-tempered ironical remarks of a very simple kind. With an excitable people, such as they are, perfect coolness and command of the temper when they are effervescing or clamouring are indispensable. Ignorance of the language spoken has its advantages as well as its drawbacks. It is even necessary sometimes to assume a greater ignorance than you possess. On more than one occasion at Kámdesh, a furious conclave has been completely discomfited by my quietly bringing a chair, sitting down in a convenient position, watching the proceedings with a sympathetic interest for a few minutes, and then turning to my book.

Once the rascal Mersi had the assurance to harangue a small crowd, inflaming them against me, close to my house. I stepped up to the orator, nodded pleasantly to him, and offered the Káfir salutation for "How are you?" &c. He was so embarrassed that all his eloquence left him, and the people laughed heartily, enjoying the fun of my supposed unconsciousness of what was going on. Another time a man, peacocking before a group of women, shouted to me to leave the valley within a day, or he would—and he made a sign with his hand of plunging a dagger into his stomach. I went up to the man, touched the place he had so violently indicated, and told him to go to Gokal Chand for medicine. That man was shouted at by his fellows for weeks afterwards. It is needless to multiply instances, for any Englishman with the faintest sense of humour can always score off wild men up to the actual outbreak of hostilities, provided that he keeps cool. No particular amount of courage is required, for anxiety is a transient emotion, and goes away of itself after a day or two. The real cause of my troubles in Presungul was my own illness, which prevented me from restraining the first beginnings of the outbreak. After my recovery, it had made too much headway, and there was no remedy, for the people had gone mad. Truthfulness is very important. The Káfirs used to test my word by coming back a week or two after they had been told stories of things which appeared marvellous to the verge of impossible in their eyes. They would with assumed ingenuousness revert to the former conversations, and would cross-examine me with great skill. I always took care that numbers and other facts never varied in my answers.

The people gradually came to trust me to a considerable extent. At first they would never give sheep or other provisions without the money being paid down on the spot ; but later on, men would go for weeks without taking the price of their property. They treated me, in fact, as a kind of bank.

A traveller cannot, in short, be too rigid in keeping all promises. I adopted the plan of insisting upon having my own way, as far as possible, whenever my fixed determination had been definitely announced, even when a persistence in my resolution might appear almost churlish. On the whole, the results of this experiment were good, but it taught me caution, and the necessity of never declaring a fixed resolve except after proper consideration.

Lastly, it is always of the utmost importance to try and discover the drift of public opinion. It is dangerous to disregard it merely because it often appears illogical or inconsequential, although it may be politic to set it at defiance on exceptional occasions, if you feel sufficiently sure of the ground beneath your feet. A greater mistake cannot be made than to strive unduly to win the affections of the people. The thing itself is practically an impossibility. If you retain their respect and confidence, and possibly their gratitude also, nothing more is necessary. The only way to gain the love of their hearts is voluntarily to abdicate the heirdom of centuries of civilisation, to sink to a lower level of conduct, to approve of what cannot be defended, and to affect an indifference to most of the Christian virtues. It is well also to remember that you cannot change the nature of an adult, however much you may be desirous of doing so. Wild men may be controlled or influenced by the methods universally known, but their instincts are immutable.

EFFIGIES.

CHAPTER XXIII

The Káfir Pantheon—Difficulty of investigation—Scepticism—Bashgulis and Presuns contrasted—Theology—List of the chief deities—Story of Bagisht —Legends of Imrá—Imrá's sacrifices and temples—Imrá's handwriting —The mysterious hole—Imrá's iron bar—Other places sacred to Imrá— Gods grouped for worship—Sacred stones outside temples—Moní—Other deities—Dizane —Nirmali—Krumai.

THE Káfir religion is a somewhat low form of idolatry, with an admixture of ancestor-worship and some traces of fire-worship also. The gods and goddesses are numerous, and of varying degrees of importance or popularity. Probably Imrá the Creator, Moní (commonly spoken of as "the prophet"), Gísh the war-god, Bagisht, Dizane, Krumai, and Nirmali are common to all the tribes, but there are several inferior deities, or godlings, who seem to be peculiar to particular localities. It is probable, almost certain, that the same god is known by different names in different tribes; but even if we allow for this, there must still be many gods who are unknown or disregarded except by particular tribes, or even in particular villages. In Presungul every village is supposed to be under the care of one special god, whom the villagers worship and honour above all others. The god Arom is the tutelary deity of the Kám tribe; but he appears to be rather unpopular, and to be chiefly sacrificed to when a peace is concluded.

The difficulty of getting information from the Káfirs about their religion is very great. In Presungul the people at first protested against my being shown their gods at all, and it was only after they had been assured by my companions that I was a Káfir like themselves that they gave a somewhat reluctant consent. The Bashgul Káfirs had no objections of this kind; indeed, they seemed to take a peculiar pleasure in showing me their little temples, and in inviting me to be present at their ceremonies. On those occasions they were in the habit of watching my face narrowly, as if anxious to discover from my features my opinion about their observances. With them the chief difficulty was that they seemed to know so little about their own theology. People were constantly referring me from one man to another for information, but each succeeding informant seemed to know less than his predecessor, while the little he had to tell was only extracted after the expenditure of much time and trouble. Cross-examination of a Káfir irritates when it does not bore him or send him to sleep. If pressed with what he considers tiresome questions, the man not unfrequently jumps up and makes a clean bolt of it. My information was mainly derived from the little stories of the gods which were related to me and to other listeners in the evening round a fire by Utah, the high-priest, and by Karlah Jannah, who was a born story-teller; but the latter, unhappily, was extraordinarily impatient of anything like interruption, and equally disliked subsequent questions designed to clear up doubtful points in a narrative. Dán Malik of Kámdesh was the man who, by common repute, knew more about the principles of his religion than any other person, but it was impossible to obtain much information from him. He had a habit of always turning the tables upon me by plying me with questions; besides which, he seemed to think that the most interesting points for discussion were whether the English or Russians were created first by Imrá? which country was first created? how many daughters Bábá (father) Adam had? and many other similar speculations, which he would return to again and again, to the exclusion of all other religious questions.

It must be remembered that the Bashgul Káfirs are no longer an isolated community, in the strict sense of the word. They frequently visit Chitrál, and have dealings with other Musalmán peoples as well. Many of their relatives have embraced Islám without abandoning the ties of relationship. One of the results of this free intercourse with Musalmáns is that Bashgul Káfirs at the present day are very apt to mix up their own religious traditions with those of their Musálman neighbours. This greatly confuses matters, and it is hopeless for me to try to write anything final, or even moderately comprehensive, concerning the religion of Káfiristán; a modest record of what I actually saw and actually heard is all that can be attempted. Possibly a better acquaintance with the Bashgul language might have made many things clear

to me which now remain dark, and perhaps had my interpreters been better the same result might have followed ;
but it appears to me that the chief reason why I discovered
so little about the Káfir faith is because the Káfirs themselves know so little on the subject. It would seem that
in Káfiristán the forms of religion remain, while the philo-
sophy which those forms were originally intended to
symbolise is altogether forgotten. This is not, perhaps,
surprising in a country in which there are no records of
any kind, and everything depends on oral tradition.

The Bashgul Káfirs, or at any rate the younger portion
of the community, are inclined to be somewhat sceptical.
They are superstitious, of course, but sacred ceremonies
are frequently burlesqued or scoffed at when two or three
waggish young men get together. Gísh is the really
popular god of the Bashgul youth. In their worship
of him there is great sincerity. A young Káfir once
asked me if we English did not prefer Gísh to Imrá (the
Creator), as he himself did, and many Káfirs have expressed their disappointment on learning that Franks
knew nothing of Gísh.

The older people are devout in their respect for all the
gods, but Bashgul Káfirs seem ready to abandon their
religion at any time without much regret. They leave
it, as they return to it, chiefly from motives of material
advantage, and rarely appear to trouble themselves about
religious convictions. The purest form of the Káfir religion is probably to be found in the Presungul. The Kám
told me that although the Bashgul Káfirs had no objection to my bringing fowls into their valley, the Presungulis would never permit it in theirs. In Presungul
there is a distinct atmosphere of religion. Devil's vil-

lages abound, the old watercourses are currently believed to have been built by gods or goddesses; miraculous imprints of divine or demoniac hands are shown on rocks; there is an iron pillar which is said to have been placed in its present position by Imrá himself, and a sacred hole in the ground, to look down which is certain death to any one. Large tracts of fertile lands lie undisturbed by the plough, because they are consecrated to Imrá. Most important of all, the valley possesses a famous temple of Imrá, renowned throughout all Káfiristán. The Presuns, unfortunately, speak a language which every one declared that it is impossible for anybody to acquire unless he has been actually born in the valley. For my part, no single word used at any of their sacrifices remains in my memory. To me the invocations and incantations were merely soft, musical mewings. The Presuns were very friendly after a short acquaintance, and looked upon me not only as a very great man, but also as one who might be trusted; but the fatal language difficulty always prevented my learning much from them.

In the Káfir theology there appears to be both a heaven and a hell. It divides the universe into Urdesh, the world above, the abode of the gods; Míchdesh, the earth; and Yurdesh, the nether world. Both the heaven and the hell for mortals is in Yurdesh, which is reached through a great pit, at the mouth of which a custodian named Maramalik, specially created by Imrá for the purpose, is always seated. He permits no one in Yurdesh to return to the upper world.

When a man dies, his soul or breath—the word *shon* has both meanings—enters into one of the shadow forms we see in dreams, which then becomes a *partir*. Good

people appear to wander about as shades in a paradise in
Yurdesh called Bisht, while, as a common Káfir phrase
goes, "Wicked sinners are always burning in fire" in
Zozuk (hell). Káfirs have no intense fear of death,
although they cannot understand suicide. The idea of a
man killing himself strikes them as inexplicable. They
are never melancholy. The gods are worshipped by
sacrifices, by dances, by singing hymns (Lálu Kunda),
and by uttering invocations (Namach Kunda). Fairies
and demons are propitiated by sacrifices. The only
phrase known to me which is comparable to our "pro-
fane swearing" is "Shut Imrá di psálá" (May the curse
of God strike you).

The principal gods and goddesses are :—

1. Imrá.	10. Nong.
2. Moní.	11. Paráde.
3. Gísh.	12. Shomde.
4. Bagisht.	13. Saranji or Sauranju.
5. Arom.	14. Dizane,
6. Sanru.	15. Nirmali, ⎫ Goddesses.
7. Satarám or Sudaram.	16. Krumai or
8. Inthr.	Shumai ⎭
9. Duzhi.	

Besides gods and goddesses there are demons, the
chief of whom is Yush, and fairies innumerable. The
high-priest of the Kám instructed me as follows.

Imrá is the creator of all things in heaven and earth.
By the breath of his mouth he endowed with life his
"prophets" Moní, Gísh, Satarám, and the rest; but
Dizane sprang into existence from his right breast.
Placing her in the palm of his hand, Imrá threw her
violently upwards. She alighted in a lake, and was

there concealed and released in a manner to be described presently. Of the inferior deities or "prophets," only Bagisht was born after the manner of mortals, and not created at once by Imrá's breath. Besides creating the godlings, Imrá also created seven daughters, whose special province it is to watch over the work of agriculture with a protecting hand. As the time for sowing approaches, goats are sacrificed in their honour, in order that crops may be ample and the earth beneficent.

Imrá also created fairies and demons, but the latter gave so much trouble to the world, that Moní, with the divine permission, almost entirely exterminated them. One terrible fiend, a devil of the worst type, on one occasion was dancing before Moní. The prophet removed a screw or plug from the demon's body surreptitiously. He repeated the act until seven screws had been withdrawn, when the body of the Evil One fell to pieces. From the fragments of the body, seven in number, seven fresh demons sprang to life, but Moní slew them all with his sword.

The story of the birth of Bagisht was told as follows by the Kám priest :—

"In a distant land, unknown to living men, a large tree grew in the middle of a lake. The tree was so big, that if any one had attempted to climb it, he would have taken nine years to accomplish the feat ; while the spread of its branches was so great that it would occupy eighteen years to travel from one side of it to the other. Satarám became enamoured of the tree, and journeyed towards it. On his near approach he was suddenly seized with a mighty trembling, and the huge tree burst asunder, disclosing the goddess Dizane in the centre of its trunk.

Satarám had, however, seen enough; he turned round and fled in consternation.

"Dizane began to milk goats (a question as to where the goats were, in the water or on the tree, was thrust aside with a wave of the hand). While she was engaged in this occupation, a devil observed her. He had four eyes, two in front and two behind. Rushing forward, he seized Dizane, while she bent her head to her knees, quaking with terror. The fiend tried to reassure her, saying, 'It is for you I have come.' She afterwards wandered into the Presungul, and stepping into the swift-flowing river, gave birth to an infant, who at once, unaided, stepped ashore, the turbulent waters becoming quiet, and piling themselves up on either hand, to allow the child to do so. The country people were astounded at the prodigy. They hurried to the scene, and on the river-bank found a little boy seated on a stone. The child then started down the river by himself, leaving all spectators bewildered. He had gone only a short distance when he met a man who asked him his name. He replied, 'You know my name; I do not.' The stranger then informed him that he was Bagisht, and that he would always be known by that name thereafter."

To understand the Káfir idea of Imrá the Creator, some more stories must be told. Many of them are bald and inconsequential; others illustrate the fact that the Káfirs have endowed Imrá with many of their own special characteristics. Of the first kind the two following stories will be sufficient. (a.) Once upon a time Imrá and the devil (Yush) rode a horse-race. Imrá's horse was made of gold, the devil's of iron. For some time neither gained an advantage; but Imrá created innumerable rats, which burrowed into the ground and made an immense number of holes, over which the devil's horse stumbled and blundered, allowing Imrá to win easily. (*b.*) Imrá once gave a book to the devil, and after a time demanded it back again. The devil refused to give it up, on the plausible ground that it had been given to him and was his. Then Imrá and he had a fight; the devil was killed, and the book recovered.

The following are better stories. (1.) Imrá and all the prophets (the narrator of this story was a Persian-speaking Káfir, who used the Persian word for prophet to denote all the gods except Imrá) were seated one day at the mouth of the valley up which runs a road from the Skorigul to the Presungul. The goddess Krumai, in the shape of a goat, came over from Tirich Mir[1] and went among them, but none recognised her except Imrá, who took an opportunity, when she was not looking, to push her into the mountain-stream. Struggling out of the water, Krumai ran diagonally up the steep rock, leaving the marks still visible in a vein of mineral of a colour different from the rest of the rock. When she got to the top she began kicking down showers of stones on to the gods below, to their great annoyance. Imrá told them that the goat was Krumai, and added that he alone had been clever enough to discover that fact. On hearing this they all adjured Krumai to behave better. She thereupon assumed her proper shape, came down amongst them, and subsequently entertained them all at

---

[1] Tirich Mir is a sacred mountain. At Badáwan (Ahmad Diwáná) there is a small square erection in the usual Káfir style, like the pedestal of an effigy. This is surmounted by what is said to be a model of Tirich Mir. Before this curious shrine goats are sacrificed to the gods and fairies supposed to live on the mountain.

a sumptuous banquet which she brought from Tirich Mir and served on silver dishes.

(2.) Imrá one day sat himself on the rocky spur at the junction of the Kti and Presun rivers. He was engaged in making butter in a golden goat-skin churn. From the skin three women emerged, who went and populated different countries. Imrá then ádded water, and a fourth woman was created, who settled in Presungul.

(3.) Once Imrá took the sun and the moon from the heavens and the world became buried in darkness. Everybody died except one man, who prayed to God for a little light. Moved by pity, Imrá gave the man a bit of the sun and a bit of the moon, which he fastened on each side of him, and then, mounting his horse, rode away. Wherever he went there was just sufficient light for him to guide his horse. After a time he reached Presungul, when Imrá appeared in front of him. "Hullo," said the man, "who are you?" "I am Imrá," was the reply. The horseman was speechless with awe and astonishment. "Let us perform the ceremony of friendship," suggested Imrá, but the man pointed out that he had not a goat. "Never mind that," replied Imrá, "I will soon fetch one." Saying which he stepped over to the mountains by the Zidig Pass, and returned with a fine goat. "But," objected the man, "where is the knife to sacrifice it with?" He had no sooner uttered these words than the goat began to dig up the ground vigorously with its forefeet, shaking its body all the time as a wet dog does. At the bottom of the shallow hole made by the goat a knife was revealed. Imrá seized it, and he and the man went through the ceremony of swearing brotherhood. When it was over Imrá said, "Now what are you going

x

to give me?" "I have nothing," replied the man; "what can I give?" "You have your horse," persisted Imrá, "give me that." "But I shall have nothing to go about on," protested the man; "no, I cannot give you my horse." Thereupon Imrá summoned an angel, who quietly stole the man's horse and led it away. As it was being carried off the horse cried out, "I have a sword in my ear; pull it out and kill all your enemies." Imrá drew the sword out of the horse's ear, and used it against his enemies. He subsequently replaced the sun and the moon in the sky, and light was restored to the earth.

(4.) A good story was told me about the sacred tree, whose branches were seven families of brothers, each seven in number, while the trunk was Dizane and the roots Nirmali; but the record of this story was lost in a mountain torrent.

(5.) After Imrá created the world, Bábá Adam and his wife were in Kashmir. They and their forty children were on one occasion sleeping in pairs, and when they awoke no single pair understood the language of another pair. They were then ordered by Imrá to march off in couples and populate the world. They went most un- willingly, declaring that Kashmir was good enough for them; but of course Imrá's orders had to be obeyed.

(6.) The reason why iron is found in some countries is that Imrá, some time or other, cast a devil made of iron into each of those countries. This was told me in the course of conversation, and my companion, Karlah Jannah, was astonished that I had never seen a certain iron bridge in Kashmir which he averred was made out of the body of a devil.

(7.) Once Imrá and all the godlings were seated on a hilltop, while in front of them were a golden bed and a golden stool. "These belong to me," observed Imrá. "Not at all," cried the others, "they belong to us all in common." "Very well," rejoined Imrá, "we will soon see who has the power to use them to the exclusion of everybody else." With that remark, he sat himself on the beautiful bed. All the other gods looked confounded, no one venturing to say anything.

(8.) On a second occasion, Imrá took the sun and the moon from the sky, and fastening them one on each side of him, rode into the centre of the mountains behind Kstigigrom in Presungul, where he went to sleep. But he had been watched by seven devils, who finding him fast asleep, carried away the horse and fastened it in a house. Of course all this time the world was in darkness, and the gods were blundering about on the road, falling and hurting themselves. "What shall we do?" they cried in despair. Presently one of them (I forget which) fancied he perceived a track of light. This was really the path taken by the horse. Following it up, the god came to the house where the horse was confined, and through a crack in the door saw what had happened. He went back at once and told his brother gods. They all went in a body, broke down the door, and liberated the horse. While they were leading him out, the horse observed that he had a sword in his ear which should be pulled out, and that with it the devils ought to be put to death. The gods at once obeyed this injunction. Afterwards the sun and the moon were restored to the heavens, and the world was again illuminated.

(9.) The following story seems to show that other gods

besides Imrá are possessed of creative powers to some
extent. Inthr made Badáwan (Ahmad Diwáná) his
resting-place, and there created vineyards and pleasant
. places, but Imrá suddenly declared the place was his.
Inthr refused to give way, and a severe fight ensued, in
which he' was worsted, and was compelled to retreat
down the valley a short space, when he created the hill
south of Badáwan, and also the Skorigul Valley. But
Imrá again attacked him and once more drove him away,
so that he was compelled to abandon the Bashgul Valley
altogether, and fly for refuge to the Tsárogul.

(10.) But Imrá often helps his people. Once upon a
time there was an enormous snake which inhabited the
Minján end of the Bashgul Valley. He used to lie in
wait for travellers on the top of certain high rocks still
pointed out, as are also the tracks by which he used to
descend and eat up the unlucky strangers. The tracks
indicated are some light quartz veins which show distinctly against the darker ground of the rocks. Imrá,
pitying the people, sent a messenger to the snake ordering him to desist from the evil practices, but the snake not
only paid no attention to Imrá's remonstrances, but ate up
the messenger who conveyed them. Then Imrá came himself, and slew the snake by cutting off its head. The
large tarn above Badáwan was formed from the blood
which flowed from the snake's head. The very spot
where the fabulous reptile was killed was shown me by a
Káfir.

Imrá is sacrificed to very frequently, sometimes from
motives of simple and general piety, especially by the
older and more thoughtful members of the community;
sometimes for particular reasons, such as recovery from

sickness, thanksgiving for seasonable weather, and for other material benefits. At the religious dances he is not more honoured than many of the other gods and goddesses. He receives three rounds, but there is none of the enthusiasm which is infused into the dances for Gísh, or the light-heartedness which accompanies the comical steps and posturings in honour of Krumai. Possibly in former times Imrá the Creator was chiefly worshipped, but at the present time Gísh is certainly the popular deity in the Bashgul Valley, while Imrá probably retains his proper ascendency in the Presungul, and in some other places. Cows are commonly sacrificed to Imrá everywhere in Káfiristán.

Imrá's temples are in every village, and are also met with far away from any dwelling-houses. They sometimes contain a wooden idol, sometimes merely a block of stone. In Kámdesh there are two principal places where sacrifices are made to Imrá. One is a little temple at the top of the spur on which the village is built, the other is a simple stone some 3 feet by 1 foot by 1 foot, which is placed on end under a mulberry tree 400 feet lower down the slope, close by a very sacred pool. The stone is blackened with the blood of countless sacrifices, while the shrine above the village is comparatively rarely visited.

The chief temple to Imrá is at Presungul, at Kstigigrom, which is undoubtedly the most sacred village in the whole of Káfiristán. The temple itself is an imposing structure, elaborately ornamented. It is between 50 and 60 feet square, and about 20 feet high. On its east side it has a square portico which covers as much space as the temple itself, and is supported on carved wooden pillars, forming a kind of rough colonnade. The portico is open to the east and south, but is boarded up on the north side. Its height is a few feet below that of the temple, and when I saw it the roof was in a dangerous state of disrepair. The carving of the pillars is supposed to be very fine. They are all fashioned after one of three designs. A favourite one is to have a row of rams' heads, one on each side of the column, extending from the top to the base. Another popular design is to carve at the foot of the pillar an animal's head, from which the horns are made to extend the entire height of the pillar, crossing and re-crossing each other at intervals, and ending above in points, between which a grotesque face appears with hands grasping each horn a few inches from the top. The third variety is of the common basket pattern. Under this portico many sacrifices are made. A large offal heap to the south showed that the offerings were cattle. There is a sacrificing stone in the colonnade, and near it one or two niches for idols. The east side of the temple, on to which the portico is built, has seven famous doors of large size, and above each another smaller door. Of the seven large doors five cannot be opened; they are securely fastened up. The other two, at the south end of the east front, are thrown open on solemn occasions, when the people are allowed to enter and view the holy place. On these two doors, and in a line with them on the dummy doors and in an intervening space, are eight huge wooden figures of Imrá. The effigies are hewn out of the wood, and stand in relief against the great planks which constitute the greater part of the front or east wall of the temple. The figures are probably seven feet high, and represent Imrá seated and working a goat-skin butter churn. The face of each is prodigious. The square-cut chin reaches within a hand's-breadth of the goat-skin on the god's knees. The brows and nose are, in the majority of the figures, scored with lines, while those on the two practicable doors have rough iron bells suspended between the eyes. The goat-skin churns are represented as carved all over. Above the faces of the images a large circular head-dress appears, with a horizontal line of carving across the middle, and vertical cuttings running upwards and downwards from it. Between several of the figures there are vertical rows of what appear to be intended for cows' or rams' heads. From one of these rows the heads can be drawn out of their sockets, and the glories of the interior be partially disclosed. Above the big images is a board ornamented with small figures and horns. On the outer side of the temple, to the north, are five colossal wooden figures which help to support the roof. On the south side the ornamentation is almost entirely confined to the upper part of the wall, which consists of a series of carved panels. On the west there is little or no attempt at ornament of any kind.

I was only permitted to view the interior through the peep-holes already referred to, which afforded me merely a tantalising glimpse. In the centre of the floor there is a square fireplace, from the four corners of which pillars extend to the roof of the building. On each of these pillars more than one subject had been carefully cut. For instance, on one of them were two huge faces. Facing the entrance there was in the middle of the west wall a structure which looked like an altar. It was built of clay and provided with a wooden shelf. Above this, on the wall, was something which at first sight looked like a square cloth of a chequered pattern, but which I eventually satisfied myself was a design painted in squares. On the same wall, to the south, were other similarly designed but differently shaped paintings, and drawings of animals done in the usual Káfir conventional style. I could just see a portion of the top of an idol of Imrá occupying the north-east corner of the temple. Projecting from the top of the temple and corresponding with this spot, there was a small wedge-shaped wooden structure which looked like a canopy over the idol. As far as could be seen, the walls of the temple were adorned all round with carved hats of an irregular half-spherical shape, stuck on the ends of poles. The whole temple must have occupied a great deal of time and labour for the Presuns to complete, so simple are they and so rude are their tools. It is regarded by them and by all other Káfirs as a stupendous monument to the glory of Imrá.

Close to the south wall of the temple, outside, is a small square wood and stone erection about four feet high and of the usual construction, with poles surmounted by rams' heads at each corner. Upon it are certain stones, believed by the Káfirs to bear the impressions of Imrá's hand in the shape of sacred writing. These supposed writings consist merely of a curious arrangement of a dark lustrous mineral in a greyish-blue stone. The stones themselves are smooth and water-worn, and the dark lustrous flaws are like the wavy V's which children use for depicting birds. People in bad health often sacrifice to these stones with the very best results.

A short distance from the temple, in short thick grass
near the river, is the famous hole. All that is to be
seen is a patch of jungle-grass, limited in extent, and
easily overlooked. The village Utah, or priest, particularly requested me not to approach the spot; he appeared
gratified at my reply, that as a guest of the tribe, I
would not think of doing so. The place had already
been examined by Afghan raiders, brought into the
country by the Wai tribe, and the priests possibly
thought that if other people went away unharmed after
seeing the sacred hole, their fables might be exposed.
The sceptical Afghans, it was admitted, did not suffer
in any way, so the revised legend about the hole now
is, that any Káfir looking down it dies at once, and
that Christians are also Káfirs. The old story was that
every one looking down the hole saw the nether world
and died forthwith. An old Káfir once assured me
that he had seen with his own eyes a man killed in
this way. Occasionally, not more than once in many
years, a horse is obtained and sacrificed at this spot.
The officiating priest moves backwards, not daring to
look behind him, and cautiously removes a few of the
stones which encircle the orifice. Then, taking some
of the horse's blood, he throws it backwards over his
shoulder, and after replacing the stones, quickly moves
away.

Close by the temple, in a house in the village, there
is a miraculous iron bar placed in its present position
by Imrá himself. Its guardians conducted me with
some reluctance into the apartment where the bar was
said to be buried under a heap of juniper-cedar branches.
The proprietor of the house, a great and holy man,

seemed greatly relieved on finding that I listened to all he had to say about this iron pillar, and yet showed no inclination to verify his statements by searching the heap of branches.

Besides the great temple at Kstigigrom, there are other temples to Imrá in probably every village in Káfiristán ; also at particular places, such as Ahmad Diwáná, below Purstám, on the left bank of the Bashgul river, and many other spots. These temples or shrines are small, and have no peculiarity to distinguish them from those of the other gods. They are about five feet square and perhaps six feet high.[1] The lower two-thirds or three-fourths are made of rubble masonry, built between wooden frames of squared timbers. The top part is often entirely of wood with a door or window in front, through which the idol, or the sacred stone which does duty for the idol, may be seen. In some cases poles are placed at the corners of the wooden roof. The poles are sometimes surmounted by fragments of iron, such as tongueless bells, iron skull-pieces, and other similar objects, placed there to commemorate some successful raid during which they were obtained and brought back as trophies.

Imrá almost always has a shrine to himself. So also have Gísh and Moní, although not invariably. The other gods are often associated ; three, four, or even five being worshipped in one idol-house, the breadth of which

---

[1] The dimensions of these shrines are given from memory only. The references in my diaries generally run : " Imrá's shrine usual size and shape ; " " Imrá's house ordinary pattern," and so on. These objects were so commonly seen that I must have imagined they had been described over and over again in my different diaries, but no actual measurements are anywhere recorded.

is then proportionately enlarged, and each idol appears at its own particular window. At Kámdesh, near the east part of the village, is a very sacred spot with a temple to Gísh fitted with a door, which is removed for a limited period each year. At three of the corners poles project upwards, two of which are crowned with caps, one of iron, the other of mail, brought back from some successful foray; the third is hung round with a bunch of tongueless, roughly-made iron bells, which are carried about and clashed together at a particular festival. Immediately facing Gísh's shrine is a similar but smaller structure, dedicated to Moní. It is occupied by three stones in a row, the middle and largest being worshipped as Moní. At Imrá's shrine at the top of the village, a conventionally carved face appears at the little door; but the popular place for sacrificing to him is at the foot of the village, where, as before mentioned, there is a simple block of stone under a mulberry tree, which has been already referred to. Near it also there is a sacred muddy pool, dug out of the hillside and protected by a door.

To the north of the east part of the village of Braga-matál there is a shrine on the hillside which is hung about with juniper-cedar all along the front. It has five windows, from four of which idols look out into the world. To begin from the right, there are Dizane, Shumai or Krumai, Saranji, and Satarám. Dizane's idol has a round face with white stones for eyes, and an irregular white quartz fragment for a mouth. She has a cheerful, and even comical appearance, while the others, having the usual extensive flat surface for the lower part of the face and no mouths, either because time has removed

them, or because the shadows conceal the short lines
intended to represent teeth and lips, look extraordinarily
solemn.

In Presungul the idol-houses are much more carved
and ornamented than in the Bashgul Valley, while the
god is often shown seated under a wedge-shaped roof,
and sometimes engaged in playing a musical instrument.
At Deogrom there is a Monitán (Moni place, *i.e.*, shrine)
where the "prophet" is made of an extraordinary shape.
He is furnished with large circular eyes with a dot in the
middle ; he has cat-like moustaches, and appears to be holding his head in his hands, the face peering out between
the points of long horns, which, starting from below,
cross and recross each other till they reach the god's chin.
Occasionally the shrine is placed on the top of a village
tower in Presungul, a plan I have seen in no other district.

The only really elaborate shrine with which I am acquainted in the Bashgul Valley is Dizane's at Kámdesh.
It was built by men brought from Presungul for the
purpose. It is covered with carving, and has the wedge-
shaped roof so common in Presungul, and practically
never seen in the Bashgul Valley except at this place.
Along both sides of the base of the sloping roof poles
are fixed, and support wooden images of birds, said to be
pigeons. This is really a very pretty little temple. Some
of the shrines, however, are allowed to fall into a dilapidated state, as, for instance, at Ahmad Diwáná ; but'
they are not necessarily unpopular on that account. It
seems to be no one's business to repair isolated shrines,
and in the Bashgul Valley no Káfir is fervid enough or
sufficiently public-spirited to do the work. In Presungul
they are always in good repair.

DIZANE'S TEMPLE.

To face page 396.

Besides the idols or sacred stones in the idol-houses there are a large number of other sacred stones set up in different places to which sacrifices are regularly made. Some are said to be of divine or supernatural origin; some have been placed in their present position to be worshipped; others have been erected to the memory of ancestors. It is the first two varieties only which are referred to at present. Besides the Imrá stone at Kámdesh, there is another famous stone at the meeting of the Kti and Presun rivers, which is said to have been placed there by Imrá himself, and there are many others all over Káfiristán. Bagisht has a popular place of worship at the mouth of the .Skorigul. Duzhi and Bagisht have sacred stones near Urmir village, and numerous other instances might be cited. Sometimes a sacrifice is made to one of these stones from a long distance, as, for instance, from the top of Kámdesh village to Bagisht's shrine at the mouth of the Skorigul.

It would seem that Moní, called emphatically "the" prophet, ought to be ranked next to Imrá. He is worshipped with more respect than enthusiasm, especially at Kámdesh and Bragamatál. In Presungul he retains his rightful position in the Káfir Pantheon. Traditionally, he is the god always selected by Imrá to carry out his orders to exterminate demons, and so forth, and there are few stories related of him in any other connection. In spite of the popularity of Gísh-worship, Moní appears to be the chief of the inferior deities. In almost every village he has a shrine. At Kámu his little temple is more ornate than that of any other god, but at all places he is occasionally sacrificed to by pious persons, when he indicates, in a way elsewhere described, that he is desirous of a sacrifice. In Presungul, at the upper part of the valley, there are two small patches of glacier several miles apart and opposite to one another. They are called Moní's marks, and are affirmed to be the places where the god stands to play the game of aluts. At the village of Diogrom I was shown a block of stone of no great size, an isolated fragment of gneiss. Its presence in the village was accounted for in the following way. Once upon a time, for some reason not stated, Moní found himself in Zozuk (hell). He wished to get out, but could not. An eagle at length offered to carry the prophet up to the earth, but Moní doubted the bird's ability to perform such a feat. The eagle, however, made good its words, and placing the prophet on one wing, and the stone on the other as a counterpoise, flew up through the earth and emerged at Diogrom, where he deposited the prophet and the stone, which remains to this day to testify to the truth of the narrative. At the religious dances Moní is honoured equally with the other gods by being given three rounds, but there is nothing peculiar about the ceremony.

Gísh, or Great Gísh, as he is always called, is by far the most popular god of the Bashgul Káfirs. Every village has one or more shrines dedicated to his worship. He is the war-god, and however sceptical the Bashgul youths may be on some points, they are all fervid in their admiration for, and devotion to Gísh. In order to compliment a Káfir and to make his eyes glisten, it is only needful to compare.him to Gísh; and it is impossible to say a more acceptable thing to a Káfir woman than to call her "Gísh Istri"; that is, Gísh's

wife.   Gísh in the Káfir idea was not born of a woman.
His life was derived direct from Imrá ; by a word he
was created.   He lived on this earth as a man.   He
was first and foremost a warrior, a man of iron nerves,
fierce and sudden in his terrible onslaughts.   He spent
his life in fighting, and died as a hero should.   In his
furious lightning-like attacks and in his desperate enter-
prises he was successful above all others.   He is the
Káfir type of a true man, and can never be sufficiently
honoured.   Fabulous numbers of enemies felt the weight
of his fateful hand.   He killed Hazrat Ali ; he killed
Hasan and Husain ; in short, he killed nearly every
famous Musalmán the Káfirs ever heard of.   After
killing Hazrat Ali, he struck the head about with a
polo stick, just as the Chitráli princes play polo at the
present day.   Some say Gísh's earthly name was Yazíd.
Several villages pride themselves on possessing two idol-
houses dedicated to Gísh.   At Kámdesh there is only
one, but an extraordinary number of bulls and male
goats must be sacrificed before it every year.   The front
of the shrine is black with blood.   Dozens of goats are
killed there at a time, and the temple is drenched with
the ladlefuls of blood cast upon it.   The initiatory sacrifices for the Jast ceremonies are performed at Gísh's
shrine.   That grimy little temple must have looked
upon many other ghastly ceremonies, the worst of which
perhaps is when a wretched Musalmán prisoner is brought
there for a regular service, in which probably nearly the
whole of the village participates, and is then taken to the
coffin-box of some dead warrior and there slain to appease
the indignant ghost of the deceased.   For the last eleven
days of April, and during the first four days of May 1891,

every morning and night for a full hour slaves beat drums in honour of Gísh. During the same period, and for four additional days, the "inspired" priest, Shahru, having taken the tongueless iron bells already referred to from Gísh's shrine, went about the village clanging them against one another. He carried them on three iron rings six inches in diameter, three bells on each ring, and occasionally dusted them with a small branch of juniper-cedar. At night he deposited them in any house he chose, when the delighted householder at once sacrificed a male goat and made merry with his friends. During his wanderings about the village, Shahru was followed by troops of little boys, to whom he occasionally threw handfuls of walnuts, and then chased them with pretended ferocity. If he overtook one of them, he gave him a slight bang with the bells. The children all the time imitated the bleating of a goat. On May 1, 1891, Shahru was more than usually inspired. He came towards my house early in the morning, his face whitened with flour plastered on with ghee. He was rushing about in the maddest way, clashing the bells and brandishing his dancing-axe. The muscular exertion he underwent was remarkable. He threw himself about like an untiring acrobat, while his voice was prodigious. He was followed by the high-priest, all the Kaneash of the year, a small ordinary crowd, and groups of little boys. The great men spoke soothingly to the "possessed" Shahru, and recited at intervals religious responses to the glory of Gísh. My dogs rushed at Shahru with open mouth and loud outcry. I hurried to the rescue with whip and whistle, for dogs are impure in Káfiristán, but Utah and the others had driven them off before

SHAHRU CHASING THE CHILDREN.

To face page 402.

Shahru hurled his bells at them, missing them inten-
tionally, I am sure. This wild impostor, as he undoubtedly was, was an excellent fellow at bottom and
a great friend of mine. He would never do anything,
even in his most inspired moments, which he thought
would trouble me. A few minutes later he came to see
me, his faced washed and his manner placid, but before
he recovered his ordinary sanity, he ordered a man named
Nílíra to sacrifice a bull to Gísh. The mandate was at
once joyfully obeyed, as had been two similar orders on
the preceding day. During this time of the year the
door of Gísh's temple remained open; Shahru simply
took away the door, ultimately replacing it on July 9th.
In the month of September, for ten days, drums are
beaten morning, noon, and night in honour of Gísh.
Every small raiding party which has been successful in
that it has killed some one, after some preliminary formalities, is taken to the gromma, where the heroes, with
their female relatives, dance solemnly to Gísh. At all
the spring and other religious dances, the moment the
drums begin to beat a particular measure, the pipers
cease, and the spectators know that a Gísh dance is
about to be performed. Usually the utmost enthusiasm
prevails, the lookers-on stimulating the dancers with shrill
cat-calls. Every dancer braces himself for a supreme
effort. The whistlings cease as the performers begin to
shuffle with intense solemnity, while the spectators follow
with excited glances every movement of the dance. In
Presungul, Gísh seems to be much less admired than
among the Siah-Posh tribes. Only male animals are
offered to Gísh, such as bulls and goats. Certain smooth
holes in rocks are often pointed out as Gísh's cannon.

Bagisht is a popular deity. He presides over rivers, lakes, and fountains, and helps good men in various ways in their struggle for wealth and power. It is more particularly because the Káfirs believe that by sacrificing to Bagisht they will become rich that they are assiduous in his worship. To the miraculous birth of this god reference has already been made. Like all the other godlings, he is believed to have lived in this world as a man, and to have become deified after his death. I am not aware of any temple erected to Bagisht; if there is one, it has escaped my memory. There are three celebrated places where he is particularly worshipped. One is at the mouth of the Skorigul, where a simple stone marks a sacred spot visited by large numbers of people, who sacrifice sheep there. Another is in Presungul. The third is at Wagúk, which, from the description of the journey related to me, appears to be in Badakhshán, or somewhere west of Minján. Utah Ding went there, taking a big male goat as an offering. He plumes himself on having made the journey. Another place sacred to Bagisht is about half-a-mile of the river channel in the Kunar Valley, just above the village Nári. There is a stone at the foot of the hill by the village of Urmir where sheep are sacrificed, and the only other place, to the best of my knowledge, is above the village at Kámdesh near Imra's little temple, whence offerings are made to the sacred stone at the mouth of the Skorigul. Just at the rise to the bridge which spans the Bashgul river at the village of Bagalgrom, there is a blood-smothered stone where sacrifices are also made to Bagisht. The usual offerings to this deity are sheep, although goats also are sometimes given.

AROM'S SHRINE

To face page 409.

No one ever mentioned the name of the god Arom to me until I had been in Káfiristán several months. Nevertheless, he is, as before mentioned, the tutelary deity of the Kám. His shrine, a simple wooden framework enclosing a large fragment of stone, is made of short beams, square-hewn, and placed over each other in pairs alternately. In shape the little shrine resembles one of the ordinary effigy pedestals, but is somewhat larger, and wood only is used in its construction. When a war is brought to a successful close and terms of peace are agreed upon, the animals which ratify the treaty are taken to Arom's shrine and there sacrificed. The number of animals demanded from the opposing tribe depends entirely on the strength it retains. If very weak, many bulls would have to be given, while, if peace were made on equal terms, a bull would be exchanged between the late belligerents. The high-priest, knowing that I was interested in the Káfir gods, once hurriedly came to inform me that Arom had seven brothers. There, unhappily, his knowledge ended. He did not know the names of any of the seven, or anything else about them. When the time comes for the Kaneash to cast aside their distinctive garments, a portion of the ceremony which has to be gone through before they can assume their ordinary clothes is for each of them to sacrifice a male goat to Arom. This is before they shave their heads and beards.

Of the gods Sanru, Satarám or Sudaram, Inthr, Duzhi, Nong, Shomde, and Paráde, I know little or nothing. Sanru was declared by some to be the father of Saranji, although other informants had assured me that all the inferior gods, except Bagisht, were created directly by Imrá. Satarám is the weather-god. He regulates the rainfall. Inthr seems to be chiefly famous because he fought with Imrá, as already related, and had to retreat from Badáwan to the Tsarogul (Péch). Duzhi has a shrine near Urmir village. It consists of a stone, and is close by Bagisht's. Nong and Shomde are deities peculiar to the Presungul. . The latter is the tutelary deity of the village of Diogrom. About Paráde I could never learn anything. I discovered his existence by learning, on one occasion, that he had expressed a desire, by means of the swinging bow, to be given a sacrifice. But all my questions concerning him were of no avail. No one knew anything about him except that "he was created by Imrá."

Dizane is a popular goddess, and is worshipped wher-ever I have been in Káfiristán. The Giché, or new year festival, is entirely in her honour, and she also has special observances during the Dizanedu holidays. Everybody who has a son born to him in the preceding year offers a goat to Dizane at Giché. Dizane takes care of the wheat crop, and to propitiate her, or to increase the produce of wheat-fields, simple offerings are made unaccompanied by the slaughter of an animal. A great irrigation channel is shown the traveller in Pre-sungul, which it is affirmed that Dizane herself con-structed. There is also a good bridge in the same district called by her name. When the men of a tribe are away raiding, and the women collect in the villages to dance day and night to propitiate the gods and sing their praises, Dizane is one of the chief deities they supplicate for help. Her hymn goes something like this: "Send my man home safe and unwounded;" while to Gísh, for instance, they sing: "Send us many goats, and cows, and other plunder." The legend which ascribes Bagisht to Dizane as her son has already been referred to, as well as the mythological story which makes Dizane the trunk of the fabulous tree whose roots were the goddess Nirmali, while the branches were seven families of brothers, each seven in number. Some Káfirs affirmed that Dizane was the daughter of Sataràm. She may have been originally the goddess of fruitfulness. She usually shares a shrine with other deities, but at Kámdesh she has the pretty little temple, previously described, all to herself. There, at the Munzilo festival, those Kaneash who live in the upper village have to sleep in the open.

Saranji is the tutelary deity of the village of Pontzgrom. She has a little shrine on the top of the village tower, and a second near the mouth of the Pontzgul. She is also worshipped in the Bashgul Valley.

Nirmali is the Káfir Lucina. She takes care of women and children, and protects lying-in women. The women's retreats, the "pshars," are under her special protection.

The goddess Krumai I thought was a god for several months, but after seeing her effigy in one of the dancing-houses in Presungul, no doubt could remain concerning her sex. She is worshipped everywhere probably, but I have never been present at any sacrifice in her honour. She lives, according to some authorities, on Tirich Mir, but she dwells in my memory chiefly by reason of a comical dance performed in her name, which always winds up the performances at the regular ceremonies, when each important deity is danced to in turn.

CHAPTER XXIV

WE now come to the fairies. These aërial spirits are everywhere in Káfiristán. They have to be propitiated in order that the millet crops may be good. A fire is lit in the centre of the growing crop, juniper-cedar, ghee, and bread are placed upon it, and a certain ritual intoned. No animal is sacrificed. At the time that the ceremony to the fairies is being prepared, certain thick bread cakes have to be offered to Yush, the devil. So also when Dizane is being invoked to protect or improve the wheat, Yush has to be simultaneously propitiated. There is a certain powerful fairy called the Charmo Vetr, who lives high up the Kutaringul, a ravine which empties its waters into the Bashgul river between Mirkani and Arandú. This *vetr* (fairy) continually receives offerings of goats and kids from the Kám tribe, and in return has given that people great help against its enemies. My tent, owing to the great heat in Kámdesh, was pitched for some time under a magnificent deodar tree above the village. In the branches of this beautiful cedar a fairy dwelt, and in addition there was an Imrá stone concealed somewhere in the foliage. For these reasons cheeses for

412

sacrifices and other offerings could be left there unguarded by mortals, for no one would dare to steal the property placed in this manner under supernatural protection. The fairies are often mischievous, and at sacrifices frequently cause the inspired priest much anxiety. He is constantly impelled to rush forward to save the basket of flour from being carried off by them. They also take a particular delight in annoying him. Sometimes he is pushed violently about, and has his raiment torn to ribbons by malicious fairies. I have often watched these men when they were on the look-out for *vetrs*, and have admired their dramatic start of surprise and fear when the fairy manifested its presence. On the whole, however, the Káfir fairies, if properly propitiated, are more benevolent than malicious. On the night preceding the Dizanedu festival there is an annual dance in honour of the fairies.

The demons and their chief, Yush, are rather dubious spirits. In discussing Yush with some of my Káfir friends one day, it seemed to me that they had some reluctance in describing his appearance. As the thought occurred to me I inquired, "Is he like me?" "Oh, no," was the diplomatic reply, "he is not like you; he is like the private English soldiers Shermalik saw in India." From this I discovered that Yush is red in colour. He loves to seize travellers at night and destroy them, but if a man is wearing his dagger he is never molested. In most of the stories in which Yush is introduced he is made to appear as a foil to Imrá. So with the other devils. The end of such narratives generally is that the devils are cut to pieces. In Presungul we passed several ruins which looked like deserted villages, the inhabitants of which had been content with very small houses. My companion explained that those places were the remains of Yush villages, formerly built and inhabited by devils. On a block of stone in Shtevgrom village, there is what is said to be the impression of Yush's hand. It is of colossal size, and has five fingers besides the thumb. Towers and tunnels are also pointed out as having been constructed by Yush. The devils are often connected in narrative with iron or iron structures, as already mentioned. Iron bridges are made out of devil's bodies, and so forth. By the side of a track leading to the upper village at Kámdesh there is a small rough altar, always covered with the ashes of a recent fire. They are the remains of sacrifices made to Yush to propitiate him and induce him not to do mischief. When offerings are made to Dizane or to the fairies, so that the fields may yield good crops of wheat and millet, Yush has at the same time to be propitiated, as before stated. Yush seems to be always mischievous, never benevolent. His machinations must be guarded against, or he must be propitiated by sacrifices. He is probably never danced to.

There are distinct traces of ancestor-worship in Káfiristán, although it is strenuously denied by the people. The effigies erected to the memory of the dead are sometimes sacrificed to, and have their pedestals sprinkled over with blood by descendants suffering from sickness. Long fragments of stone are set on end in many places. These, no doubt, are partly intended as a kind of cenotaph, but a goat is always killed when they are erected. The Marnma festival is in honour of the illustrious dead. The two last days of the Duban are also devoted to dancing, feasting, and singing for dead and gone heroes. In Presungul there are no effigies erected to deceased relations, as is so popular a custom with the Siáh-Posh Káfirs, and it is almost certain that the same thing is true in Waigul. In Presungul there was no evidence of ancestor-worship.

Concerning the existence of fire-worship in Káfiristán, the evidence is not so convincing. Indeed, the only fact in support of it is that at all the Agars (Káfir sabbaths) a sacred fire to Imrá is lit by the Urir Jast, and must on no account be forgotten, even when, owing to sickness or other tribal calamity, dancing is pretermitted.

The functionaries of religion are the Utah or high-priest, the Debilála, who chants the praises of the gods, and the Pshur, the individual who is supposed to become temporarily inspired during religious ceremonies and on other occasions.

The high-priest, the Utah, is a very important personage. The Kám priest, my " brother," has been already described. There is another Utah for the village of Pittigul, but he is not the tribal priest, and is of small importance. The Katirs of the Bashgul Valley have as their Utah Kán Márá of Bragamatál, who is far above every one else of his tribe in wealth and importance. All the Utahs are greatly respected. In Presungul there is one to each village, and some of the elders among them are considered men of great sanctity. They are all rich men. In the Bashgul Valley the priest takes two shares of every animal sacrificed, and has other perquisites. On the march and elsewhere he takes precedence of every one. Even before he is a Jast he is allowed the privilege of seating himself on a stool outside a dwelling, which no one under the rank of Mir may do. Certain places are considered impure for him. He may not traverse certain paths which go near the receptacles for the dead, nor may he visit the cemeteries. He may not go into the actual room where a death has occurred until after an effigy has been erected to the deceased. Slaves may cross his threshold, but must not approach the hearth. The high-priest is present at all the principal religious ceremonies, and, whenever possible, officiates at the sacrifices at the different shrines.

The Debilála is also a man held in high respect, particularly amongst the Kám tribe. He recites the praises of the god in whose honour a sacrifice is being made, and at the great religious dances in the spring has a special place assigned to him in the centre of the performers and by the side of the priest, where he sings and dances. He also is debarred from using certain pathways supposed to be impure. The Kám Debilála, Arákon, was in the habit of closing one ear with a finger while singing. As the sound of his voice was in that way intensified to his own hearing, he imagined that its volume was actually increased.

The Pshur is the individual who is supposed to be the subject of temporary inspiration. He has already been referred to frequently. At times he behaves with the utmost violence, but there seems to be no rule on this point. The Kám Pshur's antics were extraordinary. He was a very muscular man, furnished by nature with a magnificent voice. Occasionally he would rush about and shout like a maniac. One of the Katir Pshurs, a Kti Káfir, was a wonderful athlete, and when "possessed" performed remarkable feats of activity and strength; but another Kti Pshur adopted other methods. He used to stare fixedly with his light blue eyes on some object invisible to all but himself, while his right arm and right leg shook violently. The Presungul Pshurs were in the habit of falling on one knee and invoking an invisible object with a trembling tongue. On the whole, the Bashgul Pshurs are despised by their fellows. The latter believe they are sometimes really inspired, but that generally they are merely liars, as the Káfirs put it in their direct way of speaking. The Presungul Pshurs are held in much higher esteem by that tribe.

The majority of the Pshurs believe in themselves to a certain doubtful extent. I imagine the Kám Pshur knew himself to be an impostor, but believed in other Pshurs, and expected some day or other to be really inspired himself. One of these individuals was really a madman, while others had practised their vocation for so long a time that they were not quite sane. The effect of a very small quantity of brandy on this Kám Pshur has already been related. Once a Pshur received from me some opium pills for a cough. The result was that he was greatly possessed all day ; he jumped and shouted, and played all manner of antics. We were on the march at the time. This Pshur was known as a terrible homicide, and was certainly half a madman. All the Káfirs we met gave us a wide berth, looking at my companion with dislike and mistrust. The Kám Pshur was turned out of Kámdesh and sent back to his own tribe, the Mádugál, because two young Kám Káfirs were killed on a raiding expedition. Possibly he had given a wrong prediction, or he should have foretold this calamity, for all the village, and particularly the fathers of the slain, were extremely angry.   It seems that the Kám, having no inspired person in their own tribe, had imported their Pshur from Mádugál; otherwise it is not clear how they could have got rid of him.   The Bragamatál Pshur, as already mentioned, originated a bloody war between the people of the Amzhi Valley, in the Waigul, and his own tribe, by a remark he made while temporarily inspired.

Besides these regular functionaries of religion, there are other individuals who temporarily act as priests. They are the Kaneash, who are on the point of completing the ceremonies for the rank of Jast.   They are considered pure, and at some sacrifices, at any rate, perform the duties of the Utah or high-priest.

Certain other individuals also have particular functions to perform.   For instance, if it is desired to find out which particular god is desirous of being sacrificed to, a particular man is called upon to supply the desired information.   Among the Kám this man was one of the Jast, named Widing Chandlu.   The following is a full account of the ceremony I witnessed on November 28, 1890.

There had been a great deal of bad weather, and a public-spirited individual announced his intention of sacrificing a goat in the hope of getting it improved. We all assembled in the living-room of his house.   The place was crowded, and among those present was Widing Chandlu.   After some conversation he got up and fetched a bow from his own house.   Arakon, the Debilála, strung the bow and then handed it back to Chandlu, who had in the interval bound his head round with a piece of white cloth.   The proceedings were opened by the high-priest, who rose from his seat and went to the door,

INVOKING THE GODS.

To face page 421.

where he stood facing us. Immediately to his right, close to a blazing fire, bowls of ghee, wine, and water, and a pile of juniper-cedar branches had been placed ready for use. Having washed his hands very carefully several times with water poured over them by an acolyte, Utah threw a few drops of water up at the smoke-hole, sprinkling also the fire and the ground on each side of him, as he repeated the word " such " three times. He next set fire to a small branch of cedar, extinguished it in the water vessel, and then sprinkled about a few drops of water from the half-burnt branch. It was then immersed once more in the water, and the bowl was placed at Widing Chandlu's right hand. Utah now took some more cedar, which he ignited and waved about while he repeated the word " such." He finished by making the peculiar sound " o-o-o-o-r-r," swinging both hands forward at the same time, at which signal all the congregation cried " i-i-i-yamach," with one voice. More cedar branches were then added to the fire, which crackled and blazed merrily, while Utah kept invoking the gods in words which were quite unintelligible to me, and Arakon, the Debilála, who was seated at my side, recited a sort of refrain, always coming in at the proper moment with the " i-i-i-yamach," chorused by the rest of the people. These particular acts accomplished, Chandlu began his own special duty. From the water vessel on his right he sprinkled the bow three times, repeating each time the word " such." He then, doubling his left fist, enclosed it in his right palm, the bowstring resting below his crossed thumbs. With elbows on thighs and wrists on knees he attentively watched the bow, while with a rapid utterance he named the Káfir

gods one after the other. Before very long the bow
began to swing evenly backwards and forwards. The
motion could only have been communicated to the bow
by a slight backwards and forwards movement of the
hands at the wrists. By closing one eye and with the
aid of a mark on the adjacent pillar, I could distinctly
see the movement of the hands; and I almost expected
Widing Chandlu to look at me and close one eye also.
He did nothing of the kind, but went on with his im-
posture in the most solemn way. The name on Widing
Chandlu's lips at the moment the bow began to sway
was held to be the name of the god who was attentive
to the proceedings. Chandlu stopped the swaying of
the bow by dancing it up and down by the string, while
he made a sound with his lips as if he were chirruping
to a canary. These proceedings he repeated several times,
until all the information desired had been communicated
by the gods. It was to the following effect:—First,
Moní was attentive, but on being asked if he would like
a goat to be sacrificed in his name, made no response,
so it was held that he had declined the honour. Then
Sataràm behaved in a precisely similar way. Finally,
Paráde accepted the proffered goat, and after a lavish
banquet we returned to our homes.

There are two wise women in the village of Purstám,
who can foretell the result of a raid by divination. They
stand opposite to one another, each balancing two arrows
in the palms of her hands. They then approach one
another, and allow the free ends of the arrows to touch,
whereupon, in a supernatural way, all the arrows shuffle
together, and it is by noticing which arrow remains
on top that they know whether the raiding party will be

successful or the reverse. The Káfirs declared that if the omen were adverse to the tribe, messengers would be sent to bring the warriors back if they had already started, or to stop them if they had not already gone.

As mentioned before, all important religious ceremonies are presided over by the high-priest, who invariably officiates at the sacrifices at the different shrines in his village. Away from the headquarters of the tribe there is usually some individual specially appointed to do the work of the Utah, and no animal is ever killed for food in Káfiristán except in the orthodox manner. On the march any one may perform the ceremony, although it is usual to invite the most important man present to do so. On such occasions, when all the proper adjuncts of the ceremony cannot be obtained, the proceedings are shorn of much of their usual detail; but even then a certain ritual has to be gone through, and the animal to be killed, if it is a sheep or a goat, must shake itself, to show it has been accepted by the god to whom it is being offered. To make it do so water is poured into its ear and all down its spine by the priest or his substitute. The Greeks, before the oracle was consulted, used to find out in a somewhat similar way if the goat, ready for the sacrifice, were acceptable; and the Indian Thugs would never sacrifice a goat to their protecting goddess Devi until it had shaken itself after water had been thrown upon it. It is not sufficient for the animal to merely shake its head to get the water out of its ears; it must shake the whole body, as a wet dog shakes itself. When it does this, a kissing sound is made by all present, and the animal is forthwith slaughtered. Sometimes there is a considerable delay in this part of the ceremony, when the onlookers appear to be reasoning with the animal upon its obstinacy, while the god is at the same time invoked to accept the offering. At all offerings at shrines juniper-cedar branches must be used. They may be supplemented by ordinary cedar, but the sacred juniper must be employed also. At Kámdesh it is somewhat difficult to obtain, and has to be brought from a considerable distance. It is stored up in houses for winter use with as much care as if it were necessary food. In the upper part of the Bashgul Valley, where it is plentiful, it is festooned on shrines and fastened round the brows of effigies ; but this is rarely done in Kámdesh, owing to the scarcity of the tree in that part of the valley.

Goats are sacrificed in considerable numbers, ten to fifteen at a time on particular occasions, as, for instance, when the Kaneash are giving their public banquets. At such times it does not seem necessary for the animals to shake themselves as a sign that they have been accepted by the gods. They are sprinkled with water during the ceremony, and are forthwith killed without any particular observances ; but single animals certainly, when away from the chief shrines, cannot lawfully be killed until they unmistakably shake themselves.

When a single animal is killed in a room, on a house-top, or when travelling, a full ritual is used if it is possible to do so. The priest always has a fragment of cotton cloth bound round his temples when out of his own house, and any one acting as his deputy for the time being also likes to bind his head in a similar way. Boots are removed and hands washed. The fire is kindled, and ghee and cedar branches are placed upon it. Water is sprinkled about on the shrine, the fire, and the animal; and indoors, is thrown up at the smoke-hole, while the word "súch" is repeated. Ignited juniper-cedar branches are waved about to the same accompaniment, and then, ghee, flour, and bread are placed on the fire. The god to be sacrificed to is then invoked, and if the Debilála is present, his praises are recited. The animal, after it has shaken itself as already described, is seized by the feet and thrown over a stool, across a man's knee, or on the ground. A dagger or knife is thrust through the neck, the point of the weapon being entered at the angle of the jaw on one side, and brought out at the other; the knife is then made to cut towards the spine, severing the arteries in that direction, and is afterwards turned round so as to cut outwards through the gullet, windpipe, and skin. Some of the blood is caught in a long-handled cup or in the palm of the half-closed hand and sprinkled on the fire, while regular responses to the priest's invocation are made by the bystanders. The animal's head is in the end forcibly dislocated, and separated from the body by a few touches of the knife. It is placed at the edge of the fire for a few seconds, just long enough to singe the muzzle, and is then withdrawn. A few more recitations are made by the priest and responded to by the people, and the ceremony is finished. The exact moment when the Pshur, if present, becomes temporarily inspired is uncertain, while the violence of his antics depends entirely on the man himself, and upon the way he is irritated or worked upon by the spirits.

Goats and kids are frequently sacrificed on the house-

z

tops, but sheep are not considered worthy of that honour. In sacrificing a bull or a cow, precisely the same formalities are gone through as have been described, except that the head is not cut off and put in the fire. The animal is killed by a stroke behind the horns with a small axe. Immediately after a sacrifice the animals are cut up. Any one can cut up a sheep or a goat, but cattle are skinned and divided by slaves. When many goats are sacrificed at one time, the bystanders draw lots who shall skin each particular animal, in the following way :— Some one collects their walking-clubs into a bundle, and then rapidly draws out the sticks and throws one or two, as the case may be, on the carcase of each animal. Each man follows his stick, and sets to work on the carcase on which it was thrown. This prevents all disputes about the distribution of the work to be done. Offerings made without the sacrifice of any animal are conducted in a precisely similar manner in all the other details.

The following is a description of the offering of fifteen goats at Gísh's shrine at Kámdesh :—The audience was small on this particular occasion, numbering about thirty, who arranged themselves in an irregular semicircle facing the shrine, with Utah in front and the Debilála and the Pshur immediately behind him. The congregation behaved like average religious audiences in England ; that is to say, without any special enthusiasm, but with a certain amount of formal decorum, while the younger people were not without a suspicion of light-heartedness. Fifteen handsome male goats were slowly driven up to the shrine by two little boys, who, considering that their part of the work was then over, ran away and shirked the religious function, as boys will all the world over. Utah

AN OFFERING AT GISH'S SHRINE.

To face page 426.

cast a critical glance round to see that all preparations
had been properly made. There was a small fire burning; it was covered with cedar branches, which emitted
a dense white smoke. A wooden vessel containing millet
flour, a second containing ghee, a third filled with wine,
and a fourth with water, were placed ready for use ; while
a prettily carved wooden utensil, shaped something like
a teapot, and furnished with a long dummy wooden spout,
held the ghee which was to be thrown upon the shrine.
From the other ghee vessel Utah took out several handfuls to put on the cedar branches and brighten the fire.
He then, in the manner of a man accustomed to perform
an important part in public, washed his hands carefully
with water poured over them by an attendant. This
operation being completed, he stood barefooted before
the holy place. He first sprinkled the goats with a few
drops of water, repeating the word " such " three times,
and taking a small quantity of the contents of each vessel,
threw it against the small closed door of the shrine, all
the time repeating a certain invocation, and at the proper
times chorusing · with the bystanders the phrase, " i-i-i-
yamach." The goats were then rapidly seized, one by
one, by young men helping at the ceremony, thrown
across a stool, and their throats cut. As the blood streamed
forth it was caught in flat wooden basins, while another
assistant secured a portion of it in a long-handled wooden
cup, which he carried to Utah, who cast it upon the
shrine, after throwing a small quantity in the fire. Each
time he did this he swung both hands forward together
and muttered " o-o-o-o-r-r," at which signal the audience
repeated " i-i-i-yamach," as before. All the time Arakon
the Debilála chanted a refrain with his hand placed in

front of his left ear, as though he were suffering from toothache, while his white consumptive face and cadenced voice gave suggestions of solemnity to the barbarous performance. When the blood ceased flowing into the wooden bowls, the goat's head was forcibly twisted round and detached from the spine, and carefully carried to Utah, who placed it just inside the edge of the fire, and after it was slightly singed withdrew it to be set aside for food. While all this was proceeding, Shahru the Pshur, who had been quietly looking on, suddenly hurled away the peaked cap (*kullah*) which he was wearing and bounded forward. He stretched his arms straight above his head, twirling his hands round, and shouting furiously. He dashed water on to the shrine, as though in burlesque of Utah's proceedings. The latter spoke what sounded like soothing words to the inspired man, which must actually have been an invocation to the god, for at certain periods the audience responded with "i-i-i-yamach." Shahru finally bent down, and rapidly swung his clenched hands between his knees and over his head several times. This done, he quietly resumed his cap, became quite sane again, and smiled blandly at me. The ceremony concluded with another short recital by Utah, with the customary response by the congregation, after which all touched the forehead just above the eyebrows with the tips of their fingers, making at the same time a kissing sound with their lips. This is the orthodox salutation of a Káfir to a shrine. The word "such" means "be pure." Once I was fishing in the Bashgul river. From curiosity, and also to guard me, a number of Kám men, headed by the priest, were seated on the rock above watching the sport. When I hooked and landed a fish, the priest invariably cried out, "Such, such, such," in a jocular way. Indeed, few Bashgul Káfirs object to burlesquing the sacrificial rites. I have seen a boy play the part of the priest in a facetious way, and one of my own followers act the Pshur, to the amusement of all spectators. Outside Káfiristán the ceremony, if performed at all, is always more or less of a travesty.

The details of the Presun sacrifices and offerings differ from those of the Siáh-Posh tribes in certain respects. For instance, there are no responses from the bystanders, although the swaying forward of the hands, which, in the Bashgul Valley, is the signal for responses from the congregation, is never omitted by the priest. The Utah, alone or in conjunction with the Debilála, performs the entire ceremony. The "such" is replaced by the word "shoo," and in adding the cedar branches, bread, ghee, &c., to the fire, the Utah makes a soft, whining, half-mewing noise, and any words he may utter are quite indistinguishable, to my ear at any rate. The Presun Pshurs never seem to be violent. They fall on one knee by the fire when their turn comes, and go through their performance in an abstracted, half-melancholy manner. I know nothing of the behaviour of the Wai people at sacrifices. When a goat was slaughtered for them at Kámdesh, they always liked to dabble some of the blood on their foreheads.

Miracles are occasionally performed. Utah has sometimes told me of such things, but I have never seen any myself. The miracle usually related was of a man under supernatural protection standing for some minutes in the centre of a large fire without being in any way injured.

Káfirs sometimes try to cheat a god. For instance,

they will wait a few hours after finding out which deity must be sacrificed to for a change in the weather, in the hope that the sky may clear and the wind stop without an offering being necessary. Once a friend of mine, named Chárá, whose little son was apparently dying from small-pox, after he had sacrificed a cow to Imrá on the boy's behalf, discovered from the swinging bow that Bagisht wanted an offering of three fine goats. He thereupon bargained with the god that he should have the goats as soon as the boy got well, but not before. The boy recovered, and I hope Bagisht received the goats. Probably he did, Chárá being a very honest fellow for a Káfir.

The Káfirs delight in stories of marvellous or supernatural things. Dán Malik told me he had seen a Musalmán doctor perform an operation with a knife on a man in the Kunar Valley, and draw out from the bottom of the incision a large centipede, which was the cause of the patient's illness. Dán Malik really believed the truth of this story. My own stories of London, its great size, the conveyance of water and gas through pipes, the use of coal as fuel, and so on, were highly appreciated. The Káfirs used to cross-examine me a long time afterwards to try and find discrepancies in the details of my wonderful stories. Probably they thought it required a great deal more credulity on their part to swallow my narratives than they exacted in trying to make me believe their fables. They believe in love-philtres and love-charms, and long to possess them. They tell of a wonderful grass which grows near the hamlet of Agaru in the Nichingul, where, if you take a gun and fire at the grass (it is not stated what prompted the first discoverer to make such a curious experiment), the broken blades, before they can fall to the ground, are seized and carried off by pigeons, large flocks of which rise at the report of the gun and fly away. Once a man managed to secure a blade of this grass and started for his home. More than ten score women, such was the potency of the strange herb, followed him with love-sick moans. As he neared his home his mother came forth and cried out, "Oh, my son, what is it you have about you which distracts me so much? Whatever it is, cast it away!" With filial promptitude the man complied with his mother's request. The fragment of grass fell in the fork of a large tree, which was at once split asunder. Much was related to me about certain magical pools of water. There were three in particular, one near the village of Pittigul, another in the Mumán country, the third on the road to Waigul. If any one approaches these pools too closely, the water becomes visibly troubled, while if an arrow were dipped into filth and fired at its surface, a mighty torrent rushes forth inundating all the surrounding country. In former times this was frequently done, but it has never been repeated of late years. My friends professed an anxiety to show me by practical demonstration that they spoke truthfully, but they took care never to carry out their expressed wish. At Pittigul they declared it could not be done, because if it were, the furious water would sweep away all the houses and fields.

CHAPTER XXV

KÁFIRS are theoretically all equal. They maintain this
principle themselves. Actually there is an oligarchy, or,
in some tribes, an autocracy. The affairs of a tribe such
as the Kám are managed by the Jast nominally, but
actually by a small group of greybeards, who at ordinary
times rule in a more or less absolute way. The Katirs
and the Mádugális submit to the rule of one individual,
unless their cupidity is aroused, when all common rules
apparently snap of their own accord.

The Kám ruling authority in ordinary times consisted
of three Jast, who were also Mírs, and the priest. They
used their power tactfully, and always knew the bent of
public opinion.

Next to this inner council of the Jast came the orators,
a troublesome class, who have wonderful influence in
exciting or convincing the people. Volubility, assurance,
and a good voice are as powerful amongst the Káfirs as
elsewhere. All the orators of real influence were Jast
also; one of them was one of the Mírs. On all questions of policy, foreign or domestic, Káfirs sit in parliament and discuss the matter noisily. Yet in ordinary

times the opinion of the inner council, most likely previously agreed upon among themselves, prevails.

A Káfir parliament is a strange sight. The clamour is wonderful. A dozen men, perhaps, try to speak at once ; each has his own little group of listeners, whose attention, if it wanders, he seeks to recall by loud ejaculations of " ai ai ! " or by little pokes in the ribs with his walking-club. If some very exciting topic is being discussed, perhaps all are talkers and none are listeners ; but, as a rule, when one of the tribal orators begins to speak, he gets the attention of the greater part of the assembly, his efforts being helped by shouted illustrations, or further arguments, by one or two of his admiring friends. Káfirs love to argue among themselves, to decide on some definite line of action. Singly they are often reasonable, but when they go off in a mob to the dancing-platform, or group themselves under a tree and begin excited discussions, it is practically impossible to foretell what they will decide. Moreover, the discussion arrived at on one day is quite likely to be rescinded on the next day, and reverted to on the third. But such occurrences are exceptional, and only happen when the people are labouring under strong excitement on some subject, such as a prospect of gain, which appeals to each individual personally, and maddens him with cupidity and indecision. Generally the Jast, or its inner circle, manage everything.

The Ur or Urir are thirteen individuals selected annually to act as a kind of magistracy in the tribe. Their chief, the Ur or Urir Jast, is an important man ; the remainder are merely his followers and assistants. The duties of the Urir as a body are to regulate the amount of water that each agriculturist is to receive from the common irrigation channels. In ordinary times at Kámdesh there is no difficulty about this; the water is brought down in canals from the snow-field behind and to the south of the village, and is ample for all requirements, but if the snowfall has been light and the summer hot and dry, great troubles arise. The women clamour for water for their parched fields, and quarrel, abuse one another, and fight viciously for the little water which remains. The Urir, either alone or with the general help of the community, keep the artificial watercourses in good order.

Another important duty they have is to see that no one picks or eats walnuts or grapes before the appointed time. Many wild stories are told of the strictness with which this duty is done. For visitors and guests great exception is made, and the people are delighted to entertain strangers just about the time when the fruit is ripe but permission to collect it has not been given. A traveller sometimes finds himself overcome with the kindness of his entertainers, who, as a matter of fact, are practising hospitality to themselves as much as to him. But with this exception, the rule is strict about the plucking of fruit. The Urir punish disobedience by the infliction of fines, which, as they naïvely put it, they " eat " themselves. It can only be the prospect of sharing in the fines which make men willing to serve in the often thankless office of the Urir. It is astonishing how well the people obey their unwritten laws. There are occasionally disputes and quarrels in consequence of the penalties inflicted, but both the punishers and the punished are obliged to be circumspect, for a public opinion which avenges any outrage on itself by promptly burning down the culprit's house and destroying his property is a power not to be lightly disregarded. If the Urir were flagrantly unjust or tyrannous, public opinion would suppress them at once; while, on the other hand, disobedience to their lawful and proper enactments would be certain to be punished. The flaw in the arrangement is that the Urir, being human, fear to offend the wealthy or the strong families; but the system seems to work very well on the whole.

The head of the Urir, the Urir or Ur Jast, is not only the chief elected magistrate, but he has other duties also to perform, of a somewhat complex nature. Generally speaking, he acts as master of the ceremonies at all the festivals and dances. He beats up recruits for the dances, and stimulates flagging energies, not only by exhortation, but also by example. He is the most earnest chanter of responses, and the most untiring dancer in the village. He has to light the fire at the gromma every Wednesday night for the weekly Káfir Sabbath, the Agar. He also seems to be the official entertainer of guests.

The election of the Urir Jast and his twelve companions in 1891 took place on March 19, at the Durban festival. I missed seeing the procedure for myself. It seems that the proceedings were of a simple character. First of all, a bull was sacrified to Gísh; after that, the Jast and the people present decided who should hold office for the following year. Finally, Utah, the priest, taking that portion of the flour which remained over from the sacrifice, carried it to the new Ur Jast's house, when the election was considered complete. It seems that all the flour not used as sacrifice is similarly carried to the Ur Jast's house. On the particular occasion referred to, this newly elected Ur Jast was absent with his flocks. So his brother at once adorned himself with a fillet, threw a scarf over his shoulder, and began to wander restlessly all over the village, as though very busy, yet apparently doing nothing, the twelve Urir stringing after him. The actual Ur Jast was sent for in hot haste, and on his arrival had to feast all comers for several nights at his house, where there was dancing, as well as other festivities. On the last day of the month, soon after noon, women from every part of the village appeared, carrying each a wicker basket full of flour to the new Ur Jast's house. The women all wore their horned caps, which, among the Kám, are only worn on occasions of special ceremony. The whole of each basketful of flour was not bestowed upon the Ur Jast, but a small quantity was carried home again by each woman, where it was used in an offering to Imrá. It was burnt with cedar branches, ghee, and bread on the family girdle. On the whole, in consequence of the contributions he receives, the Ur Jast's appointment is believed to be lucrative as well as honourable, although his expenditure on the village feasts must be considerable.

Besides the authority exercised by the Jast and by the Urir, the Káfirs are influenced very strongly by tradition and custom—the unwritten, and even unspoken laws of the people. If the perplexed stranger asks the explanation of practices and usages which are new to his experience, the reply will almost invariably be " Insta charaza " (It is our custom), and this will be said in a tone to imply there is nothing more to be said on the subject. The fear of ridicule is a powerful factor in preventing a Káfir from adopting novel procedures or inventing new rules for action. If he can refer any given question to central principles generally recognised and accepted by Káfirs, he is happy ; but if he have no good cause for action of his own initiative, he will do little or nothing ; he will wait to have the matter settled by open tribal discussion.

The tyranny of majorities is very great. As a rule, a minority gives way at once. Indeed it must be so, for the final argument is usually a threat. A Káfir is accustomed in all ordinary questions rapidly to calculate what would be his chances of success if the matter in dispute were to end in a fight, and he dearly loves to fight with all the probabilities in his favour. If physical superiority is against him, he generally gives way at once, acquiescing without rancour in the views of the majority. In his own way the Káfir has an immense amount of Eastern fatality in his disposition, and is usually intelligent enough to distinguish between what is and what is not inevitable.

Disobedience to the Jast in council is punished promptly and severely. The offender's house is burnt down, and his property is dispersed and destroyed. As the Jast come from all the clans of a tribe, their decision is the decision of the whole people ; and he must be a brave man indeed who would refuse to accept the fiat of the council. The penalty mentioned is in reality a theoretical one only, for no one ever incurs it. If he felt himself unable to obey the rule of the Jast, a man would run away from his tribe altogether. The only instances known to me where the punishment was ever threatened were two in number.

The penalty for theft is rather doubtful. Theoretically, it is a fine of seven or eight times the value of the thing stolen; but such a punishment in ordinary cases would only be inflicted on a man of inferior mark, unless it were accompanied by circumstances which aggravated the original offence. I should say, as a rule, that the loser would get his property back; there would then be high words and the prospect of a fight; neighbours would intervene, and a goat would be sacrificed by the thief. Everybody would make friends, and the sufferer would be given some slight supplemental payment, as recompense for the trouble he had been put to in recovering his property. The tribe would heavily punish any one who stole from another tribe or people with whom they were anxious to keep on good terms. Then the virtuous indignation expressed by the tribe's orators is most edifying, and the penalties are severe. In one case I know, restitution was ordered by the Jast, and a fine of fifteen Kabul rupees was also inflicted.

Murder, justifiable homicide, and killing by inadvertence in a quarrel, are all classed as one crime, and punished in the same way. Extenuating circumstances are never considered. The single question asked is, Did the man kill the other? The penalty is an extremely heavy blood-ransom to the family of the slain man, or perpetual exile combined with spoliation of the criminal's property. The man who has caused the death of a fellow-tribesman at once takes to flight and becomes a "chile" or outcast, for his clan will not help him in any way. His house is destroyed and confiscated by the victim's clan, and his property seized and distributed. If he has relatives, such as a father or a brother, who hold goods in common, it is asserted that their property is looted also; while, if it is known that their possessions are entirely separate, they must not be touched. There seems, however, to be a general impression abroad that the law in this respect is more severe to the poor than to the rich. Nevertheless, public opinion is strong enough to ensure that the shedder of blood leaves his village, in any case, without any hope of returning to it except by stealth. A murderer's family is not despoiled of his landed property. The chile or outcast is not compelled to leave his tribe. He must merely leave his village, and always avoid meeting any of the family or clan of the murdered man. If by chance he comes across any of them on the road, he goes aside and conceals himself, or goes through the pretence of hiding himself, so that his face may not be looked upon. In a village, in similar circumstances, he will hide behind a door or steal round the back of a house. His sons, those not grown up, as a rule become chiles also, and the same law holds good concerning his daughters' husbands and their descendants. Musalmán traders who have married the daughters of chiles have to behave in precisely the same way as any other chile when they visit Kámdesh, for instance.

The village of Mergrom is the largest of several "cities of refuge." It is almost entirely peopled by chiles, the descendants of slayers of fellow-tribesmen. I have known one of those people, a wealthy man, who had to avoid the Utahdári clan, go quietly to Kámdesh in the evening and hold a secret conference with Utah, the chief of the Utah-

dári, concerning questions of trade. In his case no rancour remained behind in the other clan. The man was a
ceremonial outcast, and the grandson of him who did the
deed. Nevertheless, he was as much an outcast in reality
as if he were himself the murderer.

A man may atone for the shedding of blood by paying
a large sum of money or in kind. This is so rarely done
that there is even some doubt about the exact amount
required ; but it was generally stated to be 400 Kabul
rupees in cash, and 400 Kabul rupees' worth of property, clothing, and what not. It is also said that if this
kind of atonement is made, it reflects so much honour on
the family of the man who makes it, that the males are
ever afterwards permitted to carry about a particular kind
of axe, to show their social importance.

In the event of a double killing—that is to say, of a
killer himself being slain by his victim's relatives—I was
told the custom was for a cow to be killed, when the representative men of each clan would each put a foot in
a pool of the animal's blood. This would constitute a
solemn peace, and an oath of a very binding character.
This Káfir custom of avenging a murder is a valuable one.
It prevents blood-feuds, which in Káfiristán would mean
the extinction of a tribe ; while its peculiar advantage is
that it does not cause any additional loss to the fighting
power of a tribe, where every single male is of great importance to the whole people. The penalty is really extremely severe. It is considered an act of virtue to dash
in and separate quarrellers. Men, women, and children
will throw themselves between fighting men with the
greatest intrepidity, and frequently get hurt in doing so.
It behoves every Káfir to prove his manhood, and show

he is not a "slave," by trying his utmost to injure his enemy up to the time the goat, the peace-offering, is sacrificed, while everybody is interested in preventing him from seriously hurting his foe. His family fear that he may become a chile and lose his property, while all other Káfirs are impelled by public opinion to play the blessed part of the peacemaker. I have sometimes in argument put imaginary cases; for instance: Suppose a man in defending his life from a murderous attack, happens to slay his assailant, why should he become a chile? The reply at once was, "He should have disabled his enemy, and not killed him." About accidental deaths I am in a little doubt. I know a man, the son of a friend of mine at Kámdesh. When a boy, this man by ill-luck killed a little girl. He was hurling stones, one of which struck her so that she died. None of the family would even look in the man's face. If he were sitting in a verandah talking to me, none of the Demidári would enter. He lived away at the village of Pittigul. I do not think, however, that he was regarded as a chile.

The punishment for a murderous assault is decided by the Jast. For instance, a man once stabbed Dán Malik. The culprit nearly killed Dán Malik, and had to pay as compensation a large number of goats. Grievous injury would always be paid for. Slight hurt would be atoned for in the usual way, the man in the wrong having to provide the goat for the reconciliation feast. Sometimes the general indignation of the community causes a kind of lynch law to be employed. The chief man at the village of Kamu was caught by the husband in an intrigue with a woman. The husband was soundly beaten by the seducer and his followers, but the whole village turned out, the peccant individual's house was burnt down, and he himself put to flight. It was only after much intercession that he was allowed to return to and remain in the village.

On one occasion a Káfir, in the hope of getting a reward, went and told the Mehtar of Chitrál of a pretended plot against the life of his son, Shah-i-Mulk, declaring that he himself was the man who had been bribed by the Kám to strike the fatal blow. Although retribution was ordered by the Jast, the village really went to the man's house and comprehensively sacked it of its own accord, all being actuated by the same impulse.

The ordinary punishment for a man caught in adultery is a fine in cows. In the Kám district six cows have to be paid; in the Katir district only three. In this case also a man's clan will not protect him, so that he must pay the penalty as soon as he is able. When the woman runs away from the husband, the penalty is, of course, greater, for there is the value of the woman herself to be taken into account. As before mentioned, the women often try to entangle men in order to get cows for their husbands, but when this is not the case, the women seem to escape with little or no punishment if the fine is paid. The fine seems usually to soothe the husband's jealous feelings.

Among the curious penalties are fines for eating certain fruit before the prescribed date; fines for making fun of any of the Urir within nine days after their appointment, and so on.

Besides the solemnity of an oath of peace made by two men, each putting the foot in the blood of a cow sacrificed to Imrá, ordinary vows may be made by sacrificing a goat. Similarly, men may be released from a vow in an identical way. Indeed, there are few ceremonies of any ordinary kind which cannot be done in Káfiristán by sacrificing a goat. I have been assured that a very binding oath is made in the following way :—Suppose a man is accused by another of stealing a cow, and is desirous of refuting the charge in the most convincing way possible, he shaves his head, even the karunch or scalp-lock, and also shaves off his beard and moustache. He then strips himself absolutely naked, and, led by a friend to Imrá's shrine, makes oath that he is innocent of the charge brought against him. He then puts on his clothes and goes home to sacrifice a goat. His late accuser also has to sacrifice a goat. I have never myself witnessed this ceremony, or that of swearing with a foot in a pool of cow's blood. My information is derived from conversations on the subject.

A man often insists on having his debts paid him, but I have never heard of anything like interest being charged. Káfirs are frequently most generous in their lending. Suppose, for instance, a poor youth wins some great competition like throwing the "shíl." As a result of his victory he has to feast the village. Some one or other is certain to come forward and help him to do this, often with the absolute certainty of never being repaid. Káfirs are most lavish and generous in loans of this description. On the other hand, I have known a rich man belonging to a powerful clan trump up a claim on a suddenly enriched man of no importance (the Káfir who first went to India with me), that the father of the latter, before he died, had borrowed from the former many goats. It seems every one knew this was false; but the man having once advanced the claim, had to maintain it with threats of violence, until at length the other man, having no family or clan behind him, found it well to compromise the matter by handing over one or two goats in payment of a demand for several score. A powerful family, being creditors of a poor man, on the death of the latter seized the daughter, and kept her more or less as a bondswoman, until she ran away to Chitrál with her lover, who was not satisfied with mere access to his sweetheart.

The great majority of debts are almost certainly never paid at all, the debtors being usually very poor people. They probably attach themselves to their creditors in many ways, and perhaps pay back in unacknowledged servitude the amounts they owe. In any civil disputes about property the disputants fight, are separated, sacrifice a goat, and friends settle the matter. I saw this procedure carried out. A quiet argument was the first stage, abuse and a broken head the second, the inevitable goat and a reconciliation the third. The man who was actually in the wrong had to pay for the goat.

In all other disputes the good old law of the strongest winning always prevails. It is that which makes the headman with many sons and grandsons so important a personage, since he can bring so much force to bear on those numerous minor questions between men of the same clan which so constantly arise, also in disputes with families in other clans, which are not of sufficient importance for the whole clan to interest itself in. Wealth is also very important. The very rich man who is popular in the tribe because he keeps going through ceremonial feast-giving is certain to have a large number of ordinary supporters on almost any question, in addition to the number to be got by bribery. The poor man of unimportant family, no matter how brave he may be, is no match for a rich man who is not a coward.

The law of Káfir inheritance starts with the assumption that a woman cannot hold property. She has no rights of any kind, and cannot inherit. The property left by a father is divided equally among the sons, except that the eldest has his share increased by some single article of value, such, for instance, as a cow or a dancing-robe; while the youngest inherits his father's house. It might seem that by inheriting the house of his father the youngest son has a distinct advantage over his brethren. This, no doubt, is true, but still the eldest of the brothers is the head of the family. I do not know to what this curious custom of the youngest inheriting the house property is due, nor could any one explain it. It may have been originally intended to prevent the youngest, while a weakling, from being thrust out of the house by his elder and stronger brothers. Of course, as the sons grow up, they settle in houses of their own, which always remain theirs. The inheritance is strictly confined to legitimate sons by free mothers. Slaves' sons would not count. If there are no children, the deceased's brother would take all the property. If there were only one son, and he very young, the brother would, as a kind of guardian, practically do as he chose with the property, provided always that he gave away large amounts of it in feasting the tribe. The wives in such a case as this would also be his to dispose of. He would keep them himself, or sell them in marriage. The mother of the heir would probably remain with her son in any case. If the heir is a son, he may dispose of his stepmothers. I do not know if he ever sells his mother in marriage. I know she is often re-married, and it is probable her price goes to the son. In one case, elsewhere referred to, the son himself married one of his stepmothers. In the failure of the immediate near male relations, the estate would fall to distant male relations, and in failure of all such, to the clan. Never, in any circumstances, does it go to relatives by marriage, which, indeed, might mean its going out of the tribe altogether.

CHAPTER XXVI

The Jast—Compulsory feasts in connection with becoming Jast—The Mezhom
—The Sanowkun—Wheat growing by the Kaneash—Minor ceremonies—
The Duban festival—The Munzilo festival—The Mírs—The Urir Jast
—Poor freemen—Recapitulation—The family—Authority of the father
—Succession to the headship—Family quarrels—Polygamy—A typical
Káfir family.

AN individual cannot become of great importance in the
tribe until he is a headman or Jast, one of those individuals who are permitted to wear the women's coroneted
earrings through the upper part of the ear, and to wear
whatever gorgeous dress he can procure for religious
ceremonies and dances—a man to be admired and envied
by all who have not attained the same rank, and one to
be always treated with respect, and given precedence.
Little boys can become Jast, that is to say, they can go
through the prescribed ceremonies, attain the earrings,
and probably be given a place in the dances also, but
they will not be considered as other than boys while
they are boys. They act sometimes as acolytes, and
hold water for the priest during certain special ceremonies and feasts, at which none but the Jast and the
priest may be present. Amongst the Kám it takes nearly
three years to become a Jast, and involves the giving of
twenty-one feasts, ten to the Jast and eleven to the tribe
at large. There are also several complicated ceremonies
to be gone through. Among the Katirs their necessary
observances can be completed in about two years.

The feasts are most expensive. Amongst the Kám, many men utterly ruin themselves in becoming Jast, spending their substance to the last goat, the last cheese, the last pound of ghee, and take praise to themselves for having done so. The feasts are not left to the discretion and liberality of the individual. If he were to offer cattle in poor condition, or male goats of inferior size, he would be immediately heavily fined. While going through the ordeal, the man himself or his immediate relations are all conscious of the dignified position the family is attaining. They often, at such times, profess a liberality they are far from feeling. More than once or twice has a goat been promised by one of them, but I never expected it to be sent to me. A man cannot go through the ceremonies by himself; he must have a female coadjutor. She may or may not be his wife, but usually is not, for the expense of two persons of the same family giving these compulsory feasts at the same time is so great, that there is only one man in the Kám tribe, Torag Merak, who can bear such a strain on his resources. An arrangement is usually made between two men, by which one of them goes through the Jast ceremonies with the wife of the other, whose husband will be associated with the first man's wife in similar feast-givings as soon as the flocks have had time to recover the drain to which they have been subjected. The initiatory proceedings are sacrifices of bulls and male goats to Gísh at the chief shrine. The animals are examined with jealous eyes by the spectators, to see that they come up to the prescribed standard of excellence. After the sacrifice the meat is divided among the people, who carry it to their homes. These special sacrifices at the shrine recur at intervals; but the great slaughterings are at the feast-giver's own house, where he entertains sometimes the Jast exclusively, and sometimes the whole tribe, as already mentioned. At Gísh's shrine, after a big distribution at the giver's house, one or two goats are offered to the war-god, the meat is distributed and carried away, while tchina cakes, cheese, salt, and wine are consumed by all present. New arrivals sit down quietly and look expectant. They have not to wait long before they are attended to. Handfuls of tchina cakes, very thin, either circular, with a diameter of two inches or so, or oval, with a maximum measurement of three inches by one and a half inches, and small cubes of cheese, are brought round on trays, with salt. The wooden wine-bowl circulates at intervals. Little family parties may be seen, the gaffer with a small cake in his left hand heaped up with salt, into which he and his four or five grandchildren dip as they eat.

The only privilege the woman gains is that she is allowed to wear markhor or goat's hair round the top of her dancing-boots, and to have a share in the dancing, when, at the completion of all the formalities, there is a ceremonial dance at a particular festival.

For the general distribution of food to the villagers considerable preparation has to be made. The slaughtering of the animals and the cooking are done in the afternoon for the following morning's feast. I witnessed one of these preliminary slaughterings. The place selected was on two or three contiguous house-tops, which afforded a level space of some twenty yards in length and twelve to fifteen in breadth. There were several large stone pots (valued at two or three cows apiece) boiling on their

respective iron tripods, each of which was declared to
be worth one cow, so valuable are utensils of all kinds
in Kámdesh.   Two or three slaves attended to the fires.
Seated in the shade of a wall were all the notables of
the village, while sauntering about with the high slow
tread of mountaineers were many friends and neighbours
of the feast-giver.   They were so numerous that they
had great difficulty in avoiding the large wooden bowls
full of blood, which stood about in different places where
animals had been slaughtered.   Streams of half-congealed
blood marked the positions where the carcasses had been
dragged on one side to be skinned and dismembered.
Several dogs were furtively lapping at the semi-solid
stream, keeping a wary eye on passers-by, who occasionally aimed at them a blow or a kick, and drove them
off howling dismally.   There were fifteen big male goats
and five bulls killed on this occasion.   From the number
of people present, and from the way they behaved, the
spectacle was evidently regarded in the light of a highly
popular show.   The goats were slowly driven forward
one by one, rapidly seized, and thrown across a stool, in
which position their throats were cut.   The string of
goats was quickly disposed of.   They were patted and
petted, and stood perfectly quiet awaiting their turn.
Only the last two or three struggled and tried to break
away, although the smell of blood was overpowering.
The bulls were seized one by one by the horns and the
heads depressed to the ground by a Káfir, the animals
not making the slightest resistance.   Then a second
man with a small narrow axe, which, however, never
missed its mark, knocked them down dead, or paralysed
them by a single blow behind the horns, the blood spurt-

PREPARING FOR THE FEAST.

To face page 452.

ing forth copiously. Generally, one or two additional blows were given while the bull lay prostrate. All the time this was going on, the feast-giver was standing before one of the fires over which the pots were boiling, and kept adding certain branches and crying "Yamach!" stepping back every now and then for a handful of blood to throw on the fire, and for a goat's head to singe in the flames. No one joined in the responses, as all do before the idols, but the individual had the entire ceremony to himself. The carcases were dragged or carried away to be hung up and divided, in the case of goats, or to be skinned and knifed on the ground, in the case of oxen. In spite of the bowls placed to receive it, blood covered the whole of the ground, the headless carcases quivered as though still alive, and the smell of raw meat became intolerable. The rapidity with which the animals were killed, and their bodies scientifically cut into joints or properly shaped fragments, was remarkable. One of the most unpleasant of the sights was to witness the workers consume, with much relish, the stray portions of raw fat. The women of the household stood by in readiness to receive into their conical baskets the omentum and its fat, and showed much housewifely anxiety in watching its course from the animal's body until it was safe in their custody. This was the show to which all Kámdesh had gathered. Those who could not find room in the confined space on the housetop sat in groups some distance off, talking politics, discussing one another's garments, or else performing friendly offices for one another which need not be more particularly mentioned. The public banquet is a common sight. It takes place on the housetop of course, as there alone can sufficient level space be procured. The spot is arranged for the company by having deodar poles, six inches in diameter, placed opposite to, and about four feet distant from, one another. On them the guests seat themselves, about twenty-five on each pole, and cooked meat in fragments is brought round in the usual conical baskets used by the women. The servers were the men and women of the family. The number of seats being limited, there is usually a crowd of men waiting patiently until those being served are satisfied. Every ten minutes or so the latter are replaced by onlookers or fresh arrivals. Bread is handed about in the shape of small chappaties, ten inches in diameter, made with tchina flour. The business-like manner in which people came, sat down, were fed, and then went away without paying any kind of compliment to their hosts, was very curious. These feasts vary in magnificence. A man's entertainment may not fall below a certain standard, but it may be as expensive or ostentatious as he likes. A very rich man will supplement these average banquets by giving wine or other luxuries. On certain days meat is always consumed; on others it is not eaten at the place of entertainment, but great heaps or portions skewered together are in readiness for the guests to carry home with them, while bread, ghee, &c., are partaken of at the house. A miserly Káfir, a man remarkable for covetousness in a nation where cupidity is esteemed a virtue, will do his utmost, will try every shift and expedient, to render his feast a success. He thinks nothing of ruining himself completely to become a Jast, and ever afterwards refers to his impoverished condition with a proud humility,

AT THE PUBLIC BANQUET.

To face page 456.

expecting, and generally getting, the sympathy and admiration of his audience at every such allusion. Not unfrequently, as one of the periodic food distributions are drawing to a close, some man, often a visitor from some other tribe, will suddenly raise his voice and sound forth the praises of his host, dilating on his bravery and generosity, on the wealth of his family, and the proud position they hold as dispensers of food largess. The Kám folk are particularly proud of their general entertainments, and frequently asked me if in my country they gave away in "charity" as largely as the Kám did.

The entertainments given to the Jast alone are considered by the people to be most imposing and exclusive functions. They are named the Mezhom. As the number of the Jast is limited, an array of seven male goats and one bull is sufficient for each day's entertainment. I was invited to take part at a Mezhom, a compliment of an unprecedented kind. When I reached my host's house, the verandah was thronged with people, and one or two carcasses of goats were lying about. A small party of slaves were drumming and piping before the door of the living-room, which had all its furniture removed and long planks substituted for the convenience of the Jast, who were seated in a dignified, expectant manner all round the room. The smoke-hole opening had been enlarged till it was about four feet each way. Utah the priest, who was also the candidate for the Jast honours, was busily engaged tending the sacred fire burning on an upturned iron girdle resting on an iron tripod. He was adding ghee, wine, portions of chappaties, and tchina flour to the flames. At the threshold, which was raised $1\frac{1}{2}$ feet above the ground level, as is the case in Káfir houses, sat a well-known Jast. The goats, brought one by one to be sacrificed, had merely their heads thrust into the room, when the Jast above mentioned at once seized and killed the animals, catching the blood in wooden vessels. Utah took a handful of blood as it was flowing from each goat, and added it to all the other things on the fire. The Debilála continued singing the praises of the gods, while at each addition of blood to the fire, at a signal from Utah, the whole audience chorused a response. The several heads were then singed in the fire. The usual response "i-i-i yamach!" was repeated twice by every one, and two of the Jast, in my corner, piped a monotonous bar or two on the reed instruments. In the verandah, the slaves, every now and then, came in with terrible effect. In the enclosed space, their music had a surprising clangour, and drowned the Debilála's chant altogether. After all the seven goats had been killed, the ceremony was practically at an end. An old woman brought in a basketful of earth to throw over the blood on the floor. She had, no doubt, been through the necessary feasts, or she could not have been present in the room. So also with the little boy who, acting as an acolyte, poured water over Utah's hands. The entertainment wound up with a general feast. The people outside in the verandah who caught glimpses of the strange and rather gruesome entertainment, considered themselves honoured and gratified. The Káfir who went to India with me explained that he liked such shows, just as I liked the Calcutta theatres. The feast-givers are known as Kaneash, while those who have already completed their virtuous work are known as "Sunajina."

The Kaneash have a complicated ritual to go through

quite apart from the food-giving ceremonies already described. As the time approaches when they may don the
earrings, the formalities become more and more complex.
On February 11, I was camped a short distance from
Kámdesh, and my friend the priest, who was also a Kaneash, sent a breathless messenger to inform me that I
must be present at an important function at his house
that evening, called the Sanowkun. We hurried back to
Kámdesh, calling on our way on Utah, who was found
busy with the garments he was to wear in the evening.
At the time appointed I found Utah's living-room full of
guests seated on planks placed against the wall, or on
stools, wherever there was sufficient room for them. In
the middle of the hearth a fire was blazing brightly.
Against one of the centre wood pillars Utah was seated.
It was the hour of his triumph. He was a simulacrum of
a man in that he closely resembled one of the decked-out
effigies. He had on a thick stumpy turban, having in
front a fringe of cowrie shells strung together with red
glass beads, and furnished with a tail. A plume-like
bunch of juniper-cedar was stuck in the front of this
striking head-dress, between the folds of the cloth. His
ears were covered with a most complicated collection of
earrings of all shapes and sizes. About his neck was
a massive white metal necklace, brass bracelets rudely
stamped with short lines and marks adorned his wrists,
while he had on his feet the ordinary dancing-boots with
long tops, ending in a markhor hair fringe. He wore a
long blue cotton tunic, reaching nearly to his knees, and
the curiously worked black and white nether garments
made for these occasions at Shál in the Kunar Valley.
Perhaps the most striking part of the costume was a

Badakhsháni silk robe of the usual gaudy pattern, which
was thrown negligently across the shoulders. In his
hand was the dancing axe of his fathers. He was bursting with pride and delight at his own appearance. After
a short interval, Utah being unable to officiate as priest, a
Jast stepped forward and acted as deputy. He bound a
white cloth round his brows, took off his boots, washed
his hands, and began the night's proceedings by the sacrifice of two immense billygoats, the largest I have ever
seen, the size of young heifers. The sacrifice was conducted in the usual way with the customary details. The
special feature of the ceremony was the dabbling of some
of the blood on the forehead of Utah and on the forehead
and legs of his son Merak, who, seated opposite his father,
was still weak and ill, for he was only just recovering
from small-pox. For the boy, this proceeding meant that
he might thenceforth wear trousers. Besides the ordinary flour, bread, and ghee, placed by the fire ready for
the sacrifice, there were some enormous chappaties, about
15 inches in diameter, like those given to elephants in
India. At this point these were lifted up, a sprig of
blazing juniper-cedar thrust in the centre, and they were
then solemnly circled round Utah's head three times and
made to touch his shoulders, while the deputy priest who
handled them cried " Such, such ! " The same thing was
then done to the boy. After an interval for refreshment
there was dancing ; but just before they commenced, a
visitor from Bragamatál burst forth into panegyrics upon
Utah and on his dead father, and spoke of the immense
amount of property which had been expended on the
feast. This fulsome flattery was rewarded according to
custom by the present of a lungi or turban cloth, which

THE SANOWKUN CEREMONY.

To face page 462.

was taken from the waist of the little boy, Utah's son, who was still suffering from the effects of small-pox. The fire was then taken away and four or five visitors were provided with turbans and dancing-boots, as well as scarves to wear over their shoulders or round the waist. Utah's sister and her little daughter, aged twelve, then made their appearance in full dancing attire. As soon as all were ready, pine-wood torches were lighted, and the dancers began the usual 1, 2, 3, pause, 1, 2, 3, pause. Utah with the Debilála and the Pshur took up a position in the centre of the room on the hearth, while the others danced outside the central pillars of the room. The first dances, three in number, were to Gísh, the war-god, and then the Pshur, who had been unusually quiet all the evening, saw a spirit, and behaved in his most furious manner. His frantic gestures in the direction of the smoke-hole made Utah and the Debilála at once enlarge the opening by pushing up the covering with their axes; he then seized the ghee vessel and carried it off, to prevent the spirit getting hold of it. He breathlessly explained that in order to obviate a great calamity to Utah and to himself, a goat must be sacrificed on the morrow. He was finally interrogated in a formal way by his brother ecclesiastics, they and the company generally chorusing responses in the usual manner, at regular intervals. After Imrá had been danced to, Dizane was honoured in the same way, the Debilála chanting her praises while he danced. Then succeeded dances to other deities.

The following day music and amusements for the young were continued all day at Utah's house, and then early on the morning of the 13th, he, with the assistance

2 B

of many of his friends, ceremoniously changed his turban for a broad-brimmed crownless hat, into the front of which a sprig of juniper-cedar was thrust. This changing of the head-dress is called the Shara'ute. In their uniform, which they wore till the spring, Utah and his brother Kaneash, of whom there were three more, were considered "pure." Great care had to be observed that their semi-sacred garments were not defiled by coming into contact with dogs. The Kaneash were nervously afraid of my dogs, which had to be fastened up whenever one of these august personages was seen to approach. The dressing has to be performed with the greatest care, in a place which cannot be defiled by dogs. Utah and another had convenient dressing-rooms on the top of their houses, which happened to be high and isolated, but another of the four Kaneash had been compelled to erect a curious-looking square pen made of poles in front of his house, his own roof being a common thoroughfare. The ceremony of the Sanowkun is always performed in much the same way, although sometimes the details are slightly varied.

Another curious duty undertaken by the Kaneash is to grow a miniature field of wheat in the living-room of the house. On February 25th I went to visit one of them. Against the south wall of the room there was a little mound of earth some three feet by two feet, about one foot high, and levelled on the top. In this tiny field wheat was growing; the young shoots had already attained the height of two or three inches. No woman has anything to do with this wheat-growing; it is all done by the Kaneash alone, and among the Kám is remarkable as the only agricultural operation the

men ever attempt. Just in front and to the east of
the tiny field was a flat stone and an iron tripod, on
which some pine sticks were placed ready for lighting.
In front of this miniature altar was a stool, with a flat
piece of wood in front, which was to serve as a footstool.
The Kaneash every evening goes through the following
rite. He seats himself on the stool and takes off his
boots, while some friends or relations light the fire,
bring forward a wicker basket piled up with cedar
branches, a wooden vessel containing water, a small
wicker measure with a handful of wheat grains in it,
and a large carved wooden receptacle full of ghee. The
Kaneash, having washed his hands, assumes the crownless hat he must never be without except in his own
house, and begins by burning and waving about a cedar
branch while he cries "Such! such!" He thrusts
this into the water vessel before him, and then burns a
second branch completely, after waving it as before,
and sprinkles it with the now holy water. He then
proceeds to sprinkle the cedar branches, the fire, and
the ghee vessel. Next, he piles cedar branches in the
fire with a few wheat grains and a handful of ghee, and
begins his incantation while the flames are dancing
merrily and the smoke rolling upwards in clouds. He
pays tribute to all the gods in regular order, every now
and then pausing to sprinkle and cast his offering on
the fire, as at the beginning. The temperature of the
room gradually grows terrific, for the ordinary house-fire
is blazing on the hearth all the time. The scene altogether is a strange one; the walls of the room are frequently adorned with grotesque figures painted in black
on the clay-coloured ground. The sprig of cedar worn

in front of the hat shows that the wearer is an ordinary notable who has become a Jast. If he has gone through the ceremony before, he wears two sprigs of cedar. This is very rare indeed, but while I was in Kámdesh Torag Merak, who was a Kaneash, had his head-dress adorned with three sprigs of cedar to show it was the third time he had completed the food distribution. His associate was his own wife. These facts were sufficient to tell the initiated that Torag Merak must be the richest man in the whole of Káfiristán, in all probability. The woman associate of the Kaneash does her killing and feasting at her house on the day following his. She has no wheat-growing to do, nor does she make offerings to the gods.

There are all manner of side ceremonies connected with the Jast. I went on one occasion to see a man who was just beginning his feast-giving. One of the Kaneash officiated as priest, which all, during the period of purity, are capable of doing. A bull and some goats were sacrificed. Into the flowing blood arrows were dipped, and then, at the end of the proceedings, were fired away promiscuously. A vessel containing blood mixed with water was afterwards emptied ceremoniously by ladlefuls on the ground, and subsequently a tub with like contents was similarly emptied. No one seemed to know the meaning of all this, or else none could or would explain its meaning; but on the whole I am inclined to think that, allowing for my difficulties of understanding the language spoken, it is probable that the original meaning of many of their ceremonies has been lost by the Káfirs; that they continue the ritual handed down from their forefathers without troubling about its meaning, and, like most other people, mistake the ceremony itself for the principles it symbolises. In the year 1891 the Kaneash began their final duties on the 11th of February. None of them were permitted to leave the precincts of Kámdesh, except for one particular sacrifice at Urmir, until May 10. On the latter date the four put off their crownless hats until they were finally wanted for a particular dance, and went about with their heads bound round with a big piece of white cloth, put on as a crown would be worn. They continued to wear the rest of their uniform for an indefinite period.

The Duban festival at Kámdesh began on March 21 in 1891. This is the period of the spring dances, and Káfirs come in from the outlying villages to participate in them. The Kaneash all have to be present to take part in the performances, which were curious. On the 22nd the serious business of the festival began. The dancers, all of them Jast, having arrayed themselves in Sultánzari over-garments, gaudy turbans used as scarves, their heads adorned with white turbans into the front of which were thrust sticks ornamented with the crest feathers of the pheasant, danced round and round to so slow a measure that they hardly appeared to bend the knee or to move forward. They were preceded by the four Kaneash of the year, attired in their official dress with the crownless hat, and were followed by more or less of a rabble, hunted up by the Ur Jast, who acted as a kind of master of the ceremonies, to swell the throng. The procession tramped slowly round the dancing-house. In the centre of the dense crowd was a man beating a drum, and the Debilála hammering incessantly at a small one. This surprised me greatly, for, as a rule, it is only slaves that beat drums.   These two individuals kept chanting, line by line, what I believe was a hymn of praise to Imrá. Just as they reached the last word of the line, the rest of the performers broke in with a " Ai-inge-e-e-e yuma derinja tunamach ! "   This went on for an indefinite time apparently, the only variation being that occasionally the leading four, the Kaneash, faced round and led the procession, creeping backwards instead of forwards.   All the performers were most solemn in feature, while the leaders bore themselves with much dignity.   At length an end came to this part of the show, and Utah proceeded to the door at the east end of the building, and with his back to the opening, faced the fire and had water poured over his hands.   A bowl of water was then handed to him, which contained a sprig of cedar.   With the latter he sprinkled water about three or four times, much of it falling over the bright dresses of the Jast.   Each time he repeated the word " Such ! "   Then he commenced naming each god in turn, thus : " Ai Imrá tunamach ! " (This is in your praise, O Imrá), and so on—the whole audience chorusing the usual responses, " i-i-i-yamach ! " There was no sacrificing, and consequently no sprinkling of blood.

An interval followed, during which late arrivals, all important men, began, with the help of admiring friends, to robe themselves, covering their everyday dirty garment with bright-hued silks from Peshawar and Badakhshán. When all were ready, a single line of Jast stood ranged round the dancing-house, all facing inwards, all dressed in their best attire, and each holding his bright dancing axe over his shoulder.   Utah and the other three Kaneash, having exchanged their crownless hats for the cowrie-fringed turbans, threw each of them a Badakhshán silk robe over his shoulders, and placed themselves at the top of the room. Curiously enough, Utah, of the four, was the only dancer, and the other three, from age or other causes, preferred to lean against the pillars in the centre and look on. The Debilála and the Pshur occupied a position in the centre, and in front of Utah. A big log fire was blazing between them. Between the line of Jast, ranged round the centre group, and the spectators, were a number of women dancers, who were grotesque and dirty to look at, in spite of the ornaments on their persons. The spectators crowded every corner of the building, while its two open sides were filled up for the most part by girls and young women, who packed themselves between the timbers of the heavy open frame-work, and climbed into all manner of difficult places where one would expect to see adventurous boys. The latter, however, were, almost without exception, in the place of honour on the floor of the house. Dances in honour of Gísh, Dizane, Imrá, Krumai, &c., were then gone through. The Duban dancing continued until February 27.

The last appearance of the Kaneash as exalted individuals is at the Munzilo festival in August. A careful description of that event, at second-hand, went down the Bashgul river with my lost note-book. But the chief points connected with it were as follows :—

Each of the Kaneash had to dance with his female associate. On the first day, No. 1 danced with his feminine coadjutor; on the second day, No. 1 and No. 2 both danced with the partner of the latter; on the third day, Nos. 1, 2, and 3 all danced with the last named's associate; and on the final day, all the Kaneash danced with No. 4's partner. Each day, while the man distributed food in the morning, the woman, his ally, provided the evening meal. The Kaneash have to sleep out of doors throughout the festival, the two belonging to the upper village at Dizane's shrine, the other two near the shrine of Gísh, the war-god. All the Kaneash have to shave their heads, moustaches, and beards, leaving only the karunch or scalp-lock. At these final feasts cheese was given away to every one, and the most arduous efforts had to be made by the food-givers to get a sufficient supply of the article. For many days before the Munzilo they were busy buying up all the cheeses they could obtain anywhere, an immense number being required to meet the extraordinary demand.

Another and nominally higher grade than the ordinary Jast is called by the Kám Káfirs " Mír," by which they mean king. To attain this dignity a man must first become a Jast. He then, at or about the Nilu festival, gives a great feast. The following year at the same date he entertains the whole of the village for two days. At the third Nilu, he has one more food distribution, after which he is a Mír. The outward and visible sign of this rank is, that he is permitted the privilege of sitting on the national four-legged little stool outside a house or verandah; but I do not think there are any other tangible advantages in being a Mír. In Kámdesh, in 1891, there were three men who enjoyed the title, while a fourth was qualifying for it. The priest of the tribe, even before he becomes a Jast, is allowed the royal privilege of seating himself out of doors in the way described. Any one may sit on planks or benches or stools inside a house, but the unique position of occupying a stool outside the house is reserved for the Mírs and the priest. One woman had also attained this exalted rank. She never did any field-work, but appeared to pass the whole of her time availing herself of her peculiar right to seat herself outside her own door.

The men of the very highest importance in Kámdesh in 1890-91 were all Mírs, but the individual who was qualifying for the rank, although a man of great distinction in his own clan, could never have become, in any circumstances, of much consequence in the tribe. All the Mírs were greybeards. I do not know if there is any age qualification for the position, but possibly it is one of the many unwritten laws of the Káfirs, that it would be presumptuous for any middle-aged man to seek the distinction.

The Ur or Urir Jast is an official elected annually, who holds an important position in the tribe. Indeed, during his year of office he is the equal of the Jast, but as he is a kind of magistrate and master of the ceremonies combined, he will be more particularly described when I come to the Káfir method of internal government.

There is a class of the community of which mention has already been made. It has no distinction or distinguishing name, but consists of men of no family or position whatever, who are also devoid of wealth. They are not slaves. They have no flocks nor herds of their own, merely a little land which their community cultivates. It is from this class that the shepherd or "pᴜtsa" is obtained. During the winter months he takes care of the goats, and receives for the whole winter one animal for every twenty in his custody. He often attaches himself to an important man as his henchman, and performs all the duties, of a servant without receiving that title.

A Káfir tribe, such as the Kám, is composed of the following social grades :—

    (1.) The Mírs and the priest.
    (2.) The Jast, and the Ur Jast (an Members of the
        official).   same class.
    (3.) Members of important clans.
    (4.) Members of very small clans or groups of families.
    (5.) Poor freemen, patsas or shepherds.

The family is the unit of the Káfir body politic. As the importance of a clan is dependent, to a very great extent, upon the number of families of which it consists, so the importance of a family is similarly dependent upon the number of adult males it can produce, to back an argument or support the head of the house in all his contentions.

The head of the house is autocratic in his own family. All his descendants give him respect and obedience during his life, and honour his memory when he is dead. If a son believes himself to be dealt with unjustly by his father, and is hopeless of redress, he may leave the tribe altogether and turn Musalmán for a time. He rarely opposes his father actively or threatens him, although he may threaten to make family affairs uncomfortable or disastrous unless his grievances are remedied. In some instances, however, when the father's actions have been of a particularly gross character, the son, backed by public opinion, may, and does, openly quarrel with and threaten his father. For instance, one of the brothers of Kán Márá of Lutdeh ran away with his own daughter-in-law. His outraged son insisted upon getting about

eight times the usual number of cattle paid as compensation for such offences, and swore that unless this demand
were at once complied with he would not allow his father
" to remain alive " in the valley. The penalty was paid.

When the father of a family grows senile, his authority materially lessens. On his death, if there be more
than one grown-up son, the first-born (provided always
he is not the progeny of a slave mother) becomes the
head of the family, but his authority is not very great.
Brothers try to hold the family flocks and herds in
partnership as long as they can, but quarrels generally
arise, which usually end in the property being equitably
divided, and each one going his own way. The disadvantage of separating until separation can no longer be
avoided is so well recognised, that great efforts are made
by relations and fellow-clansmen, or other friends, to
patch up any quarrel which occurs. Separation means
weakening the family, and if none of the brothers have
sons old enough to help in tending or herding the flocks,
it also means great inconvenience, for no man can leave
his grazing-grounds to go to his village unless he leaves
a deputy behind him, either as paid servant or as partner.

Peacemakers in Káfiristán have always plenty to do.
Brothers continually quarrel. The two most famous
young warriors of the Kám tribe were brothers named
Shyok and Din Malik. Together they owned a great
deal of property. The former was the Ur Jast of the
tribe in 1891, and both were saving up to become Jast.
A terrific quarrel broke out between these two concerning the ownership of a paltry sheep-skin bag. The
high priest with great difficulty succeeded in patching up
a peace, but assured me it would only be of a tempo-

rary nature. Just as I was leaving the Bashgul Valley, a serious dispute broke out between the priest and his two brothers, the latter alleging that the former had received many presents from me which he had not shared with them. They demanded that the flocks and herds should be divided, and insisted on separating from their illustrious brother unless he came to terms with them.

Káfirs are polygamists. If houses are plentiful, as in Kámdesh, one man while young or middle-aged may have several homes—two or three, that is to say—for inferior or slave wives do not require separate maintenance; but as he grows older his sons will occupy his houses, and he will probably be content with one for himself, which the youngest son will inherit, as will be explained in dealing with inheritance.

A typical powerful Káfir family was that of Dán Malik of Kámdesh, or that of Kán Márá of Lutdeh. Dán Malik was a very old man belonging to the important Demidári clan. Although not so wealthy as Torag Merak, he was of more weight in the tribal counsels, not only because of his deserved reputation for shrewdness, but because he had three stalwart sons, and four or five grandsons on the verge of manhood. In 1891 he was undoubtedly the chief man of the Kám tribe, but since then, he and two or three of his grandsons have been killed, and no doubt at the present time Torag Merak, my shifty "brother," is the most powerful man in the Kám tribe. Dán Malik lived in a single house with his aged wife and several little grandchildren, whose fathers, two of his sons, had been killed on the frontier. His three surviving sons lived in houses of their own, near at hand, each ruling his own family, but all looked up to Dán Malik as a final court of appeal in all matters. All the property of the family was held in common, and no dispute ever appeared to rise about its distribution, although two of the sons were both turbulent and avaricious, and all were of middle age.   The average woman is of no importance in a family except as a field-worker and as a bearer of children ; she need not therefore be further referred to in this connection.

CHAPTER XXVII

Káfir villages—Women's quarters—The fort village—Villages built upon defensive positions—Populous villages—Walled villages—Undefended villages—The one-room house—Centre pillars—The roof—The smoke-hole—Houses of the better class—Katir houses—Houses of the Presun Káfirs—A Káfir tower—The dancing-place or "gromma"—The Nirmali house—Pshals—Cooking utensils—Store vessels—Káfir fire-irons—Fixed furniture—The bedstead—Tables and stools—The "Sheni"—Cupboards and other receptacles.

KÁFIR villages are built in various ways, according as they are liable to attack by a numerous enemy or by small raiding detachments. Other considerations also must have been taken into account in settling the plan of the different villages. The chief of these must have been whether the inhabitants were numerous and brave enough to protect themselves by numbers alone, or would have to rely partly or chiefly upon natural defensive positions or on fortifications. Another important question to be decided would be the total amount of arable land available for the community. In places where the cultivatable ground is inconsiderable, the houses are generally piled on top of one another, or built in the strangest positions, in order that the fields may not be encroached upon. In some instances the configuration of the ground has rendered a particular plan necessary. In many cases several of the above considerations sometimes have determined the site and arrangement of the village.

In one respect all Káfir villages agree with one

another, and that is in having the women's hospital, or Nirmali-house, placed at some distance from the other habitations. From the position of many of these buildings the inference is irresistible that the villagers are much more anxious to keep the female inmates far removed from the ordinary dwelling-houses than they are afraid of having them captured by an enemy.

The following are the chief varieties of Káfir villages :—

The fort village is peculiar to the Katir tribe. In the Bashgul country, Ptsigrom in the Skorigul, Pshui, Apsai, Shidgul, and Bádámuk are of this kind. These villages are built in an oblong figure; the houses, two or three stories high, surrounding a centre courtyard, which is partially occupied by a dancing-place and a rude altar, while the dancing-house or gromma, which is used in the winter and in bad weather, is close by. The exterior of such a village offers to an enemy an unbroken front, as all the windows of the rooms, looking outwards, are very small. There is usually only one entrance gate, or at most two, in which case the second not unfrequently, as at Bádámuk, leads into dark passages difficult to penetrate at any time without a guide. The main entrance is capable of being quickly and effectively closed. Such villages are usually built on the bank of a river flowing through the Káfir equivalent for a plain. When besieged, the inhabitants obtain their water from the river by means of a tunnel, which leads from the central courtyard to the river's edge, and ends in a covered way made of roughly hewn timbers. These fort villages contain from 120 to 200 different families, and are all greatly overcrowded. The

houses which form the four sides of the oblong figure
have low cellars like chambers underneath them, into
which sheep, goats, and cattle are driven when an
attack is imminent. The corners of the village are

APSAI VILLAGE.

generally strengthened by towers, and at Bádámuk and
other places, where there are steep slopes in close
proximity, one or two detached three-storied towers are
built up the hillside as an additional security. A great
deal of wood enters into the construction of these

villages. On the courtyard side the dwellings or rooms are often furnished with verandahs or wooden galleries open in front, the uprights and frames of which are often rather effectively carved in the ordinary basket-work pattern, or with purely conventional heads of animals. The different floors of a house are reached by solid ladders, that is to say, by planks shaped by the axe alone, and deeply notched at proper intervals for the feet. The quaint carvings, and the irregular outline of the inner aspect of the houses caused by the verandahs or galleries, render these villages some-what picturesque, but they are grimed black with smoke, the open spaces are littered with the bones and horns of animals killed for food, and the general appearance is squalid and depressing, while the stench is sometimes hardly bearable.

Of villages built upon defensible positions good examples are to be found at Purstám, Bajindra, and Gourdesh. The houses at Purstám are clustered together on the east face of a steep detached rock, inaccessible from every other direction. The lowest habitations are on the bank of a side branch of the Bashgul river. The road up the rock between the houses is extremely steep Half-way up is the dancing-house with its wooden plat-form adjoining. Bajindra is one of the most curious villages in Káfiristán. At that place advantage has been taken of the flat upper surface of a huge detached piece of rock, and upon it some thirty different domiciles have been crowded and superimposed one on the other. The only way to reach the houses is by a bridge which con-nects the village with the hillside behind. This bridge can be easily broken away, and then the houses are

2 C

absolutely inaccessible. The drawback to the position is that the river is a little distance away, and there is no other water supply for the people. There are two or three little hamlets in the Skorigul built precisely after the fashion of Bajindra on fragments of rock, but they are all on the river-bank by the water's edge. The village of Gourdesh is a densely populated cluster of some twenty-five houses, built on the knife-edge of a rocky spur which projects into the Gourdesh Valley, and compels the river to flow in a pear-shaped course round its base. This spur, 200 or 300 feet high, is precipitous, except at its point of connection with the main range of hills, where there is a watch-tower, and where the village can be easily defended. To enable all the houses to perch on the rocky ledge many ingenious contrivances have had to be adopted. In some instances the verandahs or wooden galleries are supported on long wooden pillars, the bases of which fit into crevices in the rock. An additional appearance of insecurity has been produced in some places where the sustaining pillars, having proved too short, have been supplemented by the placing of smooth water-worn stones beneath them. The insecurity of this arrangement is, however, more apparent than real, for experience has taught the Káfirs so much skill in the management of weights, that even the most fragile structures they erect rarely, if ever, collapse. Villages like Gourdesh cannot possibly grow larger, and in consequence they are greatly over-populated.

Places like Kámdesh, Bagalgrom, and Bragamatál (Lutdeh) depend for their protection on the strong arm of a numerous population rather than upon fortifications or the happy selection of a good defensive site. Any detached towers which such villages may possess are more for use as watching places than for defensive purposes, although they are capable of being employed for the latter purpose also. In some portions of Kámdesh the houses are built in regular terraces, which rise one above the other like a giant's staircase, or they are made to overhang steep drops or low precipices. They are likewise crowded into many awkward and inconvenient positions, with the obvious intention of not curtailing or interfering in any way with the cultivation. In many other villages the same cause and the same result are seen to a very much greater extent. Kámdesh, Bagalgrom, and that portion of Bragamatál which is, on the right bank of the river, are built on no regular plan, houses being erected wherever there is room for them. That part of Bragamatál which is on the left bank is laid out in the form of half a regular hexagon, open towards the south. The enclosed space is occupied by the gromma and dancing-platform, and by detached clusters of houses.

The only regularly walled villages with which I am acquainted are in the Presungul. Their general construction is as follows. The houses are packed together on and in the substance of a mound or rounded hillock. Many of the rooms are underground. At the foot of the slope, a short distance away, there is a protecting wall topped with brushwood. At Pushkigrom, the lowest village in the valley, the arrangement is somewhat different. There the houses are built on a slope which is surmounted by watch-towers, from which extend walls which run down to and encircle the houses. This surrounding wall is strengthened with barricades at different points, and looks very strong.

There are some villages in Káfiristán which are both small and defenceless, and are also easily accessible. From such places the inhabitants must bolt at once if a' formidable enemy makes his appearance. There are others which could be defended if the people were brave, e.g., Kstiggigrom in the Presungul. There, however, the villagers prefer to retire to a large cave overlooking their homes, where they cannot be followed. From that safe and elevated position they have more than once watched their houses being sacked and burnt. Other small villages seem to find a sense of security in the fact that they are more or less hidden away in the hills, or up difficult and unpromising ravines. Of these, as of all other villages in Káfiristán, it may be said that they find their chief protection in the easily defensible nature of the main roads of the country.

The simplest form of house consists of one apartment, oblong or square in shape, and measuring some 18 by 18 or 18 by 20 feet. It is usually well built, of cedar timber, and rubble stones embedded in mud mortar. The timbers, fashioned with the axe alone, and roughly morticed together at the angles of the building, form a series of wooden frames upon and between which the masonry is built. These wooden frames are about nine inches apart. The thickness of the walls is about five inches. They are well plastered with mud both inside and out, and are strong and durable. There are sometimes two doors, but usually only one. The door is a solid piece of wood, shaped by the axe alone. There are no hinges, but small projections from the upper and lower edges are made to revolve in sockets in the doorframe. The Káfir slaves, if we consider the indifferent tools at their disposal, are extremely clever at carpentry. In addition to the door or doors there is often a little window. It is usually fifteen or eighteen inches square,

A CORNER IN KÁMDESH.

and is closed by a wooden shutter revolving on pivots. The doors are fastened by a wooden bolt, which is made to run easily in a grove cut in the solid substance of the door, and thence into a socket in the door frame. The bolt has vertical notches all along one side. Just above the groove in which it works is a small round hole in the substance of the door. This is the keyhole. The key is a piece of iron wire, about the thickness of the top of the little finger, and more than a foot long. It is bent back in such a way that it is somewhat of the shape of a pot-hook, and can be pushed through the keyhole, and then if it is turned downwards, the end can be made to catch in the slots in the bolt, and the latter can be pushed back and the door opened. Sometimes, however, it is a very tedious operation to get the end of the iron wire to catch in the notches of the bolt. I have often watched a tired-out woman come home from field-work and spend a wearisome time before she could get the arrangement to act. When my own bolt proved recalcitrant, I was accustomed to solve the problem by lowering some small boy into the room through the smoke-hole to open the door from the inside.

In the centre of every room, at each corner of the square hearth, are four wooden pillars, which are often elaborately carved. These pillars are usually between five and six feet apart, and are either rounded or more or less square in shape. Their diameter varies from nine to fifteen inches. From the lateral walls of the apartment two large beams cross over, and are mainly supported on the top of the hearth pillars.

Boards covered with beaten-down earth form the roof, but they do not fit accurately, so that snow-water and rain find easy access into the room. The only way to minimise this discomfort is to keep adding earth to the roof, and to get it beaten down or trampled by men or goats. The roof is the worst feature of all Káfir houses.

As they are all made in the way described, and are all flat, there is not one which is even moderately water-tight. It is necessary that they should be flat, for contiguous roofs form the only level spaces which can be found in some villages where corn can be winnowed or thrashed, or fruit be spread out to dry.

The smoke-hole is over the middle of the hearth. It is usually about a foot square, and has enclosing boards which project a few inches above the level of the roof. It is closed by a flat board with a long handle in the middle being placed over it. The long handle hangs down into the room, whence it can be pushed up and the smoke-hole opened. The hearth square in the centre of the room is raised a few inches above the level of the surrounding floor, and, like the latter, is made of beaten earth. The height of a room does not exceed seven or eight feet.

The foregoing description applies to the house of an average poor Káfir of the Bashgul Valley. In such an apartment he brings up his family. There would probably be also a stable or rough kind of shed leaning against one wall of the house, and more or less completely closed in by mud walls, or by screens made by twisting twigs together.

A better kind of house in the Bashgul Valley consists of two stories, the upper part being reserved for the dwelling-place, and the lower half being used as a cow stable or a wood store. The best built habitations in the Bashgul Valley are those used by the wealthy Káfirs of the Kám tribe. Such dwellings consist of three stories. The top floor is the living place, the middle story is the store-room, while the bottom room is employed as a cow stable or wood store in the winter. In this variety of house a verandah is almost always projected from the top storey. These verandahs, or open wooden galleries, are well-made structures, closed on all sides except in front. They are frequently elaborately ornamented with carving. The projecting floor of the verandah is supported on long wooden pillars, the lower ends of which are securely kept in their proper position on the ground by the nicety with which the weights above are adjusted. The roof of the verandah is upheld by the wooden framework of the structure, and by a row of pillars which runs down the centre of the floor. Frequently all the pillars and the front of the verandah are prettily carved, and its roof-beams, which are allowed to project a foot or more beyond the walls, are fashioned at the ends into effective, if grotesque, animals' heads.

In the Katir part of the Bashgul Valley the houses are, on the whole, distinctly inferior to those of the Kám tribe, for instance. This is more particularly the case in the fort villages, where the exigencies of space require that each floor, consisting of verandah and living-room, shall house an entire family. But however the rooms may be arranged, and however large or small a house may be, the principle on which it is built remains the same. It is either one cubical apartment or several apartments superimposed, and with or without verandahs.

The houses of the Presun or Viron Káfirs differ in many respects from those already described. Perhaps the most obvious and striking peculiarity of the Viron houses is that their accommodation is principally underground. This arrangement is more particularly noticeable in the upper, and consequently colder, part of the

BUILDING A HOUSE.

To face page 488.

valley. In that position, also, wood being scarce, it is sparingly used in the construction of the walls. The timber used is not shaped with the axe, as in the Bashgul Valley, but is used in the form of round poles. The large proportion of mud and rubble to timber gives the houses a somewhat badly built appearance. There are no verandahs to break the ugly lines of the buildings. In the lower part of the valley, at Pushkigrom, wood is abundant, and the domiciles are built almost exclusively of round poles, very little masonry being used in their construction. The villages themselves are either built on a hillock or on a slope. There is one exception to this rule in the case of the village called Diogrom, which is on level ground close by the river. In the villages of the upper part of the valley, that part of the houses which emerges above ground is very like the doorways which open on to the lanes, being rarely more than 3 feet 6 inches or four feet high. The houses are packed together closely, and the paths between them are hardly broad enough for a man with moderately broad shoulders. Many of the houses have three apartments, one below the other, one being half underground, and the other two completely so. I carefully examined the house of the Shtevgrom priest. From the roadway, a 3 feet 6 inch doorway opened on to a short ladder, by which the floor of the dwelling-room was reached. That apartment was twenty feet square, but only seven feet high. The roof was supported by numerous pillars, all of which were grotesquely carved into a supposed resemblance of gods or goddesses. Four pillars, carved with more than usual care, bounded the hearth in the ordinary way. Each was made to resemble, more or less, a man on horseback. The horseman was given an enormous face, shield-shaped, 1½ feet long by ten inches at the broadest part, the brows. The chin was not more than an inch and a half from the top of the diminutive horse's head. The rider's left hand rested on the horse's neck. What at first sight looked

THE HIGH-PRIEST'S HOUSE.

like an enormous ear, turned out to be the horseman's right arm grasping a weapon. The tiny animal itself was given a little stand, such as a toy horse has. The nose of the effigy was scored by parallel lines, intersected at right angles by similar parallel lines. All the other pillars in the room were similarly carved into grotesque male or female forms, except that they were not provided with horses. Above the hearth, which was seven feet square, there was a wooden structure four feet square, which projected above the level of the roof about four feet. This was roofed, and in one corner of it there was a smoke-hole of a foot square. This peculiar chimney is very common in Presungul. From the dwelling-room a ladder led into a lower apartment, which was not more than five feet in height. There was yet another room, lower still, which was reached in a similar way. There it was possible to stand upright. From this lowest apartment a tunnel ran under the village wall to the river-bank. A second tunnel, which I was solemnly informed had been originally constructed by Yush (the devil), burrowed under the village tower or citadel.

A Káfir tower used for watch and ward is from one to four stories in height. It is of square shape, and commonly ten feet by ten feet. The door is always some considerable height above the ground, and is reached by a ladder, which can be drawn up in time of need, when the men inside are completely out of reach. The floor of each of the upper stories has a large square aperture in the middle, and each is usually provided with a ladder. The top of the tower, the three or four feet which constitute the parapet, is a little wider than the rest of the building, and projects about a foot outwards on every side. The roof of the tower at the foot of the parapet is pierced by a series of holes all round, which enable the defenders to see clearly all the walls of the tower, and to command its base. Such structures are sprinkled all over the country, and are, as a rule, extremely well built.

The dancing-place is always the most important spot in

a Káfir village. There is usually only one, but Kámdesh and Bragamatál have two each. A dancing-place should consist of a house to be used in winter and in bad weather, a boarded platform, and a level piece of ground, on which particular dances are performed, furnished with a rude stone altar. A description of the upper Kámdesh dancing-place will also apply, with some modifications, to all similar places in the Bashgul Valley. The whole place is called the gromma, a name evidently derived from the word "grom" or "brom," the Bashgul term for a village. A Káfir who had been to India with me always called the gromma the "church" when he spoke Urdu. To the north of the Kámdesh dancing-place is the gromma or dancing-house. It is twelve feet high, thirty-five feet long, and thirty feet broad. Its sides are barred, not closed, by heavy square beams, between the intervals of which spectators can thrust their heads and shoulders restfully. During a spectacle these apertures are generally crowded with the heads of girls and women. Down the centre of the gromma run two rows of massive pillars, which support the heavy roof. They are about six feet apart. The central four are quite plain, except at the top, where they are ornamented with carved horses' heads. The remaining four are completely covered with the ordinary basket-work carving. In the middle of the roof there is a four feet square smoke-hole. Bordering the gromma to the south is the largest level space in the village. It is about thirty yards square. On it there is a rude altar, formed of two upright stones, with a horizontal one on top. On this altar there is almost always to be seen the remains of a recent fire. To the east this space is continuous with

a platform, which is carried out from the steep slope and
maintained in that position by wooden pillars and beams.
It looks, and is, a shaky structure.   A railing runs round
its three dangerous sides.   Seats are provided on it in

CORNER OF A VILLAGE WITH ALTAR STONE.

the shape of long planks of comfortable breadth, a few
inches off the floor. These platforms are always to be
seen if the village is built on the side of a hill. Most of
the shrines at Kámdesh are provided with a platform

which only differs from that at the gromma in point of size. In villages built on the flat, such as those in the upper part of the Bashgul Valley, the platforms are lifted off the ground on trestles. They are, indeed, an essential part of every dancing-place, because certain ceremonies cannot be performed except upon them.

The gromma of a Presun (Viron) village differs considerably from those of the Bashgul Valley. In the first place, they are nearly all of them half underground. That at Diogrom, for example, is like a huge bear-pit, and is reached by long passages sloping down from the village level. They are very large, as they are used for guest-houses, and are capable of holding a large number of people. In one corner they generally have a small shrine, containing a quaintly carved idol of some god. The four central pillars are hewn into marvellously grotesque figures, the huge shield-shaped faces of which are more than two feet in length. The arms are made to hang from the line of the brows, while, if a goddess is represented, the long narrow breasts, which look like a pair of supplementary arms, start from between the arms and the brows. There is never any doubt, however, about the sex of an effigy of this kind. The knees of the figures are made to approach one another, while the feet are far apart, as if, indeed, the god or goddess was swarming up the pole backwards.

There is a building peculiar to all Káfir villages. This is the "pshar" or Nirmali house, the lying-in hospital. It is always placed on the outskirts of a village, and not infrequently is outside it altogether. In the Presungul, for instance, at one place it is on the opposite side of the river to the village. In the Bashgul Valley it is usually a very badly built, low, single, square apartment, into the construction of which very little wood enters. It is there distinguished by having two or three sheepskins fastened to a pole and stuck on the roof. It has no windows, and is a squalid-looking place, blackened by smoke and disfigured by the abominable sheepskins. In the new hamlets springing up in the Skorigul the pshar is the merest hovel, half underground and yet incompletely sheltered. In the Presungul these places are much better built. They are commonly placed near or on the river-bank, and apparently consist of two or three rooms in a line, the doors all facing towards the water. The unpleasant sheepskins are not employed to indicate the buildings, their peculiar shape and their isolated position being quite sufficient for that purpose.

There is another class of buildings in Káfiristán which so enter into the inner life of the people that they require a full description. These are the pshals. The word *pshal* literally means a stable, but it is used by the Bashgul Káfirs to designate their dairy farms and their grazing-grounds, as well as the buildings in which the herdsman confines his flocks and watches them by night. The life of the average well-to-do Káfir is about equally divided between the village and his pshal. Indeed, if he have no brothers or relations or friends in partnership with him, and have no sons, or only young ones, he must pass the whole of his time with his flocks, except in the winter, when a patsa or shepherd is usually hired. Some tribes have their winter pshals almost as far away as the summer pshals; the Kám, for instance. Others, like the Presuns, have them almost at their doors, where the collection of stables and goat-pens is twice as big as the

village itself, and to all appearances is just as well built.
The Katirs of the Bashgul Valley are in this matter
something between the Kám and the Presuns, and have
some winter pshals close to the village, and others far
away.   On the summer grazing-grounds there is every
variety of building, from the hut made of a few branches,
with rough goat-pens attached, which is the commonest
form, to the strongly-built regular pshal, with its artful
arrangement of stones on the top, which in the dusk
appear like men on the look-out on the roof.   Not infrequently the night pens are erected close to a shallow
cave, or near some shelving rock which can be partially
enclosed by branches, and so made into a little dwelling
and store place for butter and ghee.   The best pshals are,
however, permanent structures, and a great deal of labour
and a considerable amount of skill are expended in building them.   The winter pshals of the Presuns are somewhat smaller than those of the Bashgul tribes, and are
arranged in labyrinths where a man may hide himself in
complete security.   Much of my time has been passed
with the herdsmen of the Kám and Katir tribes, and
many days have been spent in different pshals.   They
are generally well built, practically on the same pattern
as the houses, and, as in the case of the latter, the weak
point is the roof, which lets snow-water and rain through
easily.   The average size of a pshal is about twenty feet
square.   It has no ornament of any kind.   Inside, raised
about three feet from the ground, there are usually platforms made of, and closed by, wattles.   These are for
the kids.   In another part of the interior, also raised
some feet above the floor, is the common couch for the
shepherds and their visitors, which is made of light

elastic branches. In the winter several men and women sleep together on one of these couches, which are about nine feet long by six feet broad. In the summer the women, having the field-work to do, rarely visit the distant pshals, except to carry flour and other provisions to their relatives. Underneath the raised structure referred to more than a hundred goats, without counting the kids, are often packed just before it gets dark. The coughing and restless moving about of the animals, the bleating of the kids, with the stagnant odorous atmosphere, make a night in a pshal an experience not readily to be forgotten. There is a large fireplace in one corner, which in the winter always contains a blazing fire, in front of which the Káfirs sit cooking their food and talking cheerily till bedtime. Just outside the pshal there is a huge heap of brown aromatic ordure, which is increased every morning by the daily sweepings.

The cows are mostly kept in the villages during the winter, for protection and stall - feeding, but if a man have large herds he only brings some half-dozen or so to the village, and keeps the rest at different pshals. . Their stables are similar to those used for the goats and sheep, except that the internal arrangements are different. The calves are kept apart in little enclosures which run down one side of the building. At the pshals a Káfir is always on the look-out for thieves and enemies day and night. He never takes off his dagger, even at night, and during the day may constantly be seen watching his property fully armed with matchlock and other weapons.

In many Káfir houses a large heavy shelf, five or six feet from the ground, runs across the room and rests against the wall opposite to the door. It is embedded in

2 D

the substance of the building; it is some two feet broad, and two and a half or three inches thick. One or two small pegs are knocked into the mud walls and serve as nails on which small articles may be hung. On the hearth there is either an iron tripod or three small carved dogs of soft stone on which cooking-vessels may be placed. The iron tripod is somewhat of a luxury, as iron is an expensive commodity, and is not produced in Káfiristán. The stone dogs are very commonly seen, but in the poorest houses the people have to be content with fragments of rock to stand their pots upon. The cooking-vessels are either made of clay or of a peculiar soft stone obtained in various places in the country. For all ordinary purposes crocks are used. The other variety is inconvenient except for big feasts. The stone vessels are always of large size, and are said to be very expensive. A large carved iron plate, somewhat like a Scotch griddle, but rather larger and without the big handle, is used for cooking chappaties (unleavened bread cakes). It has a small iron handle fixed to the edge, to enable it to be carried about conveniently. To turn over the cakes while they are cooking, small iron spuds are employed. Dough is kneaded in long and shallow wooden trays, which look smooth and well finished, although axes or knives are alone used in making them. Carved wooden vessels of all sizes are used to hold milk, honey, wine, and other articles of food or drink. They are more or less cylindrical in shape, and are nearly as deep as their greatest diameter, which is about midway between the top and the bottom. An extraordinary amount of labour is sometimes expended in carving these vessels. They are sometimes adorned with pretty patterns, and are generally provided with two handles placed opposite to each other. These are usually wrought in the shape of rams' heads. Occasionally a few fragments of brass are inlaid in the handles. Some are quite plain except for the carved handles, but the majority have a band of carving extending an inch or two below the brim. They are made by laboriously cutting them out of blocks of walnut-wood. The ornamenting must be a labour of love, so prettily and carefully is the work done. Some of these vessels are very graceful in outline.

Large plain wooden, tub-like vessels are to be seen in most well-to-do houses. They are capable of holding several gallons of wine. At large gatherings they are placed in convenient positions for having their contents dipped into, and handed round in bowls and drinking cups. Clumsy long-handled cups are used for skimming purposes and for tasting a stew. Wine is sometimes handed round in shallow tin bowls, but these are rare as compared with those made of walnut-wood. Flour and small quantities of grain are carried about in shallow wicker baskets, of which the diameter rapidly diminishes from the brim to the small flat base. These baskets are of different sizes and are used as measures.

The fire is usually tended by hand, but the Káfirs have small weak tongs, besides certain nondescript fragments of iron, by which the ashes can be raked and explored. Usually, however, sticks or half-consumed brands are employed for the purpose.

The ordinary furniture of a room consists of bedsteads, stools, and little tables, while planks are often employed as benches. When used for that purpose they are raised three or four inches off the ground by stones, for Káfirs dislike high seats almost as much as they dislike the absence of seats altogether. These benches are usually seen in verandahs. In a room, if there is a deficiency of stools, men sit upon billets of wood, two or three inches thick, or on pieces of firewood.

The bedstead is of the common Eastern pattern, similar to the charpoy of India. It is usually too short for Western tastes. It is of rough construction, but is not uncomfortable. The wooden framework supports the interlacing strips of narrow hide, or the goat's-hair ropes on which the sleeper lies. The bedding consists of goat's-hair mats or Presungul blankets, and whatever spare clothes are available for such purposes. There are no pillows of any kind. Káfirs do not undress on going to bed. They loosen their clothes, and in the villages the men take off their daggers. At the pshals they merely draw them to the front so that they lie between the legs. The bedstead is used as a couch for distinguished visitors, the national broad-edged bud-zun, a Chitrál robe, or a blanket being spread upon it. Although intended as a seat of honour, it is best avoided, as it usually swarms with vermin. A baby's cradle is simply a diminutive charpoy turned upside down, and swung by having the four legs attached by string to a hanging rope. When the child is a little older, the cradle can be reversed and turned into a small ordinary bedstead.

The tables used by the Bashgul Káfirs are of wicker-work. They are small and not more than ten to twelve inches high. The round tops are about fifteen inches in diameter. They are contracted in the middle, and exactly resemble the little stands used by sweetmeat sellers in India. An extremely well-made little table is occasionally seen in the Bashgul villages. It is manufactured by the Wai tribe. The three legs are of iron curiously wrought. They clasp and hold in position a shallow carved walnut-wood bowl. This little table is about twenty inches high, and appears to be of Greek design. It is rigid, however, and is not made in such a manner that the legs can be folded up.

The stools for which Káfiristán is famous are small, but of varying degrees of smallness. They are made in the same way as the bedsteads, but are square. The seat is about fifteen inches both ways, and is commonly made of interlacing narrow strips of leather. It is usually about nine inches from the ground. All Káfir houses possess a certain number of these little stools. They are also used to a limited extent in the Kunar Valley by the Gabar villagers and others.

The large oblong box called the " sheni," besides being used as a coffin, is also employed as a receptacle for the storage of grain and other property. My dwelling-room at Kámdesh possessed two of these somewhat depressing-looking objects. The shenis are always long enough for a corpse, but are not all of the same size. Some are very large ; all are heavy. The average size is probably six feet to seven feet long, two feet six inches broad, and some three feet six inches to four feet high. They are made with axe and knife alone. The sides, ends, lid, and bottom are neatly fitted, and perforated projections from one board pass through a hole in another board and are secured with a peg. The ends serve the place of feet, the bottom board being fixed to the same five or six inches from their lower edge. By this means the box is raised off the ground. It is, of course, far too heavy to be carried about. The various boards of which it consists are carried separately and the whole fitted together in the house. After serving its purpose as a store-chest it can be taken to the shenitán or cemetery, and used as an above-ground coffin.

On the rare occasions when I have been permitted to enter a storeroom in Káfiristán, I have more than once noticed a cupboard fixed on a shelf some distance from the floor. It was like a small sheni. The front was provided with two equal-sized folding doors, prettily carved.

The other receptacles for food stores are large stone or wooden vessels, which are ranged along the shelf already referred to as being opposite to the door, and goatskin bags and sacks. Wine, honey, butter, ghee, grain are all kept in goatskins of appropriate size. Some of the sacks are so large that when full of grain or flour they constitute a heavy load for a strong man. If all his store places are full, a Káfir is not particular where he keeps his property. I have been to visit a sick old man, and found the floor of his room covered with cobs of Indian corn to the depth of a foot. The legs of his bed were fitted into cleared spaces, and the cobs around him were nearly on a level with the bed itself.

CHAPTER XXVIII

Káfir clothing in general—Dress of the Siáh-Posh—The goatskin—The
"Budzun"—Sewing—Women's cotton clothes—The horned head-dress—
Gaiters of the women—Káfir boots—Hunting-boots—Imported dress—
Scarcity of clothing—Dress of the slaves—Siáh-Posh blankets—Winter
clothing—Dress of the Kashtán—Toilette of a Kashmir "masher"—
Dress of the Presuns—Dress of the Wai—A Jast hat—Dancing-turbans—
Dancing-boots—Dancing ornaments of women—Two strange figures.

WITH the exception of very young children, none of the
Káfirs go naked. The sexes are clothed differently,
although they have one garment in common. Rank is
usually indicated by the ear ornaments worn by the men,
and not by dress. Clothing is varied but slightly, and
in the case of women not at all, in accordance with
the season of the year. For special festivals particular
costumes are worn, or elaborate additions are made to
the ordinary attire.

There are distinct sumptuary laws relating to clothing.
The Afghan "postín" (sheepskin coat) seems to be prohibited altogether, but, with this exception, the rule
appears to be that within certain limits any man may
wear what he chooses, provided that he first obtains the
sanction of his fellow-tribesmen by feasting them. For
instance, one man always wore red trousers at particular
dancing festivals. Although a good warrior, he was not
particularly distinguished above his fellows in that respect. He presented six cows to the village, and was
then permitted to wear the bright coloured garments

he longed for, of which, by the way, he always seemed particularly shy, and invariably covered as much of them as possible with his long Chitráli robe.

Different tribes have recognised peculiarities of dress. In some cases these differences are slight, in others they are remarkable. All the tribes that use dark-coloured garments appear to wear nearly identical clothing, while the other tribes have distinctive costumes.

Woollen cloth is manufactured in Káfiristán. All cotton clothing, and all silk, velvet, and so on, used for the making of the headmen's dancing-dresses, are imported. The thick blanketing used is woven on looms by female slaves. There appears to be nothing of the nature of what we call fashion. The clothes are shaped and sewn. There is no difference between indoor and out-door clothing. No clothing is removed in saluting or in visiting. In making vestments and women's caps, ordinary needles and thread, brought into the country by pedlars, are employed. The gaudy dancing-dresses are looked upon as valuable property, and descend from father to son, although a certain amount is said to be put in the coffin-boxes with the corpse of a great man. There is no particular uniform worn by fighting men or by the priests, but the latter have a wisp of cotton cloth twisted round the head coronet-wise, or they use some other kind of distinctive head-dress.

A man who has killed a certain number of enemies, not less than four or five, is permitted to use the blue turban taken from a dead Musalmán, as a shawl or wrapper. The long narrow turban-cloth is cut in half, and the halves sewn together side by side, so as to give a shawl of the necessary breadth. The men are very proud of wearing these sheet-like wrappers, and stalk about in them in a highly dignified way.

The great majority of the male Káfirs wear nothing whatever on the head, either in summer or in winter. When it is very cold or very hot they protect the head and face with anything they have. There seems to be no prohibition against wearing head coverings, but they can only be obtained with great difficulty. A favourite head-dress is the soft roll-up Chitráli cap. This can be worn in all but the hottest weather, and is soft and comfortable, but it is practically only obtainable by the Bashgul Valley Káfirs, and only by a small proportion of them.

To speak generally, the women are well and sufficiently clothed. The legs are often encased in gaiters, and the feet covered with soft reddish leather boots, according to the time of year, and the nature of their work, but more often than not they go about with bare legs and feet.

Having spoken generally of the clothing of the Káfirs, particulars may now be given. It will be convenient first to describe the dress of those tribes which, from their custom of wearing sombre-hued garments, are included under the name of Siáh-Posh Káfirs. These tribes include all those who inhabit the Bashgul Valley, the Katirs, the Kám, the Mádugál, the Kashtán, and the Gourdesh, as well as those branches of the great Katir tribe who live in the western valleys which run down from the Hindu Kush, and are known respectively as the Kti, the Kulam, and the Rámgul or Gabarik Káfirs. Subsequently the dress of the Wai and of the Presungul Káfirs will be described.

The simplest and commonest form of dress of the Siáh-Posh—of the males, that is to say—is the goatskin. It is worn by boys and by poor men at all times. It is also used by the great majority of all classes of the

BOYS IN GOATSKINS.

people when engaged in raiding or hunting, or when herding or watching their flocks. In the villages, only those in poverty appear in this dress, except on the death of a near relative, when it is assumed as a mourning garb. When employed in this way, it is merely thrown across the shoulders, over whatever other clothes are being worn. The goatskin is a shapeless wrapper, girdled at the waist by a leather strap. It only partially covers the neck and chest, and in men reaches about half-way down the thigh. In extreme cold a cape of the same material is added, and rough sleeves also, which are sewn into the body portion by huge stitches an inch or an inch and a half long, made by boring holes and then passing a stout thread through them. Imperfect as must be the protection which this primitive garment affords against rigorous cold, I have frequently seen Káfirs on the war-path or during hunting expeditions trudge through the snow with no other clothing except perhaps goat's-hair gaiters and boots. Owing to its scanty dimensions, and also on account of the defective method employed in curing hides, which leaves them stiff and unmanageable, it is difficult for a man to arrange his goatskin decently when he sits down for formal conversation, while in climbing trees he has necessarily to abandon such attempts altogether. However, in villages it is comparatively rare to see men, even slaves, wearing this garment, except with cotton trousers as well.

Although there is a thick blanket-like cloth made in Káfiristán, yet fragments of goatskin are almost invariably employed for all the various purposes for which pieces of cloth are usually required; such, for instance, as to make small bags, to bind up wounds or sore places, or to protect broken limbs from injury by the sustaining splints. Infants are also carried about wrapped up in portions of goatskin. The fashion is to wear the hairy side of the goatskin outside; indeed, in rain or snow it would be the only way to prevent the leather from spoiling ; but in severe, dry cold the hairy side is sometimes worn inside.

Another strictly national garment of the Siáh-Posh Káfirs is called the "budzun" in the Kám tribe. It is worn by all females, and by many men as well. Its colour is a very dark brown ; its shape is peculiar. On a woman it reaches from the neck to the knees and covers the shoulders, but leaves the neck and a wedge-shaped portion of the upper part of the back uncovered. This particular form of the back part of the garment permits the head of a baby, carried at the back inside the dress in the usual Káfir way, to protrude into the daylight ; yet there is no difference between the budzun as worn by the men, who never carry children in this way, and that worn by the women. The budzun opens all down the front. The men rarely confine it at the waist, but generally wear it thrown loosely over the shoulders. The women, on the other hand, always keep it closely and decently adjusted to the body ; they usually fasten it about the level of the breast by a large brass pin, or with a wooden substitute that looks like a small packing needle, and at the waist, by a long, dark red, flat girdle about an inch and a quarter broad, ending in black or red tassels. The bottom of the dress has a regularly wavy outline, and is edged with red. The most striking peculiarity of the shape of the budzun is the way in which the absence of sleeves is compensated for by the large flaps which overhang the armholes. The Siáh-Posh Káfirs of the western valleys have proper sleeves to the budzun, which in all other respects resembles the Bashgul garment, except that it is slightly lighter in colour, while the edging is different in tint, and is narrower. The women bunch up their budzuns through the girdle, and in the respectacles thus formed, carry various articles, such as walnuts, food, and similar small articles.

A Bashgul woman's mourning garment is simply a tattered budzun, worn cloak-fashion over her every-day dress, and a special cotton head-dress, which will be referred to when we deal with funeral customs.

If we put aside those articles of attire which are used merely for ornament, there is no other clothing, that I am acquainted with, which is made in Káfiristán from materials manufactured in the country itself, except the caps of the women, their leggings, the soft red leather boots worn by both sexes, and the goat's-hair gaiters and foot-coverings worn by the men when travelling through the snow.

All the sewing seems to be done by the men, who may often be noticed leisurely at work on the small cotton caps worn by the women. Old men often used to come to sit with me, and frequently brought their "work" with them. Distinguished warriors who are also dandies are permitted to have their shirts rather prettily embroidered in colours, both back and front. One of these young braves once told me, with a chuckle, that the personal badge he himself wore had been worked by a "yar" (i.e., friend), mentioning another man's wife, but I never saw a woman using a needle.

The women's cotton clothes consist of a cap and of an under garment. The latter, however, is only worn by the females of comparatively wealthy families. The cap is a square piece of cotton cloth, folded in and sewn at the corners, so as to form a square head-dress about an inch and a half high. It is worn at the back of the head. Below the Katir part of the Bashgul Valley the cap is worn on all occasions except at particular festivals and religious ceremonies, when the peculiar horned head-dress is used. Among the Katir tribes the custom is different. The horned cap is worn in the fields, and for all outdoor occupations, while the cotton head-gear is reserved for the house after the day's work is done. The assumption of a head-dress marks the age of puberty; before that event occurs the girls simply bind the head at the level of the brows with a double string, occasionally orna-mented behind with flat button-like silver beads.

The cotton under-garment or shift is of the same length as the budzun, or a little longer; it often shows an inch or so below the woollen tunic. It is provided with sleeves, and is often rather prettily embroidered at the edges with blue. Poor women can never afford this luxury, so that in the fields under a blazing sun they must always work in their heavy hot clothing, while their more fortunate sisters can slip off the budzun down to the waist, and still be sufficiently protected by the cotton under-garment. Káfir women, though anything but moral in their conversation and behaviour, are never indecent in their clothing.

The horned head-dress is a very peculiar article of attire. It consists of a pad six inches broad from front to back, made of hair covered with black net. This pad rests on the top of the head. From each side in front project upwards and outwards two horns about seven inches long. From the base of these front horns two others run backwards and downwards over the pad, parallel to each other, and two and a half inches apart, tapering slightly to a blunt point. All the horns are about an inch in diameter at the base, and are made of the same material as the pad. At the front of the pad, resting on the brow of the woman, is an ornamented square iron bar five inches in length and about a third of an inch in thickness, and immediately below this is a spiral iron ornament, three inches and a half from side to side and one inch in diameter. Some of the coils are round, others are flat. The latter have rough designs punched on their outer surface. Running backwards on the top of the pad there is another iron ornament, lighter and smaller than that for the brow. It is about two inches long and half an inch in diameter. To the end of this are attached four or five common brass thimbles and perhaps a coloured bead or two, and then a couple of brass spirals which look like springs, three or four inches long, finished off at the lower end by two or three more brass thimbles with round brass bells fastened inside them. At the base of the front horns two or three cowrie-shells are often sewn on as an additional ornament. I have seen on the brass thimbles short English inscriptions, such as "For a good girl." These were the only printed or written words I ever found in Káfiristán. The western Siáh-Posh women wear an identical head-dress, except that it is narrower and the front horns are much shorter, not more than half the length of those worn by the women of the Bashgul Valley. These short horns sometimes peep out from a covering of cotton cloth enveloping the whole head-dress. The back horns are also comparatively small. One woman at Lutdeh ornamented her cap with a string of cowrie-shells twisted round the base of the front horns.   In the Katir district of the Bashgul Valley the peculiar appearance of these horned head-dresses is often enhanced by the custom many women adopt of slipping cotton-bags over the horns to keep them from dust and damp.   The material for the horned caps is made by female slaves on very light looms constructed of a kind of cane.   The entire apparatus is easily held between the knees, and the weaving is done by the fingers exclusively.   A slave informed me that the net-like cloth thus manufactured is also useful for protecting the eyes from snow-blindness.

The gaiters worn by the women are made of precisely the same material as the budzun.   They extend from just below the knee to the ankle.   They have a reddish stripe along the vertical edges, to which are fastened strings for keeping them in position.   There seems to be no rule about wearing these rough, coarse, woollen gaiters.   In hot weather they are rarely seen, while even when it is cold many young women seem to prefer marching and working without them.

The boots made for the Káfirs by the slaves are of soft reddish leather, reaching to the ankles, and are fastened by leather thongs.   They are highly esteemed by the surrounding Musalmán tribes, and are often given by a Káfir to his Musalmán friend or "brother." They are by no means uncomfortable to wear for short journeys, but for long distances they are insufficient protection to unhardened Western feet.   The Káfir methods of curing leather are defective, and, as a result, their boots cannot be worn when it is raining, and have to be taken off and carried whenever the ground is wet from overflow from irrigation channels, or for any other reason.

For the snow the Káfirs cover the legs and feet with a thick material woven from goat's-hair, which has the especial advantage of being warm, while at the same time it is not spoilt by damp.

A Káfir youth starting on an expedition to cross a snow pass or kill markhor would generally be attired as follows :—The head would be covered with any cloth the sportsman possessed, in addition, perhaps, to the very popular soft brown roll-up Chitráli cap. The body would be clothed in a goatskin coat, usually open at the neck and leaving the arms bare, but possibly fitted also with a cape and sleeves. A leather belt would not only keep the body garment in position, but would also support, on the right side, the inevitable dagger, and on the left a set of bandoliers. The legs would in all probability be protected by the goat's - hair leggings already mentioned, and the feet by coverings of a similar material. In the case of an ordinary poor man, the leg from the middle of the thigh, where the goatskin coat ends, to just below the knee, where the leggings begin, might be altogether bare. The above articles of attire comprehend all the clothing made by the Siáh-Posh themselves. The goatskins are prepared by anybody. The women's horned caps, the woollen cloth for the budzun and leggings, and the goatskin gaiters, as well as foot-coverings of all kinds, are manufactured by the slaves exclusively, while the cotton cloths and cerements are sewn and fashioned by men of all classes.

Of imported articles of dress the Káfirs are very fond, the men of the Bashgul Valley favouring brown Chitráli robes and caps, while the western Siáh-Posh tribe, and indeed all Káfirs, appear to prize chiefly the black

2 E

woollen robes made in Minján, and no doubt in other places as well. A Siáh-Posh Káfir, well dressed, according to his own idea, wears a cotton shirt and trousers, a Chitráli cap on his head, a Chitráli or similar robe flowing from his shoulders, footless Chitráli stockings and soft red leather Káfir boots; in short, with the exception of his boots, the whole of his dress is either imported or made from imported materials.

The budzun, though still worn by a few old Káfirs of conservative instinct, has been almost completely ousted, in the Bashgul Valley at any rate, by the long Chitráli or Minján robes, which are now worn by all those rich enough to wear what they please. The arms are very rarely thrust into the unnecessarily long sleeves of the "shukr." The garment is preferably hung loosely on the shoulders, and a characteristic gesture is the one-handed hitch up of the robe by the collar part (the other hand being usually occupied with the walking-club) as a young or youngish Káfir springs out through the doorway of a house or darts away at the close of an interview. The long arms of the trailing garment are often tied up at the wrists, and then used as convenient bags for the reception of small quantities of fruit, grain, flour, and so forth.

The Káfirs like a certain coarse cotton cloth made and sold to them by their Musalmán neighbours, and infinitely prefer this rough variety to much better specimens, the product of Indian looms. They maintained that the cotton they procured was both stronger and warmer than mine. The trousers they fashion are short and very wide, while the shirts are worn in the usual Oriental way, outside, not tucked into the trousers. If

a man have only enough cotton cloth to make one garment he uses it for trousers, as then he can wear his
goatskin coat open in the hot weather.

It is always a matter of considerable difficulty for Káfirs
to get sufficient clothing. Hardly any man has more
than one suit of cotton clothes; so, on the rare occasions on which it is being washed, such, for instance, as
his undertaking a long but peaceable journey, the man
has in the meantime to keep very much out of the way,
or must appear in public with a Chitráli robe bound
tightly round him. On meeting a man thus clad, it
would be a relevant and proper thing at once to ask him
where he was going, and how many days he expected to
remain away. The women generally have but one budzun
after they have arrived at full growth, and their clothing
is sometimes desperately tattered and torn, as well as
dirty. Many of them, indeed, look as if they were in
mourning for deceased relatives when they are merely in
their usual everyday attire. But if the inhabitants of the
Bashgul Valley are hard put to it for clothing, the Siáh-
Posh of the western valleys are frequently in still more
desperate straits, according to all accounts. It is said
that one of the commonest reasons for their selling their
young female relatives is to procure clothes. Some of
them are compelled to substitute for a body-garment a
strip of turban or other cloth with a slit in the middle
through which the head is thrust, the sides of the body
as low as the waist remaining uncovered. For head-
covering they frequently have a wisp of cloth bound round
the brow, and, Chitráli caps being unattainable, they have
either to go bareheaded, or else to bind anything on their
heads which is at hand, as the poorer Bashgul Káfirs are

also compelled to do ; but with this trifling exception, and in the slight difference in the edging of the budzun, and the presence or absence of sleeves to that garment, there appears to be but small difference in the dress of the different tribes which collectively constitute the Siáh-Posh Káfirs.

Oddly enough, the slaves are by no means the worst dressed among Siáh-Posh communities. This may be because they are the manufacturers of so much of the clothing worn. A slave cannot be detected by any peculiarity of his attire. His budzun is precisely the same as everybody else's, nor has it any distinctive marks or badges of any kind. Nevertheless, he is usually readily recognisable after a little practice, on account of the more or less degraded type of his features. There is one point, however, about the slaves. They never in my recollection are seen wearing a Chitráli or Minjáni robe or a Chitráli cap, or indeed any regular head-covering.

The only blankets made by the Siáh-Posh are of goat's-hair. They may be warm, but look rough and most uncomfortable. Indeed, though used as blankets, and spread as such on beds, they look far more like door-mats.

Cold does not seem to affect the Káfirs in any way ; indeed, they are hardly less scantily clad in the winter than in the summer. Except when wearing goat's-hair foot-coverings, which are hardly ever used in the villages. they discard boots altogether in the snow, lest they should be spoilt, and the men go about bare-legged. The women also trudge to the water-mills with a similar absence of all protection to the legs and feet. Children used to come to see me clad merely in short goatskins, open everywhere, except at the waist.

There is one tribe of Siáh-Posh called the Kashtán. They inhabit the village of that name, which is close to Kámdesh. They formerly had another village called Dungul in the Dungul Valley, from which they were ejected by the Pathans. It appears that a long time before this event the Dungul villagers were in great fear of their Pathan neighbours. During the winter months the Káfirs were so entirely cut off from the rest of the tribe at Kashtán that, to avoid wounding delicate susceptibilities, they adopted the Pathan dress more or less completely. This compliment failed in securing the desired result, but some of the refugee Dungul women still wear in Káfiristán the ordinary attire of a Musalmán woman. That they are rather proud of the distinctiveness it gives them is certain, while one or two incidents have come under my notice which incline me to think that the Bashgul Valley Káfirs, at any rate, certainly admire the blue costumes of the Gabar Musalmán women of the Kunar Valley.

With the scanty toilette at his disposal it might seem that a Káfir youth of the "masher" type would find small opportunity of satisfying his ideal ; but human nature seems to be much the same everywhere, and a blue shirt, or some special mode of wearing his apparel, supplies the Káfir dandy with the solace which young men of his age and temperament undoubtedly require. I have watched a youth at the end of a march dress himself in the clothes he had carefully carried over his arm throughout the day. He first went down to the river and washed until he was reasonably clean. Then he arranged his long scalp lock with a piece of wood, in place of a comb. The piece of wood was not run through the hair, but the lad tossed his wild, wet locks back with his left hand and then forward on to the stick in alternate motions. Next, taking a pair of footless Chitráli stockings, he drew them on to his legs with great circumspection, and tucked the extremities of his coarse loose trousers into the tops of them. Lastly, he put on his single upper garment, an ordinary shirt-like thing, and fastened his dagger belt round the waist. But this was by no means so simple an operation as it sounds. The shirt or upper garment had to be pouched up, so that the folds fell in a particular way, and the plaits on the hip required to be drawn down tightly, but with regularity and smoothness. When all was finished he strutted about before me, taking steps about six inches long.

On account of the sad colours they use, and by reason of the excessive dirtiness of their cotton garments, a Siáh-Posh crowd, except when arrayed for a religious dance, presents a sombre and squalid appearance. The women are fantastic without being always picturesque. Separately they are often comical. They sometimes appear as if they were arrayed in an Inverness cape. At other times, from behind, one would imagine they wore a frock-coat and boots, an illusion which their somewhat lengthy stride helps to increase. When, startled from field-work, while wearing the horned cap, they suddenly look up from a bent posture, their resemblance to some kind of black goat is certainly curious. On the other hand, the sight of a tired woman, with a heavy load in the conical basket on her back, and possibly a lusty infant at her breast, crawling wearily home from work, is very depressing. I believe the black garments of the Siáh-Posh are preferred by the people because they hide the dirt, and in wet weather the filthy water-drops from the sooty ceiling, better than lighter-coloured clothing would.

The Presun or Viron people wear a dress entirely different from that of the Siáh-Posh. It is made exclusively of thick grey blanketing, which has a ribbed appearance. The men wear a kind of wrapper coat with sleeves, confined at the waist with a leather strap supporting the dagger, which no Káfir likes to be without. The coat is open in front almost to the middle of the body. It reaches to the knees. Long wide trousers of the same material as the coat cover the legs as far as the ankles. They are folded on themselves, and secured in that position by narrow coloured woollen tape wound round and round the leg, which enables them to be tucked comfortably into the ordinary soft leather boots, worn according to circumstances. No head-covering of any kind is used except by a few on religious ceremonial occasions.

The women wear a kind of skull-cap, small and round, which fits on to the back of the head. Girls not yet arrived at puberty—and it is astonishing how old-looking and big some of these girls are—wear merely four large cowrie shells on a string which passes over the crown of the head and behind the ears. The body-garment is very long and grey. One might almost call it a gown which reaches to the ankles. Into the back of this garment woollen cloth of a dark brown, or even black colour, is often woven. This is done, so they say, to hide the dirt marks caused by sitting on the ground. When it is very cold the women wear a couple or more wrappers. Babies are not tucked into the back of the dress, as is the custom in the Bashgul Valley, but are taken care of by little girls, who carry them on their backs slung in a small blanket.

There appears to be no cotton cloth in the Presun Valley. The clothing of the people is all made by themselves. The thick heavy robes of the women, hanging about the legs, cause them to take short mincing steps, very different from the more or less manly stride of the Siáh-Posh women.

The Presun people use blankets made of the same material as the other clothing. They are some five and a half feet in length, and about four feet wide. They consist of two lateral pieces sewn together with strong rough stitches. They are often elaborately embroidered at the ends in square patterns of blue and red chequers. For their excellent woollen cloth the Presun people are as famous as for their elaborate wood-carving. The heavy loose clothing of the Presun people gives its wearers a certain air of clumsiness, which their stolid-looking faces accentuates.

A detailed description of the Wai people's dress was unluckily lost with a notebook carried away in a torrent. This loss has to be supplied chiefly from memory, but partly also from a few notes found in my diaries. The Wai men affect white cotton clothes, and blue and other colours, whenever they can procure them. There is nothing remarkable about the cut of the upper garment or shirt and the short wide trousers. I well remember three splendid-looking men of this tribe, with high aquiline features, marching up the Kámdesh hill with a slow, decided, almost stamping tread, their shoulders thrown back, their chests expanded, their mouths half opened for easy breathing.

They seemed too proud or indifferent to show the slightest curiosity on meeting me. They wore white cotton shirts and trousers, and had blue shawls carried over the shoulders, the weather being hot. I have also seen Wai men on one or two occasions in goat-skin coats, or wrapped in the blue shawls made from Afghan turbans; but I have no recollection of any distinctive thick garment, nor of any peculiar blanket. The women wear, at times at any rate, shallow turbans of white or drab-coloured cloth, with strings of cowries in front of each ear, and necklaces of red and white beads. From the centre of the front of the turban there projects a small red tuft. Their clothing is of light-coloured material. At a short distance they appear to have a body-garment and a skirt reaching to the knee. Coming closer to them, the observer perceives that they are hard put to it to procure clothes, and that their light-coloured garments are of poor quality. They have a small pad fitted on the lower part of the back, which supports the apex of the conical baskets they use, in which custom they differ entirely from all other Káfir women I have seen.

It will be convenient to describe ornaments and dan-cing-costumes together. The particular dancing-dresses are never used for any except ornamental purposes.

There is one particular crownless hat furnished with a short tail. It is exclusively worn by men who, after much feast-giving, are on the point of assuming the ear-rings, which proclaim the fact that they have become Jast, or headmen. This peculiar hat consists entirely of a brim about two and a half inches broad, which is apparently composed of layers of cotton webbing, some-

thing like the "Nawár" tape used in India for making
beds, except that it is only about half as broad.   Into
the front of this hat, between the layers of the webbing,
a sprig of juniper-cedar is thrust, or more than one in
the case of men who have been through the Jast ceremony more than once.   This particular hat is never
worn at dances.   It is the only unusual and ornamental
article of dress which is not also employed in adding to
the spectacle of a religious ceremonial dance.

Káfirs at their dances, and at no other times, wear
turbans.   These turbans are generally white, and are
tied round the ordinary "kullah" or peaked cap.   Being
usually somewhat skimpy, they require to be adjusted
with considerable nicety.   Those about to become Jast
put aside at dances the crownless hat already described,
and replace it with a large turban furnished with a short
tail behind, and decorated in front with a fringe of cowrie
shells strung alternately with red glass beads.   Into the
front of the turban are fastened sticks tipped with the
crest feathers of the manál pheasant, a very popular ornament.   Some peacocks' feathers we took up from India
were greatly admired when used in this decorative way.

Those who are headmen are entitled to wear, through
the upper edge of the cartilage of the ear, the small silver
earrings, somewhat resembling a baron's coronet, which
almost all Siáh-Posh Káfir women possess; while from
the lobe of the ear depends a narrow twisted silver bar
about two inches long, terminating in a ring two-thirds
of an inch in diameter.   Those completing the observances required for the rank of headman wear such a
complicated collection of brass earrings, in addition to
the above, that it is impossible to describe them.   They

look like gigantic Indian puzzle-rings open. The neck is not uncommonly encircled by a silver, or what looks like a silver, fluted ornament, solid and heavy like those worn by Hindu women. The wrists may be adorned with brass bracelets rudely stamped with short lines and marks.

The body-garment used at dances consists of a long flowing robe with sleeves. It reaches to the heels, and has to be tucked up through the iron-studded leather belt or its substitute to prevent the skirt trailing on the ground. Káfirs love to have their robes inordinately long in the skirt and the sleeves, so that they may in one garment possess as much valuable cloth as possible. The robes are made of Badakhshán silk, sham kinkob or sultánzari from Peshawar, cotton velvet, or coloured cloth, according to the wealth of the owner. He may, in addition, wear a spare piece of silk, or a cloth belt worked with cowrie shells, sashwise over one shoulder and under the opposite arm. The trousers worn are of coarse cotton, and are made wide and short. They are often tucked into the pretty Chitráli stockings. Men about to become Jast wear a special pair of trousers made for the Kám people by the inhabitants of Shál in the Kunar Valley. These trousers are only worn in conjunction with a certain long blue coat reaching to the knees, which hides the nether garments except below the knees, where the latter are prettily embroidered in a black and white chequered pattern. They do not extend as low as the ankles, and have deep lateral slips of four or five inches long at the bottom on both sides.

The dancing-boots worn both by men and women who have gone through the necessary ceremonies for the rank

of Jast are elaborate and peculiar. The part corresponding to the golosh of English boots is ornamented in red
and straw-coloured squares, and the whole boot is decorated with red woollen rosettes; while from the long
soft drab-coloured uppers, which reach nearly half-way
to the knee, depend long fringes of white goat's hair
or markhor's hair dyed red at the tips. This fringe falls
over the ankle part of the boot, and increases its fantastic
appearance. The boots are secured to the legs and ankles
by narrow woven tape.

The above description applies, first, to men of the
Jast class, and second, to those completing the observances by which alone this rank can be attained. At
the spring religious dances it is these classes which
supply the performers almost exclusively, although occasionally young men of good family and renowned in war
are invited to supply vacant places in the throng. Each
dancer is provided with the peculiar-shaped dancing-axe
described elsewhere.

But although a headman may array himself in this
fashion for the great festivities in which he occupies so
prominent and striking a position, there are yet many
gradations of style, according to the wealth of different
individuals, or, in ordinary dances, according to the tribal
status of those taking part in them. Some men only
add a silk or other turban cloth worn scarfwise over one
shoulder and under the opposite arm. Others may wear
as their sole ornament a kind of fillet, consisting of two
rows of flattened half-spherical silver buttons behind and
at the side, while the part for the forehead and brows is
of some black material, or is merely a double string, such
as girls wear. Some appear in footless Chitráli stockings

as their only additional ornament. Nearly all wear soft leather boots, but a certain number dance in bare feet only.

On certain particular occasions the women actually wear the men's ornamental costumes in addition to their own. At the village of Lutdeh, for instance, after the men of the district had started for a raid, and the women had abandoned their field-work and were collected in the village dancing day and night to their gods for the success of the expedition, many of the women were arrayed in men's dancing-robes worn under the budzun, and only partially displayed by the budzun being slipped off one shoulder and down to the waist. Many also brandished daggers or twirled dancing-axes; but this was the only occasion on which I witnessed this curious observance.

For ordinary ceremonial and other dances women appear in various degrees of finery. The horned caps already described are sometimes adorned by having a piece of coloured silk or white cloth bound round the front horns. Large silver blinkers are worn by the lucky few who possess them. They appear to be only permitted to women who bring them as part of their dowry on marriage. All women wear the serpentine earrings. They are heavy, and depend from the lobe of the ear. A string over the top of the head helps to sustain them. These earrings, like the small coroneted variety, are worn at all times; the blinkers, on occasions of great importance only. Women never, except in such instances as those already mentioned, wear any special garment for dancing; but the budzun is sometimes slipped off one shoulder so as to show the white cotton garment beneath; but even that is unusual. As a rule, only ornaments are worn. Of these, the most common are silk or coloured cloth sashes, or else belts studded with cowrie-shells hanging from one shoulder; or perhaps a small turban cloth wound round the waist, on the top of which may very likely be seen a band of cowries prettily worked on cloth, while suspended from the lower edge are a number of metal discs, odd-shaped implements like trepanning-saws, and hollow metal balls, which clang and clash with each shuffle of the dancer. In front a couple of ends of cloth covered with cowrie-shells sometimes hang down from the belt. Girls, if adorned at all, merely wear a few cowries and beads, and the ordinary beaded band round the head.

When arrayed for dancing, the women wear their belts so low that their waists appear of a prodigious size. No doubt the Káfirs consider this in itself a point of beauty in a woman. Women who have gone through the regular feast-giving may wear, on high occasions, the strange hairy dancing-boot, just as the men do; in other cases they jerk and shuffle about in the ordinary boot of the country, or with bare feet merely. Nobody seems to pay the least attention to the dancing women. They are neither admired nor disparaged; they are simply ignored. At religious dances they move outside the circle of posturing, stamping men, and often seem to have a bad time jammed up between dancers and spectators.

In addition to the more characteristic ornaments worn by Káfirs, there are many others in the shape of cheap rings with imitation stones, worth about a penny a dozen, and strings of beads and such like articles, which are brought by pedlars from Peshawar and other places. The Wai women have a peculiar kind of earring, large, flat, and more or less like a kidney in shape.

In the Presungul one day, while nursing a sprained heel tendon, I saw a man clothed in a long red coat, his head covered with an Afghan kullah and turban. In his hand he carried a long spear, while across his back was a double curved bow and a quiver full of arrows. He stamped along vigorously, making the most of certain bells he had about him, which clanged at every step. He made a profound obeisance at an Imrá shrine close at hand, and at once started off again energetically. In my disabled state it was impossible to get near enough to him to examine his ornaments. He was the owner of the house which contained the iron pillar, and was travelling down the valley on duty, inspecting all the herds in the country, to select the two fattest cows for sacrifice at Imrá's shrine. Another fantastically ornamented figure—the equivalent, I was informed, of the man becoming a Jast in the Bash-gul Valley—accompanied me on the last march from Presungul to Kámdesh. We were supposed to be "shadowed" at the time, and probably for that reason there is no account of the man's ornaments in my diaries. I only remember that he wore, among many other articles, the kidney-shaped Wai earrings.

CHAPTER XXIX

The position of women—Marriage—Polygamy—Exogamy of clan—Divorce—
Family life.

KÁFIR women are practically household slaves. They
seem to have no civil rights of any kind. To all intents
and purposes they are bought and sold as household
commodities. While they are young their life is one of
incessant labour and trouble. In some cases the entire
work of agriculture is in their hands, as well as all carrying work, except the very heavy kinds for which they
have no strength; such, for instance, as dragging timbers
from the forest for house-building operations. Probably
for the same reason the men alone do the threshing of
the corn. Women are rarely actively ill-used; they are
merely despised. The only females who receive any
share of respect are the aged, the mothers and the
grandmothers of the tribe. They, especially if they
have been through the Jast ceremonies, do receive a
certain amount of consideration. Young women are of
course sought after by the men, who are ever ready to
indulge in an intrigue, but even with this object they
appeared to be valued merely in proportion to the difficulty involved in making conquests of them. A Káfir with
three or four young wives is still always on the look-out
for love-charms or philtres. He will ingenuously explain
that he does not wish his own wives to get more fond
of him, but longs to attract and fascinate other women.

THRESHING.

To face page 530.

Young women are very immoral, not because their natural average disposition is either better or worse than that of women of other tribes and races, but because public opinion is all in favour of what may be called "gallantry." When a woman is discovered in an intrigue, a great outcry is made, and the neighbours rush to the scene with much laughter. A goat is sent for on the spot for a peace-making feast between the gallant and the husband. Of course the neighbours also partake of the feast; the husband and wife both look very happy, and so does every one else, except the lover, who has to pay for the goat, and who knows that he or his family must also pay the full penalty sooner or later. There is no getting out of that, for his clan will not help him, unless the husband demands a higher penalty than that sanctioned by custom—namely, the payment of six cows. There are several households in Kámdesh whose sole property in cows consists of the number thus paid. Among themselves the women are wonderfully helpful and kind when there are no disputes going on about the irrigation of the fields or other business matters. They are very industrious and work incessantly. They start off at daybreak, and drag their wearied limbs home from the fields just before it gets dark. They are fond of their husbands, and are devotedly attached to their children, especially to the boys. In other respects they are like women generally; some are good and some are bad.

Marriages are very simple affairs : they are actually the purchase of women by men. When a man wants to marry a particular girl, he sends a friend to her father to ask his consent and arrange about the price. On the latter point there is often much haggling. When the amount to be paid has been settled, the suitor visits the girl's house ; a goat is killed, then there is some feasting, and the marriage is completed. Many a young girl is married before she has arrived at the age of puberty ; indeed they generally are. Infants in arms are sometimes married, or at least affianced, to grown men. It is comparatively rare to find a girl of twelve who is unmarried. A young woman who remains unmarried must be a hopelessly bad character. If an unmarried girl were found to be misconducting herself, she would probably be only scolded by her parents, and the matter would be hushed up. Full-grown young women, and even middle-aged women, are sometimes married to boys, for the former are field-slaves quite as much as wives, so that an orphan lad who is the owner of fields must marry in order to get his land cultivated. As the Káfirs are polygamists, there is no hardship involved in this custom—to the boy.

All well-to-do Káfirs have more than one wife, but rarely more than four or five. It is considered a reproach to have only one wife, a sign of poverty and insignificance. There was on one occasion a heated discussion at Kámdesh concerning the best plans to be adopted to prepare for an expected attack. A man sitting on the outskirts of the assembly controverted something the priest said. Later on the priest turned round fiercely and demanded to be told how a man with " only one wife " presumed to offer an opinion at all. The spectators laughed at the interrupter's presumption, and partly hustled, partly led him away, for he had to pretend a desire to assault the priest in reply to the scorn poured out on him. The man's conduct was excused to me on the ground that he must be mad. As a matter of fact, he was right about the expected attack, and the priest was wrong. The price paid for a wife depends entirely upon the status of the suitor. If a poor man, he would have to pay eight cows; if fairly well-to-do, twelve. If the girl's father were very wealthy, he would probably refuse to entertain a poor man's proposals at all. If both families were wealthy and important, the suitor would have to pay a very large price, but not nearly so much as he would ever afterwards declare he had given, for he would almost certainly get with his wife a female slave, certain silver ornaments, or sundry measures of corn. In such an instance as this, the Káfir love of bragging would have to be allowed for. Both families would try to exaggerate their own importance by the fables they told about the marriage expenditure. Although a man may marry a woman with the full consent of all concerned, and although she may bear him children, neither she nor her children would be allowed to leave her father's house until the last penny of her price had been paid. It is not quite certain, however, if sons would not belong to the father. Daughters certainly would not. It is paying the full price which gives the man the right to take his wife to his home for her to work in his fields.

As mentioned before, a man may not marry in his own clan, nor in his mother's, nor in his father's mother's, but he may marry all sorts of female connections by marriage. A brother takes over his dead brother's wives to keep himself, or to dispose of as he thinks fit. A woman in Káfiristán is really a chattel. She cannot inherit; she has no property even in herself.

Divorce is easy. A man sells his wife or sends her away. An old Káfir, after telling me he had had altogether twelve wives, added that he had only two remaining. He explained that some had died, while he had tired of the others and had sold them. If a woman behaves very badly, and her husband, although he dislikes her, cannot dispose of her, he may send her back to her parents. I remember an instance of this kind. The woman was the prettiest I ever saw in Káfiristán, and would have been considered a beauty anywhere, but she was so bad and troublesome that no one would take her. She was sent back to her father's house and worked for him. If any one were found intriguing with her, he would have to pay the usual fine to the husband. If a girl were born to her, the woman would keep her; if a son, the husband would claim him. When a woman runs away with another man, the husband tries hard to get an enhanced price for his fugitive wife. His power to do this, and the power of the seducer to resist any unusual demand, depend very greatly upon the respective importance of the two families, i.e., the number of men each can produce as family connections to argue the question. If both men were of the same rank, the price the husband originally gave for the woman would probably suffice ; but endless squabbles, followed by peacemakings, would have first to be gone through. Although divorce is theoretically so simple, and usually is so in practice, yet with well-born wives the woman's family and public opinion have sometimes to be considered. If the woman had misbehaved badly in the Káfir sense, there would be no difficulty in the matter, but if the husband simply tired of her and wanted to get rid of her out of the village, there might be obstacles raised by her family against his doing so. But this reservation would apply only to a very few families in the Kám tribe, for instance. The power a Káfir has over his wife to beat or otherwise ill-use her is also limited by public opinion. It is a sacred duty for all Káfirs to separate quarrelling persons, so that if a husband and his wife were quarrelling, the neighbours would step in and insist on being peacemakers. Husbands who, on returning from a journey, receive hints, but not proofs, that their wives have been behaving badly and unprofitably, do maltreat them, but the punishment has to be inflicted secretly, late at night, and as a rule is not very severe. Káfirs rarely divorce their wives unless the women run away from them. Young boys who find themselves married to old women, when they grow up commonly acquiesce in the arrangement, and procure younger wives as soon as possible.

The family life of Káfirs is kindly on the whole. A well-to-do man with several wives may have two or three different homes. In Kámdesh, where there are plenty of spare houses, this is certainly the case. The women seem to get on very well together. It is not invariably the youngest and prettiest wife who has the most influence, except with old men. Middle-aged men sometimes, though rarely, are influenced by a woman's force of will rather than by personal attractions, especially if the woman is the mother of many children. Husbands and wives enjoy playing with the baby together, and will glance significantly and delightedly at one another when their offspring makes some admirable childish remark. All very young children are spoiled, both boys and girls, but very soon the girls are neglected and the boys indulged. A Káfir asks nothing better than to carry about or be followed by a tiny son. He allows himself to be bullied and tyrannised over by the mannikin in a most amusing way. If he have not a son to play with, he will sometimes take care of a little girl with a natural fondness, but without any pride. A small child may, as a rule, have anything it cries for, from an enormous meat-bone bigger than its arm to a bundle of lighted faggots from the fire. Indeed, everybody is kind to children. A little slave-girl on her way to be sold is treated with as much apparent affection and pride in her baby tricks as if she were her conductor's own daughter. As soon as girls grow to the age of eight, they begin to experience the evil destiny assigned to their sex. The women of the house are always very respectful to their lord and master, and hover about serving him and his, even when they appear scarcely able to stand. They fare very badly and only get coarse food themselves, except when feasts are going on, when at the end they eat up the scraps. There is, however, every variety of attitude in the way different men treat their wives, except that none are treated too well. Boys generally tyrannise over their mothers, mothers are often stern and harsh with their daughters, while the husband and father is a very great man indeed, and much puffed up with his own importance in his own house. A Káfir woman and her dirty little baby, when looked at aright, are just as charming to watch as similar human pictures anywhere else. Men often fear their mothers-in-law as well as their fathers-in-law in a very amusing way. Sons are, as a rule, kind to their aged mothers. One poor old woman had a bad fall, breaking her arm and lacerating the deep-seated blood-vessels. The bleeding was stopped for a time, but without permanent success. The woman's son, a well-known warrior, was greatly concerned about his mother for three days, during which period he was very miserable. On the fourth day, however, he came to me to say that he had work to do, and so doubtless had I also ; that if it seemed advisable to cut off the old woman's arm, he wás quite willing that it should be done, but that it was no good trifling any longer. He then went away and began to prepare the funeral feasts, which were really wanted a few days later. Connections by marriage are looked upon as relatives and kindly treated. Old people of both sexes are devoted to their grandchildren, especially the old men. The old women are often so physically exhausted after their hard life that they appear to be emotionally dead a long time before they actually expire. Káfirs have a natural turn for politeness and ceremoniousness, odd as it may sound to say so ; and this, in spite of the furious quarrelling which occasionally arises, makes their domestic affairs run smoothly on the whole. Young boys soon learn to be wonderfully independent, and are placed in charge of their father's flocks at an absurdly early age, while those belonging to important families quickly acquire habits of command and a sober style in business matters. The worst feature in the domestic life of the Káfirs is the idea they seem to have that anything is good enough to feed a child upon. The little children are, on the whole, even worse fed than the poor women. A goat's hoof, the dirty rind of cheese, or any other garbage, is thought good enough for children.

CHAPTER XXX

THE greater part of the external trade of Káfiristán is
carried on through the Musalmán villages on its frontiers.
Some of these villages are inhabited by Káfirs who have
changed their religion, or whose ancestors did so; while
others are inhabited by non-fanatic Musalmáns, such as
the so-called Gabar people of the Kunar Valley or the
Moghli Shiahs of Minján. There is a certain amount of
trade also done in the Chitrál bazaar. Pedlars, bringing
small wares and ornaments from Peshawar or Badakhshán,
also enter Káfiristán to ply their vocation. The Minjánis
travel into all Katir districts—the Rámgul, the Kulam,
the Kti, and the Bashgul—and also trade in the Presungul. They never visit the Kám or the other Siáh-.
Posh tribes. The western Katir sell young female
children to the Minjánis, but of late years this traffic
has decreased considerably, although the Kti people in
particular are always on the look-out to steal little girls
and sell them in Minján. The Minjánis bring in black
woollen robes (shukrs), coarse cotton cloth, wooden
combs, cheap Badakhshán silk over-garments, small trinkets, and salt, which they exchange for wool and hides,
honey, and ghee. They carry back enormous loads of

hides and wool, and regard the Minján Pass as merely an incident of the journey. In the evening they sit quietly by themselves in the Káfir villages, waiting for some one to give them food, for which, of course, no payment is ever made. With Presungul the principal trade is salt; with the other western Káfirs, salt and clothing. The salt is sold at about the equivalent of eight seers for one rupee. The Presuns buy it by the slab, the standard unit being an irregular-shaped fragment of rock salt, some three and a half inches thick and a span and a hand's-breadth in its greatest length.

Besides salt, cheap stuffs for dancing-dresses, cotton cloths, needles, thread, beads, brass thimbles, pewter rings, and other personal ornaments, iron, lead, and other metals, gunpowder, and matchlocks have also to be imported into Káfiristán, since none are produced in the country itself.

In the Gabar villages of the Kunar Valley salt is sold at eight or ten seers to the Kabuli rupee, if coins are used. One seer of ghee will purchase four seers of salt. A roll of coarse cotton cloth made locally, twelve inches broad by twenty-four yards in length, is worth one rupee. Of better qualities of cotton, which are brought from Peshawar, the price is four or five yards, according to quality, for one sheep. If the Káfirs have a few rupees, as a rule they do not care to trade with them, as they believe they get better bargains by bartering goats, sheep, and ghee.

The Káfir exports consist chiefly of ghee, hides, wool, goats, sheep, honey, and walnuts, in the order named. The soft leather boots made at Kámdesh are also highly appreciated by the Musalmáns on the borders. In ex-

change for such commodities they appear to have little
difficulty in getting iron, gunpowder, and matchlocks; it
is simply a question of price. The lower Bashgul Káfirs
get their iron from the valley of Damir chiefly. Chitrál
is too long a journey for most Káfirs, because nearly all
porterage is done by women; but the Katirs go there a
good deal, for salt particularly. In the Kunar Valley, in
peace time and in the winter, a large number of Káfir
women are to be seen. They carry ghee, walnuts, and
other articles. The pedlars are few in number. They
bring all manner of trashy goods into the country—sham
jewellery, imitation kinkob, common kullahs, cotton
velvet, cheap silks, glass beads, brass thimbles, sometimes with English inscriptions on them, and all manner
of worthless-looking small articles for personal adornment. They get enormous prices for such small wares,
if the intrinsic value of the articles be alone considered;
but if the cost and labour of a long journey, and the
constant danger the men run of being robbed be also
taken into account, the actual profits gained must be
very small. If they were not hospitably entertained
wherever they go, such trading would be impossible.
Indeed, prepared food or fruit is never bought or sold
in Káfiristán. Strangers or natives can always get
enough to eat in ordinary times. In this respect the
difference between Chitrál and Káfiristán is very great.

Among the Káfirs themselves all business is done by
barter. A cow is a standard of value, being reckoned
at twenty Kabuli rupees; a goat is three rupees, and
a sheep two. It does not necessarily follow that these
animals can be obtained at the prices mentioned. If
one asks the price of a matchlock, he will possibly be

told it is worth one or two cows, as the case may be—
that is, twenty or forty rupees. A drum might be valued
at a goat, and so on. Grain and flour are measured
in shallow wicker baskets, of which there are three
particular sizes. The exact amount each basket was
supposed to hold and its price was one of those
secrets the Káfirs never divulged to me. Everything
depended upon the amount of heaping up which was
allowed. The same may be said of a goatskin sack
of grain, flour, honey, or ghee. All such measures
must be estimated by the eye and then bargained for.
No one will believe that there can be any curiosity
about measures of quantity, except when the idea of
purchase is also in the inquirer's mind. Rough scales
and weights are in common use. There is probably
a set in almost every household in the Bashgul Valley.
Smaller and somewhat more accurate scales are employed
for precious articles, such as silver. I have a small
weight in my possession which is a tiny brass model
of a kid, but the usual weights are fragments of stone.

Káfirs are clever at all trade tricks. They sold me
several ornaments as silver which are really of base
metal. They took silver from me to fashion into earrings, and brought me articles made of a kind of pewter.
The Jast bari who did this kept all his processes a
profound secret. All I ever learned about the silver-
workers and brass-workers was that they are decidedly
clever, and immovably reticent about their occupations.

With regard to the other trades, the slave women
weave the woollen cloth on small upright looms, identical in principle with those seen in India.

Nor could I perceive any difference in the manner

of working iron. There was a regular forge, an anvil

SLAVE WEAVING.

fixed upon a huge block of wood, an adjacent trough
full of water, and a blast-furnace. The bellows were

a pair of goatskins, emptied and inflated alternately. The smith at work had hammers of different sizes for the various manipulations required. In short, everything was such as would be seen in an Indian smithy.

The Káfirs are indeed well skilled in many of the ordinary trades. The Presuns are far behind the Bashgul people in this respect, but they also are far removed from savage simplicity. The bootmakers are very skilful. They make good strong soft leather foot-coverings, very durable if they do not get wet. Leather curing is not properly understood, and all leather articles soon get hard, when they crack and spoil. Much of a Káfir's spare time, and he has a great deal of it, is passed with a goatskin, which he rubs and twists between his hands, or gets some one to help him pull at and stretch. This is amateur skin-curing, but everything connected with the curing of cowhides is done by the slaves, the skilled artisans. Ropes are twisted from goats'-hair, and are fairly strong, though rough-looking and cumbersome.

Crocks and other potter's vessels are well made. They are of the usual Oriental pattern.

Wood-carving cannot be called an art; it is merely a trade. There are a limited number of patterns, and nothing whatever is left to the worker's imagination; so also with the wood sculpture and effigy-making. Everything is stereotyped and conventional. All this work is done by the carpenter slaves, the men who also make coffins and shape the timber for house-holding.

There is no special trade of building. Every one can build a house, although the carpenters must make the door frames and windows, and hew into proper form the roof-boards and pillars. Farm and dairy work is done by the people, who are all equally expert. The implements are made by the carpenter and blacksmith slaves.

There is very little differentiation of trades. The carpenter does wood-work of every description. The blacksmith can often act as silversmith; at any rate the silversmith can always do the work of the blacksmith. The leather-worker makes belts, pouches, boots, and certain parts of musical instruments. The versatility of the craftsmen prevents anything like supreme excellence being maintained in any one branch. The nearest approach to new ideas in the manufacture of novel forms of utensils which my visit suggested to the Káfirs was in utilising my empty jam tins. These were in one or two instances fitted with small iron rings at one point of their circumference and carried about as drinking cups, being fastened to the owner's girdle by a thong of leather. The best carpenters and wood-carvers in Káfiristán are to be found in the Presun Valley; the best iron-workers in the Wai country, while the best bootmakers and leather-workers are in the Bashgul Valley.

The chief crop produced in Káfiristán is a kind of millet, called in the Punjáb "tchina." Others are wheat, barley, and Indian corn. Rice is not cultivated. A considerable quantity of wheat is grown, but it is somewhat of a luxury, and is reserved for guests and feasts. Tchina (millet) is the staple food of the people. Indian corn is produced in considerable quantities; barley less than any of the other food grains. Field operations begin at different dates in different localities, in accord-

PLOUGHING.

To face page 549.

ance with their altitude and aspect. The amount and
duration of the snowfall naturally determine the dates
of the spring sowings also. Kámdesh village is between
6000 and 7000 feet above the sea-level. On April 4,
1891, ploughing began in that village, while on October
2, 1890, I had watched the Indian corn crop being har-
vested. In the same place, on September 7, 1891, the
wheat and tchina crop were cut. The wheat was being
dried on the house-tops preparatory to being winnowed;
the tchina was being threshed. At the beginning of
April 1891 there was still a good deal of snow all over
the cultivated fields. It melted wonderfully quickly, and
little torrents, streams, and runnels were draining away
from the arable land. At the Sheikh hamlet of Agatsi,
on the opposite side of the river, some 1800 feet lower
than Kámdesh, the fields were already green with the
young wheat, which had been sown before the snowfall.
At the end of September 1890 we had seen people
ploughing in the Pittigul Valley.

When the ploughing began the land was very soft
from the lately melted snow. The ploughs used are
so light that they can be easily carried over a woman's
shoulder. They are furnished with an iron tip, and
have a prominent heel which stands high out of the
shallow furrow. They are of rough and primitive construction. Two women manage a plough, which is drawn
by a small ox. The animal's movements are controlled
by one of the women placed on the off side, who grasps
in her hands a long handle, fixed at the other extremity
to the yoke, which works on the ox's neck just in
front of the hump. With the leverage afforded by this
long handle the woman seems to have no difficulty in

keeping the animal on a level course, or in turning him
as she pleases. The plough itself is controlled by the
second woman, who works alongside instead of behind
the handle, which is fore and aft, and made to be grasped
with both hands. After traversing the small field a few
times, the women change places, so as to equalise the
labour. Stooping over the handles sideways is more
arduous than directing the course of the ox, although
the woman staggering along and pushing against or
dragging at the animal's neck with the long yoke-pole
appears to be doing more work. Musalmáns beyond
the border always maintain that in Káfiristán a woman
is harnessed to the plough with the ox, but this is not
true. In the Kám tribe a man never touches the plough
handle, but in other places men do work in the fields,
even when they are not slaves. Musalmáns within the
borders of this country, as at the little settlement near
Gourdesh, plough in the usual way, one man doing all
the work and driving a pair of oxen. At this place the
two systems may be seen in operation in adjacent fields.

No time is lost in getting the seed into the ground.
On April 5, in a particular field near my house, the
plough started breaking up the ground. On the following day the seed grain was being sown. After the plough
had done its work, strings of women, in an irregular line,
began breaking up the clods with hooked sticks or
with implements like blunt axes, furnished with wooden
handles and iron heads. Another instrument looked like
a light open crutch without the arm-rest, and was used
upside down. One woman worked the single end, while
a second, with ropes fastened to the forked extremities,
dragged it up after each plunge into the broken-up furrow.

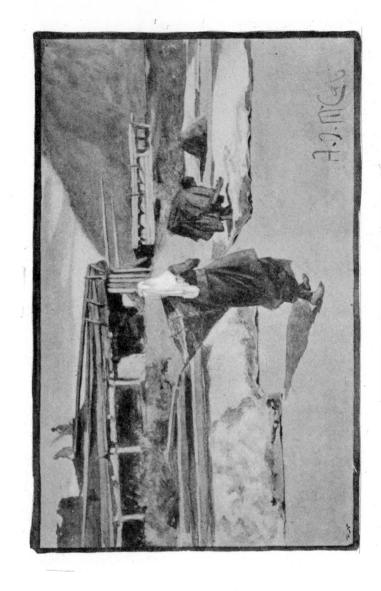

SPREADING GRAIN ON THE HOUSETOPS.

To face page 553.

The sower casts handfuls of grain in what seemed a very niggardly fashion from a small goatskin bag carried in the left hand. On May 5, 1891, all the Kámdesh fields were ploughed, and in several places the crops were showing above the ground. The women were hard at work carrying manure.

On May 14 the women were weeding. They worked eight or ten in a line, except when the space was very limited or the slope very great, when they worked singly or in couples. Each used a stick which had an off-shoot from the end at right angles to the handle. They were kneeling, stooping, or sitting, but a few, especially the old women, were bending down in the characteristic attitude of female field-workers in England.

By May 18 the wheat had grown up several inches. Such of the women as were not weeding were busily occupied in manuring the fields with stable and latrine refuse, which was carried in their conical baskets and then distributed in handfuls over the crops.

In July irrigation of the fields was necessary almost everywhere. The quantity of water allowed to each was regulated by the Urir, but in 1891 there was a good supply of water, and consequently no fighting and quarrelling among the women, as there frequently is in years of drought. The women turn the water into their fields and regulate its flow in a very deft way. Their only implement is a short hooked stick, but they thoroughly understand what they have to do.

On September 7, on my return to Kámdesh, the wheat was already cut and threshed. The grain was spread out on blankets on the house-tops to be picked, cleaned, and winnowed. The tchina was being threshed. The

2 G

flail is a long stick with a strong curve at the handle end. It is used by twirling the wrist backwards in a circular way, while the hand never relaxes its grasp. The implement is continually being shifted from one hand to the other. Little friendly parties are made up for threshing, which is usually the men's sole share in the work of agriculture. The workers circle round a heap of grain in a regular manner, bending and swinging their flails in unison, often forming a very graceful picture. On October 2, 1890, I marvelled at the huge loads of this crop which the merest "slips of girls" contrived to carry up the severest slopes.

Winnowing is done with a small wooden vessel, shaped like a flat-bottomed boat, and furnished with a handle five inches long projecting from the square stern. A woman ladles up the grain and the wind does the rest.

When necessary, at the mouth of ravines and valleys, and in other situations, fields are carefully terraced, especially in the Presungul, where the natural difficulties of the country have made the inhabitants skilful and painstaking agriculturists.

To speak generally, the Káfir cattle are good. They are inferior to good English breeds, but reach the average of those seen in Kashmir. A certain number specially fattened for sacrifice to Gísh in connection with the Jast ceremonies are really handsome animals, as big as English beasts, and much resembling them in shape and colour. Seeing them in India, one would conjecture that they were English, or at least half English. Some varieties are humped.

The beef obtainable in Káfiristán is extremely tough, a quality which is due no doubt to the method of killing cattle, and to the fact that the meat is never hung. Káfirs like it, but then they also eat the flesh of cattle which die from disease.

In the autumn, when feeding is difficult, horse-chestnut branches are utilised as fodder. A certain amount of stall-feeding is practised. At the end of a day's weeding, the long grass stalks are collected into bundles by the women to be carried home, dried in the sun, and stacked for winter use. These grass stacks are very common objects. In the Presungul they are built on the top of the pshals. In Kámdesh they are often built on specially prepared platforms. My kitchen in Kámdesh was made by building up walls under one of these platforms. Until the stack was nearly consumed the kitchen was the only place which could be relied upon to be always dry.

Every man in Kámdesh who possesses cows brings as many of them as possible into the village during the winter, partly on account of the facility for feeding the animals, and partly because the ghee and cheese making may be done there comfortably.

The goats are a fine breed. The males in some instances attain a prodigious size, especially those reserved for sacrifice and fed up with that object.

The sheep are very poor. It is rare indeed to get any of even comparative excellence. They are ill-fed, and consequently are diminutive, thin, and bad eating. Their flesh is not much liked by the people, but a certain number have to be kept for the sake of the wool.

Butter is churned in goatskins. The ghee is made in the usual way by driving off the water of the butter by heat. The Káfirs are famous for their ghee. It is rarely adulterated, and is of excellent quality. In the summer months, while the men are away at the dairy farms, they live almost entirely on butter-milk, bread being difficult to obtain, and animals being comparatively rarely killed for food.

For cheese-making the following is the process. A short length of goat's intestine (challah) is fully inflated, and tied tightly at both ends with goat's-hair. It is hung up over a fire for days, months, or even for a year. When wanted for use, it is untied and well washed. It is then placed in a dried hollowed-out pumpkin filled with water, which is covered with a wooden top and placed by the fire from morning till midday. Equal portions of this, of water and of " aillah " (the residue in cheese-making), are then mixed together and poured into the vessel holding the milk. The whole is stirred and set down by the fire, and in two hours the cheese is ready to be worked.

One day I went to see wine being made at Bináram, a hamlet close to Kámdesh. The arrangements were very simple. A flat-topped boulder conveniently placed by the roadside formed the floor of the wine-press, and one side of a second boulder did duty for one of its walls. The other walls, more or less semicircular in continuous outline, were made by stones placed one on the top of the other and raised to a height of two and a half feet, the interstices being filled up with clay. The greatest length of the vat was about five feet six inches, and its greatest breadth about four feet. The floor sloped naturally, and at the lower end, in front, an aperture had been left, partly closed by a little brushwood, from under which a deeply-grooved piece of wood, with its edges still further deepened by clay from the vat, protruded, and afforded

WINE-MAKING.

To face page 559.

an outlet for the expressed juice. At the time of my arrival a considerable quantity of grapes had already been thrown into the receptacle, and a woman kept emptying into it fresh basketfuls which she brought up the steep hillside from below, where the vines grew. When everything was ready, and the vat was full of grapes, its owner laid humorously violent hands on a big man who was looking on. He was persuaded to tread the grapes. They took him aside and carefully washed his legs and feet, and then put him into the press. He enjoyed himself thoroughly, treading with so much vigour that he had to be frequently checked to prevent the juice from overflowing the receiving vessels. These were at first large wooden cups, which when full had their contents ladled back into the press. This was explained to me as a "necessary custom always observed." Then goatskins were filled with juice through a kind of wooden funnel. That was all. The first sweet grape juice in the goatskin is very pleasant. In eight or ten days it becomes sour by fermentation, and is then wine. There is no process of straining, and the fluid is most uninviting in appearance. Probably it is to remove the scum from near their lips that the Káfir always blows into the winebowl before drinking. The wine is usually poor and thin, but even then is usually diluted with water. Wine which had been kept for two or three years was, however, clear, and sometimes distinctly strong. Some Europeans think ordinary Káfir wine pleasant to drink. I have never seen a Káfir drunk.

When the juice is nearly all extracted from the vat, a semi-solid residue remains. This is taken out, a small quantity at a time, and placed on a flat stone, some two feet or so in diameter, with a raised edge of clay two inches high all round. Here, protected by circles made of twigs, two large stones are put on the top and pressed down by a long pliable pole used as a lever, one end being firmly buried in the ground, while a number of men hang with all their weight on to the free end. The amount of force used can be easily regulated by the number of men employed. This dried residue is made up into cakes for food. It looks and tastes most unpleasant, but it is nevertheless highly appreciated by Káfirs, who believe that it possesses most sustaining qualities.

CHAPTER XXXI

IT is probable that there is no single tribe of Káfirs at the present day which is at peace with all the other tribes. Some of their wars, if wars they can be called, have continued for generations. For instance, that between the Kám and the most western Katirs, the Rámgulis, is said to have lasted over a hundred years. As the two districts are far apart, very little damage is done by one tribe to the other. Years probably pass without a single man being killed on either side, or a single head of cattle being captured or lost. The one dangerous place for both people to meet is in the Presungul, or on the road from Presungul to Minján, because the Presungul people are not strong enough to protect sojourners in their country. In the upper part of the Bashgul Valley, Kám and Rámguli can, and do, meet. Each may want to murder the other, but such an act would be followed in all probability by war with the Bashgul Katirs. The murdered man's tribe would hold the Lutdehchis responsible for their fellow-tribesman, while the Lutdeh men would possibly declare war or exact compensation from the murderer's tribe. In a wild country like Káfiristán such events do happen, though rarely.

For instance, a Wai man murdered a Rámguli at Lutdeh, and then fled to his own country. Shortly afterwards the Bashgul Katirs raided the Wai country, and the murder, although it was not the stated reason for the attack, no doubt influenced them considerably when they had to decide in what direction to raid after Gísh had, through the Pshur, ordered them to get more sacrifices for his shrines. The murder of a Káfir in the territory of a people, or by a member of a tribe, with whom his tribe is at peace, is not necessarily followed by war. As an example, two Káfir youths were killed by a distant tribe, through whose valley they were travelling to try and murder in a third tribe closely connected with the other. The Kám did not want war just then, so the affair was compounded in the following way. The fathers of the two young men who had been killed went to the valley where the event had occurred, and after much negotiation obtained two persons, a man and a woman, whom they conducted a short distance on the road home to Kámdesh, and then slew. Thus their honour was satisfied and the two tribes remained at peace.

A man of any position who has been killed must be atoned for by blood. In 1891 some Kám Káfirs were hunting some Jandúl Musalmáns down the Kunar Valley. The Jandúlis ran for shelter to the Mehtar's new fort at Nursut, which was garrisoned by Chitráli soldiers. The fort door was banged to just as the last Musalmán, closely followed by the leading Káfir, passed through.

It was a near shave, and the Chitráli at the gate had to fire, killing the Káfir, to keep him from entering.

Time passed on until, in 1893, I found myself at Chitrál on a special mission from the Government of India to the Mehtar Nizám-ul-Mulk. One day a messenger came to me from a well-known Káfir named Shyok, who sent word that, as an old friend of mine, he was anxious not to cause trouble of any kind in the then critical state of affairs at Chitrál, but that the man who had been killed at the Nári fort was a member of his (Shyok's) family, and although the slain man was an individual of no tribal importance, yet Shyok must have a Chitráli to kill. In the circumstances, to prevent complications, and particularly out of friendship with me, Shyok was prepared to accept any Chitráli, a slave even, but a Chitráli of some kind or other he must have. As I knew Shyok to be remarkable for cupidity even among Káfirs, it seemed as if there should be little difficulty in settling matters by paying him a ransom for the slain man; but on broaching the subject to my Káfir son Shermalik, who had been sent to see me as Shyok's ambassador, he remarked, " You know Shyok well. There is nobody in Káfiristán so avaricious as he is, yet if you offer him a lakh of rupees he cannot accept it. For his honour's sake he must have a Chitráli to kill in front of the dead man's coffin." All my arguments and persuasions were in vain. Shermalik said that the Mehtar would understand the situation, and would readily supply a victim if advised to do so. How the affair ended I do not know. Probably Shyok or some of his friends caught some unhappy Chitráli and killed him, and the Mehtar winked at the deed, if he heard of it at all.

While on this subject the following incident may be recorded. At the end of 1891 old Dán Malik was killed in the Kunar Valley during a treacherous raid on the Káfir grazing-grounds there by Umrá Khan of Jandúl. Some time afterwards a Pathan was caught in the Kunar Valley by some of Dán Malik's relatives and taken to Kámdesh, where the poor captive was placed on the ground in front of Gísh's shrine. The whole village assembled there, and a regular worship of Gísh was conducted in the orthodox way by the high priest. At its close the prisoner was taken to the Kámdesh cemetery and stabbed to death in front of Dán Malik's coffin.

It is open to doubt if, among themselves, Káfirs have any custom equivalent to a declaration of war. War begins with a raid by one tribe on another. When a people intend to participate in an existing war, or to start one on their own account, they sometimes, at any rate, merely content themselves with killing some members of the tribe they dislike. Probably there has been some anterior straining of the intertribal relations, and such an act of war is held to be quite sufficient without any formal declaration of hostilities. With Musalmán enemies the procedure is different. At one time during my stay in Káfiristán there was a fierce dispute between the Kám and the Mehtar, which culminated in the former threatening to send the latter a bullet or bullets, which was equivalent to a breaking off of all negotiations, and a notification that war had begun. Sometimes it is said arrows are sent by Káfir tribes to intimate to the recipient that hostilities had commenced, but of my own knowledge I can say nothing on that point.

The commonest cause of war among Káfirs themselves is robbery. One tribe knows that another tribe has fine flocks and herds, and decides to make a raid. Sometimes the Pshur starts a raid, as in the case already referred to, by declaring, during temporary inspiration, that the gods order it. Another cause is the general excitement of a tribe seeking to find some outlet for its energy. As an example of this, on one occasion, in 1891, the Wai retaliated on the Bashgul Katirs for raiding, by secretly marching down the Nichingul and exterminating the hamlet of Sunru, the lowest settlement of Katirs in the Bashgul Valley. In their rage at this reprisal the Katirs very nearly attacked the Kám, declaring that the latter were cognisant of the whole affair. They contended that the Kám had permitted the Wai to raid on them through Kám territory, and ignored altogether the fact that the Wai men must have marched through the Mádugál country also ; but then they were friendly with the Mádugális. On another occasion the Kám very nearly attacked the Wai because they believed the latter might possibly have been implicated in the killing of two Kám men.

All Káfir tribes are extremely jealous of one another, no matter how they may have intermarried. Káfir hates Káfir far more intensely than he hates Musalmáns, and this sentiment is always liable at periods of unusual excitement to start internecine strife.

With foreigners the Káfirs are, as often as not, the actual though remote aggressors. Ambitious Musalmán chiefs may raid into Káfiristán, burning with the desire to earn the title of Gházi, and fanatics may be maddened by Mullahs to draw the sword for Islám, proselytise, or

exact tribute from the infidel, or die the pure death of
the "martyr"; but the Káfir is an uncomfortable neighbour at all times.   He is incessantly robbing, blackmailing, or murdering on the frontier unless completely
overawed by the power of some particular chief, as the
Bashgul Katirs were by the Mehtar, Amán-ul-Mulk, of
Chitrál, or the Kám by the Khan of Jandúl.   Many
of the attacks by Musalmáns on Káfiristán have been
in revenge for murdered relations and plundered cara-
vans.

A Musalmán people entering on a Káfir war would be
careful to keep their design as secret as possible.   The
Káfirs, although their suspicions might be aroused, would
receive the first definite intimation that war had begun
by the irruption of the enemy into their territory.   In
1891, at the end of the year, Umrá Khan lulled the Kám
tribe into false security by lying promises and honeyed
words.   Then he suddenly raided the Narsut grazing-
grounds with great success.   That is the origin of the bitter
strife which until last year was raging furiously.   From his
own point of view Umrá Khan acted with statesmanlike
astuteness, and his action would be applauded by general
Musalmán opinion.   A Musalmán is under no obligation
to behave honourably in his dealings with "infidels."

All the neighbouring Musalmán tribes have an intense
hatred of Káfirs, with the exception, perhaps, of the
Kunar Valley Gabar villagers and the Minjánis.   This
does not arise, I am convinced, from religious prejudices
so much as from the injuries they have received from the
Káfirs through long ages.   Similarly, the Káfirs love to
dance to Gísh after killing Musalmáns, but their hatred
of Afghans is far more a race hatred than religious

fanaticism. Even in times far remote it may be doubted if race antagonism was not at least as strong as difference of creed in keeping Afghan and Káfir at bitter feud. Both are brigands by instinct, and both are careless of human life. Perhaps the Káfir is the worst of the two in both respects, but the Afghan makes the account more than even by his added perfidy and cunning.

As war, and not peace, may be said to be the normal condition of Káfiristán, peace arrangements may be considered before methods of warfare are described. Peace generally happens when two tribes feel themselves equally exhausted, or when one tribe has proved itself overwhelmingly superior to the other. Peace might sometimes be defined as a cessation of hostilities for a longer or shorter period, rather than as peace in our sense of the word. Among themselves it is probably arranged in the first place by some neutral tribe friendly with both. The ratification of such preliminaries depends greatly upon the peace-offerings suggested, which the stronger tribe receives, giving nothing in return. Within the present generation the Kám have been at war with the Wai, the Kashtán, the Mádugál, and the Bashgul Katirs, in addition to their other long-standing feuds, which have never yet been settled. At the different peace-makings, the Kám and the Katirs exchanged a cow for a cow, showing that they considered themselves still equal in strength, while the Wai paid the Kám four cattle and the Kashtán paid eighteen cows and eighteen axes, in this way indicating that they were more desirous of peace than the Kám. Of what the Mádugál paid I have no record. The animals in each case were sacrificed at Arom's shrine.

I am not sure how Káfirs come to an end of hostilities with a Musalmán people, but they no doubt send and receive messengers, and the Káfirs probably ratify their promises by sacrificing a goat. When war was imminent between the Kám and the Chitrális in 1891, as soon as wiser counsels prevailed on both sides, several Káfirs went to see the Mehtar, and solemnly promised to abstain from killing Musalmáns in Chitráli territory, and agreed to pay tribute in kind for grazing rights in the Kunar Valley; they confirmed their promises by ceremoniously sacrificing a goat at Chitrál.

It generally takes time for a Káfir, unless utterly crushed, to make up his mind for peace. His furious resentment against his enemy is not quickly cooled down to the overture-making point. After desultory but not bloody warfare on the frontier, and after experiencing inconvenience in not being able to get supplies as usual from over the border, he gradually comes to entertain an idea of the desirability of peace.

After a war there are no blood-feuds. The high priest of the Kám had respect and friendship for Karlah Jannah of Badáwan, notwithstanding the fact that the latter killed the former's brother during the last war between the Kám and the Bashgul Katirs.

In their intertribal fights the Káfirs are always desirous of getting outside help. The Mehtar of Chitrál has on more than one occasion allied himself with the Kám against other Káfir tribes, and among the never-ending family quarrels of the Bashgul Katirs, he succeeded in obtaining for himself a preponderating influence in that part of the valley. The price paid for the Mehtar's help was usually all or most of the prisoners taken, and a certain number of " beautiful" girls in addition. The late Mehtar was generally willing to send a force to co-operate with the Kám in a raid on those terms, and was paid in a similar way for his support of one of the factions of the Bashgul Katirs. The Wai Káfirs invaded the Presungul with the help of an Afghan force, on the terms that their allies might keep all the plunder they could get.

When attacked by foreigners, who are always armed with much better firearms and other weapons than the Káfirs possess, the latter usually adopt purely defensive tactics. They hold positions, form little ambuscades, and so forth, but are always prepared to fall back before the superior strength of the enemy. They seek to cut off stragglers and harass the invaders in every possible way. Then, when the enemy, from accumulated losses, lack of supplies, or hopelessness of further successes, begins to retreat, the light-footed Káfirs attack him on all sides like a swarm of hornets. Dogged resistance is turned into furious bravery. A Káfir never fights so well as when the advantage is on his side. He plays a winning game splendidly. Each man tries to emulate the traditional heroes of his tribe, and will perform the grandest deeds to gain the admiration of his fellows. I was told of the man Shyok that on one occasion he dashed single-handed into a group of the enemy, stabbed right and left, and escaped uninjured. He is a man of enormous strength, and in spite of his weight is as active as a leopard.

The most common plan of carrying on hostilities is for small parties of Káfirs, two or more, to penetrate into the enemy's country and kill sleeping men or women, or

form small ambuscades, and then, if successful, hurry
back at full speed to dance to Gísh. On such expeditions the Káfirs exhibit the most extraordinary courage
and powers of endurance. In the recent Kám-Jandúl
war they killed several people close under Umrá Khan's
fort at Jandúl. Their wonderful walking powers enable
them to travel distances which seem almost incredible.

On a disturbed frontier many little groups of thin,
worn-out-looking men may be met marching rapidly
but wearily homeward. They represent the unsuccessful
warriors. They have to carry their own food, as in the
enemy's country it is nearly impossible to get supplies of
any kind. There is a particular cake which Káfirs carry
on their expeditions. It is made of the refuse from the
wine-press mixed with flour and ghee. They believe
also in the sustaining powers of cream-cheese. They
carry as much as they can, but must often be half-
starved before they get home again. Indeed, they look
so always, and come back very thin.

When a successful little party has come back, the
fact is soon known throughout the village. The warriors,
arrayed in much finery, with dancing-axes in their hands,
are conducted to the dancing-platform, and in company
with the women of their family dance to great Gísh. In
the intervals of the dance the women throw wheat grains
upon the heroes. The dancing is only performed when
small bands return. If a large raiding party or small
army comes back victorious, there is no dancing, nor
is there any if a Káfir has been killed. The dancing
of the returned warriors is strictly a family affair, and
few outside the men's intimate relations take the trouble
to go and see it. In the daytime, when news is brought

RETURN OF A WARRIOR.

To face page 573.

that a victorious party is near at hand, the women run
delightedly to wash their faces, fill small wicker baskets
with wheat, and go out to meet the braves. The men of
the family go also. Proud fathers lead in their sons, who
are either kissed actually, or a yard off, by nearly every
one they meet. The Gísh observances are more fully carried out at Kámdesh than at Lutdeh. There is always
some kind of dancing, but at Lutdeh there is little or no
dressing up of the principal characters.

In fighting among themselves, Káfirs pursue the same
tactics as against foreign enemies. A Káfir will fight just
as resolutely in defence of his property as to save his life.
When every fighting man of the Bashgul Káfirs went to
raid the Amzhi Valley of the Wai, they must have out-
numbered their opponents by five to. one; yet the latter
followed them up, got in front of the returning raiders on
the hillside, and in their frantic attempt to get back their
flocks and herds, engaged in severe hand-to-hand fighting. As a rule, a Káfir always loves to have numerical
superiority on his side. I know an instance where six
men hid in the long grass on the edge of a field where
a Sheikh and his wife were working. Watching their
opportunity, they rushed at the man and seized his
hands in the old "Thug" fashion and then stabbed him
to death, catching and killing the woman subsequently.
On another occasion a small party concealed themselves
for days near an enemy's goat-pens. Every night they
surrounded the place. At length one night a man
emerged to fetch water from the river. As he was stooping down to fill his pitcher he was seized by the arms and
killed. The assailants then sat down to watch again.
The men in the goat-pens, four or five in number, suspi-

2 H

cious of the delay of their companion, then came forth
armed with guns, when the others decamped and raced
back to their village. Káfirs spare neither man, woman,
nor child ; all alike are considered mortal enemies. One
Kám man I know, who used to twist his moustaches as
only famous warriors may do without being jeered at,
based his claim to renown on the fact that he had murdered nine women and one man. With Afghans, the
moment one of their number has been killed by a Káfir,
all turn out, seize their arms, and follow the assassin in
the hope of catching him. Káfirs sometimes take advantage of this and form a big ambush. Two or three of
their number then go out in the hope of killing an
Afghan. If they succeed, they run back through the
ambush, which is then ready for the pursuers. I know
one instance in which the manœuvre was terribly successful. The Afghans on their part are not one whit behind
the Káfirs in ruthlessness.

Káfir weapons are the dagger, bows and arrows, spears,
and matchlocks. The peculiar shape of the Káfir dagger
is too well known to require an elaborate description.
The commoner and cheaper varieties are about a foot
in length ; from the top of the hilt to the point of the
blade is just under thirteen inches. The blade is eight
inches long, and gradually tapers from the hilt, where it
is just over an inch in breadth, to the point. It is double
edged, and a little over a quarter of an inch thick at the
hilt. It is grooved down the middle and both sides,
nearly to the point. The hilt guard is five and a quarter
inches from side to side, and ornamented at each extremity by a circular convex brass button, firmly riveted
to its upper surface. Three and a half inches above the

guard, and parallel with it, is another cross-piece of iron, very strong and carefully ornamented. Between this and the guard, the shaft of the hilt is so fashioned that four fingers may close on it firmly, each in its own groove. The weapon as a whole is much more powerful than it looks. The riveting of the blade to the handle allows a slight movement of the blade, which gives a deceptive appearance of weakness. The sheath is made of iron or brass with an inner backing of wood. The back of the sheath is incompletely closed by metal, and permits the wood lining to be seen. The top of the sheath has an ornamented brass collar, while at the lower end it terminates in a metal knob with a constriction just above, which is often tightly bound round with brass wire. Costly daggers have brass sheaths, which are frequently ornamented with silver studs at the top.

Káfir bows are distinctly feeble-looking, but a skilful man will shoot with fair accuracy up to eighty yards. The arrows are unfeathered. They are twenty-four inches long. The shaft is made of reed, bound in the middle and at both ends with very fine string. The arrow-head is of a peculiar shape. It is three-sided, and has three sharp edges which meet at the point, and are peculiar from the fact that their other extremity is prolonged backwards from a quarter to half an inch beyond the base of the bayonet-shaped arrow-head. This must make the arrow very difficult to extract from a wound. The sharp edges are two and a half inches long.

The spears are fitted with a straight blade pointed at the end, and are often ornamented with a brass stud or two. At the base they are furnished with a stout prong for thrusting into the ground. A peculiarity of some of the spears is, that a single prong is substituted for the straight double-edged blade mentioned above.

The Káfir matchlocks are purchased at the frontier. None are manufactured in the country itself. They make extremely bad shooting, and cannot be trusted to go near a small mark—an envelope, for instance—at a greater distance than twenty or thirty yards. Káfirs brag a good deal about the power of their fire-arms, but I have watched them practising at a mark using a rest, and have seen them shoot markhor many times, and I should much prefer them to shoot at me with a matchlock at forty or fifty yards, than to have a good man aim at me with an arrow at the same distance when I was not looking. For the matchlocks, the Káfirs carry leather pouches for ammunition, flint and steel of an ordinary description, and bandoleers, which at a short distance look like Pan-pipes.

KÁFIR ARCHER.

Shields are all imported, and are more for ornament than for use. There are very few swords, and mutilation of a dead enemy is never practised. What swords there are, have been received by their owners as presents from Musalmán chiefs.

The Kám are very proud of possessing a cannon. It is kept in the ground-floor of a house at the top of the village. It was made by Dir men, who were brought to Kámdesh for the purpose. It is very solid and heavy. The metal on the outer surface is rough and knobby. The length of the barrel is three feet six inches, and the diameter of the muzzle four inches. A leaden ball and a block of wood are said to be fired simultaneously by this weapon. It is carried about from place to place on cross-pieces of wood, and requires for its transport three-score or fivescore men, according to different informants. It has been in action and performed prodigies, according to the Kám, notably on one occasion during a siege of the village of Apsai in the last Katir war. It must be fastened to a tree in order to fire it. It has no stand or carriage of any kind. The Kám are inordinately proud of the possession of this weapon, but I doubt if they would care to use it again, except for the sake of its moral effect.

The dancing and other axes are not intended for fighting purposes, although the small variety might be so employed on an emergency. The walking-club of which Káfirs are so fond, and which they delight to ornament with carving about the handle, is only used in quarrels. I was told that an ordinary head would smash the club unless the latter were shortened in the grasp, and merely the thick lower end used to strike with.

CHAPTER XXXII

THE Káfir year, at least in the Bashgul Valley, is divided into 360 days, and marked by special festivals. These festivals are twelve in number, and start with Giché, the first day of the new year. The following list gives all these particular days, and the dates on which they occurred in 1891. The festivals marked with a dagger (†) are those at which I was present with the Kám tribe :—

1. Giché †	. . . . . .	January 16.
2. Veron	. . . . .	February 3.
3. Taska and the throwing of the Shíl † .		February 18.
4. Marnma	. . . . .	March 8.
5. Duban †	. . . . .	March 19.
6. Azhindra †	. . . .	April 4.
7. Diran †	. . . . .	May 9.
8. Gerdulow .	. . . .	June 5.
9. Patilo †	. . . . .	June 30.
10. Dizanedu †	. . . .	July 9.
11. Munzilo	. . . .	August 17.
12. Nilu †	. . . . .	September 17.

After Nilu there is a long interval—120 days, it is said—until the next Giché or New Year's Day.

For the purposes of the calendar only three seasons are enumerated, namely, Wazdar (Summer), Sharwar

(Autumn), and Zowar (Winter), each of which is computed at 120 days. There is a word in the Kám language, "Wazat," which means spring-time, but it is not referred to in counting up the year.

The holidays of the other tribes in the Bashgul Valley were not coincident with those held at Kámdesh, although, as a rule, there was only a difference of a few days in point of time. I do not know why identical festivals were not held on the same date in all the villages. Presumably it had nothing to do with the influence of varying altitudes in the sowing and reaping of crops, nor with any desire on the part of the different tribes to show their complete independence of their neighbours in every particular; while it may have been the result of an amiable wish to receive or pay visits from or to distant villages on the recurrence of the annual festivals, which would be impossible if the feast-days clashed.

In addition to the holidays enumerated in the above list there is a series of rest-days or Sabbaths, which occur every Thursday during the time field-work is in progress. These rest-days are called Agars. In 1891 the first Agar was on April 3, the last on September 17. They usually began at Kámdesh on a Wednesday night, when a fire was lit at the dancing-place in honour of Imrá, and the people danced and sang to the music of drums and pipes. The duty of lighting the fire for the Agar devolves on the Urir Jast, and was never neglected, even when the village was in mourning for the death of a warrior, or was depressed by reason of epidemic sickness or similar calamities. I failed to discover anything concerning the origin of these Agars. Their observance may have become a national custom, the origin of which is as difficult to determine as the Sabbaths of other ancient peoples. As the Kám people were averse to starting on a journey on the Agar days, and as all the women left their field-work altogether on those occasions, it is possible that the Agar was originally considered an unlucky day. This, however, is mere conjecture ; my imperfect knowledge of the Káfir tongue and the inefficiency of my interpreters may have combined to prevent my arriving at the truth, quite as much as the dislike of the people to being cross-examined and their impatience at being questioned on points they assumed that everybody understood or ought to understand. As far as the women were concerned it was only field-work which was stopped, for they were constantly to be seen carrying stones or earth for building operations, and engaged in other coolie labour.

In the upper part of the Bashgul Valley the Agar usually fell on a Saturday. Although the Kámdesh Agar usually began on a Wednesday evening, this was by no means invariably the case, the alteration of the day being usually dependent on some other festival falling on the Agar day, and so necessitating the change.

Káfir festivals frequently begin in the evening, and thus a so-called one-day festival often lasts for two nights and one day. I was never able to count up the Káfir calendar satisfactorily, even with the help of the most intelligent of my Kámdesh friends, and failed entirely to discover how the days were fitted in so as always to make the Giché, the new year, fall on the same date. The impression left on my mind was that the Kafirs did not trouble themselves about such niceties, yet when away from their villages, the men with me always

NEW YEAR'S DAY CEREMONY.

To face page 583.

knew accurately the number of days intervening before the next festival. The following are the principal
festivals :—

(1.) Giché, New Year's Day. The surrounding Musalmáns call this the Káfir Eed. In 1891 the Giché
ceremonies were shorn of their customary splendour on
account of the severity of the weather and the unusual
snowfall. All men who had had sons born to them
during the year took a goat each, and in the course of
the day sacrificed it at the shrine of the goddess Dizane.
In the evening and throughout the night there were
feastings and rejoicings in most houses at Kámdesh.
At the first glimpse of dawn on the morning of the 17th,
in spite of a heavy snowstorm, men and women issued
from every house carrying torches of pine-wood, and
marched up the hill crying " Súch, súch," and deposited their brands in a heap in front of Dizane's
shrine. The blaze was increased by ghee being thrown
on the fire. The Debilála chanted the praises of the
goddess, the people joining in the refrain at regular intervals. I saw very little of the ceremony, because on
account of the heavy fall of snow no one came to show
me the road. I awoke and hastened up the hill at the
first cry from the shrill female throats, but being almost
immediately caught in a snow-drift, it was necessary for
me to turn all my thoughts and all my energies to getting
out again. In the far distance the huge bonfire could
be faintly seen through the falling snow. The sight was
a pretty one even in my miserable plight, the outline
of the intermittent blaze being broken by the trees which
it fitfully illuminated.

(2.) Veron. This festival is of inferior importance,

and such Káfirs as happened to be absent from their villages made no attempt to hurry back for it, as is their usual custom when a feast-day approaches. On this day the thirteen Urirs entertain the whole of the village, probably in consideration of the fines they have collected in virtue of their office.

(3.) The Taska day is looked forward to with considerable interest by all Káfirs. In 1891 the festivities began in the evening, when a goat was sacrificed at almost every house in Kámdesh. A peculiar feature of this festival is that during its continuance little boys are not only permitted, but are encouraged, to use vile abuse towards grown-up men. During the evening of the 18th of February, the boys from the upper village collected near my house to shout out foul remarks concerning the men of the east village, whence the same kind of language was used in response. This continued all night, and early on the morning of the 19th, the boys, now reinforced by grown-up youths, went round from house to house shouting obscene abuse against the owners. This was supposed to be very amusing, especially when the chief of the headmen was assailed. During the day there were one or two dances in different places, but there had been recently so terrible a mortality amongst the young children from small-pox, that the people were too depressed to indulge in the snowball fights which in happier years mark this anniversary. On the 20th the Taska festivities wound up at the dancing-house with a subdued revel called the Prachi Nát (Prachi dance), said to be indulged in by boys of the lower orders exclusively. My friends asked me not to go to that performance, and I complied with their request; but previous to this, in the afternoon, there was a great dance in the gromma, at which the Kaneash were present in their robes, and all the Jast who participated in the revels were gorgeously attired. All the functionaries of religion were also present. Gísh seemed to be the most honoured of the gods on this occasion. The proceedings began with dances in his honour, and ended up in a similar way after Dizane and Imrá had also received three rounds each.

On February 21, 1891, the first day after Taska, the annual competition in throwing an iron ball called the shíl took place, according to custom. The occasion is always observed as a general holiday. The shíl is about the size of a lawn-tennis ball, and is faceted all over in an irregular manner. It is one of two precisely similar balls said to have been made by Imrá when he created the world, and only one of which is used for the throwing competition, the other being buried under a stone in the middle of a spring of water near the top of the village hill. I was informed that in very ancient times the two shíls were discovered rolling over and over in a running stream, and were then taken out and reverently preserved by certain Kám Káfirs, who appear to have known by direct inspiration what the iron balls were, and what they were for. On the present occasion the shíl was produced by the holder, Chandlu, the Debilála's brother. For a whole year it had reposed out of sight in a bed of wheat. When it was brought again into the light a goat was sacrificed, and the flesh partaken of by such of the Jast as chose to be present. The throwing took place at a position near the upper village, where a contiguous line of house-tops afforded a more or less level space, and in the presence of a large number of spectators. The weather was unpleasant, but the competition must take place, no matter how bad it may be. All the ambitious and stalwart youths of the tribe, and many visitors as well, took their stand one by one behind a particular mark, whence, starting at a furious pace, each hurled the iron ball as far as his strength permitted, all the spectators shouting out "Onsht, onsht!" (up with it, up with it). This was intended to incite the competitors to the utmost effort, and certainly added to the general excitement. All were urged to join in the sport, myself among the rest, but I well knew that throwing such a weight in lieu of a cricket-ball would almost break my arm, so I prudently refrained. After several hours had passed, during which innumerable young men had thrown the shíl as often as they liked, a young tribal hero made his appearance and threw a grand throw amid thunders of applause. One of the orators springing upon a fragment of rock spoke excitedly and fluently in praise of the thrower. The hero himself, a famous warrior, tried to look modest, but only succeeded in looking intensely gratified. Another young man subsequently made a still better cast, and remained the victor; but he was not nearly so popular as his more distinguished adversary, whose continuous attempts to make a still better throw were greeted with enthusiastic shouts of "Shámish!" (Well done!) In the end both young men divided the honours, and feasted the whole village, although the actual victor of course retained possession of the shíl for the year. Like Henry Morton after the Wapinshaw, the winner has to entertain the vanquished. He has also to feed the whole of the village as well. A friend of mine, named Aza Kán, had on several occasions proved himself the best man in the tribe at throwing the shíl, but on this occasion he refused to compete. When asked the reason, he replied that he had already been the victor on five different occasions, and did not care again to undergo the expense of feasting the village. Some Káfirs on hearing that in my country the winner of an athletic competition such as this would probably receive a prize, disapproved strongly of such a custom, remarking that as Imrá had made a particular man's arm strong, therefore that man should give a feast in honour of Imrá. Concerning the possibility of an individual of some other tribe winning the competition, they told me that in such a case the man would be allowed to give a feast, but he certainly would not be permitted to take the shíl away to his home.

The shíl-throwing is an ancient custom, and is said to be observed by all the tribes of Káfiristán. It appears to be in praise of Imrá, and is called the Shílarigajar.

(4.) The Marnma festival took place at Kámdesh on March 8, while I was away in the Kunar Valley. By all accounts the observance was both curious and interesting. On the evening of the 7th, the women cooked rice and bread, and then, early in the morning, taking a small quantity of the prepared food with ghee and wine, placed the whole in front of the family effigies. The faces of the images were also smeared with ghee. After a short interval the food on the ground was destroyed and flooded away by a gush of water from a goatskin. The women next repaired to the pshar or Nirmali house, where they feasted and amused themselves with loud laughter. They then started for their respective homes singing. The men and women chaffed one another indelicately on the road, the former offering the latter neck ornaments or other small articles to be danced for. Later on, near each house, a small portion of prepared food was placed on the ground in the name of each deceased relative that could be remembered, and was in its turn swamped away by a gush of water. The food which remained over was then feasted on, and I was assured that joy and contentment reigned in every household, the atmosphere of which no doubt reeked with the appalling remarks which appear to be inseparable from Káfir gaiety and festivity.

(5.) The Duban is the great festivity of the year. For it there is an elaborate ritual and a tedious ceremonial. In 1891 it lasted from March 19 till the 29th, both days inclusive. On the first day the Urir for the year and their chief or Jast were elected. The 20th was an off-day. On the 21st the regular dancing at the gromma began, with its concomitants, slow processions round and round inside the building, hymn-chanting, and the strange antics of the buffoon priest. The 23rd, the 24th, and the 25th were the chief days, and of these the last-mentioned was the most important. Then the violence of the " low " priest was as extraordinary as his physical endurance was marvellous to behold. On the 26th the regular dancing to Imrá and the inferior deities was poorly attended, and on the 27th it ceased altogether. The 28th and 29th were devoted to feasting, dancing, and chanting in honour of the illustrious dead.

(6.) The Azhindra fell on April 6th. There was no dancing. The event of the day was a procession down the Kámdesh hill to the shrines—represented by upright stones—of Bagisht and Duzhi, which are situated near

the river-bank and close to the village of Urmir.   For this
ceremony the rule which prohibited any of the Kaneash
from leaving the village until the Diran festival is relaxed.
After a bull had been sacrificed to Bagisht and a large he-
goat to Duzhi, the company engaged in a game of aluts,
while the carcasses of the animals were being skinned and
cut up into portions for each man to carry away with
him.   Several games were played simultaneously.   For
the chief of them Utah and the Debilála chose sides.
All those too old or too inefficient to play themselves
crowded round to watch and applaud the players, headed
respectively by the high priest and the precentor.   Then
came the feasting on a horrible mess compounded of the
liver and other inner parts of the sacrificed animals,
cheese, cooked fat, and I know not what else.   A second
ceremony was then gone through before Bagisht's shrine
in the way of a recitation by the Debilála, and responses
from the congregation.   After that the young men of the
village drew up in line, and raced through a terraced
field of wheat to a stone about 120 yards off.   This race
was quite as much a part of the business of the day as
any other of the ceremonies.   Finally, all started together
to return to Kámdesh, singing.   One man sang a line by
himself, then everybody sang the next line, and so on.

(7.) The Diran marks the date when the Kaneash are
permitted to leave the village and go where they please.
There is also a procession up the hillside to Imrá's idol
temple on the top of the Kámdesh spur.   All proceed in
regular order, headed by the high priest, who at intervals
sprinkles water with a sprig of juniper-cedar from a
wooden bowl.   Each time he does this he cries " Súch,
súch ! " (be pure, be pure), while a singer, not the

Debilála, sings a hymn of praise to Imrá, all the congregation joining in a regular refrain. Drums and pipes also lend their aid. When Imrá's shrine is reached, a cow is sacrificed with the proper formalities, and a large number of wicker baskets heaped up with flour are placed before the shrine, each having on the top a bread-cake shaped like a rosette. Following this, the assembly moves a little to the north, and a goat is sacrificed to Bagisht in Katirgul. There is no temple erected of any kind at the place, the theory being that the sacrifice is offered direct through the air to the distant shrine. While the carcasses are being cut up, the people are amused by an archery display by the best shots in the village. Sides are formed and a regular competition is gone through. The sacrifice on this occasion is presented by the Urir Jast.

(8.) Of the Gerdulow festival nothing is recorded in my journals, except the name and the date. I was away from Kámdesh when it took place, and no trace of anything concerning it can be found in any of my various diaries. It is probably of secondary importance.

(9.) The Patilo was observed in 1891 by dancing. The proceedings began at night, and dancing was kept up with great spirit both at the upper and lower village dancing-places. It was to the glory of Imrá, and was accompanied by drums and singing. The spectacle was extremely picturesque, the silent dancers being only clearly seen as they emerged from the gloom into a limited space illumined by a large fire, whence they circled back again into darkness.

(10.) The Dizanedu occurred on July 9. For two days previously, men and boys had been hurrying in

from all sides bringing cheeses and ghee. Every pshal
or dairy farm contributed. At two o'clock the male
inhabitants of Kámdesh went to Dizane's shrine to
sacrifice a couple of goats, and make offerings of portions
of cheese and bread-cakes. Then the whole company
returned to Gísh's temple. An immense pile of fine
cheeses was heaped upon the wooden platform close by,
and from each one a shallow circular fragment was cut
out. These convex pieces were placed on the cedar
branches with bread-cakes and ghee during a regular
worship of Gísh. This ceremony over, the people collected into groups, scales were produced, and all the
cheeses were cut into portions. Each share was weighed
separately, the make-weight being neatly skewered on to
the big pieces with little bits of stick. While this was
being done the goat's flesh, divided into " messes," was
being cooked in two large vessels, the green twigs used
to bind together the different shares simmering away
merrily with the meat. Women brought bread from
the different houses, and ultimately stood in a row in
the background, while their male relations thoroughly
enjoyed themselves. There was a regular religious
ceremony performed by Utah, and just before this began,
Shahru, the mad priest, at the invitation of the oldest of
the Mirs, replaced the shutter which closed the tiny
door or window of Gísh's temple. This shutter had remained on the top of the shrine ever since Shahru had
removed it early in the year.

There was dancing on the 11th, both at the upper
and lower village dancing-platforms, to a certain slow
measure called the " Prem dem nát," while on the 12th
the whole of the village collected at the lower dancing-

2 I

place to view the performance called the Stritilli nát. This was one of the best sights I saw in Káfiristán. Being in the open air a very large number of spectators could assemble, and the terrible atmosphere of the gromma had not to be endured. The performers were arrayed in all their finery, and consisted entirely of the Jast supplemented by three women dancers. Upon this festival it is the custom for the upper and lower villages to entertain one another in alternate years. Great cheerfulness prevails, and not a little horse-play is indulged in. On this occasion, as so frequently happens at Káfir gatherings, the proceedings which began in sport ended in what promised to be a determined fight between the east village and a mob who attacked it in sport. At one instant matters looked very serious indeed, but happily daggers had been discarded, and only sticks and branches of trees were used as weapons. The women behaved with extraordinary courage, dashed among the fighters and dragged away husbands and brothers by main force and disarmed them. Those not engaged in the turmoil, together with many visitors from Lutdeh, at length succeeded in restoring order, though not before many shrewd blows had been given and received. The affair was not without its humorous aspect also. An important man, such as the priest, or one of the most respected of the Jast, would rush among the combatants and harangue them. Finding his admonitions disregarded and himself hustled, he would seize a club and become as mad as the most furious in the throng. The women were very much in evidence all day. They appear to have the privilege of seizing men and ducking them in the streams on this anniversary. My Baltis had to run hard to escape being

THE STRITILLI NÁT.

To face page 592.

treated in this way.   As I was tramping up the hill to my tent at the top, a young woman and a little girl flung water over me, and many others seemed half inclined to follow the example, but the spectators, in horrified accents, protested so strongly against the proceedings, that I was allowed to pass.

(11.) The Munzilo was held on August 17 in 1891. I was away from Kámdesh at the time.   It seemed to me, from descriptions at second-hand, that it was mainly occupied in the final ceremonies for the Kaneash, which are referred to in their proper place.   It lasted several days, and the deities chiefly honoured were Gísh and Dizane.

(12.) The Nilu festival began late on the evening of September 17.   On the 18th, little boys of from six to twelve were the only performers.   They collected about four in the afternoon, and were slowly and carefully dressed up by amused relatives, in whatever would answer the purpose of adornment.   After the little fellows had finished dancing, there was a worship of Imrá, without the sacrifice of an animal, and in the evening a second fire was lit.   On the 19th there was a men's dance, with intervals for chants in honour of Gísh, Dizane, and other deities.   A dance to the glory of Krumai closed the proceedings.   In the morning everybody appeared to be listless, not to say bored with the whole proceedings, and sacrifices were offered to all the gods collectively.

CHAPTER XXXIII

WHILE pregnant a woman still continues her daily avocations, although as time advances she is naturally exempt from the heaviest kind of labour. When the birth of the child is imminent she goes to the Nirmali house, where her child is born. She remains there twenty days if her baby is a girl, or twenty-one days if it is a boy. Then, after a ceremonial ablution, she goes home, when she is allowed a further rest of twelve days before she resumes her ordinary work.

The naming of children is peculiar. The instant an infant is born it is given to the mother to suckle, while an old woman runs rapidly over the names of the baby's ancestors or ancestresses, as the case may be, and stops the instant the infant begins to feed. The name on the reciter's lips when that event occurs becomes the name by which the child will thenceforth be known during its life. As a consequence of this custom, it not unfrequently happens that several members of a family are compelled to bear the same name. In such cases the children are distinguished from one another in conversation by the prefix senior or junior, as the case may be.

Káfir men and women are known by their own particular name affixed to that of their father; thus, Chandlu Astán means Astán the son of Chandlu. In the case of very popular names, the grandfather's cognomen has frequently to be employed also to distinguish the various individuals; thus, Lutkám Chandlu Merik means Merik the son of Chandlu, the grandson of Lutkám. Occasionally, though rarely, the mother's name is used along with the father's; so Bachik-Sumri Shaiok means Shaiok the child of Bachik and Sumri. There is no objection in Káfiristán to a child's bearing the same name as its father; indeed, one constantly hears of Merik Merik, Gutkech Gutkech, and similar instances of father and son bearing identical names.

If a Káfir turns Musalmán, he of course assumes a Musalmán name also, but his tribe always speak of him by his Káfir name only.

Many Káfirs are known by some adjective defining a physical peculiarity being prefixed to their true appellation. The commonest prefixes of this kind are red, stout or sturdy, lame, one-eyed, thin, and tall.

The following is a list of some of the more common names of Káfirs :—

MALES.	FEMALES.
1. Utahding.	1. Sumri.
2. Shyok.	2. Azakanni.
3. Málkán.	3. Kazan.
4. Bachik.	4. Baza.
5. Málding.	5. Saggi.
6. Bilizhe.	6. Kazhirbri.

MALES.	FEMALES.
7. Sunra.	7. Gumli.
8. Palúk.	8. Kori.
9. Dimu.	9. Dimilli.
10. Mirján.	10. Ilkani.
11. Garak.	11. Wazbri.
12. Mori.	12. Mirza.
13. Karuk.	13. Mirkani.
14. Sámar.	14. Málkanni.
15. Azá.	15. Tromgatti.
16. Aror.	16. Bangu.
17. Kuli.	17. Arubri.
18. Widing.	18. Wázi.
19. Arakòn.	19. Chabri.
20. Aramallick.	20. Marangzi.
21. Katamir.	21. Muzik.
22. Tong.	22. Sunik.
23. Utamir.	23. Gumali.
24. Chárá.	24. Areni.
25. Baril.	25. Aurulli.
26. Malik.	26. Boza.
27. Basti.	27. Konzo.
28. Chimiding.	28. Tramgudi.
29. Samata.	29. Bodza.
30. Barmuk, &c., &c.	30. Maláki, &c., &c.

Babies are often suckled until they are two or three years old or more. Women are hospitable to hungry infants other than their own. I have several times seen them quiet other people's children by suckling them. Babies, of course, accompany their mothers everywhere. The infant is carried inside the dress in front when the woman is going to or returning from the fields, for at these times her back is always occupied with the conical basket, or is bending under the weight of heavy loads. While the mother is actually tilling the land the baby is

generally transferred to the back, its head appearing at
the wedge-shaped opening in the dress. The child's face
is often congested as if suffocation were imminent. It
always looks wretchedly uncomfortable, but is happy
enough. On the 32nd day after birth there is a head-
shaving, but there is no special ceremony for the occasion, nor any feasting. Some bystander simply wets the
head all over with water and then shaves away all the
hair, except from one patch in the centre of the crown, one
and a half inches by one inch, which is left untouched.
The head-shaving is, I believe, an invariable custom
both for boys and girls. When the children attain to
three or four years of age they are often left at home
in the charge of their father, or for some old gaffer or
gammer to look after; but the little girls very soon
begin to learn field-work, following their mothers, with
miniature conical baskets on their backs, and tiny knives
thrust into their girdles behind. The little boys go
about the village with toy dancing-axes made of reeds,
or pretend to play the aluts game. Wherever they
wander they are certain of a kindly reception.

Among Káfirs there is no particular ceremony for a
girl on reaching the age of puberty. For boys there
are particular formalities which must be observed before
they are permitted to wear the virile garment—loose
trousers. The usual custom is for boys to be taken to
Dizane's shrine at the Giché festival arrayed in these
emblems of manhood; a sacrifice is made, and there is
a feast, lavish or penurious according to the wealth of
the parents. The sons of poor people are often allowed
to associate themselves with the ceremonies carried out
by youths of richer families. The boys who take part in

the Sanowkun of a Kaneash are exempted from further observances ; but it is probable that, even in such cases, an offering is also made to Dizane at the proper time. I have seen boys under twelve smeared with blood at the Sanowkun, boys who certainly had not reached the age of puberty. Outside Káfiristán, on a visit to Chitrál, for instance, boys may wear trousers, but must not do so in their own country until the proper observances have been complied with.

Boys and girls do not play at the same games. The girls play at ball, at a kind of knuckle-bones, in which, however, walnuts are used, and at swinging ; while any boy amusing himself in any of these ways would be despised. From the age of five upwards little girls play untiringly with a bouncing-ball made of wool. The object is to keep it bouncing regularly, while between each pat the player spins round once. The girls' game at knuckle-bones is played with an uneatable kind of walnut. Several of these fruits are spread out between the legs of a player. She tosses up one with her right hand, catching it in her left, and while it is falling snatches up the others in a particular order and arrangement. Swinging is the most popular amusement of all for girls, who swing by the hour. They sing shrilly all the time without cessation. Young women often join in the sport, and on Agar days in May dozens amuse themselves in this manner. A tree on a steep slope is usually selected. A big girl seats herself on the swing-rope. A crowd of girls then join hands and drag her up the slope as far as they can. When let go she swings far out, perhaps nearly to the top of a tree lower down the hill, and is much put to it to keep her dress decently arranged. All the time she sings with the other girls some snatch of song in alternate lines.

Boys play very rough games. A favourite pastime is for a boy to make a sudden dash at another boy looking in another direction, or while engaged in the same trick on a third, and throw him down. At the shîl competitions, between the intervals of the throwing, it was common to see half-a-dozen boys hurled to the ground at a time. We were on house-tops at the time, and at one place there was a sheer fall of thirty feet. Some of the players fell actually on the edge of this drop. None of the grown-up men and women took the slightest notice of the children. I asked a man if it never happened that a boy fell over and was killed. He replied that it did occur occasionally, but not very frequently.

A game constantly played at the same time of the year is merely an imitation of the national dance. But this is an exception to all other children's sports, because girls and boys play at it together. A number of youngsters of both sexes march or trot round and round in a circle singing. At a distance they look as if they were all affected with a shockingly bad limp. They carry sticks over their shoulders, and although the singing is most discordant, they keep capital time.

Boys play a game with walnuts in the following way. A circle a foot and a half in diameter is levelled on the hillside, the slope behind forming a vertical back wall to the circle of some three or four inches in height. In the middle of the circle there is a hole one and a half inches in diameter and three or four inches deep. The players standing downhill, five feet or so, take any number of walnuts up to a handful and try to throw them into the hole. Those which remain outside are then thrown at with another walnut. If the player hits one, he continues his hand; if he misses, his place is taken by another boy. This game is played with considerable skill, the real test of which is the throwing at the walnuts which remain outside the hole. The boy throwing invariably first wets the walnut he is about to cast with his tongue, then, taking steady aim, raises his hand well above his head and throws hard.

At Kámdesh the boys one day started playing another game on my house-top. It surprised me that no one was hurt. During the game three boys were sent flying off the roof. Fortunately the fall was not more than twelve or fourteen feet, and was into heaps of snow many feet in depth. In the distance the same game was being pursued with vigour on the tops of houses two and three stories high, but perhaps for my benefit the young Káfirs outdid themselves in their rough-and-tumble amusement. They were soon more or less completely smeared with blood from cuts on shins, fingers, &c. The game was played as follows:—One side, consisting of four boys, faced an equal number of adversaries, whose object it was to defend a goal marked out by a circle a foot in diameter. Each boy seized a big toe with the hand of the opposite side and hopped about on the other foot, which was kept in front. If he released the big toe or was thrown down, he had to stand aside and become a spectator until the round was finished. He was permitted, however, on occasion, to place the held foot on the ground and rapidly pass the foremost foot behind it, and might then do his best rushing about in crab-like fashion and fighting, but he must still never let go the

BOYS' GAME.

To face page 602.

big toe for a single instant. The plan of operations
was usually for the whole of the attacking side except
one to hop forward and try fully to occupy their opponents, or knock them over and put them out of play,
and in this way allow their own "back" to get through.
Sometimes the scrimmages were most exciting. The
long scalp-lock is justly considered the best of all possible grips. More than once the attacking back had got
right through and nearly reached the goal, when one of
the opposite side caught him by the hair, swinging him
clean off his feet, and in one instance off the roof as
well. It was impossible not to admire the perfect
temper and good-nature of the boys. They dashed at
one another like little furies, with fierce and determined
faces, in more than one instance streaming with blood;
but the moment the round was over they were as happy
and jolly together as possible. Their keen sense of
justice was admirable to witness. In the whole course
of the game there was not a single dispute. Several
men looked on, cheering the performers with laughter
and applause, but they were never appealed to in a
single instance to decide any point in the game.

A favourite amusement of the boys is shooting arrows.
A dozen little Káfir boys found a dead crow near my house.
This was a great find. They stuck it up, and at about twelve
paces riddled it through and through with arrows. The
worst shots were not more than a few inches out. It was a
curious reflection for me, that any one of these children,
in an ambush, could send one of their iron-tipped arrows
through a man's heart. I subsequently heard of an instance where a Káfir boy, hardly more than thirteen,
killed a Pathan in the way mentioned. The bows are

weak to look at, but shoot very well. The usual game is for the boys to divide into two parties and shoot at marks, which consist of two pairs of sticks stuck into the ground, twenty-five or thirty yards apart. At such ranges the shooting was sometimes wonderfully accurate.

The boys are very fond of rough-and-tumble fighting, one section of a village against another. I have watched the boys at Kámdesh amusing themselves in this way at my next-door neighbour's. They would tumble from the house-top into the room below, then out of the verandah on to the raised platform, and thence down the notched ladder and along the edge of a little cliff which bounded the level space on which my house was built. Once there, that round of the game seemed finished, and there was nothing for it but to begin all over again. One boy was dragged a dozen yards simply by the hair of his head, while another urchin was pulling his legs in an opposite direction. He was only about nine or ten years old, but he never made a murmur. Why his hair did not come out was a wonder. Many a time the boys, tumbling down the ladder, had hair-breadth escapes from being killed or maimed for life. No one, except my own followers, seemed to think that anything unusual was happening. One of my men rushed forward to interfere, and got laughed at by all the spectators. The boy is father to the man, and this Spartan form of enjoyment, the ferocious looks, the absence of anything like laughter, the savage cries and fierce blows, must teach the Káfir youth to endure anything. The tortures which English boys occasionally inflict on one another are as nothing to the sights we witnessed. As soon as it was all over, victors and victims alike showed by their manner that nothing unusual had occurred.

It will be convenient here to describe also the amusements of the men. The shíl-throwing has been already described at page 585.

In the early spring, every day and almost all day, archery is practised as a sport. The men and lads divide into two parties, and shoot at marks placed on opposite slopes of a gully, or some other convenient spot. They consist of a single stick about two feet high, and are usually about eighty yards apart. Almost everybody joins in the game. Those who are too old to play, and others who come late, are enthusiastic spectators, cheering every good shot. There is almost always some one among them accustomed to public speaking. Such a man, when some particular cleverness has been shown, will break out into laudations of the marksman, particularly if the latter belongs to some well-known family or is a famous warrior. Such a one will be greeted with a speech running something like this :—" Oh, well done! well done you, thou son of rich parents." Being proclaimed the son of rich parents was always considered a high form of praise. The mark itself was very rarely hit, never more than two or three times in an afternoon, but comparatively few shots were very wide of it. The two sides fired alternately, man by man. The moment a man had shot his arrow he scampered off to the mark, apparently quite heedless of those behind who were still shooting. There was often some very careful measuring required to determine which of two or three arrows sticking in the ground was actually nearest to the mark. No disputes. ever arose. If there were differences of opinion, some bystander was appealed to, and his decision was invariably accepted as final.   An amusing point of the game was to see a man at the mark pointing out to one of his own side, about to shoot, the exact inch on the mark he was to strike, as though hitting the stick anywhere was not a piece of the greatest good luck.   The method of counting the score was decidedly faulty, for an arrow which almost grazed the mark and went on for two or three yards, might in the result be counted after others which plumped into the ground a yard from the base of the stick, and were consequently not nearly such good shots.

A moderately popular game played by men is to dig two holes, a couple of inches in diameter and six yards apart, on some house-top, and then roll walnuts from one hole to the other.   The object is to get the walnut into the hole, or as near to its edge as possible.   The particular skill required is to judge the necessary strength, and to allow for the irregularities of the house-top.   Sides are formed, and great excitement is shown at a promising shot.   The men on the same side as the roller judge whether to leave the nut alone or help it by brushing out of its way small obstacles, such as dust or bits of twig. They behave very much like curlers in Scotland on similar occasions.

Men also play a kind of " touch " ; only, instead of the hand being used, it is necessary to tread with the foot on a man's instep to make a capture.   This leads to some modification of the English game.   For instance, a man on a lower roof may be pushed back by the others, and so kept in a position where he cannot possibly put his foot on any of theirs.   He then has to dodge about for a chance of getting on a level with them.

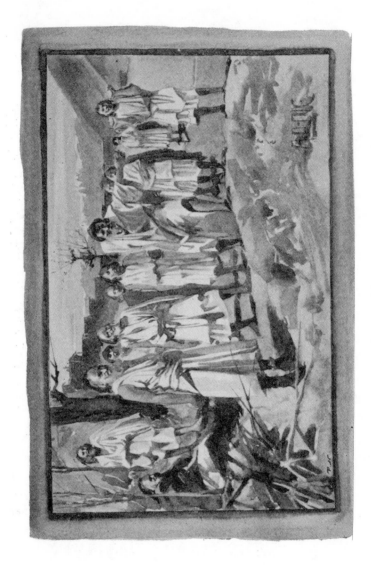

THE GAME OF "ALUTS."

To face page 611.

A very good and extremely popular game is called "aluts." It is exactly like quoits, flat stones being used instead of the quoit. Whenever a number of Káfirs are collected together on level ground, and have nothing to do, they almost invariably start this game. The marks are placed twenty-five to thirty yards apart. The details of play and the manner of counting exactly resemble those of the English game, except that in Káfiristán any number almost may play at a time, and there is no pedantic strictness about the exact spot where the flat stone must leave the player's hand. It is capital sport to watch, all participating are so keenly interested, while many display remarkable skill in dropping their stones on to the mark, or in knocking aside those of their opponents. I myself could never cast the heavy flat stones so that they did not turn over in the air, and consequently could never take part in a game. At such games as this Káfirs are seen at their best. Every one is excited, but thoroughly good-tempered. A really good shot is frequently applauded by friends, foes, and spectators equally. There is never any occasion for an umpire. The players are wonderfully fair and just. The most important men of the tribe often act as leaders of the opposing sides in the aluts game.

Young men occasionally amuse themselves with athletic exercises, stone-throwing against each other, running and jumping, and also display their activity in various other ways, such, for instance, as by holding a short stick tightly with both hands and yet jumping over it backwards and forwards. Occasionally they try simple acrobatic feats. At one of their friendly competitions at Purstám held in my honour, several Kám men actually competed with Rámgulis, their hereditary enemies. The most remarkable point about the display was the extraordinary equality of the competitors. In one event, three standing jumps, the winner cleared about twenty-five feet, but nearly all the rest were within a few inches of him. So also with several other of their contests. Like other young men, Káfirs are fond of skylarking, and their frolics are apt to end in fighting; but as in the villages they almost always put aside their daggers before they begin, peace is usually restored by the bystanders before much harm is done.

All young Káfirs, both men and boys, wander about their villages with the Eastern variety of the stone-bow, with which they shoot at small birds, bits of twig, or anything which they find suitable for a mark. The weapon is identical with the Indian "galail." They are fairly expert in its use, but not nearly so accurate as some Chitráli boys I have watched shooting apples off a tree.

Swimming is an amusement, as well as a necessary part of a Káfir's education. On inflated goatskins a man will cross rapid streams, taking with him a goat, or even a cow. A party on the march always has one of these goatskins as part of its equipment. When wanted for use it is inflated by means of a reed. Sometimes exciting scenes are witnessed where a man, after swimming a swift-flowing river, has to make frantic exertions to prevent himself being carried down-stream on to rocks. Káfirs seem insensible to the coldest water.

Dancing enters greatly into the inner life of the Káfirs. It is a religious exercise, a spectacular performance, and an amusement, but it is possible that there is no such thing as purely secular dancing. In Eastern countries

SHOOTING WITH STONE-BOW.

To face page 612.

religion is so mixed up with the manners and customs of a people, that it is often difficult, and sometimes impossible, to separate them. So with Káfir dancing. Children play at dancing; boys on the march will frequently stop for an instant or two, shuffle a few steps, stamp a little, and then go tramping on with an entire absence of anything like self-consciousness. For instance, a youth may be seen lying on a bank resting his load, while all the time his limbs are twitching to the rhythm of a song he is singing aloud or to himself. Yet in all these instances the performers are probably practising a religious exercise, even though they may be unaware of the fact themselves. Káfirs dance when they are happy, and when they are plunged in grief at the death of relatives. When any one is sorely hurt from an accident, or when he is sick or dying from smallpox, or some other disease, people congregate in his room to amuse him, as they say; but my own idea is that it is to help the individual's recovery, that it is a form of supplication to the gods. At funeral ceremonies people caper about while the tears may be streaming down their cheeks. The Káfir gods are propitiated by songs, dancing, and feasting, which includes sacrifices, and never in any other way.

In any description of Káfir dancing it is necessary to describe also the occasion which gives rise to the exercise. The chief of these are :—

1. The dances of the Jast to the gods.
2. The dances to the illustrious dead (ancestor and hero worship).
3. The homicides' thanksgiving dance to Gísh.
4. The women's dance to the gods while the men are raiding.
5. The dances on the death of a Káfir.
6. The dances in celebration of the erection of effigies.

2 K

These religious exercises are performed inside the gromma, or outside in the open air, according to the season of the year. The gromma has already been described. It is a big square building with two rows of wooden pillars running down the middle. A large fire is lit on the hearth, and the musicians are stationed at the east of the building. Facing them on the opposite side of the fire is the priest gorgeously dressed, while on his right and left are the Pshur and the Debilála respectively. These form an inner circle which is surrounded by a single line of the Jast, all decked out in every scrap of finery they possess. The dancing begins with three rounds to Gísh, succeeded by a similar number to each of the other deities, and winding up with the dance to Krumai.

When all are ready and in their places, the band strikes up. The drums have been already described. The pipes are simple hollow reeds about a foot long furnished with two holes besides the end apertures. One of the ends is shaped as though to fit the mouth; but, curiously enough, it is the opposite end which the player puts to his lips. Only two, or at most three, different notes can be sounded by manipulating the two holes and the shaped extremity. The pipes are always played by amateurs. The music is most feeble and discordant. My ear could never distinguish between the different tunes which were being played. The time is accurately kept by the drums. It was only by noting the difference in the rhythm of the drum-taps that I could ever tell one dance from another.

The pipes do not play, and the audience indulge in preliminary catcalls for the Gísh rounds. Then the spectators become silent and the dancing begins. All the Jast stand looking inwards towards the fire, and at

Kámdesh seem to take their time from the priest, who with the Pshur and the Debilála are inside the circle. All the performers begin by twisting rapidly their shining dancing-axes, which they hold vertically by the lower end. The Kám priest is a famous dancer. He begins by shuffling in such a rapid manner that he seems to vibrate from head to foot, as if he were standing on the floor of an engine going at full speed along the line. After a time he stops vibrating, and stamps vigorously forward towards the fire, and finally dances back to his former position, kicking his toes quietly at the fire as he retreats. The Jast begin when the priest begins. Their step is a jerky shuffle with a side movement of the toes of one foot to mark the third beat of the drum. Then when the priest, changing from the stationary to the progressive style, dashes towards the fire, they all turn to the right, lower their axes and plunge onwards as though they were trying to smash their fantastic boots on the earthen floor. When the priest stops at the fire and begins to dance backwards, they all turn inwards again, and keep time with him by leisurely forward kicks, until the moment comes for the energetic shuffling to recommence. Occasionally, one of the Jast while stamping round will turn and go backwards a few steps, holding his axe horizontally above his head with both hands, and jerking it sideways in time to the drums. Another will jerk his disengaged hand sideways in front of his left shoulder, but this is the exception.

In the dances to Imrá, Dizane, and the other deities, the pipes wail tunelessly, and are supplemented by hand-clapping on the part of the dancers, during the shuffling stage, but not by the audience. Krumai is always the last of the deities honoured, although her dance does not necessarily complete the ceremonies. The Káfirs are so indefatigable that they sometimes go through the list of the chief deities over and over again. There is no standing in one place nor any shuffling in the Krumai dance. At the first beat of the drums and squeak of the wind instruments, all the dancers begin to trot round the building, some with swoops like old-fashioned waltzing, others going sideways, fast or slow according to taste. On one occasion a huge man was particularly noticeable. His idea of the thing was a high-actioned step which brought his knees alternately to the level of his waist. He attempted no other step, but went round and round with an air of complete self-satisfaction. At the same dance one or two of the other performers did equal honour to themselves and me by dancing in front of me with delighted grins on their faces. This was a compliment to a guest. I cried "Shamish!" (well done!), as politeness demanded, and away they went again. The Krumai dance is the only frivolous part of these performances. The men's faces are usually as stolid-looking as their father's wooden effigies, except that the exercise is so severe that it makes even the hard-trained Káfirs sweat profusely. In fact, these dances are really solemn occa-sions. All those taking part in them do·so by virtue of their rank as Jast. They know that the eyes of the natives, envious or admiring, are upon them the whole time. They have the look of men conscious of the exalted position they occupy, and equally aware of the responsibilities it entails.

In strange contrast to the other dancers is the Pshur.

At Kámdesh this man used to appear in his dirtiest
dress, if, indeed, he had more than one, and without
dancing-boots. He swung about at his pleasure, and
looked as if, being overcome with wine, he had wandered
into the sacred circle by accident. There was always a
chance of his diversifying the proceedings by seeing a
fairy and amusing us with his antics.

The Debilála, on the other hand, danced heavily but
reverently, and after the Gísh rounds sang the praises
of each god in succession.

Often several women are associated with the dance.
Their place is outside the Jast, between the latter and
the spectators, where they are sometimes greatly crushed.
Their appearance is not pleasing. Their dirty faces, unkempt hair, and general slovenliness are but slightly
relieved by the fillets of the girls, the horned caps of
the women, and the slight attempts at ornamentation
of all. One woman perhaps binds a piece of bright-
coloured silk round the horns of her head-dress, others
wear sashes of fragments of cloth or old turbans,
covered in some instances with ears of wheat, which
look quite pretty; but the dirty clothes, especially any
underclothing showing beyond the edge of the upper
dress, combined with the general sombre colouring of
the women's clothing, make the female dancers very
depressing objects. However, no one takes any notice
of them, everybody's attention being reserved for the
parti-coloured men. In the dance the women move in
ungraceful jerks, each step being hardly an inch in length.
They vary the monotony of this movement by turning
slowly round and round, heavily and awkwardly, the
hands being carried breast-high.

The outdoor dances of the Jast are much the same as those performed in the gromma, except that the priest does not play so prominent a part in them. He takes his place in a single ring with the others, and the movements are the same as those already described.

These annual observances are enacted with the usual feasting, but instead of taking place inside the gromma, the dancing is performed on the roof, and the proceedings are shorn of much of their picturesqueness by the absence of all bright-coloured dresses, which it appears can only be worn in the service of the gods. The only decorated people at the Kámdesh ceremony on March 28, 1891, were a man named Samatu Malik, who composed the hymn; a Jast named Mír Ján, who acted as his assistant, and the Ur Jast, who, in virtue of his office, wore a turban and a sash. No dancing-boots were worn. When I reached Kámdesh gromma to see the show, a troop of men were stamping round the smoke-hole on the roof to the accompaniment of a large and a small drum. The two hymn-composers chanted a sentence together, and all the throng sang a response in unison, and so on. At intervals there were scramblings for walnuts, much consumption of cheese and other viands, and wines; while several young women were incessantly employed in fetching snow for the spectators to eat. The proceedings were as follows. Samatu Malik in the centre of the crowd began a chant in praise of a mentioned name. It consisted of a string of five or six words. All the rest then sang an evidently well-known response. After three or four sentences had in this way been chanted and responded to, all began stamping in time to the drum-taps, bending over to watch their feet at the same time. Then, after a moment or two, all with one accord, still chanting and chorusing, began to stamp, step, limp, or prance round and round, each according to his own taste. At intervals a dancer would turn round and proceed backwards, setting, as it were, to the man behind him, the two jerking their hands rhythmically, or a group of four or five would participate in a vigorous ground stamping. No women took part in the dancing.

There is nothing distinctive about the homicides' thanksgiving dances to Gísh. Each of the returned braves (at Kámdesh) decks himself out as well as he can, and, carrying a dancing-axe, goes with the women of his family to the dancing-place. Any clothes brought back after stripping the slain are thrown down in front of the rude altar there, and the men, heading the string of women, dance the prescribed number of rounds to Gísh. In the intervals the women shower wheat grains over the heroes. The solemnity of all concerned—men, little girls, and women—is very great. Generally, after the wheat has been thrown and before the dancing is resumed, some old man eloquent shouts out the praises of the warriors and of their forebears in a tone which might often be mistaken for anger by the uninitiated.

I once arrived at Lutdeh, as already related, while the tribesmen were absent on a raiding expedition. The following is an account of what I saw, copied from my diary :—

"The women, according to custom, have abandoned their field-work, and are all congregated in the village. For the greater portion of each day and for the whole of each night they employ themselves solely in dancing and feasting. They have elected three Mírs, the chief of whom is Kán Jannah's wife. These three persons direct the revels, and contribute greatly towards the feasting. Kán Jannah's wife is carried from one place to another as a 'flying angel' on the shoulders of a stalwart young woman, each of the other Mírs holding one of her hands. Whenever these four with their escort attempt the bridge, each time I feel absolutely certain that an accident is inevitable. The little party staggers over the narrow shaking bridge, and then starts off at a run, to the outspoken delight of the onlookers. Occasionally the women dance on some convenient house-top. In the afternoon they invariably feast and dance under the big mulberry tree in the east village, and use the east or west village dancing-place according to the position of the sun. During the night all congregate at the east village dancing-place.

"Although they all seem abandoned to feasting and holiday-making, they are nevertheless engaged in strictly religious ceremonies. To watch them at night, when the majority are obviously thoroughly tired, leaves no doubt in the mind on this point. I have more than once secretly approached the dancing throng at midnight and in the early morning, and have observed by the fitful light of the wood fire how exhausted and earnest the women looked. One young woman, shrugging her shoulders in time to the music, had streams of perspiration rolling down her face, although she was all muscle apparently. The exertions these women undergo are astonishing to see. Many of the very old women have to give up from sheer exhaustion, but the middle-aged and the young work away singing and dancing

THE WOMEN'S DANCE TO THE GODS WHEN THE MEN
ARE RAIDING.

To face page 622.

hour after hour and night after night. I feel sure they undergo quite as much exertion as their male relations who are absent and fighting.

"The dancing measures are marked by a drum and by general chorusing, or, when the slave-boy drummer gets tired, by the cadences of the voices alone. Those in whose cause he labours might at night be thought the creatures of a dream. Very old women and girls of ten or twelve, comely faces and hideous old crones, every description of form and figure is represented in the singing, shuffling crowd. The aged are very earnest and solemn; the young girls, on the other hand, are ready to seize every opportunity to make improper remarks to any male spectator of whom they do not stand in awe. Still the great majority of the dancers at all times attend strictly to the dancing. On my arrival at Lutdeh, on taking my seat on the dancing-platform, a very large number of the women gave me the customary greeting of welcome as they passed me dancing, but afterwards took little or no notice of my presence, while none showed the slightest sign of shamefacedness. They evidently believed themselves to be engaged in an occupation which did them infinite credit in every way. I could read as much in their faces and in their gestures.

"All wore horned caps except the little girls, and, with the same exceptions, nearly all wore gaiters and soft leather boots or dancing-shoes. Every woman had on the national budzun, worn according to the amount of finery she had to display. For instance, one had donned a gaudy silk robe belonging to her husband. She wore it underneath the budzun, one side of which was slipped off the shoulder to show the splendour of the under-

garment. Others not so well provided had to be content
with showing their cotton shifts in a similar way, or
with hanging a pretty scarf embroidered with cowrie
shells from one shoulder. A large number carried
dancing-axes, and not a few had daggers. One old
woman drew her dagger and flourished it clumsily before
my eyes for some minutes. The other dancers seemed
to admire the action, and passed behind her, leaving her
to fascinate me. Every scrap of ornament a woman or
her family could boast of was produced and worn.
Certain brass axes with a little horse on their upper
edge were delightful objects, and my praise of their
beauty was highly appreciated. One carried by a pretty
girl, half married to Utahding of Kámdesh, I admired
very much. The girl was delighted, and sang more
shrilly and shuffled more vigorously than ever, while a
little girl, the daughter of Gazab Shah, shouted out
excitedly that the axe belonged to her family, and was
only lent to the other girl. There were about half-a-
dozen women with the blinker ornaments.

" The dances were to Imrá, Gísh, Dizane, and the
other deities in turn. After each dance there was a
short rest, after which the women collected again in the
centre of the platform. Then one or two recited a well-
known line with all the refinements of anthem-tortured
words, to which the remainder sang a response, and all
facing to the right, started off, shuffling or lightly stamping in the various figures of the dance. That to Gísh
was all shuffle, with a rapid twist of the toes outward at
each step, to keep time with the drum."

Before the funeral dances are described, the kind of
dancing which takes place in private houses, for Jast

ceremonies, or to amuse sick people, may be briefly noticed.

For the Jast ceremonies the ritual is much the same as that carried out at the gromma. The Kaneash who gives the entertainment dances between the hearth pillars with the Debilála and the Pshur, while the others dance round the room close to the line of spectators, seated on benches or stools along the walls. After the fire has been taken away, some five or six men, visitors or villagers, are provided with dancing-boots and turbans, pine-wood torches are lighted, and one or two women of the entertainer's family make their appearance, ornamented, to the best of their powers, with shell and other decorations, and usually wearing a cowrie-adorned belt, from which depend metal discs, trephine-shaped iron ornaments, and hollow metal bells, which clang and clash with every movement of the dancer. Then the drums start the usual one, two, three, pause; one, two, three, pause; and the movements begin. The central three shuffle, stamp, and cross over; then back again to their original positions. The circle of men outside the hearth push, stamp, and plunge round the room from right to left in the manner already described. The women dance very slowly, revolving in a jerky, clumsy manner, and moving in the opposite direction to the male dancers. When any of the latter move in a reverse way from their usual direction, they continually overtake and pass the women. The exercise is of a severe kind, and even the leanest Káfir soon begins to shine with his exertions.

This is a type of all other dancing in houses, although details vary, and the dancers are not necessarily dressed up, as they must be on the more important occasions. The stamping is such a strain on the feet, that boots are generally, though not invariably, worn. Often at private dancing-parties the music is supplied by a kind of harp, the boat-like stand of which is held between the musician's knees, who helps the instrument with his voice. He is voluble in utterance, and has all manner of little affectations, such as musicians seem to have all over the world.

There are many kinds of dancing, to each of which particular names are given, but they depend more on the place where, or the occasion upon which they are held, than on any particular step or movement. All dances on the wooden platform are known as "Dam Nát," while those on the solid ground adjoining are called "Zhige Nát." All the Agar celebrations are of the former variety. On June 30, at Kámdesh, I went to see one of two dances going on at different places at the same time, called "Patlo Nát." It was late at night, and the scene was more than usually picturesque, because the only light came from blazing logs a short distance away. None of the dancers were ever in anything but a fitful light, while the great majority were in absolute gloom. To the accompaniment of drums, a refrain was sung and responded to by Samatu Malik, who was in the centre of a densely packed crowd of men who circled round him. One of the most effective movements was a kind of solemn prance, each man with his stick over his shoulder.

A dance called the "Presun dam Nát" is danced by hopping solemnly twice on one foot, while the knee of the other leg is kept at the height of the waist.

The only example of the Wai people's dance I have

seen was an imitation given me by a Kám boy. He held a dagger at arm's length. He kept flourishing the point, which was held downwards, by a movement of the wrist alone, and hopped twice on each foot alternately, dancing round and round, occasionally backing for a few steps and then going forward again.

The Presun dancing has been already described.

Káfirs are greatly addicted to music and singing, and have considerable aptitude for both arts. Besides the drums and pipes already alluded to, and the small harp briefly mentioned, they have a kind of large black guitar, and little fiddles which can be played skilfully. The fiddles are of rough construction, but Samatu Malik would sometimes play pretty airs upon them. One in particular, called Shah Katur's air, which Malik heard during a visit to Mastuj, was quaint and pleasing. Some of the men have agreeable voices, but the women's are always hopelessly discordant. The chanting of songs is very monotonous and wearying.

CHAPTER XXXIV

THE funeral ceremonies of the Káfirs are curious and fantastic. I have only witnessed those of the Kám tribe, but probably all the Siáh-Posh have similar observances.

If a young child or an infant dies, it is merely taken to the family receptacle at the cemetery and put in it. It is probable that no formalities of any kind are gone through for any individual under the age of puberty in girls, or unless the boys are entitled to wear cotton trousers.

On May 13, 1891, Dán Malik's little grand-daughter, aged about ten, lay dying. She was on a bed, and only semi-conscious. The room was full of relations and friends. The men on one side of the room were busily occupied sewing clothes for the corpse. A crowd of women, closely packed, were at the foot and sides of the bed, and filled the air with lamentations. The atmosphere of the room was such that on entering it I broke out at once into a profuse perspiration. It was useless to beg that the poor child might be given a fair chance. The women trooped out in dozens into the verandah when asked to do so, but returned as soon as we left, and pressed round the bed as before.

The following day the girl died, and the body was carried to the cemetery. I watched the mournful pro-

cession from an adjacent house-top. First came several
men carrying the corpse in a blanket, not shoulder-high,
but at arm's length and close to the ground. Then followed male relations and friends, looking very mournful.
Lastly, the women followed singly or in pairs, weeping
aloud. The blanket sagged down so much in the middle
that it was impossible to see how the corpse was dressed,
only the waxen features, the head covered with some
white cloth, and the feet encased in red leather boots,
being visible. It was impossible to intrude one's curiosity
at such a moment, but Utah told me that the body was
simply placed in a coffin-box without ceremony of any
kind.

In December 1890 I witnessed the ceremonies observed on the death of the old wife of Torag Merak.
The dead woman had occupied the highest position
among the women of the village. On adjacent house-tops
nearly all the notables of Kámdesh assembled. In the
centre of the concourse, on a bed supported at each
corner by a slave, lay the body of the deceased, covered
over with bright-coloured turbans. The head was
adorned with a kind of crown of sprigs of juniper-cedar,
and monstrous imitations of feathers made by fastening
bits of red cotton round sticks. The eyebrows, closed
lids, and grey cheeks were exposed to view. The blinker
silver ornaments were placed one on each side of the
head, as with the body in a lying posture they could not
be fixed as they would be worn during life. On the feet
were dancing-shoes fringed at the top with markhor hair.
At the foot of the bed were a second pair of dancing-
boots of similar make. Festoons of wheat hanging from
the bed proclaimed to all that the deceased during her life

had given freely of her substance. Underneath the bed several women of the house were seated weeping and wailing, while many more surrounded the bier, circling slowly round it. One of the women, the deceased's daughter, stood on the left of the corpse, holding the bed-frame with both hands. She appeared to be the chief mourner. In the intervals of the music she addressed her dead mother in accents of shrill praise and lament, often without paying the slightest heed to the formal speeches presently to be referred to. None of the women wore their horned head-dresses or other ornaments. As the feeble pipes and drums marked the time, the throng of women moved slowly round the bier sideways from left to right, their hands uplifted to the level of their shoulders. With outspread fingers they incessantly turned the palm first towards themselves then towards the corpse, a gesture supposed to indicate " she has gone from us." Beyond the circle of women were a few men closely related to the dead woman. They also edged round sideways, and made a similar gesture to that of the women, except that the hands were twisted at the level of the brows, and the action was much more energetic. Outside these men a few couples danced round merrily in the usual stamping way. In the intervals of the music the bed was placed on the ground, and some one of the spectators, usually Samatu Malik, declaimed short staccato sentences praising the virtues of the deceased, her lavish feasts, and extolling her family and kindred.

On September 9 the heads of two young men were brought into Kámdesh by some friendly Káfirs of another tribe, as already related. The two lads had been killed on a raiding expedition, and the heads had been severed from the bodies and brought in as an act of kindness to the parents. The heads were met just outside the village by a multitude composed almost entirely of women, weeping and lamenting with loud outcries. The heads of the youths were then escorted to their fathers' homes, where they were placed on beds. This happened in the morning.

In the afternoon, about four o'clock, the heads were taken in procession to the lower village dancing-platform, where a large crowd had collected. Each head was on a bed covered with bright-coloured cloth, such as turbans or pieces of silk, so arranged that the absence of the bodies could only be told by the ease with which the heads could be carried about. The Jast were seated all round on benches, the women sat on the ground. Female relatives of the deceased sat on the edges of the beds and kept bending forward, slowly shaking their heads from side to side, and apostrophising the dead faces exposed to view. Each woman had a ragged garment over her ordinary dress, and allowed her hair to escape from its cotton cap and fall down her back. The men over their woollen robes wore each a goatskin as a mourning vestment.

The outcry of the women was very great, yet at a word of command it ceased almost entirely. Then lame Astán stepped forward, buried his face in his sleeve, and appeared overpowered with grief. In a broken voice he proceeded to harangue the heads, extolling their bravery and the fame of their families. At intervals in his speech he cried out, "Well done! well done!" After he had ended, the beds were raised shoulder-high, drums were

2 L

beaten by four slaves, accompanied by a couple of reed pipes, and the throng of women circled round and round, stepping to the music, and twirling their hands shoulder-high in the usual manner. Then Astán and two other elders came forward and joined in the slow dance. It was a strange sight to see these three men dancing outside the circle of women, their tears flowing freely, their aspect that of extreme sorrow, while their movements were such as we associate with lightness of heart. They twirled their hands at the level of their brows, but were occasionally so overcome with emotion that one hand had to be raised to the face, and one only was left to twirl.

This dance over, the beds were again placed on the ground. The widows and near female relations, who had been standing round with their hands on the framework of the beds, or who had remained seated disconsolately on the ground, resumed their proper positions on the edge of their beds, and began to lament afresh. Their wailing is not a "boo-hoo-hoo," but is more like a regular chant, each line ending in "o-o-o-o, o, o, o," the voice gradually descending the scale and getting slower at each successive "o." Silence being again demanded, Samatu Malik advanced, and addressed the heads until it seemed as if he would never stop. Meanwhile, wine and refreshments were being handed round to the whole company.

At length even the Kám chief orator had said all there was to say, and Nílira's head was carried away. After the lapse of a short interval Sunra's head was also carried off, the women accompanying them as far as the shenitán or cemetery, but most of the men and all the

Jast took leave of the ghastly relics in a field just short of the final resting-place of the dead. The form of parting salutation was the motion of wafting a kiss, the head and lips only, not the hands, being used for the gesture. The next proceeding was to dress up two straw figures in the houses of the parents of Nílira and Sunra. These effigies were gorgeously attired, wore turbans, and were girdled with belt and dagger. They received just as large a share of the women's attention as the heads had.

The same evening there was a great firing of guns from the Jinjám direction, which proved to be a funeral procession bringing the body of a famous warrior named Basti, who had died of fever at Bazgul, his own village, to the tribal headquarters, Kámdesh. Basti, it seems, had been a very "good" man—that is to say, a splendid fighter—and therefore his remains were brought to Kámdesh, where alone a hero's funeral could be properly conducted. The upper village at once began to fire guns, and large numbers of people, Jast and simple, started off to meet the procession. Far ahead of the rest were a number of women, who declared their affliction by deafening cries. All the women nearly related to the dead Basti were led by the hand by female friends. Then, in the midst of a large concourse of people, much firing of guns, and the wailing of women, Basti's body was carried on its stretcher to a house in the upper village, where some of his relatives dwelt. The head was crowned with a large turban, the face exposed, and the body covered with bright-coloured cloth. A bed having been substituted for the stretcher, the women took their places on it in the customary manner. After a time, when it was thought their grief had found sufficient expression, silence was enjoined, and Samatu Malik was invited to say a few appropriate words. He stepped to the foot of the bed and burst into tears. Then, in broken accents, he began his address to the dead man. Cheering up at the sound of his own high phrases, he praised the prowess of the dead Basti and the fame of his family, until he was quite exhausted.

When he had ended it was quite dark, and most of the men, having finished their wine, walked sadly away. Late into the night somebody was still declaiming between the pauses of the lamentations of the women. The next morning Basti's corpse was carried to the upper dancing-platform. It was dressed in fine clothes, with feathered sticks thrust into the folds of the turban. Out of each red leather boot also protruded one of these ornaments. A cowrie-shell scarf was laid over the breast, and one or two men deposited their shields on the bed as they passed by. But Basti had lost all his goats and become very poor before he died, so that his bier was quite outdone in splendour by those holding the stuffed figures intended to represent Sunra and Nílira, which were also brought to the dancing-place at the same time. The three beds were raised shoulder-high, and the music, dancing, and feasting were resumed. In fact, the greater part of the day was spent in listening to orations, in slow dancing, and in lamentations by the women. During the morning a group of women came bringing Nílira's young widow, with her hair down her back, abandoned to grief. She went through the form of kissing all the figures.

In the afternoon three cows were killed in front of the three biers, and Nílira's straw figure and Basti's corpse were taken away to the coffins, but Sunra's straw figure was kept for. another day's ceremony, for Sunra belonged to a great and wealthy family, and there was to be more feasting on his account. Many animals were slaughtered by Dán Malik, Sunra's grandfather, in order to keep up the position of the family. All night long the wailing over Sunra's straw representative continued, and early on the morning of September 9 an old woman was declaiming his genealogy with untiring persistence, while a crowd of women and many men, seated on the benches, listened to her words in rapt attention. When she was at fault for lack of matter, she repeated her last line over and over again until a fresh idea, or a new way of expressing an old idea, formed itself in her brain, but she seemed to have considerable power of ringing the changes on the names of all the boy's ancestors on both sides. Each fresh arrival, man or woman, went through the form of kissing the straw figure before selecting his or her seat. It seemed to be proper etiquette for the men to drop their walking-clubs while performing this ceremony. When the time for refreshment came, the men trooped off willingly enough, as did most of the women also, but a few of the latter, near relatives of the deceased Sunra, had to be greatly persuaded before they would consent to be supported away and leave the lay figure which did duty for their dead relation. A certain number always remained with the figure till the end of the day, when it was carried off to the cemetery.

On September 10 it was the turn of Basti to have his grass figure taken to the dancing-house, and for his relations to distribute wine and food, while the usual weeping, oratory, and dancing went on. But as he was a great warrior, the ceremonies in his honour transcended those for the well-born but youthful Nílira and Sunra. As Basti's dummy was being carried to the dancing-place a regular fusillade of matchlocks was maintained. The young men had no such honours allowed them. Indeed, except when the heads were first taken to their homes, I do not think a single gun was fired in their honour.

At the dancing-place, as soon as Basti's effigy arrived, the drums and pipes struck up a lively measure, and the dancing began. The dressed-up figure on the bed, with feathered sticks in turban and in boots, was raised by four men, not slaves, but people of importance. They danced the bed round and round, first to the right and then to the left, moving with a couple of springs in each foot, which makes a very lively measure. At the same time they jerked the bed up and down, so that if the dummy had not been well secured it would certainly have been thrown off. As it was, its position continually shifted, and it had to be replaced at each pause in the dance. After a time the exercise became less violent, the bearers being content to stand still, or merely jog the bier slightly in time to the drums and pipes. The other dancers were in three circles. The innermost was of women dancing and making the funeral gesture. The middle one was of men edging sideways and twirling their hands in front of their foreheads. The outermost comprised the bulk of the dancers, who moved briskly in pairs or singly. Several carried matchlocks, one carried a quiver of arrows, another a spear, and many had shields. All the Jast who took part in this circle dance went singly, as did the shield-bearers also. The latter seemed to have a particular step of their own. They kept waving

WOMEN WAILING OVER THE EFFIGY.

To face page 638.

their shields above them in a semicircular sweep and turned half round as they did so. The remainder danced in pairs in the usual way.

Soon after mid-day the straw figure, which after ten o'clock had been consigned to the care of toothless but marvellously fluent old crones, was carried away to the cemetery under a great deal of gun-firing. At the coffin-place the straw figure was burnt, as Sunra's and Nílira's had already been burnt. The dead Basti's homicides were variously estimated, but all agreed that they were between thirty and forty in number.

When a body is placed in the coffin, the clothes in which it is dressed are left with it. Thus the two heads and Basti's corpse would have all their silk vestments placed in the coffins with them. Should any one steal this property, it is generally believed that he would shortly afterwards sicken and die. When the straw figures are done with and burnt in front of the coffins, their clothing is taken back again to the houses. Women are buried wearing their serpentine silver earrings and other ornaments. In answer to my questions, I was informed that slaves do undoubtedly steal these valuables occasionally, but do so knowing that if they are caught they will be exposed to the vengeance of the relatives of the despoiled dead. Several bodies are put in the same receptacle. It is only a very "big" man who is given a coffin all to himself. Besides clothes and ornaments, small wooden vessels, containing bread broken up in ghee, are placed in the boxes for the use of the dead. At the shenitán (cemetery) many of the coffins are decayed by age, and their contents are exposed to view. These consist of bones and the wooden vessels referred to. The boxes are never renewed,

I think. All the pathology Káfirs know is derived from inspections of the coffin-boxes. They knew all about "stone in the bladder," and explained to me that they derived their information from the inspection of the contents of the boxes at the shenitán. As a rule, no attempt is made to decorate the coffins, but there are exceptions to this, notably at a place close to Purstám, where there is a coffin under a shelving rock by the roadside. It is ornamented with a gaudy turban-cloth depending from under the lid. It had on the top the white stones Káfirs are so fond of placing in that position, probably for ornament, but possibly also to keep the wood from warping. There were two flags resting against the coffin, one white and the other red, fixed to the end of long poles ; also against the rock were placed three poles, the upper halves of which had been reduced to half the size of the lower halves.

The shenitáns are generally formed on a rocky spur close by the village. Sometimes they are on the flat just off the road. At Bragamatál the cemetery is immediately above the west part of the village, and so inconveniently near to the dwelling-houses that if the wind is in a particular direction the result is appalling. At that particular place, also, some of the coffins have small wooden canopies built over them, a plan I have seen adopted nowhere else. The choice of ground for a cemetery seems to be made with the idea that it must be quite near a village, and yet must not be on ground capable of being cultivated. These places are considered impure, for neither the Kám priest nor the Debilála may even walk on the roads leading to them.

When the death of any one of importance occurs in a

THE SHENITÁN (CEMETERY).

To face page 642.

village, it is often signified by the firing of a gun. On the death of a wife, the husband, after feasting the village, goes into seclusion, and remains in his own house for some thirty days. This is also done by a wife for a dead husband. Friends go to visit the bereaved people, to cheer them up and condole with them. I went to a house once where there was a woman whose husband had been recently killed. The place was darkened, and in addition to the usual mourning dress, she had on her head a square of cotton cloth, and what looked like a small bag depending from it over her left ear. Mourning garments are worn for a long time, possibly until the effigy is erected. Among the Kám all relations wear them, but among the Katirs it seems sufficient for the eldest son, the head of the family, to assume them, even for the death of a father. After a death, the room in which the person died is purified by pouring in water through the smoke-hole by means of a wooden trough of a particular pattern. It is then sufficiently purified for every one except the religious functionaries, who will not enter the apartment until an effigy has been erected to the deceased.

One year after the death of a Káfir of adult age an effigy has to be erected to his memory. This is both a duty and a privilege, and consequently has to be paid for by feasting the community. The style of image to be erected depends entirely on the amount of food to be distributed. One day's feasting is sufficient for a flat, common affair, but to have the effigy placed on a throne or astride a couple of horses, a three days' banquet would certainly be required. The chief expense in food distribution is not at the time of a relation's decease, but a year

later, when the effigies are erected. Women as well as
men are glorified after death by pious relatives, and in
this way may be placed on an equality with men by being
given a throne to sit upon. Káfirs repeatedly assured me
that women's images were never placed on horses; but I
have myself seen an outrageous figure of a woman seated
astride a couple of horses. Some of the wooden images
are of a very large size; indeed, there are very many
varieties, each distinguished by a particular name. They
are either kept under open sheds or are exposed to the
air. To describe these images minutely would take up
too much time and space. They are all carved on conventional models, and are made solely with axes and
with knives. The more ponderous kinds are roughly
fashioned in the forest, and are then brought into the
village to be finished. Some of the best images have
a mannikin seated on the left arm holding a pipe, others
have similar little images perched on the chair handle.
Several of the large images have all manner of quaint
designs and carvings over their bodies. Some even look
as if the carving were intended to imitate tattooing, such
as the Burmese are so fond of. The people have a good
deal of superstition about these effigies. Bad weather,
which occurred while a slave was carving some images
for me to take to India, was ascribed to the fact that
images were being taken from the country; it was asserted
that similar natural phenomena had marked the carrying
away of an effigy to Peshawar by Mian Gul. The images
are often decorated with wisps of cloth bound round the
head, and, where the juniper-cedar is easily obtainable, by
sprigs of that tree fastened to the brows. The faces of
the effigies are carved precisely like the idols, and simi-

larly white round stones are used for the eyes, and vertical cuts for the mouth, or rather the teeth. The effigies are provided with matchlocks or bows and arrows, axes and daggers, carefully but grotesquely carved, and commonly have a cartwheel-shaped ornament in the middle of the

EFFIGIES.

back. The effigies of males are given turbans, while those of females have a peculiar head-dress, which is possibly a rough imitation of the horned cap. To get a proper idea of these images photographs or drawings must be studied. There are no effigies in Presungul, and it is said that they are unknown in the Wai country also. It is probable, therefore, that they are peculiar to the Siáh-Posh tribes.

Another form of memorial to the dead is a kind of menhir. It is about three feet high, and specimens are to be seen all over the country. There is but little ceremony in erecting them. A goat is sacrificed, some of the blood is thrown on to the stone, and that is all.

In the Dungul Valley, in one of its more open spaces, there is a detached fragment of rock half buried in the ground. About and around it stones have been carefully piled so as to form a narrow oblong structure with a flat top some two and a half feet from the ground. It presents an appearance identical with the structures so constantly seen in Astor and Chitrál, except that instead of being built against a rock, it is isolated and can be walked round. I asked a Káfir companion for what it was intended. To my surprise he gave me the same answer always given to similar inquiries in Astor and Chitrál : that it was intended for coolies to rest their loads upon. But there are no coolies and no loads in Káfiristán to justify the erection of resting-places for burdens; this particular structure was the only one of the kind I have noticed in the country.

A very common way of commemorating the dead is by the erection of small effigies on the end of poles, which are supported on a pedestal some three feet high and two feet square. The poles are also squared, and bear on their front surface a number of horizontal notches which correspond with the number of homicides the man committed in his lifetime. Such memorials seem to be exclusively erected to the memory of warriors, and I cannot remember seeing them anywhere except in the lower part

MEMORIALS OF THE BRAVE.

To face page 648.

of the Bashgul Valley, in the Dungul Valley, and in the Kalash village of Utzún.

A very elaborate monument is a gateway standing by itself in a more or less isolated position—that is to say, away from houses. It consists of two square masonry pillars between five and six feet high, connected together by a wooden door frame. The wood-work is embellished with carving. From each pillar springs a squared pole surmounted by a small effigy, represented as seated in a chair or on a horse, and furnished with weapons carved in the ordinary way. The poles are notched horizontally, for the reason already stated. Between the two effigies a figure of a mannikin is often placed on the top of the doorway, playing some musical instrument to amuse the dead hero. Such monuments can only have been erected after the expenditure of much labour. They are very effective in appearance.

CHAPTER XXXV

Sport in Káfiristán—Partridges—Pheasants—Bears—Markhor—The commonest diseases—Small-pox—Ulcerative disease—Goitre—Medical acquirements of Káfirs—Astronomy.

THERE is good sport to be obtained in Káfiristán. The rivers teem with fish. Partridges, pheasants, and pigeons abound. There are also a few teal and other wild-fowl. The big game consists of bears, leopards, markhor, and wild sheep. There are, I believe, no ibex in the country, or at any rate in its eastern half.

The partridge is the "chikor," the red-legged variety. They exist in such swarms that in some places the traveller puts up coveys every few yards. The birds were almost tame in the beginning of the winter, and several were shot from my cook-house in the middle of the village of Kámdesh. The Káfirs shoot them sitting, with their matchlocks. One of their methods of approaching them is to put on a long horned cap and then move slowly along in a stooping position. The birds are supposed to mistake the sportsman for some strange animal, their curiosity is aroused, and they permit him to get near enough to use his matchlock with effect.

Another plan adopted at Agatsi was for the shooter to carry in front of him an oblong cloth shield painted over with circles dotted in the middle. Behind this screen he warily stalks a covey. When well within range, he fixes the screen on his head by means of a cord, and takes a steady pot shot at the birds But powder and shot are so valuable that Káfirs comp. atively rarely go partridge-shooting.

The magnificent manál pheasants are stalked and shot sitting, or are hunted about in the snow by bands of yelling Káfirs, till the birds are exhausted, when they lie up in stone heaps, and are easily surrounded and captured alive.

Bears are shot with matchlocks or riddled with arrows.

Markhor are hunted with dogs, and killed with bows and arrows or matchlocks. In the winter, at the lower part of the Bashgul Valley, markhor are to be found in very great numbers. They are hunted for food, and the slaughter is often prodigious. In one place in the Katirgul there is a wall of stones and bushes, flanked at each end by square enclosures concealing deep pits. Markhor and wild sheep are driven by a crescent-shaped line of Kafirs across the river and against the wall. The animals dash away right and left into the enclosures, where they fall into the pits and are killed. Hunting markhor with trained dogs is very hard work. The dogs are fine big animals, of a breed for which the Káfirs are renowned. My experience of this form of sport made me ever afterwards confine myself to more legitimate and easier methods.

I have several times seen Káfirs miss a markhor at twenty yards. I have also known them miss at greater ranges with my express rifle, declare they had killed the animal in a position whence it could not be recovered, and a few days later relate to me fables about the body having afterwards fallen into the torrent, and having been swept away; from which it may be gathered that they possessed real sporting instincts, which only require development. Arrows are not much employed in markhor-shooting, although they are said to be of great use in killing wounded animals.

The commonest diseases met with in Káfiristán are fevers, chest complaints, small-pox, and a peculiar ulcerative disease. Influenza was epidemic in the winter of 1890-91. Sore eyes are most common, as well as the lid deformities which result from these affections. Rheumatic diseases afflict the aged. Goitre is very prevalent among women. There are also lepers and epileptics. Those complaints which require surgical operations for their cure are tumours, cataracts and other eye diseases, and stone in the bladder. Fractures of bones, dagger and other wounds are seen as frequently as might be expected.

At first the people were astounded at my cures, and used frequently to exclaim, "This Frank is indeed a great man," but later on they were much less interested, and finally took everything as a matter of course. They almost resented Gokal Chand's skilful treatment of chronic eye diseases, arguing that if a man's or woman's eye could be restored to sight by a simple-looking operation, that therefore old-standing cases of diseased eyelids ought to be equally quickly cured. They soon learned the value of quinine in periodic fevers, and of iodoform in ulcerative throat diseases. It is not necessary to write much about the complaints which Káfirs suffer from, for they are the same in Káfiristán as elsewhere.   Exception must be made in cases of small-pox, ulcerative disease, and goitre.

The ravages of small-pox in Káfiristán are very great, while the mortality among children is extremely high. Large numbers of one-eyed people are met with, and many blind, who owe their misfortunes to small-pox ; while one of the most pitiable sequels of that disease is the suppuration of joints.   Káfirs are ignorant and care-less about infection, and the clothes of a man who has died from small-pox are cleansed in a perfunctory manner, and worn by any other man who has had the disease. Isolation is never practised.   Inoculation is the only preventive measure adopted, and although it undoubtedly helps to spread the disease, it is a most useful custom.   A man who understands the method, usually a Musalmán, is induced to enter the country, and crowds of children are taken to him to be inoculated.   Guns are not allowed to be fired in a village while small-pox is raging.   In the sick-room a big fire is lit, and in the evening friends and neighbours collect and dance in the hope of help-ing the invalid's recovery.   Goats and cows are sacri-ficed or promised to the gods with a similar object. The fearful atmosphere of the crowded sick-room, with its fire and the effluvium, combined with the cooking and feasting, may be imagined.   I was never able to face it.

There is a particular form of ulcerative disease pre-valent in the Bashgul Valley, and in Chitrál also to a less extent.   It appears to confine its ravages to the face, mouth, and throat.   There is hardly a family which has not one or more of its members afflicted in this

2 M

way.   I imagine this disease is a kind of "rodent ulcer." The hospital assistant at Chitrál informed me on my return from Káfiristán that the complaint is very common in Chitrál, and that he cured it with iodide of iron and cod-liver oil, and used iodoform as a local medicament.

Goitre is a common disease, but is almost exclusively confined to women.   I saw only one man suffering from it, and his goitre was of trifling size.   Women sometimes have very large goitres, but nothing like the immense tumours to be seen in Chitrál.   Before I went to Káfiri-stán, Chitrális declared to me that no Káfir suffered from goitre, because he drank wine; and it is really a fact that it is only those in the Bashgul Valley who never drink wine, namely, the women, who are afflicted with goitre.   The Káfir women work in the fields, and the Mehtar's queens do not, but both get goitre.   It is the freedom from this disease which the Káfir males enjoy which is so puzzling.   They certainly drink a little poor wine, generally with water, but that presumably cannot afford.them protection against goitre.   They lead a free, open-air life, but so do the Chitrális, who yet have en-larged necks.   Bashgul men and women live under the same conditions of life, drink from the same streams, and eat more or less the same kind of food.   Why should one sex enjoy an immunity from a disease which is denied to the other, and which is denied to both sexes in the adjacent valley of Chitrál?

Káfirs have little or no medical knowledge.   What little they do know has been learned from their Musal-mán neighbours.   Firing is their remedy for pains of every kind. Some men are scarred all over the body from the use of cautery irons. A headache, a pain in the abdomen, the agony of sciatica or of a wrenched or fractured limb, are all alike treated by firing. They have no knowledge of purgatives. All wounds and sores are treated by being packed up tightly in dirty fragments of half-cured goatskins. Fractures are bound up carefully with wooden splints, narrow and numerous, but at the slightest onset of pain these are taken off and the cautery iron is applied. After spending a long time in adjusting and "putting up" a fracture, it was nothing uncommon to find that an hour or two later my excellent bandages and splints had been taken off for a few hours, to rest the patient. There is this to be said for the Káfir method, that it cannot possibly cause gangrene of the fractured limb, which is often the result of tight bandaging among other ignorant people. Truth compels me also to say that the terrible consequences I foretold to the Káfirs in the way of permanent deformities, if they persisted in disregarding my instructions, only occurred in one or two instances.

The Káfirs appear to have no method of exorcising disease, although many fables are current of the magic power and wonderful charms possessed by Musalmán physicians.

The Káfirs seem to have little knowledge of, and to take small interest in, the heavenly bodies. One of them, an intelligent man, once instructed me that there are seven heavens riveted together by the North Star. He said there was another star which performed a similar function, and pointed vaguely to Cassiopœa, but was obviously uncertain in his mind where the second rivet was to be found. The Káfirs know the Pleiades, which they call Laruk, and Orion's belt, which they name Turík. The Great Bear they call the "Prusht" (bed), and say that the first star of the tail is the husband, the second the wife, and the third the lover.

THE END

INDEX

Bold type indicates an illustration